D0720775

Humana Festival 2011
The Complete Plays

Humana Inc., headquartered in Louisville, Kentucky, is a leading health care company that offers a wide range of insurance products and health and wellness services that incorporate an integrated approach to lifelong well-being. By leveraging the strengths of its core businesses, Humana believes it can better explore opportunities for existing and emerging adjacencies in health care that can further enhance wellness opportunities for the millions of people across the nation with whom the company has relationships.

The Humana Foundation was established in 1981 as the philanthropic arm of Humana Inc., one of the nation's leading health care companies. Located in Louisville, Kentucky, the site of Humana's corporate headquarters, the Foundation's mission is to support charitable activities that promote healthy lives and healthy communities. The Foundation's key funding priorities are childhood health and education, health literacy, and active lifestyles.

For more information, visit www.humanafoundation.org.

Humana Festival 2011
The Complete Plays

Edited by
Amy Wegener and Sarah Lunnie

New York, NY

Copyright © 2012 by Playscripts, Inc.
All rights reserved

Published by Playscripts, Inc.
450 Seventh Avenue, Suite 809
New York, New York, 10123
www.playscripts.com

Cover Design by Andy Perez
Cover Image by Josh Cochran
Text Design and Layout by Gabriella Miyares

First Edition: April 2012
10 9 8 7 6 5 4 3 2 1

CAUTION: Professionals and amateurs are hereby warned that plays represented in this book are subject to a royalty. They are fully protected under the copyright laws of the United States of America and of all countries covered by the International Copyright Union (including the Dominion of Canada and the rest of the British Commonwealth), the Berne Convention, the Pan-American Copyright Convention and the Universal Copyright Convention, as well as all countries with which the United States has reciprocal copyright relations. All rights, including professional and amateur stage rights, motion picture, recitation, lecturing, public reading, radio broadcasting, television, video or sound recording, all other forms of mechanical or electronic reproduction, such as CD-ROM, CD-I, information storage and retrieval systems and photocopying, and the rights of translation into foreign languages, are strictly reserved. Particular emphasis is laid upon the matter of readings, permission for which must be secured in writing. See individual plays for contact information.

LCCN: 95650734
ISSN: 1935-4452

ISBN-13: 978-0-9819099-8-1

Contents

Acknowledgments

The editors wish to thank the following persons for their invaluable assistance in compiling this volume:

Jennifer Bielstein
Molly Clasen
Michael Bigelow Dixon
Dominic Finocchiaro
Adrien-Alice Hansel
Kory P. Kelly
Rachel Lerner-Ley
Marc Masterson
Mik Mroczynski
Lila Neugebauer
Janice Paran
Andy Perez
Jessica Reese
Jeffrey S. Rodgers
Sarah Rowan
Emily Ruddock
Zan Sawyer-Dailey
Kirsty Gaukel
Whitney Miller-Brengle
Stephanie Spalding

Beth Blickers
Val Day
Polly Hubbard
Morgan Jenness
Jonathan Lomma
Kate Navin
Mark Orsini
Mark Christian Subias
Chris Till
Maura Teitelbaum
Derek Zasky
Cathy Zimmerman

Actors Theatre of Louisville Staff
Humana Festival 2011

ARTISTIC DIRECTOR, Marc Masterson
MANAGING DIRECTOR, Jennifer Bielstein

ADMINISTRATION

General Manager..Jeffrey S. Rodgers
Human Resources Coordinator ....Cora Brown
Systems Manager..Dottie Krebs
Executive Assistant.......................................Janelle Baker
Administrative Services Coordinator ....Alan Meyer

Marketing

Director ....Kory P. Kelly
Public Relations Manager....................................Kirsty Gaukel
Marketing and Sales Manager.................................Sarah Rowan
Audience Development and Special Events Manager ....Stephanie Spalding
Communications Coordinator ....Whitney Miller-Brengle
Graphic Designer ....Andy Perez
Group Sales Manager ....Sarah Peters
Group Sales Associate.......................................Chris O'Leary

Development

Director ....Schuyler Heuser
Manager of Major Gifts ....Melinda Townsend
Manager of Foundation and Government Relations ....Emily Ruddock
Manager of the Annual Fund......................Gretchen Abrahamoon
Manager of Corporate Relations ....Danielle Manley
Development Coordinator ....Andy Nusz

Finance

Director ....Peggy Shake
Accounting Coordinator.....................................Erin Bukowski
Accounting Assistant.........................Brunhilda Williams-Curington

Operations

Director ....Mike Schüssler-Williams
Operations Manager ....Barry Witt
Maintenance..John Voyles
Housekeeping....................Eboni Boone, Robert Boyd, Rhonda Burres,
Brian Coleman, Patricia Duncan, Liosha Finn,
Hank Hunter, Michelle Willis
Receptionist ....Griffin Falvey

AUDIENCE SERVICES

Ticket Sales

Director ....Kim McKercher

Senior Box Office Manager .... Saundra Blakeney
Training Manager ....Steve Clark
Subscriptions Manager .... Julie Gallegos
Senior Customer Service Representative..................... Kristy Kannapell
Customer Service Representatives .... Cheryl Anderson, Ben Bush,
Alicia Dossett, Carol Niehaus,
John Rooney, Kae Thompson

Volunteer and Audience Relations
Director ....Allison Hammons
House Managers .... Zach Chotzen-Freund, Dana Cooley,
Elizabeth Cooley, Sara Durham,
Kyle Sawyer-Dailey Ethridge, Rachel Fae Szymanski
Lobby Manager .... Kyle Haeseley
Coat Check Supervisor .... Cory Vaughn
Coat Check Attendants................ Tanisha Johnson, Kathleen Kirkpatrick

ARTISTIC

Associate Artistic Director.................................. Sean Daniels
Associate Director..................................... Zan Sawyer-Dailey
Arts Management Executive Assistant .... Meg Fister
Company Manager ....Dot King

Literary
Literary Director .... Amy Wegener
Literary Manager. ....Sarah Lunnie
Humana Festival Literary Assistant....................... Rachel Lerner-Ley

Resident Designers
Costume Designer.................................... Lorraine Venberg
Lighting Designer .... Brian J. Lilienthal
Sound Designer... Matt Callahan
Assistant Scenic Designer...............................Ryan Wineinger*

Education
Director ....Steven Rahe
Associate Director...Jacob Stoebel
Education Fellow...Julie Mercurio
Teaching Artists................................ Liz Fentress, Keith McGill
University of Louisville Teaching Artists ....Gary Brice, Conrad Newman,
William Salmons, Jacqueline Thompson

PRODUCTION

Production Manager ....Kathleen Kronauer
Assistant Production Manager...............................Paul Werner
Production Stage Manager ....Paul Mills Holmes
Resident Stage Managers.....................Kathy Preher, Kimberly J. First

Scenic

Technical Director. . . . . Jason Grant
Assistant Technical Director . . . . .Alexis Tucker
Shop Foreman . . . . Javan Roy-Bachman
Carpenters . . . . Charles Ames, Braden Blauser,
John Newman, Mercy Rodriguez,
Kristen Rosengren, Pierre Vendette
Pamela Brown Deck Carpenter . . . . .Brandon Floyd
Bingham Theatre Deck Carpenter. . . . . .Matthew Krell
Scenic Charge. . . . . Kieran Wathen
Assistant Scenic Charge . . . . Jessica Hyatt

Costume

Shop Manager . . . . Kristopher Castle
Assistant Costume Designer. . . . . Lindsay Chamberlin
Wig and Makeup Master. . . . . .Heather Fleming
Crafts Master . . . . Shari Cochran
Master Draper . . . . Margret Fenske
Head Draper . . . . Shana Lincoln
First Hands. . . . . Christi Johnson, Karen Merrill
Stitchers . . . . Elizabeth Hahn, Bonnie Jonus
Journeyman Design Assistant. . . . . .Lisa Weber*
Humana Design Assistant. . . . . Amanda Sox
Wardrobe . . . . .Asia Bloemmer, Regina Harris, Meg Kane

Lighting

Supervisor . . . . Nick Dent
Master Electrician . . . . .Lauren Scattolini
First Electrician. . . . . Rob Brodersen
Technicians . . . . Katy Atwell, Brian Hoehne, Derek Miller

Sound

Supervisor/Associate Designer . . . . Benjamin Marcum
Engineer. . . . . Paul Doyle
Technicians . . . . .Marisa Barnes, Mary Stebelton, Stowe Nelson

Properties

Properties Director . . . . Mark Walston
Properties Master. . . . . .Joe Cunningham
Guest Props Master. . . . . Alice Baldwin
Carpenter Artisan . . . . Karl Anderson
Soft Goods Artisan. . . . . Heather Jakubisin
General Artisan. . . . . .Jay Tollefsen*
Artisan/Shopper . . . . .Jessie Combest
Artisans . . . . Noah Johnson, Scott Rygalski

Video

Media Technologist. . . . . .Philip Allgeier

APPRENTICE/INTERN COMPANY

Director . . . . .Michael Legg
Associate Director. . . . . .Amy Attaway

Apprentices
Kerri Alexander, Victoria Alvarez-Chacon, Monica Bergstrand, Dinah Berkeley, Martina Bonolis, Jordan Brodess, Daniel Desmarais, Havalah Grace, Rebecca Haden, Ellen Haun, Alex Hernandez, Emily Kunkel, Devin Olson, Sean Michael Palmer, Brandon Peters, Lizzie Schwarzrock, Alex Stage, William Steele, Scott Swayze, Peter Vergari, Zachary Virden, Ryan Westwood

Members of the Apprentice Company receive additional training at the Louisville Ballet.

Interns
A/I Company. . . . . John Rooncy
Arts Administration . . . . .Sara Durham
Community Relations and Festival Management. . . . . .Brianna D'Alessio
Development . . . . .Carrie Cooke
Directing . . . . Zach Chotzen-Freund, Rachel Paul
Dramaturgy/Literary Management . . . . Mik Mroczynski, Jessica Reese
Education. . . . . Jane Jones, Christina Lepri
Graphic Design . . . . .Elissa Shortridge
Lighting . . . . Jesse AlFord
Lighting Design. . . . . Rachel Fae Szymanski
Marketing. . . . . .Elizabeth Malarkey
Media Technology/Photography . . . . Joe Geinert
Sound Design. . . . . Dan Cassin
Stage Management. . . . . Rachel Enright, Travis Harty, Caitlin O'Rourke

KENNEDY CENTER/
WILLIAM R. KENAN FUND FOR THE ARTS FELLOWS

Lighting . . . . .John Alexander
Production Management. . . . . .Jeremy Stamps
Fight Director . . . . .Joe Isenberg

Usher Captains
Dolly Adams, Marie Allen, Libba & Chuck Bonifer, Tanya Briley, Maleva Chamberlain, Donna Conlon, Terry Conway, Doris Elder, Reese Fisher, Joyce French, Tom Gerstle, Marilyn Huffman, Sandy Kissling, Nickie Langdon, Barbara Nichols, Cathy Nooning, Teresa Nusz, Judy Pearson, Nancy Rankin, Nathan Rome, Bob Rosedale, Amanda Simmons, Miranda Stone, Jenna Thomas, Christopher Thompson, Tim Unruh, David Wallace, Bette Wood

Actors Theatre's company doctors:
Dr. Andrew Mickler, F.A.C.S.
Dr. Edwin Hopson, DC, CSCS
Dr. April Hopson, DC
Dr. Bill Breuer, MCH, DC, FAPHP

* Paul Owen Fellow

Foreword

One of the true pleasures of curating the 2011 Humana Festival—and for the reader opening this volume—is the opportunity to experience a thrilling array of different voices, styles, and singular imaginations. Each of these plays creates a distinct world in its own right, and in a festival context they gain a collective power that speaks to the robust strength and diversity of American playwriting. The minds behind these theatrical events include prolific veterans and newcomers, and the plays were inspired by adventures that ranged from a summer working on Martha's Vineyard to growing up as a Filipino-American latchkey kid in the rural Midwest. They took us on epic cross-country travels as well as intensely intimate journeys of introspection. There were flights of fantasy and juicy "what-if" scenarios too: exploring the unstable reality of a science fiction writer's existence, and a couple's escape from the modern world into a community where it's always 1955. As ever, this group of Humana Festival plays forged a dynamic dialogue with the current moment we're living, and interrogated who we might become.

This diversity of thought and storytelling is reflected in the way that this work lives on in the American theatre, too. As of this writing, there have been more than a dozen productions of these plays scheduled in cities all over the country, from New York to San Francisco, Chicago to Atlanta, Minneapolis to Miami and elsewhere. The plays are being seen in varied markets, some heading to New York or major regional houses and others thriving in mid-sized or smaller venues, where they find many new audiences. These days, the ecology of new play development and production can create a web of conversation, with multiple organizations supporting the work and communities partaking along the way.

This was often true of the developmental paths leading up to the Humana Festival productions as well. For example, *Maple and Vine* was first dreamed up with The Civilians, co-commissioned by Actors Theatre of Louisville and Berkeley Repertory Theatre, and then developed at the Perry-Mansfield New Works Festival in Colorado and Playwrights Horizons in New York. Many of the plays this year benefited from innovative partnerships between the Humana Festival and university theatre departments, which enabled us to provide workshop resources prior to their Festival premieres: New York University (*Elemeno Pea*), Louisiana State University (*The Edge of Our Bodies*), University of Nevada, Las Vegas and Florida State University (*BOB*). Creating opportunities for playwrights to hear their work with their teams before rehearsals began, these collaborations were an important part of the process.

The weeks in which these world premiere productions began to take shape in the rehearsal rooms at Actors Theatre signaled a vital next step in their development. Characters were embodied by the nuanced voices of specific actors, and stage directions were translated into fully-designed physical reality for the first time. It's tremendously exciting to support a playwright's vision as a new play makes the transition from the page to the stage. In this book, you'll find ten plays that made that leap in Louisville, and were seen by spectators from 44 states and 9 countries who visited the 2011 Humana Festival. With this publication, we are proud to further expand that audience, and to celebrate these remarkable playwrights by sharing their stories with you.

—*Marc Masterson*
Artistic Director
Actors Theatre of Louisville

Editors' Note

"It's kind of funny to me when people get so suspicious of pretending," confides *Maple and Vine*'s Dean, the dapper recruiter who welcomes new neighbors into a compulsively authentic planned community where it's always 1955. "I mean, don't you think people pretend every day, without knowing it? We all imagine the life we'd like to have, and it takes a little pretend to get it." This powerful statement about the role of storytelling in determining the shape of our future lives certainly applies in Jordan Harrison's tale of a couple who adopt 1950s identities, abandoning the modern world for new (or rather, old) social strictures. But the truth of Dean's observation also resonates beyond the borders of Harrison's drama. In adventures that range from the epic to the introspective to the apocalyptic, the characters who populate the worlds of the 2011 Humana Festival of New American Plays demonstrate the myriad ways that we build and organize our lives through sheer imagination.

The Humana Festival has always been curated from an ethos that values diversity; each year we relish the opportunity to champion a range of different voices, cultural perspectives, aesthetics and original stories. This desire to celebrate rich variety precludes choosing plays that are united by an articulated theme. Yet the human mind cannot help but make connections, and read in retrospect, the plays from any given year tend to converse with one another in fascinating ways. Considered collectively, the plays of the 2011 Humana Festival found Americans in the process of trying to decide how to live in the world, and searching for ways to evolve beyond the boundaries that have already been imagined for them. We saw playwrights grappling with big questions about what happens when we push into new territory, as characters interrogated and redefined notions of family, class, social mores, the journey to adulthood, and the contours of reality itself. Together, their stories formed a snapshot of a people in progress—for good or ill, refashioning ourselves as we go.

These evolutions often happened at the level of social structures, as the plays' inhabitants found new contexts for their relationships in the world around them. *Edith Can Shoot Things and Hit Them*, A. Rey Pamatmat's tale of three kids struggling to take care of one another on a remote farm in the Midwest, struck a chord with audiences for expanding the notion of what constitutes a family. In a world where parents are largely absent or their homes inhospitable, young Kenny, Edith and Benji find "home" in each other. Social evolutions occur out of sync in Molly Smith Metzler's *Elemeno Pea*, when a weekend on Martha's Vineyard shows Buffalo-bred Devon just how unquestioningly her little sister Simone has bought into the world of her super-wealthy employer. Metzler puts the sisters' newly opposed worlds in direct conflict, as fortunes and entire futures shift in the course of one afternoon. And the discontented New Yorkers in Jordan Harrison's *Maple and Vine* make radical choices about what kind of society they want for themselves, taking on new identities and an entirely different set of rules to live by. Walking away from the world they know, they sacrifice a measure of freedom for the promise of greater contentment.

The plays contained many examples, too, of personal evolution: individuals fashioning their own identities, negotiating an often confusing world through a transforming consciousness. With bracing intimacy, Adam Rapp's *The Edge of Our Bodies* took audiences inside the experience of Bernadette, a teenager on the threshold of adulthood who ventures into New York City by herself. At once empowered and made vulnerable by her near-anonymity in the vast city, Bernadette bears witness to the night's ugliness and beauty with growing powers of perception. With eyes opening to a different plane of reality entirely, Chet Ellis, the science fiction writer in Anne Washburn's seductively labyrinthine *A Devil at Noon*, slides down the rabbit hole of his own fragmenting imagination, as the line between the material world and the fictions of his "inner space" begins to disintegrate. Both Washburn's Chet and Rapp's Bernadette struggle to find their own footing; so too does the eponymous hero of Peter Sinn Nachtrieb's *BOB*, a joyous carnival-ride-of-a-play that traces the picaresque lifelong journey of one man on a quest for greatness. In vastly varied ways, all of these plays are fueled by the restless imaginations of characters in a state of expansion, self-definition, and sometimes disorientation.

And what decisions do you make about how to live in the world—what kind of relationships do you forge—when the world is about to end? Commissioned for Actors Theatre's 22-member Apprentice Company and written by playwrights Dan Dietz, Jennifer Haley, Allison Moore, A. Rey Pamatmat and Marco Ramirez, *The End* invited audiences to consider just that question— not only from the point of view of a diverse cast of human characters, but from that of the Antichrist and the Four Horsemen. An array of scenes and monologues explore the problem of arriving at the end of time, and the drama that a paradigm shift of that magnitude might provoke. With distinct dramatic visions, the three ten-minute plays of the 2011 Festival—Laura Eason's *Mr. Smitten,* Gregory Hischak's *Hygiene,* and Marc Bamuthi Joseph's choreopoem *Chicago, Sudan*—also reflect on how catastrophe and loss can end the world as we know it. Whether connecting with a stranger over a death, discovering a bizarre parasite, or considering the personal, global, and environmental connections between tragedies on two continents, the figures in these plays are forced to make sense of the world in new ways that are painful but also filled with potential.

What do we make of all these theatrical worlds abandoned and torn down, transformed and reconceived by the people who occupy them? The plays of the 2011 Humana Festival offer a powerful reminder that it takes a little pretend to shape a life still in motion, to imagine our way into new territory that, for better or worse, challenges us to think beyond what we know. If living is in itself a creative act, maybe we tell stories in order to practice the work of inhabiting the real world—in other words, perhaps plays function as a kind of imaginative rehearsal for our lives. May the stories in this book inspire readers to conceive of as-yet-unimagined possibilities, and provide a roadmap for rehearsals yet to come.

—Amy Wegener and Sarah Lunnie

MR. SMITTEN
by Laura Eason

Copyright © 2011 by Laura Eason. All rights reserved. CAUTION. Professionals and amateurs are hereby warned that *Mr. Smitten* is subject to royalty. It is fully protected under the copyright laws of the United States of America and of all countries covered by the International Copyright Union (including the Dominion of Canada and the rest of the British Commonwealth), the Berne Convention, the Pan-American Copyright Convention and the Universal Copyright Convention, as well as all countries with which the United States has reciprocal copyright relations. All rights, including professional, amateur stage rights, motion picture, recitation, lecturing, public reading, radio broadcasting, television, video or sound recording, all other forms of mechanical or electronic reproduction, such as CD-ROM, CD-I, information storage and retrieval systems, and photocopying, and the rights of translation into foreign languages, are strictly reserved. Particular emphasis is laid upon the matter of readings, permission for which must be secured from the Author's agent in writing.

Required royalties must be paid every time this play is performed before any audience, whether or not it is presented for profit and whether or not admission is charged.

All inquiries concerning rights, including amateur rights, should be addressed to: William Morris Endeavor Entertainment, 1325 Ave. of the Americas, New York, NY 10019, ATTN: Derek Zasky.

BIOGRAPHY

Laura Eason is the author of more than fifteen plays, both original work and adaptations.

Produced full-length plays include: *Ethan Frome* (also director, Lookingglass Theatre, Chicago), *Sex With Strangers* (Steppenwolf Theatre, Chicago; Sydney Theatre, Australia), *The Adventures of Tom Sawyer* (Hartford Stage, CT; New Victory, NYC; People's Light, PA; Actors Theatre, KY; Kansas City Repertory; St. Louis Repertory; Denver Center), *Around the World in 80 Days* (also director, Baltimore Centerstage; Kansas City Repertory; Lookingglass), *Rewind* (Side Project, Chicago), *When the Messenger is Hot* (59E59, NYC; Steppenwolf; Theatre Schmeater, Seattle), *Area of Rescue* (Andhow Theatre, NYC), *A Tale of Two Cities* and *Huck Finn* (Steppenwolf), *In the Eye of the Beholder* (also director, Touchstone Theatre, PA; Lookingglass), and *Coast of Chicago* (Walkabout Theatre, Chicago), among others.

Produced short plays include: *Mr. Smitten* (Humana Festival), *Citi Moms* (Women's Project, NYC), *USA-001A* (American Theatre Company, Chicago), *Jack and the Collection* (WET, NYC), *Lost Boy in the Ruined City* (Theatre Seven, Chicago), *It Was Fun While it Lasted* (City Theatre, Miami), and *Lost in the Supermarket* (Vital Theatre, NYC), among others.

Laura's work has been developed by Rising Phoenix Repertory, Rattlestick, New Georges, New York Theatre Workshop, Women's Project, America-in-Play and MCC, all in New York, and is published by Smith & Kraus, Playscripts, and Broadway Play Publishing, where she is a former playwright of the year. Commissions include: Denver Center, Arden Theatre, Hartford Stage, Writers Theatre, Steppenwolf, Lookingglass, and Two River Theater.

In New York, she is an Affiliated Artist of the Obie-winning New Georges and an alumna of the Women's Project Playwright's Lab and America-in-Play. For six years, she was the Artistic Director of Lookingglass Theatre Company in Chicago where she is still an active Ensemble Member. Lookingglass received the 2011 Regional Theatre Tony Award.

Laura is a graduate of the Performance Studies Department of Northwestern University and has received Joseph Jefferson Awards (Chicago) for new work and adaptation. Originally from Chicago, she lives in Brooklyn, NY. More information is available at her website: www.lauraeason.com.

ACKNOWLEDGMENTS

Mr. Smitten premiered at the Humana Festival of New American Plays in March 2011. It was directed by Kent Nicholson with the following cast:

ANNA .... Cassie Beck
DR. LOOMIS .... Gerardo Rodriguez

and the following production staff:

Scenic Designer .... Ryan Wineinger
Costume Designer .... Lisa Weber
Lighting Designer .... Nick Dent
Sound Designer .... Paul Doyle
Properties Designer .... Mark Walston
Media Designer .... Philip Allgeier
Stage Manager .... Kathy Preher
Dramaturg .... Rachel Lerner-Ley
Casting .... Zan Sawyer-Dailey

CHARACTERS

DR. LOOMIS, the vet, very handsome, maybe even distractingly so, very masculine, somewhat cold at first.

ANNA, very pretty, usually a very together person but at the moment she is barely holding on, much to her chagrin.

LOCATION

A veterinarian's office.

TIME

The present.

Gerardo Rodriguez and Cassie Beck
in *Mr. Smitten*

35th Annual Humana Festival of New American Plays
Actors Theatre of Louisville, 2011
Photo by Joe Geinert

MR. SMITTEN

An exam room. ANNA, *teary-eyed, sits waiting, handkerchief in hand.* DR. LOOMIS *enters. By her reaction it is clear he is younger and handsomer than expected, and, actually, not who she expected at all. His demeanor is rather cold.*

NOTE: *As the scene progresses, it is important that* DR. LOOMIS *remains very masculine and doesn't dissolve into something softer, regardless of the direction the action takes.*

DR. LOOMIS. Hi. I'm Dr. Loomis.

ANNA. (*Surprised, unconsciously fixing her hair.*) OK. Hi.

DR. LOOMIS. Dr. Mahn-yatis is on vacation.

ANNA. Oh, they didn't tell me she wasn't here.

DR. LOOMIS. Yeah. Well. As you might have expected the news isn't good.

ANNA. (*Trying to keep it together.*) Mmm-hmm.

DR. LOOMIS. He's at the end of his life and his body is shutting down.

ANNA. (*Starting to lose it.*) OK.

DR. LOOMIS. Sixteen is a very long life.

ANNA. (*Not long enough.*) I know.

DR. LOOMIS. (*Looking over the chart.*) And Mittens seems to have been in good health // for most of his—

ANNA. (*Correcting him.*) Smitten.

DR. LOOMIS. Sorry?

ANNA. Nothing. It doesn't matter.

DR. LOOMIS. (*Looking at the chart.*) Oh, *Smitten.*

ANNA. It was the name he had at the shelter when I got him as a… (*A beat, she suppresses tears.*) Kitten. *Mr. Smitten,* actually, which, I know, is a really stupid name.

DR. LOOMIS. Well, it's not the best.

ANNA. (*A little taken aback by that.*) Well, I don't really call him that. I call him Schmitt.

DR. LOOMIS. (*A glimmer of humanity.*) That's cute.

ANNA. Thanks.

DR. LOOMIS. (*Back to business.*) Are you OK for me to go on?

ANNA. (*No.*) Sure. Of course.

DR. LOOMIS. He doesn't have much time.

ANNA. How much?

DR. LOOMIS. It's impossible to be exact, but I would guess a matter of days.

ANNA. (*Quietly.*) Oh.

(ANNA *turns away, crying silently into her hands, her shoulders convulsing.*)

DR. LOOMIS. Are you OK?

(ANNA *nods. She holds up a finger. A very awkward beat.*)

Uh...do you need a minute or...?

(ANNA *nods her head no. She tries to talk. She can't. She takes another moment. She tries to talk again. No luck. He gestures that he's going to give her a minute. She shakes her head that she doesn't need it. He sits. She turns to him to talk. No luck. He stands.*)

Really. I'll give you a minute.

ANNA. (*Muscling through.*) No. I'm OK. Really. I'm OK.

DR. LOOMIS. OK. So, it's up to you whether you want to let nature take its course or if you want to have him put down.

ANNA. Put down? When?

DR. LOOMIS. We could do it today, if you wanted to.

ANNA. Today?!

DR. LOOMIS. Or tomorrow. It's totally up to you.

ANNA. OK. (*Sniffling.*) Sorry to be like this. It's just—

DR. LOOMIS. (*Coldly.*) I understand.

ANNA. I've had him for sixteen years! When I think about what he's seen me go through—

DR. LOOMIS. (*Warming up.*) —I understand. I do—

ANNA. (*Continuing her thought.*) Six jobs, four apartments, a whole *marriage*— from first date to divorce! He's been the most reliable man in my life!

DR. LOOMIS. I know this can be difficult.

ANNA. I know I seem like a crazy cat lady.

DR. LOOMIS. (*Re: how pretty she is.*) You don't. *At all.* (*Catching himself.*) Anyway. It's totally normal. People get attached.

ANNA. When I think about coming home and that he won't be there...

DR. LOOMIS. (*Getting a little choked up but fighting it like hell.*) I know.

ANNA. How can I walk through the door and *NOT* see his little face!

(DR. LOOMIS *suddenly turns away, crying silently into his hands, his shoulders convulsing.*)

Uh...Doctor? Are you...are you OK?

(DR. LOOMIS *nods. He holds up a finger. A very awkward beat.*)

Uh...do you need a minute or...?

(DR. LOOMIS *nods his head no. He tries to talk. He can't. He takes another moment. He tries to talk again. No luck. She gestures that she's going to give him a minute. He shakes his head that he doesn't need it. She sits. He turns to her to talk. No luck. She stands.*)

ANNA. Really. I'll give you a minute.

DR. LOOMIS. (*Muscling through.*) No. I'm OK. Really. I'm OK. Very sorry about that.

ANNA. That's OK.

DR. LOOMIS. (*Pulling it together.*) No, that was totally unprofessional.

ANNA. It's OK. Really.

DR. LOOMIS. (*Explaining.*) My dog. I had to put him down day before yesterday.

ANNA. (*Very sincerely.*) Oh, I'm so sorry.

DR. LOOMIS. He, uh, he was very old, too, but… Anyway. Sorry.

ANNA. You had him a long time?

DR. LOOMIS. Twelve years.

ANNA. Wow.

DR. LOOMIS. Yeah. He was the best. Just a mutt I rescued off the street but he was… (*Really choked up again.*) The best little guy.

ANNA. I understand.

DR. LOOMIS. (*Together again.*) Anyway. Sorry. So not professional. Here I am, my first week here and I'm— Sorry. Totally lame.

ANNA. I don't mind.

DR. LOOMIS. Thanks, but, really, I'm sorry.

ANNA. It's OK. Honestly, when you came in, I was so humiliated that I was crying and everything because I am not like this. I pride myself on being together, you know? And you're so… (*A subtle physical gesture indicating he's handsome.*) I just thought, this guy is going to be a totally callous asshole. Sorry.

DR. LOOMIS. It's fine. Actually, I thought you were so… (*A subtle physical gesture indicating how pretty she is.*) That you were probably here to put down your grandmother's tabby or something.

ANNA. Nope. (*Pointing to herself.*) Total cat lady.

DR. LOOMIS. Sorry how I was at first. I was just trying to keep it together.

ANNA. It's OK.

DR. LOOMIS. Not that I was very successful. (*Pointing to himself.*) Total crybaby.

ANNA. (*Choking up, too.*) No. I understand! It's so corny, and maybe this is humiliating to admit, but he really was, like, my best friend.

DR. LOOMIS. (*Agreeing.*) Yep.

ANNA. Because people, even people you really care about, people you're close to, they can be such assholes sometimes, you know?! (*Backing off, worried* *she is sounding harsh.*) Or at least really disappointing.

DR. LOOMIS. No. It's true.

ANNA. But Schmitt was always so…

DR. LOOMIS. I know. Same with Champ. He was…he was just… (*Can barely get it out.*) *Awesome.*

ANNA. And you feel stupid about how sad you are, you know? Like you're a loser 'cause you love your cat so much but, he is, every time I come home, just LOVE, you know? Just so… (*Can't get it out.*) So…

DR. LOOMIS. (*Can barely get it out.*) *Awesome.*

(*They sit and cry for a second, moving towards each other. They hold each other for a moment, pulling each other close. Then, a knock on the door.*)

VOICE. (*O.S.*) Dr. Loomis?

(*They break apart. Suddenly, they are incredibly awkward and uncomfortable with each other and what they've shared.*)

DR. LOOMIS. Uh, yes, just a minute, I'm just finishing up in here. (*Standing, all business again.*) Well…

ANNA. Well…

DR. LOOMIS. Do you need some time to figure out what you want to do or…?

ANNA. I, uh, I think I'll just take him home.

DR. LOOMIS. Alright. They'll bring him right in to you and I'll give you something for his pain.

ANNA. OK. Thanks.

(*An awkward beat.* DR. LOOMIS *turns to leave, then turns back.*)

DR. LOOMIS. You know, we have a service. If you want to, we can come out to your house. It's just an injection, no pain. You can be with him the whole time, if you want. And then we can take him. Bring you back the ashes if you want them.

ANNA. Really? You could do that?

DR. LOOMIS. Sure. Yes.

ANNA. You or Dr. Mahn-yatis?

DR. LOOMIS. Either one of us. Whoever you would want. (*Quickly.*) Available. Whoever was available.

ANNA. OK.

DR. LOOMIS. But I know this is a hard time. So, I could also just come over to see how you're doing.

ANNA. Yeah?

DR. LOOMIS. You know, some other time besides the cat killing. Which I will happily do. Well, not happily. But.

ANNA. I'd like that. You coming over. Not the killing part.

DR. LOOMIS. Right.

ANNA. Well.

DR. LOOMIS. Well.

ANNA. Thanks.

DR. LOOMIS. So, I'll see you…when I see you.

ANNA. (*Sadly.*) Soon, I'm afraid.

> (*She starts to cry. He sits next to her to comfort her. After a moment, he starts to cry. They look to each other, realizing the absurdity and awesomeness of their mutual grief and sympathy. They start to laugh. They laugh. And laugh. And laugh.*)

End of Play

MAPLE AND VINE
by Jordan Harrison

Copyright © 2011 by Jordan Harrison. All rights reserved. CAUTION: Professionals and amateurs are hereby warned that *Maple and Vine* is subject to royalty. It is fully protected under the copyright laws of the United States of America and of all countries covered by the International Copyright Union (including the Dominion of Canada and the rest of the British Commonwealth), the Berne Convention, the Pan-American Copyright Convention and the Universal Copyright Convention, as well as all countries with which the United States has reciprocal copyright relations. All rights, including professional, amateur stage rights, motion picture, recitation, lecturing, public reading, radio broadcasting, television, video or sound recording, all other forms of mechanical or electronic reproduction, such as CD-ROM, CD-I, information storage and retrieval systems, and photocopying, and the rights of translation into foreign languages, are strictly reserved. Particular emphasis is laid upon the matter of readings, permission for which must be secured from the Author's agent in writing.

Required royalties must be paid every time this play is performed before any audience, whether or not it is presented for profit and whether or not admission is charged.

All inquiries concerning rights, including amateur rights, should be addressed to: Samuel French, Inc., 45 West 25th Street, New York, NY 10010-2751, www.samuelfrench.com.

ABOUT *MAPLE AND VINE*

This article first ran in the January/February 2011 issue of Inside Actors, *and is based on conversations with the playwright before rehearsals for the Humana Festival production began.*

"First of all, welcome. Welcome to the SDO.
I bet you're all feeling pretty anxious.
'Am I going to use the right words.'
'Am I going to walk the right way.'
I mean gosh, you've just taken a pretty huge step, right?"

As *Maple and Vine* draws us under its spell, Dean, a charismatic man wearing an "immaculate 1950s suit and well-shined wing tips," stands before the audience, brightly beckoning us toward a better future that's fashioned from the past. In the Society of Dynamic Obsolescence, it's a perpetual and compulsively authentic 1955—a carefully constructed community without lattes or cell phones, where a housewife prepares supper for her husband every night, the neighbors are neighborly, and everyone has a dossier that determines their identity. Trading the dizzying choices of the 21st century for clearly defined social roles (and the rich drama of repression), the denizens of the SDO have left the modern world for one with sharper boundaries. But what does it mean to relinquish some freedom in exchange for happiness?

With a potent mix of searching humanity and delightfully dry humor, Jordan Harrison's new play examines this question through the experience of Katha and Ryu, a thirtysomething New York City couple mired in an unshakeable urban malaise. Facing sleepless nights and the repetitive exhaustion of her publishing job, Katha loves her husband but is at a loss about how to reengage with the world—until a chance meeting with the dapper Dean gives her new hope. At first bemused by this—and, as a Japanese-American doctor married to a white woman, wary of "authentic" 1955 prejudices—Ryu begins to feel the pull of the SDO and the promise of his wife's contentment, of leaving the deadening grind of their lives behind. "Katha and Ryu describe it as a question of happiness," Harrison explains, "but I think the real question they're asking is 'How can I feel like myself again?'"

The playwright's fictional foray into a sequestered community was inspired by research on real groups that have chosen to withdraw from the modern world. Initiated by director Anne Kauffman (who helmed the Humana Festival production) with the theatre company The Civilians, the project began with "upwards of 100 interviews with the Amish, cloistered nuns, Civil War reenactors, and off-the-grid artists living in the wilds of Maine," says Harrison, "all kinds of people who retreat from the modern world for different reasons." He was brought on board in 2008, as a writer who could bring some creative distance and narrative shape to the raw material: "My job was to edit and splice all of that language into something more like a play," he recalls. Actors Theatre of Louisville and Berkeley Repertory Theatre signed on to co-commission the script, and Harrison dived in.

An initial stab at weaving the interviews together took Harrison in an entirely new direction, though, when he discovered that a tale set in an imagined context would actually serve the project better than a documentary approach. "I've taken the concerns of those who were interviewed, and invented a whole other society based on them," he notes. "There are only four or five sentences from the original transcripts that are in the play—everything else is gone—but it still feels fertilized by those ideas." Reading the interviews, Harrison was fascinated by a recurring thread: "Instead of the modern world being too noisy and fast-paced for these people, it was actually *too quiet*. They were almost frightened by how much freedom they had, and so they traded in a measure of that freedom in exchange for more of a social structure, for a community enforcing the rules."

From those impulses, the SDO was born, complete with steak-and-martini lunches, period undergarments, and an Authenticity Committee that enforces era-appropriate aesthetics, values and behavior. Here, the last half-century of history doesn't exist. "I was drawn to the 1950s," Harrison explains, "because there were such clear rules—and roles. Everyone was watching over you with certain expectations. It's tantalizing to the dramatist, because so much is under the surface that you really get to feast on subtext." Equally appealing were the period's style and otherworldliness: "It's an era that has a certain romance for me—a time when people looked good in their clothes and drank sophisticated drinks," he laughs.

The stylish, well-ordered allure of this society and its troubling limitations are two sides of the coin for the playwright—and the play stirs both feelings as we watch Katha and Ryu step away from their 21st-century lives, and deeper into their new identities as a box factory worker and housewife. "It's both a little scary and a little seductive," says Harrison. "The notion that less freedom could make you happy is a morally problematic idea, it's a controversial idea, and it's one of the things that I've been most excited about in working on this play." As Katha and Ryu begin to learn what their new neighbors have been willing to sacrifice for happiness, they make some surprising discoveries about what they themselves would do—and along the way, so do we. Harrison admits, "I'm hoping that the audience thinks, 'I would never do something like that.... Or would I?'"

—Amy Wegener

BIOGRAPHY

Jordan Harrison's play *Maple and Vine* premiered in the 2011 Humana Festival, and has been seen at Playwrights Horizons in New York, A.C.T. in San Francisco, and Next Theatre in Chicago. Jordan's other plays include *Doris to Darlene* (Playwrights Horizons), *Futura* (Portland Center Stage), *Amazons and Their Men* (Clubbed Thumb), *Act a Lady* (2006 Humana Festival), *Finn in the Underworld* (Berkeley Repertory Theatre), *Kid-Simple* (2004 Humana Festival, SPF), *The Museum Play* (Washington Ensemble Theatre), and *The Flea and the Professor* (Arden Theatre Company), which won the 2011 Barrymore Award for Best Production of a Musical. Jordan is the recipient of a Guggenheim Fellowship, a Hodder Fellowship at Princeton University, a Theater Masters' Innovative Playwright Award, the Kesselring Fellowship, the Heideman Award, Jerome and McKnight Fellowships from The Playwrights' Center, and a NEA/TCG Playwright-in-Residence Grant. He is a graduate of the Brown University M.F.A. program and an alumnus of New Dramatists.

ACKNOWLEDGMENTS

Maple and Vine premiered at the Humana Festival of New American Plays in March 2011. It was directed by Anne Kauffman with the following cast:

Katha	Kate Turnbull
Ryu	Peter Kim
Dean	Paul Niebanck
Ellen/Jenna	Jeanine Serralles
Roger/Omar	Jesse Pennington

and the following production staff:

Scenic Designer	Brian Sidney Bembridge
Costume Designer	Connie Furr Soloman
Lighting Designer	Jeff Nellis
Sound Designer	Benjamin Marcum
Properties Designer	Alice Baldwin
Media Designer	Philip Allgeier
Wig Designer	Heather Fleming
Stage Manager	Melissa Rae Miller
Dramaturg	Amy Wegener
Casting	Calleri Casting

Directing Assistant	Rachel Paul
Scenic Design Assistant	Ryan Wineinger
Assistant Costume Designer	Lisa Weber
Assistant Lighting Designer	Rachel Fae Szymanski

Production Assistant...Nick Bussett
Assistant Dramaturg...Mik Mroczynski

Maple and Vine was commissioned by Actors Theatre of Louisville and Berkeley Repertory Theatre. It was originally developed by The Civilians, and written with support from Guggenheim and Hodder Fellowships. It also received developmental support from Playwrights Horizons, the Perry-Mansfield Performing Arts School New Works Festival, and the Kesselring Fellowship through the Orchard Project and the National Arts Club.

CHARACTERS

KATHA, mid to late 30s.

RYU, mid to late 30s.

DEAN, late 30s.

ELLEN, late 30s. *Also plays* JENNA.

ROGER, mid to late 30s. *Also plays* OMAR.

NOTE

The acting edition of *Maple and Vine* is published by Samuel French, Inc. Companies producing the play should acquire that version of the script, as it includes updates the playwright made following the publication of this collection.

Jeanine Serralles and Kate Turnbull
in *Maple and Vine*

35th Annual Humana Festival of New American Plays
Actors Theatre of Louisville, 2011
Photo by Michael Brosilow

MAPLE AND VINE

PART ONE.

1.

In the darkness, we hear:
Sounds of a rainforest.

The rainforest stops abruptly, and we hear:
Sounds of an ocean.

The ocean stops abruptly, and we hear:
Sounds of a babbling brook.

And back to the rainforest.

RYU. Make up your mind.

KATHA. I've been awake for two hours.

RYU. Oh Baby.

KATHA. I've been counting the seconds between the jungle insects. There's a pattern. (*Talking along with the sounds:*) Chirp-chirp. (*Pause.*) Chirp-chirp. Then it gets longer. You don't care.

RYU. I know what you're going to say, but what if you took a pill.

KATHA. I don't want to be zonked out all of tomorrow.

(*Pause. She listens to* RYU *breathing. We hear a* WOMAN*'s strident voice from the street below.*)

WOMAN IN THE STREET. Simon. I know you're in there.

KATHA. Oh no.

WOMAN IN THE STREET. Simon buzz me in.

Why are you DOING THIS TO ME?

KATHA. She's back.

RYU. Who?

KATHA. She usually comes around 2…

WOMAN. Why are you DOING THIS TO ME?

(RYU *presses a button on the alarm clock and blue glowing numbers read* "2:03.")

RYU. She's right on time.

KATHA. It isn't funny. This is, like, the farthest I'll ever get from being at work. This is it.

17

KATHA.
I should be having a *dream*, / I
should be somewhere else, but
instead I'm just—here.

RYU. Jesus.

KATHA. No, Simon. No one deserves this.

WOMAN. (*Overlapping at "/"*)
I came all this way, I took THREE
TRAINS so I don't see how you
can be DOING THIS TO ME!

WOMAN. No one deserves this Simon.

(KATHA *continues in a clenched, terrible way—stoked by the voice outside.*)
I lie here all night thinking about
the whole day in front of me I
write imaginary emails I make
imaginary trips to the copy room
so when I actually LIVE IT it's like
I'm doing it all over again like like
Sisyphus or like Hell, I think it's
probably very much what Hell
would be like, this kind of cold
like repetition with no chance of—
peace.

WOMAN. Simon, if I have to stand
out here in the cold any longer I think
I'm really going to LOSE IT.

RYU. Baby please—
You're shaking.

WOMAN. Simon!

RYU. Who's Simon?
KATHA. Who knows.
RYU. Is he the one with the pug?
KATHA. It's not like I've ever seen our neighbors.
WOMAN. SIMON!
KATHA. And yet I feel like I know him.
RYU. Baby how about a pill.
KATHA. You're always trying to medicate me.
RYU. I'm always trying to help you. It's been six months.
KATHA. It takes as long as it takes.
RYU. Of course.
KATHA. What if this is *me* now.
RYU. No.
KATHA. Hold me for a while?
RYU. Sure. I can do that.

(*He holds her.*
KATHA *starts to suck her thumb. It helps, a little.*)

2.

DEAN speaks out to us. He wears an immaculate 1950s suit and well-shined wing tips. He takes off his hat, politely, before speaking. Revealing slick, aggressively parted hair.

ELLEN stands further off, almost out of the light. She wears a smart, feminine suit, hat and gloves.

DEAN. First of all, welcome. Welcome to the SDO.

I bet you're all feeling pretty anxious.

"Am I going to use the right words."

"Am I going to walk the right way."

I mean gosh, you've just taken a pretty huge step, right?

The first thing to remember is that all of us were newcomers at one point.

The other thing to remember—and this one really helped me—

The other thing to remember is that the 1950s *weren't in black and white.*

It sounds silly, but it's easy to think like that. All we've seen are the photographs. Old TV shows. But people in the '50s had yellow shirts and red sneakers just like you and me. So the main thing is to remember that you can live in color. You don't have to go around trying to act like someone in an old photo. I mean anyway you can't, because they're a photo, and you're...you.

That's what this place is for. So you can feel like you again.

I'm sure you all have a lot of questions.

"What do I wear?" "How do I talk?"

"How do I explain this to the kids?"

Ellen and I will help you answer all of these perfectly normal questions.

Everyone, this is my lovely wife Ellen.

ELLEN. Hello everyone.

DEAN. Isn't she something?

3.

KATHA and RYU's apartment, the next morning. KATHA sits slumped in pajamas, staring at her laptop computer. A bowl of cereal sits beside her, untouched. She looks happy in a tranquilized sort of way. Maybe she's still in bed. RYU is fully dressed. He's also looking at a laptop, but more actively—web surfing, sipping his coffee.

We hear period-sounding voices from KATHA*'s computer:*

MALE VOICE. Don't you like it?

FEMALE VOICE. Like it?

(*Soaring music plays.*)

It's more exquisite than any dress I could ever have imagined.

MALE VOICE. Puff sleeves.

FEMALE VOICE. The puffiest in the world. You are a man of impeccable taste, Matthew.

KATHA. So beautiful…

MALE VOICE. Well, you don't / want to get your dress dirty.

RYU. What?

KATHA. (*Still watching the video, rapt.*) Just, the way Matthew doesn't ever say "I love you" but you just *know?*

RYU. Who's Matthew?

KATHA. Oh, sorry. It's "Anne of Green Gables."

RYU. Didn't you already watch that?

KATHA. There are 26 installments.

(*Sheepish.*)

The things they have on YouTube.

RYU. The things people look for on YouTube.

KATHA. It's my childhood. Don't begrudge me my opiates.

RYU. I never begrudge your opiates.

(*He walks out of the room.*)

KATHA. It's a nostalgia thing. But I'm not sure whether it's nostalgia for the 1880s or the 1980s. My mother and I watched it all together on TV.

(RYU *comes back in brushing his teeth.*)

It always seemed like a nice life. Go to the one-room schoolhouse. Do arithmetic on your slate. Dip some girl's pigtails in the inkwell.

(RYU *disappears into the bathroom to spit.*)

It seemed like a nice life.

RYU. (*Off.*) I was just Googling? There are some really affordable places in Nyack.

KATHA. Nyack?

(*He comes back in.*)

RYU. It'd be quieter, we'd have space. It's just the commute.

(*She hits pause. The music stops.*)

KATHA. Space for what.

RYU. You know, space.

KATHA. (*Thin ice.*) Space for kids?

RYU. Space for whatever.

KATHA. Let's—not have this conversation now.

RYU. Why not?

KATHA. I'm getting ready for work.

RYU. You don't look like you're getting ready. You look like you're at a slumber party.

KATHA. I'm eating breakfast.

> (*She grabs her cereal bowl. She starts the video again. Soaring music from the computer.* RYU *shakes his head. He starts to put on his coat.*)

RYU. Well, see you tonight.

KATHA. Okay.

I'm home pretty late.

> (RYU*'s hand on the doorknob.*)

What's your day like?

> (RYU *starts to cry.* KATHA *hits pause.*)

Oh. Oh no.

What'd I say?

RYU. (*Holding back tears.*) It's just—it'll be like every other day—I'll get *through* it, I'll come home and then you're there isn't any—

KATHA. Here. Come here.

RYU. I'm the one who's supposed to be there for you.

KATHA. There aren't any rules.

4.

> DEAN *speaks directly to us.*

DEAN. It wasn't that the modern world was too fast, or too noisy.

In a way, it was too *quiet.*

Let me explain. In the 21st century, everything's pretty easy, right? You have your drive-thru espresso. Your drive-thru pharmacy. Or why go to the store when you can get it online? You hardly ever have to see anyone—except for all those people you've never even met who enter your life through your computer, pulling you every which way.

In the '50s it's different. In the '50s you have to go places. You have to talk to people. You pick up the phone to make a call and there's an operator on the other end and you say "Good morning." Or say you want to find something out, you go down to the library and Miss Wilkes looks it up in the Dewey Decimals. There's a separate store for meat, and fish, and fruit, and a gent behind each counter who knows your name. A man brings the milk every morning.

In the modern world, I used to make it through half the day without talking to a single soul. I used to have it so easy. And now, looking back—I realize how lonely I was.

5.

At the office, late that morning. KATHA *stares at her phone, catatonic.*

OMAR *and* JENNA *watch her from a distance.*

JENNA. What's going on?

OMAR. Haven't you noticed?

JENNA. (*Nodding.*) She should really rethink the sweater.

OMAR. No, I mean—she hasn't moved in like ten minutes.

JENNA. Why not?

OMAR. 'Cause she's depressed I guess.

JENNA. What about?

OMAR. Nothing.

JENNA. How do you know it's nothing?

OMAR. Her husband's a doctor.

JENNA. What kind?

OMAR. Plastic surgeon.

>   (KATHA *appears to be giving herself a private little pep talk. Maybe she gives herself a light slap on each cheek.*)

JENNA. Ohmygod.

OMAR. What's she doing?

JENNA. Ohmygod.

>   (KATHA *picks up the receiver.*)

OMAR. Every day she comes in later.

JENNA. I know, isn't it great?

OMAR. No, I mean: What if they let her go.

JENNA. Let her go. I'll take her job.

OMAR. (*Loving it.*) Don't be terrible! Besides, you wouldn't get it.

JENNA. Why not?

OMAR. You're too nice.

JENNA. I know, I'm nice right?

OMAR. You're too nice.

In that job you have to be able to tell people / No.

KATHA. (*Overlapping with* OMAR*'s* *"No."*) No! I will not hold!

    (*She has been put on hold. She hangs up, starts to dial again.*)

JENNA. And I suppose you can tell people No?

OMAR. (*Arch.*) Maybe.

    (OMAR *starts to leave.*)

JENNA. Fancy salad place for lunch?

OMAR. Always.

    (*And he's gone, headed towards* KATHA*'s office.*)

KATHA. Yes, you just put me on hold? Do not do that again.

———

Marcus please.

———

Katha at Random House.

———

Well I'm pretty sure he's at his desk for *me* because he left me three messages about the Labradoodle book.

———

An early *lunch*, what a luxury. You'd think the man putting together the most urgent coffee table book of our times wouldn't have time to—

———

No. I'll be here.

    (KATHA *hangs up. She stares at her phone.*)

I'll be here.

    (KATHA *sucks her thumb unconsciously.* OMAR *comes sidling up to the doorway.*)

OMAR. Katha?

Knock knock.

KATHA. Who's there?

OMAR. Omar.

KATHA. Omar who.

OMAR. (*Concerned.*) You know, *Omar.*

Oh, I get it—we're doing a thing, a knock-knock thing.

(*Short pause.*)

KATHA. You know for a homosexual you're not very funny.

OMAR. Well, you're my boss, so.

KATHA. So.

OMAR. So we don't really have that relationship?

(*Beat.*)

Are you ready?

KATHA. Ready…

OMAR. You have the Department Head meeting in ten minutes.

(*For a moment,* KATHA *seems to forget how to breathe.*)

Unless you want me to tell them you're busy sucking your thumb.

(*He exits.*)

KATHA. "Unless you want me to tell them…"

That's good. Maybe he is funny.

You're talking out loud.

(*She stares at her phone. Inhales and exhales. She picks up the receiver and dials just two numbers.*)

Yes. Put me through to Human Resources.

6.

ELLEN *speaks directly to us.* DEAN *stands farther off now.*

ELLEN. In the beginning, most people try a little too hard with the lingo.

It's easy to get carried away. There are lots of fun terms:

"Don't be a square." "Back-seat bingo."

But you don't want to use them all in one sentence.

DEAN. "Hey cat, don't be a square, how 'bout we jump in my hot rod and play a little back-seat bingo?"

ELLEN. I'm not that kind of girl!

DEAN. Oh yes you are.

(*They have a laugh at this.*)

ELLEN. (*To us again.*) That was a lot of fun, but you see the problem. You can end up sounding like you're a person at a theme party, not a person.

The most colorful slang from the '50s comes from the Beats and the Hotrodders, so nice ordinary people will want to use those words sparingly.

DEAN. What people don't realize is that a lot of the most common '50s sayings are still in use in 2011, so they'll come naturally to you.

"Cool it." "Make out." "Have a blast."

"Word from the bird."

Just kidding. I was just making sure you were paying attention.

ELLEN. Oh Dean.

Sometimes you just razz my berries.

7.

Early that afternoon. KATHA *and* RYU *in Madison Park, with hot dogs.* KATHA *isn't eating hers.* RYU *still has his scrubs on.*

KATHA. Happy? I don't know.

RYU. I mean the last time you really—felt like yourself.

KATHA. I guess when we rented bikes in Amsterdam? And we got falafel?

(RYU's *beeper beeps. He takes it out.*)

That was almost two years ago.

RYU. (*Glancing at it.*) What about Cape Cod—was that after? When we pulled the bikes over

KATHA. And we had oysters

RYU. From that stand.

(*Beat.*)

KATHA. So the secret is bikes.

RYU. Or food.

(*He takes a bite of his hot dog, trying to be jaunty.*)

KATHA. Great, Ryu.

Then we're all set, we'll just get some...*bikes* / and and

RYU. Baby.

KATHA. and some hot dogs and some Cherry fucking / *Garcia*

RYU. Baby okay / okay

KATHA. and it'll be like it never happened!

RYU. Of course it happened. It was terrible. But that doesn't mean we have to give up.

KATHA. Oh right, "Snap out of it, Katha—it's been six whole months, get over it. / Chin up, kiddo."

RYU. I didn't say that. I would never / say that.

KATHA. "Six months, time to pop out another one!"

RYU. Now you're just / being crazy—

KATHA. Maybe I don't want to love something for all that time again just to have it, to have it / stolen away!

RYU. Settle down.

KATHA. We saw him, Ryu! We saw the ultrasound! We saw him!

>   (*Quieter now. Spent.*)

He was real.

RYU. Of course he was.

He was mine too.

KATHA. I'm sorry—shit. You must get / tired of this routine.

RYU. Don't be sorry.

KATHA. I love you.

RYU. I love you.

>   (*Beat.*)

KATHA. I want us to be happy.

RYU. I think…people aren't happy. People have *never* been happy. The whole idea is a tyranny. Slaves building the pyramids. Cathedrals…*Serfs.* They didn't have enough time to ask "Am I happy?" This is not even a hundred-year-old idea: "Am I happy?"

KATHA. Maybe that's what happy *is.*

RYU. What.

KATHA. Not having enough time to wonder if you're happy.

>   (RYU*'s beeper beeps again.*)

RYU. No, that's just busy.

>   (*He looks at it.*)

I should, I'm sorry—

>   (*He stands up, brushes crumbs off his pants.*)

We'll keep talking tonight.

KATHA. You just got here.

RYU. You think it stops?

KATHA. I know

RYU. Bags of blood, and bags of *fat*

KATHA. (*"Tasty."*) Mmm

RYU. …and 15-year-olds who want boobs.

>   (*Beat.*)

I have to go back. You do too.

KATHA. No I don't. I quit.

(RYU *takes her in—she is strangely cavalier.*)

RYU. You quit?

KATHA. I quit. Finito Mussolini.

RYU. When?

KATHA. This morning.

RYU. Why didn't you say that before?

KATHA. I didn't feel like talking about it.

(*Pause.* RYU *is deeply weirded out. His phone rings.*)

RYU. Jesus.

(*The phone rings.*)

I'm going to cancel my procedures. I mean, you're clearly—

(*The phone rings.*)

You sure you're not—

KATHA. I'm not a flight risk. Go.

(*The phone rings.*)

RYU. I'll be right back. (*Answering.*) Hello?

(RYU *runs off.* KATHA *doesn't know what to do with herself. She takes a first bite of her hot dog.*

DEAN *enters in his '50s garb. He is lost, squinting at street names. There is something unmistakably, gorgeously out of place about him.*)

DEAN. Excuse me.

KATHA. (*Giving him the signal for "I just have to swallow this."*) Mmph.

DEAN. Oh, sorry.

(*He offers her the handkerchief out of his breast pocket in one smooth gesture.*)

KATHA. No, it's fine. Sorry.

DEAN. Not at all. Do you know where 200 Fifth Avenue is?

KATHA. Oh yeah, it's confusing. The entrance is on 25th. That's right by where I work. Worked.

DEAN. Well, lucky I ran into you.

(*He tips his hat, starting to go.*)

Thank you.

KATHA. Job interview?

DEAN. What? No. Why do you ask?

KATHA. Just, the suit. It must be eighty degrees out. So it's just pretty put together.

DEAN. Thank you. I have the same one in navy and dark brown.

KATHA. This whole thing you have going— (*Making a circling gesture with her* *hands, as if circumscribing his outfit.*) —it's like something out of the '50s.

DEAN. Yes.

KATHA. Is that what they're doing downtown now? Let me guess, there's nothing shocking left so the only shocking thing is to be straight-laced. We've come full circle. (*He just looks at her.*) Or is it less... (*Succumbing to self-consciousness.*) ...self-conscious.

DEAN. I'm not part of a fashion movement. If that's what you're suggesting.

KATHA. Oh I don't mean to make it sound... / superficial.

DEAN. That's all right. We're used to people being suspicious.

KATHA. Suspicious?

DEAN. Of the way we do things. Especially people who are content with the way the world is nowadays.

KATHA. "Content."

What's that like?

(*He seems to really see her for the first time.*)

DEAN. What I mean is, we're used to explaining ourselves to people.

KATHA. Who's we?

DEAN. May I sit down?

8.

DEAN *speaks directly to us.*

DEAN. I'm called back, now and then, on business. Spreading the word.

And it's not just my job to tell the rest of the world about us. I have to decide what to tell *us* about *them*. I have more access to the news, and if it's gossip about so-and-so is dating so-and-so, of course I don't tell you—but when a plane crashes into the World Trade Center I tell you, when the war in Iraq starts I tell you.

I have more access to the outside world, so it can be a struggle for me. I have a cell phone, for emergencies. I keep it in a drawer in my house. I keep the drawer locked. Just knowing it's there can be hard. It can be a distraction. That's why people today can't think straight, because there are so many distractions. They are not quiet in their mind. If you're here, you probably know that already.

It may be hard at first. I won't lie to you. When you first come to the SDO, you're used to a different kind of freedom. In the Society of Dynamic Obsolescence, there are very specific boundaries. By which I mean, if you're a gardener, you garden—you won't get invited into the house of the man you're working for. If you are a homemaker, you make your home. That's what you do. You don't start an Ultimate Frisbee team, you don't go backpacking in Thailand. Your husband and kids are going to be home soon and dinner has to be on the table. You are not free. But in another way, you're more free.

We may seem behind bars to them, but to us, they are behind the bars.

9.

KATHA *and* RYU *returning to their apartment, early that evening.*

RYU. I thought you were like college friends. I never imagined you'd befriended this—strange clean man who speaks in complete sentences.

KATHA. Didn't you like him?

RYU. I didn't like that he was trying to sell us something.

KATHA. He wasn't *selling* something. He was explaining his way of life. How long has it been since we met someone who seemed so…

RYU. Don't say happy.

KATHA. He can't be much older than us. He was *us* a few years ago.

RYU. So he said.

KATHA. And now there he is with his briefcase and his little hat, he's got it all figured out.

But it's silly, right?

RYU. It's not just silly. It's a cult.

KATHA. It's not a cult. They have non-profit status.

RYU. I'm not sure I even get it. It's like Civil War reenactors? Except for—

KATHA. Except for you live there.

RYU. Crazy.

KATHA. But I think the intriguing part is when you hear 1950s you think it's going to be all *Stepford Wives*. You think identical houses, identical cars, a kid on each lawn all bouncing their balls in unison. But it's not that. It's not just suburbs. There's a whole universe in there.

RYU. Did you just call it intriguing?

KATHA. You can be anything there. Beat poets. Secret Communists. They need dissenters too, you heard him. We wouldn't have to be June Cleaver and…her husband, help me

RYU. Ward

KATHA. Ward Cleaver.

RYU. You said "We."

KATHA. What?

RYU. "We" wouldn't have to be June—

KATHA. Oh, I mean "we" like "one." One wouldn't have to be June Cleaver.

RYU. Huh.

Are you hungry? I'm starving.

KATHA. Again?

RYU. How 'bout this. How about we order in, we get a bottle of wine, get out some actual *plates*. And then maybe later we can… (*He means have sex.*)

KATHA. I told you, it's icky when you plan it.

RYU. It's been two months.

KATHA. Six weeks.

RYU. (*Dejected.*) Got it. No sex.

KATHA. No *planning*.

RYU. Oh, fine, so I'll just come and take you in the night sometime, is that what you'd prefer?

> (*Pause. A feeling like maybe it is.* RYU *takes out his cell.*)

Sushi or Middle Eastern?

KATHA. I don't know.

Was there sushi in the '50s?

RYU. Doubtful.

KATHA. They probably didn't even have take-out. It'd be, "Honey, fix me my dinner."

RYU. Now it's starting to sound good.

KATHA. (*A deterrent.*) Remember I'd be the one doing the cooking.

RYU. You have your moments. You make a good grilled cheese.

> (*She makes an ironic "I'm the champion of the world" gesture.*)

So sushi? Say yes, 'cause I'm dialing.

KATHA. (*Almost to herself.*) I used to make a good red sauce.

RYU. Dragon Roll?

KATHA. I wonder if we could.

RYU. What.

KATHA. Do it, I wonder if we could live there.

RYU. You're being serious?

> (*He looks at her. She looks at him. He closes the phone.*)

KATHA. They do trial periods. Just six months, to see.

RYU. Six months?

KATHA. Although he said most people don't feel settled for about a year.

RYU. You're not in your right mind. You're just reaching for anything that's different.

KATHA. Dean said you might have that reaction.

RYU. Dean said——. (*He contains his sudden anger.*)

I want to make sure I understand. A man you just met in the *park* is part of this cult, the Society of Dynamic—what was it?

KATHA. "Dynamic Obsolescence." The SDO for short.

RYU. And all the members of this cult—

KATHA. Why don't we find another word besides "cult"—

RYU. And all the members of this non-cult devote themselves to recreating a rigorously detailed 1950s America.

KATHA. 1955. It's always 1955.

RYU. And you are really entertaining the idea that we would leave our jobs—

KATHA. Done—

RYU. Leave our jobs and move to this gated community that just cropped up right in the middle of a landlocked Midwestern state, where we don't know anyone and we have no contact with the outside world, and we, what, we live off the land and drink ice cream sodas and pretend there's no internet?

(*Short pause.*)

KATHA. It sounds better when you say it out loud, doesn't it.

10.

ELLEN *speaks directly to us. She smokes, wonderfully. This time* DEAN *is standing farther off, just out of the light.*

ELLEN. Here are some things you've never heard of:

Hummus.

Baba Ganoush.

Falafel.

Focaccia

Ciabatta

Whole grain bread.

(*She raises her eyebrows significantly: "Yes, not even whole grain bread."*)

Portobello mushrooms

Shiitake mushrooms

Chipotle peppers

Chipotle anything.

Jamaican Jerk.

Miso.

Sushi.

That one is hard for me.

But I do without.

You'll do without too.

Gruyere

Manchego

Parmigiano Reggiano—the parmesan in a can is all right.

No Kalamata olives

No pine nuts

No pesto

No *Lattes.*

That's hard for a lot of people.

What you get

Is salt.

You get pepper.

Mayonnaise. Mustard.

You get dried oregano. Basil.

Parmesan in a can.

Paprika, if you want a little kick.

Sanka.

It's a relief, the limitations. You'll find that it's a relief.

It may be hard to maintain a vegetarian lifestyle. Some people have tried. You're always welcome to try, if it coincides with the rest of your Dossier. For instance, it might coincide with the Dossier of a beatnik English professor— but if you're taking on the identity of an oil man or an ad executive, it would be pretty disruptive not to have steak and a martini for lunch. Disrupting means you're not period-appropriate.

One question we get a lot is health concerns.

"Do I *have* to smoke?"

"Do I *have* to drink?"

"Do I *have* to eat hot fudge sundaes."

Of course, we can't ask for more commitment than you're willing to give. But we think you will get much more out of the experience with total commitment, total authenticity.

What's a little hypertension if you're happy.

11.

Split scene: ELLEN *is rummaging through* KATHA*'s closet;* RYU *is in the living room with* DEAN.

ELLEN. Just once a year. During recruiting season.

KATHA. It must be hard, coming back.

ELLEN. Not at all.

KATHA. You don't get, I don't know, *tempted?* "Ooh, HBO." "Ooh, internet."

ELLEN. Mostly I'm just reminded how hard it was. When I see all the really desperate cases.

(*This hangs in the air.*)

KATHA. Well? What's the prognosis?

ELLEN. You can keep the ones with cotton, wool, or silk. But throw out the poly-blends.

KATHA. Throw out?

ELLEN. Or storage. But most people decide to stay after the trial period. It doesn't really matter, as long as you keep them out of the SDO. The same goes for Lycra, ultrasuede—most of it wasn't in homes until the late '60s. No digital timepieces, of course. And absolutely no Velcro *anything.*

KATHA. Isn't that always the rule?

ELLEN. Oh, you're a funny one.

KATHA. I don't know…

ELLEN. (*Cheerful in a slightly metallic way.*) No, it's good to know what your skills are.

(ELLEN *disappears into the deep recesses of the closet. A pair of sneakers comes flying on.*

From off:)

Oh dear. Most of these will have to go.

KATHA. I thought this was just a consultation?

(*Over to* DEAN *and* RYU. DEAN *makes notes on a clipboard.*)

DEAN. Of course there are certain things about your situation that will limit your Dossier.

RYU. My situation.

DEAN. Yours and Katha's.

RYU. Katha's and mine.

DEAN. Oh dear, I'm not making myself clear. When we have a mixed-race couple, that tends to suggest certain details about their Dossier.

(*He glances down at his clipboard.*)

You'd be living in the North, I imagine?

RYU. North of what?

DEAN. The Mason-Dixon.

(*Pause.*)

RYU. There's a Mason-Dixon line in the gated community?

DEAN. We have everything in microcosm, yes. So there are areas with the spirit of the South and areas that have more the feeling of the North. The Midwest. The West is still under construction, so that won't be an option for another year or two.

RYU. Well, then—I guess we would probably live in the North, yes.

DEAN. (*Looking at the clipboard.*) How do you feel about boxes?

RYU. Boxes?

(*Back to* ELLEN *and* KATHA. ELLEN *is holding up a frock on a hanger.*)

ELLEN. This one will work nicely.

KATHA. That was my mother's.

ELLEN. And this one.

(*Pause.*)

KATHA. That's it?

ELLEN. And the solid-color sweaters. I'm afraid you have a very synthetic closet.

KATHA. What am I supposed to wear?

ELLEN. I sew all my own clothes now. I'll teach you. It's simple if you use patterns, and fun. You'll want to change your hair, of course. And you'll probably want to try out the support undergarments before you get to the SDO. You can find a lot of them online. There's a whole different architecture to the undergarments. It really helps with period posture and bearing.

KATHA. Is it the same for everyone?

I mean, I'm sure the beatnik chicks aren't wearing girdles, right?

ELLEN. Beatnik chicks.

KATHA. I just don't know if the whole housewife thing is the way I want to go.

(*Pause.*)

ELLEN. Sure, smoking reefer and reading Ginsberg is fun for a day.

But you seem like you'd want something more complicated. Some repression, some rich subtext. Someone you can really grow into.

KATHA. Repression...

ELLEN. In the '50s, people keep things to themselves. They hold their heads high. People have a lot of secrets.

(*Beat.*)

I know, you think a housewife is just someone in a pretty dress. But a housewife makes things *work*. If there's a silence, she fills it. If there's a wound, she dresses it.

You're a tall girl, Kathy—

KATHA. Oh, it's "Katha."

ELLEN. (*Cheerful.*) I know what I said.

You're a tall girl. If you didn't slouch so much, (*She corrects* KATHA'*s posture.*) you could really command a room.

KATHA. And that's...allowed, in 1955?

(ELLEN *checks to make sure they're alone.*)

ELLEN. It's different for girls. It's a different kind of power. It's not about shaking a big stick. We aren't trying to be men. What we do is more indirect. But in the end, we get what we want.

(*They share a smile. Back to* RYU *and* DEAN.)

DEAN. The nice thing is you can do a trial period. So if it turns out it isn't a fit, you're free to leave at any time.

RYU. Why does that always have an ominous ring to it?

DEAN. Maybe because you're a distrustful person.

RYU. Excuse me?

DEAN. (*Warm, frank.*) How can you be any other way in a big city? Identity fraud, online profiles... All of your information is just—out there. That's one of the things people love about the SDO. There's less information. A kind of privacy long since extinct. A more innocent world to raise the kids in.

You do want children, don't you?

(*Beat.*)

RYU. We tried, once. And Katha...lost it at twenty weeks, so

DEAN. I'm sorry.

RYU. So I want to try again. But Katha—isn't so sure.

DEAN. Not yet.

(*Pause. They lock eyes.*)

For many women, that becomes very important after moving to the SDO.

(RYU *stands up.*)

RYU. I should see how Katha's doing.

DEAN. Listen, Ryu. Just listen for a second. I want to ask you something. Have you ever gone hiking for the day in the clean air and come back feeling refreshed?

RYU. Sure.

DEAN. You stand up straighter, right? You think more clearly. Everything's better when you come back, at least until that feeling wears off. So then: Why do you ever come back?

(KATHA *comes in wearing one of the dresses that passed muster. Her hair is up in a kerchief* ELLEN *gave her. She does a little twirl.*)

KATHA. (*To* RYU.) Well? What do you think?

ELLEN. I love it.

RYU. (*To* KATHA.) Can we talk alone please?

DEAN. Absolutely, what a great idea. Take your time.

(DEAN *and* ELLEN *stand a ways off, but don't exit. They watch* RYU *and* KATHA *during the following.*)

KATHA. I know what you're going to say.

RYU. What am I going to say.

KATHA. That this is all crazy,

That it'll never work,

That they're a couple of irony-free androids and what if everyone there is like them.

RYU. (*Impressed and a little bewildered.*) That *is* what I was going to say.

(*They glance at* DEAN *and* ELLEN. DEAN *waves.*)

KATHA. They're not going to be our best friends.

They're not going to be coming over for Tupperware parties every day.

It's still going to be You and Me, without all the things that make it impossible for us to be You and Me here.

DEAN. How are you folks doing over there?

KATHA. Fine, just another minute!

RYU. (*Sotto voce.*) He called us a Mixed-Race Couple.

KATHA. We *are* a mixed-race couple.

RYU. But he said it with capital letters.

(*She gives him a "You're being paranoid" look.*)

You know how much I'd be making there? Four figures.

KATHA. Money goes farther there. It's adjusted for inflation. Deflation.

RYU. I went to medical school, Katha.

KATHA. You're the one who's always talking about the hours. The emptiness. The injecting goo into trophy wives who think you're their best friend. Give it six months. Think of it like a vacation. A vacation from your life. And if you miss all that, I'm sure they'll be dying to have you back.

(*Beat.*)

Do you love your job?

RYU. No.

KATHA. Do you love your life?

RYU. No.

KATHA. Do you love me?

RYU. Yes.

12.

DEAN. The more people who come to the community, the more accuracy we're capable of. So it's not just good because Hey, the more the merrier—it's good because everyone who joins us contributes to the authenticity.

Our city planners are a good example. You see, fifty years ago, sidewalks and roads didn't used to be nearly as wide. Did you know that? And our city planners make sure that is accurately represented. A lot of times they'll work together with the landscape architects. So we have city parks that are spotless for the nice neighborhoods. Fountains and everything, really nice. And we have parks with graffiti for the neighborhoods that maybe aren't as nice. The kind where homosexuals and communists might meet at night. There might be candy wrappers on the grass. The trees might have the names of lovers carved in them. The graffiti was a lot tamer back then, of course. We have a pamphlet for that.

(ELLEN *holds up a pamphlet.*)

Some of the technology has been hard to track down. Typewriter ribbon, mimeographs. Our engineers had to learn how to replicate them. Now they can do it so it's just like new. I mean just like old.

(ELLEN *laughs wholesomely.*)

This is all to say, you might want to think about how *you* can contribute. And if you can't think of something, you might consider joining your local Authenticity Committee. Ellen can tell you about that, she's the Vice President.

ELLEN. Six years running.

DEAN. My wife, a woman of influence.

13.

Back at the office. OMAR *sits at* KATHA's *desk now.* KATHA *stands behind him, training him. They both look at the computer screen.*

KATHA. I usually dump the Unsoliciteds in this folder.

OMAR. "Siberia." Cute.

KATHA. That way they aren't haunting me before I have time to deal with them. Usually I give myself an hour on Friday morning and just burn through them. There's this one guy, Mr. Firestone? He must be in his seventies at least. He sends us all his war stories, and I mean war stories like *war.* Korea. Really, um, representational. And he always calls, asking for the hard copy back. We don't do that. He knows we don't do that. He's just looking for a way to get me on the phone—I mean you.

OMAR. Um, Katha, I wanted to thank you…

KATHA. Thank me?

OMAR. I don't want this to be weird, but you really made my career, by leaving I mean.

KATHA. Well, you can have it.

OMAR. I know I can.

KATHA. No, I mean, I don't want anything to do with it.

OMAR. You really burned out.

KATHA. I don't know if that's the word I'd—.

Fine, I "burned out."

OMAR. Do you have any advice for me?

KATHA. Advice…

OMAR. I mean, to not burn out like you?

KATHA. Um. Take breaks. Try to punch out at five. I don't know. With you I sense a… (*As though she's saying "ruthlessness."*) stability I didn't have, so.

OMAR. Is it true you're joining a cult?

(*Short pause.*)

That's what they're saying.

KATHA. Who.

OMAR. Everyone.

KATHA. If it's easier for you to believe, then yes, it's a cult.

OMAR. What do you mean easier to believe?

KATHA. If it means you don't have to wonder which of us is crazy: Me, for leaving? Or you, for working a 60-hour week just so you can pay for an apartment the size of a matchbox, while you spend the rest of what you make buying drinks to numb yourself while you complain to your husband which makes him hate you and makes you hate yourself even more because you're supposed to be this woman, this powerful woman because that's what you're supposed to BE, except for you don't feel powerful, you feel like someone who doesn't SLEEP or DREAM or do anything but just get THROUGH it.

OMAR. Wow.

KATHA. I'm sorry, that was—not really about you, was it. Good luck. With everything, Omar. Really.

OMAR. What is this place you're going, anyway?

(*Short pause.*)

KATHA. You know how you'll go hiking for the day in the clean air and come back feeling refreshed? You feel better, you think clearer. So then…why do you ever come back?

OMAR. I don't really go hiking, so.

(*Short pause. The phone beeps.* JENNA*'s voice comes through the speaker.*)

JENNA. Fancy salads?

OMAR. (*Pressing a button on the phone, leaning towards it.*) Totally.

JENNA. Is she still there?

(*He looks at* KATHA, *sheepish.*)

OMAR. Yeah, we're just finishing up in here.

(*The phone beeps a farewell sound.*)

Sorry. You were saying?

KATHA. No. That was all.

14.

ELLEN speaks out. DEAN stands farther off.

ELLEN. We take our job very seriously on the Authenticity Committee. It's not just clothes and mimeograph machines—it's about everyone's *emotional* experience. And the question we have to answer again and again is how far do you take it.

We have people from all walks of life in the SDO. And the question sometimes is how do we respond authentically to these people. For instance, we have a Japanese-American fellow moving in right now. And it's interesting, what the research tells us, what we have by 1955 is already a kind of *counter*-prejudice… People have started to feel a little uncomfortable that American citizens were interned, during the war? So prejudice might not look like "Get out of my neighborhood." It might look more like "Here, I baked you some cookies, neighbor." Of course, it isn't always cookies. (*Beat.*) It can be complicated to navigate, but authenticity is very important to us.

(DEAN *comes forward to join her. His arm around her shoulder, supportively.*)

DEAN. The SDO is...*built* on the idea of giving up one kind of freedom for another kind of freedom. Ellen and I had to give things up.

(*Beat.*)

But there's something about facing obstacles together—it has a way of binding families together, husbands and wives. You will not believe the rewards that come from authenticity.

15.

KATHA *is holding flashcards, testing* RYU.

RYU. Eisenhower.

KATHA. Easy. Vice president?

RYU. Nixon.

KATHA. First lady.

RYU. Mamie.

KATHA. Soviet president.

RYU. Khrushchev. These are too easy.

(*She flips past a few cards.*)

KATHA. Best-selling car.

RYU. Chevy?

KATHA. Buick.

When was the Evacuation Claims Act?

RYU. 1948.

KATHA. *What* was the Evacuation Claims Act?

RYU. Truman agreed to compensate Japanese-Americans for their forced evacuation during the war.

KATHA. And?

RYU. And?

KATHA. How did it turn out?

RYU. Not...well.

KATHA. (*Reading.*) "Thirty-eight million dollars were set aside for the more than one-hundred thousand Japanese-Americans who had been moved to internment camps. But this turned out not to be nearly enough compensation to replace the decimated farms and blacklisted businesses, not to mention the emotional cost of internment." This is good stuff, this will really help you create your character.

RYU. My character.

KATHA. Well, not your "character," per se, but remember they said it's good to add details, period details, to feel emotionally—.

Like maybe you have a little sister—Reiko…or Keiko—and you had to see her grow up in the camps. Maybe you have a lot of pent-up anger. Righteous pent-up anger.

RYU. You sound almost excited.

KATHA. I don't know, it might be a way to feel more connected.

RYU. Connected?

(*Short pause.*)

KATHA. I just / mean

RYU. Connected?

KATHA. how you never talk much about your heritage, it's just never been a big thing for / you so

RYU. Oh what, because I'm not, what, doing *ikebana?* You think I'm self-hating or something? "Heritage." I'm from California, Katha, / Long Beach, California—

KATHA. Fine. Fine. Forget it.

(*In the clear*)

You win. Katha is un-P.C. Bad Katha.

(*Pause.*)

RYU. Kath. What will it be like when it's just the two of us?

KATHA. You mean—

RYU. When we're alone. Will we be us, or '50s-us?

KATHA. I think the idea is, there's no difference, if we do it right.

RYU. But will they know, if we slip?

KATHA. Like will they have our house bugged?

RYU. It's a serious question.

KATHA. In fifth grade, my favorite teacher was Mrs. Hatzlett. She taught music. I loved her class. But one time, just to show my friends I was cool, I called her Mrs. Fatslett. And soon the whole school was calling her Mrs. Fatslett.

RYU. I know this is going somewhere.

KATHA. What I'm saying is, I don't think anyone remembered that I was the one who said it first, and I don't think Mrs. Hatzlett could have *known* it was

me, but—she knew. She could tell something was different because of the
way I was, around her. So what I'm saying is, I think they'll know like *that*. If
we've been breaking the rules.

    (*Pause.*)

RYU. But what about, for instance, in bed.

KATHA. Oh.

RYU. Do we have to be period...

KATHA. *Oh*

RYU. ...appropriate? I mean, do we have to not do things we might normally
do?

KATHA. Like?

RYU. Like most of what we do!
I was reading, oral sex was illegal in 36 states.

KATHA. That doesn't mean people didn't do it.

RYU. (*Conspiratorial.*) True.

KATHA. As long as we can make sure it's accompanied afterward by period-
accurate feelings of shame and confusion...

RYU. So it's only bad if we feel good about it?

KATHA. Yes. I think that's right.

RYU. But we're doing this to be happy in the first place...

KATHA. Right.

RYU. I'm so confused.

KATHA. I love you.

RYU. I love you too.
Let's have shame-free oral sex, while we can.

KATHA. What if we had a Safe Word.

RYU. A Safe Word. Like S&M?

KATHA. Like, absolute emergency, one of us needs to acknowledge the 21st
century—absolutely *has* to talk about sushi or hybrid cars—

RYU. Or oral sex.

KATHA. But only for emergencies.
It would have to be a word no one would ever say back then.

    (*Pause.*)

RYU. "Facebook."

KATHA. Wasn't that a word?
It just meant something else.

RYU. "Twitter."

KATHA. Also a word.

RYU. This is hard.

> (*Pause.*)

KATHA. "iPad."

RYU. "Xbox."

> (*She makes a face.*)

"Kim Kardashian."

KATHA. Something with some dignity.

> (*Short pause.*)

RYU. "Hybrid car."

KATHA. Too clunky.

> (*Short pause.*)

"Portobello."

RYU. Too whimsical.

KATHA. "Latte."

RYU. Too lame.

KATHA. "Hillary Rodham Clinton."

> (*Pause.*)

RYU. "Hillary Rodham Clinton."

KATHA. It has *heft*, right?

RYU. You wouldn't say that by accident.

KATHA. It's modern, it's shrill—I already kind of miss it.

RYU. You sure you want to do this.

KATHA. Yes.

Are you sure?

RYU. (*"You promise?"*) Six months.

> (*She nods.*)

Goodbye Hillary.

KATHA. Goodbye Hillary.

RYU. Hello Ike.

> (*Short pause.*)

KATHA. "I like Ike."

"I like Ike!"

> (*He joins in. It grows into a joyful, impulsive dance.*)

BOTH. I like Ike!

I like Ike!

I like Ike!

I like Ike!

(*Blackout.*)

16.

DEAN *speaks out.* ELLEN *looks on from a distance.*

DEAN. A lot of people ask me, Dean, isn't it hard pretending all the time?

And what I tell them is I tell them about a TV show called "The Adventures of Ozzie and Harriet." Most of you have probably heard about it, even if you haven't seen it. Nowadays you have TV shows about people who solve crimes using ESP, and people who solve crimes with math, and people who solve crimes with talking cars. But back then people just wanted to see a family, like their own family but a bit nicer, like their own family but a bit more attractive.

(*Lights rise on a modest but attractive 1950s living room.*)

And what was so special about this TV family the Nelsons is that they weren't actors, not really. They were themselves. They used their own names. Ozzie, Harriet, David, and Ricky. They got up every morning and drove to the studio a few minutes away, and they ate their breakfast in a dining room modeled after their own dining room, but a little bit cleaner.

(KATHA *enters, wearing a housedress and a short new period haircut. She goes by* KATHY *now. She pulls the curtains open and looks out into the sunny morning.*)

And they acted out their own problems and obstacles, only those problems were a little smaller, a little simpler, so you could be sure to solve them in a single episode. And a curious thing: The longer they pretended, the less they could tell what was pretend and what was real.

(*The doorbell rings.*)

KATHY. Who could that be.

DEAN. So it's kind of funny to me when people get so suspicious of pretending. I mean, don't you think people pretend every day, without knowing it?

We all imagine the life we'd like to have, and it takes a little pretend to get it.

(KATHY *opens the door.*

There are two beautiful bottles of fresh milk resting on the welcome mat.)

End of Part One.

PART TWO.

1.

Sounds of a factory—a nice, clean, civilized factory. ROGER *is showing* RYU *around. They both wear dungarees, work shirts, and suspenders.* (ROGER *is played by the same actor who played* OMAR. *Much more stoic now.*)

ROGER. [We call that the Crow's Nest. Managers can see pretty much everything from up there. Who's working and who ain't, if you catch my drift.[1]] This floor is all Boxers. Lots of fellas start out here. The Packers are one floor down, and below that you've got Secretarial.

RYU. Specialized.

ROGER. There you go.

(ROGER *picks up an un-made cardboard box. While he's talking, he assembles it with effortless quickness and grace. Almost involuntary.*)

First thing is to make sure you do the narrow flaps first, before the wide flaps. Then you want to add a dot of glue to each corner. Dot dot dot dot. No more than a dot or it turns into a mess. Now it's time for the wide flaps. Then you got your tape, make sure it's nice and wet. Then it goes snip, and down the chute.

RYU. Got it.

ROGER. Why don't you do one for me.

(RYU *starts to make a box. He folds the narrow flaps first.*)

Good…

(RYU *continues with* ROGER *watching closely.*)

RYU. So. Is this…fulfilling?

ROGER. What?

RYU. Here at the factory— is it gratifying?

ROGER. I'm not sure I know what you mean. The work isn't too hard. You get thirty minutes for lunch. The owner is nice.

RYU. Yeah?

ROGER. He says hello when you pass him in the hall. Every June there's a picnic at his place. His wife makes potato salad and there's a three-legged race. Madge and I won last year.

RYU. (*Sincere.*) That sounds…good.

ROGER. You came from the big city, right?

---

[1]   Optional cut. (In the original production, Roger led Ryu downstairs from the "Crow's Nest" to the Boxing floor.)

RYU. That's right.

ROGER. What'd you do back there?

RYU. (*Not looking at* ROGER.) Taxi driver.

ROGER. Must meet some crazies doing that.

RYU. It was all right.

ROGER. You folks find a place to stay?

RYU. Yeah, over on Maple and Vine?

ROGER. Over by the high school, right?

RYU. It's two blocks away. Little yellow house.

ROGER. Oh yeah, that used to be the Gibson place.

RYU. Oh. Where'd they go?

　　　　(*The slightest pause.*)

ROGER. Moved somewhere bigger, I imagine. Very ambitious guy, Donner Gibson. Had a mulatto wife, but she was so light you might not even know it. Probably fooled some people. Gibson was at the steel mill, last I heard. They like to move people up over there. Here too. You won't be a Boxer for long if you've got the drive. And nobody doubts you little guys have the drive, right? Not anymore.

　　　　(*Beat.*)

I mean after the war.

RYU. Oh, right.

ROGER. *Kamikaze.* Those little guys had drive, you gotta hand it to them.

RYU. (*Playing along, hoping this will end.*) Oh, yeah, you better watch out.

ROGER. There you go. So, I'm gonna leave you to it. If it takes you more than 30 seconds a box, you're probably too slow. And you'll keep getting faster. Just give me a holler if you need anything.

RYU. Okay, thanks.

　　　　(RYU *finishes the box. He lifts it up. A feeling of small satisfaction.*)

2.

KATHY *has been setting out hors d'oeuvres. She wears a cocktail dress. Something smooth is playing on the hi-fi.*

RYU *comes in, wiping sweat off his brow.*

RYU. Hi.

KATHY. How was your first day?

RYU. Well it's not exactly rocket science, but—I started okay and I got better. Thirty seconds a box. It's more physical than you'd think.

KATHY. I can see that.

RYU. You fall behind and forget about it.

KATHY. Better wash up. The Messners will be here any minute.

RYU. Shit, I forgot.

KATHY. You'll be fine, it's only cocktails. Just put on a clean shirt. And a spritz of that cologne I got you.

(*The doorbell rings.*)

Oh dear, that's them. Hurry—oh wait, do these look okay?

RYU. (*Smirking.*) You cooked?

KATHY. I cook every night, remember?

(*She winks at him.*)

RYU. Oh, yeah.

KATHY. Try one.

RYU. What are they?

(*He pops one in his mouth.*)

KATHY. Pigs in a blanket.

RYU. (*With a mouthful.*) Sauce is good.

KATHY. (*Proud.*) It's ketchup and mayo.

(*Ding dong. The doorbell again. KATHY goes to the door, RYU heads off.*)

Coming!

(*She opens the door. DEAN and ELLEN are standing there. ELLEN holds a wrapped present.*)

DEAN. Hello, hello!

KATHY. Ellen, Dean. Won't you come in? Oh—

ELLEN. (*Handing her the gift.*) It's just a little something for the house.

KATHY. You shouldn't have.

(*ELLEN looks around. She might be inspecting things for authenticity, but disguises it as the curiosity of a houseguest.*)

ELLEN. Looks like you're all moved in...

KATHY. We're nearly there, yes. (*Comically miming a pain in her back.*) Oof.

DEAN. "Oof"?

KATHY. All those boxes. But the neighbors have been wonderful. Heavy lifting. Bringing *pies*.

DEAN. Well what d'you expect? They're your neighbors.

KATHY. We just never had such—visible neighbors! (*Almost to herself.*)

Audible maybe.

ELLEN. (*Still inspecting.*) It's a charming house. I've always thought it was charming from the street but this is even nicer…

KATHY. Please, won't you sit down.

What can I get you all to drink?

ELLEN. Dubonnet, please.

DEAN. Yes, I'll have a Dubonnet too. With ice.

ELLEN. (*Nodding.*) Ice.

KATHY. Two Dubonnets.

> (*Just as* KATHY *heads off to make the drinks, something strikes the outside of the window.*)

ELLEN. What was that?

DEAN. I think it was…something hitting the outside of the house.

> (*Something hits the window again. It's a pebble.*)

ELLEN. Oh how strange.

DEAN. I better go see what it is.

KATHY. (*Reentering with drinks.*) Did that come from outside?

DEAN. Probably just some neighborhood urchins.

ELLEN. Be careful, Darling.

DEAN. Don't be silly.

> (*Another pebble.* DEAN *goes out the door.*)

ELLEN. Oh how strange.

> (*Maybe it doesn't sound like* ELLEN *thinks it's all that strange.*
> *Light shifts to outside the house.* ROGER *is there, in the shadows, pebble in hand.*)

DEAN. How dare you.

ROGER. How dare I?

DEAN. Ellen is in there, we're with friends—this is very embarrassing.

ROGER. You made your excuses.

DEAN. How did you know I'd be here?

ROGER. You always check in with the newbies the first week.

And he said Maple and Vine.

DEAN. You did your homework.

ROGER. You wanted to see me too.

DEAN. What are you talking about.

ROGER. That's why you placed him on my floor.

DEAN. They all start out in Boxing, especially the Negros and Orientals.

ROGER. Or else in Packing—or the steel mill, or anywhere! But no, he's right there with me, on my watch. Like some kind of message.

DEAN. I told you to leave me alone, remember?

ROGER. Guess I forgot.

> (*He pulls* DEAN *into a kiss. They kiss forcefully, angrily.* ROGER *starts to touch* DEAN.)

Say it.

DEAN. Say what.

ROGER. You know what. Say it.

DEAN. (*Barely audible.*) I want you to fuck me.

ROGER. What was that?

DEAN. I want you to fuck me.

ROGER. What are we going to do about that?

> (*Short pause.*)

DEAN. The park at midnight. Ellen sleeps like a log.

ROGER. I remember.

> (*Beat.*)

God I miss fucking you.

DEAN. I'm not like you. I don't need this.

ROGER. Could have fooled me.

DEAN. Get the hell out of here.

> (*Back inside the house.* KATHY *has just opened the present.*)

ELLEN. It's a tea cozy.

KATHY. Oh, how wonderful. We don't have one!

ELLEN. It's supposed to be a frog.

KATHY. I think I see it.

ELLEN. It's, what's the word, abstract.

> (RYU *enters.*)

RYU. Hello Ellen.

> (ELLEN *bows slightly.*)

ELLEN. Hello.

KATHY. Look what Ellen brought us.

ELLEN. I have a friend who knits them, she's very talented. You'll meet her soon.

> (DEAN *reenters.* RYU *shakes his hand.*)

RYU. Mr. Messner.

DEAN. Please, Ryu. Call me Dean.

ELLEN. Is everything all right?

DEAN. Of course. Fellow lost his way, he was looking for Elm. So I told him he had his trees mixed up.

(*DEAN laughs at his own joke.*)

ELLEN. You should have invited him in.

DEAN. Oh, no. He didn't look like a very sociable fellow, I'm afraid. Not one of ours.

KATHY. I should say not, throwing rocks at people's windows. Hasn't he heard of a knocker?

(*We hear a buzzer from offstage.*)

Oh, those are my crab puffs.

(*She goes. A short but heavy silence.*)

ELLEN. (*To DEAN.*) They loved the cozy.

RYU. We did, we loved it.

KATHY. (*From off.*) We did!

ELLEN. Tell me, Ryu—Did everyone make you feel at home at the factory?

RYU. Very much. The Floor Manager was nice. Fellow named Roger.

ELLEN. (*This might be directed toward DEAN, lightly.*) How nice.

RYU. He seemed sort of…preoccupied with my heritage?

ELLEN. Some people are still adjusting. To think, just a few years ago we were putting you people behind fences, and now you're working right there alongside us. Isn't it grand. *America.*

(*KATHY returns with the crab puffs just in time to hear this. She and RYU share a wide-eyed look across the room.*)

KATHY. I'm a little nervous how these turned out, this is a brand-new recipe for me.

DEAN. It smells delicious.

KATHY. I know crab is a trifle *exotic,* but you put cream cheese in anything and it's bound to turn out well.

DEAN. Mmm.

ELLEN. Well, aren't these nice and simple.

RYU. These are *really good,* Honey.

(*Short pause. ELLEN sees that DEAN is unusually quiet, she'll have to keep the conversation going.*)

ELLEN. You should come with me to the Authenticity Committee sometime, Kathy.

KATHY. (*Non-committal.*) That sounds…nice.

ELLEN. Monday, Wednesday and Friday nights in the school gymnasium.

We'd love to have you.

> (DEAN *and* RYU *chew solemnly.* ELLEN *discreetly corrects* KATHY'*s posture.*)

Remember. Stand tall.

> (*There is a kind of cut—Lights down and up again quickly. Everyone is playing charades now. They're all a bit tipsy.* ELLEN *takes the game very seriously, her true colors showing. It's* KATHY'*s turn, she mimes a movie camera.*)

ELLEN. Movie!

Four words.

Fourth word.

Four syllables.

> (KATHY *acts bored. She mimes looking at a watch. She taps her foot.*)

RYU. Um.

"Waiting."

"Boredom?"

> (KATHY *acts even more emphatically bored.*)

"Impatient."

ELLEN. (*Chastening.*) Four syllables.

> (KATHY *makes a gesture for clearing the first attempt away, starting over. She starts to wrap her arms around herself, rather embarrassed, as if to suggest a couple making out.*)

DEAN. "From Here To Eternity!"

KATHY. YES!

> (ELLEN *and* RYU *look at* DEAN, *incredulous.*)

DEAN. I love that movie.

> (*Another cut, lights abruptly down and up. The two couples are now slow dancing to a waltz on the hi-fi.* RYU *is struggling. Still, it's fun.*)

DEAN. It helps to count at first.

DEAN & ELLEN. One-two-three, one-two-three.

RYU. One-two-three, one-two-three.

DEAN. With the emphasis on the *one*-two-three.

RYU. *One*-two-three, *one*-two-three.

KATHY. That's it.

DEAN. (*Speaking in waltz rhythm.*) And then, when you're comfortable with that...

> (*He gives* ELLEN *a twirl.*)

ELLEN. Ta da.

(Another cut, lights down and up. Everyone in different positions, a bit drunker now. RYU *is pouring himself another drink.* ELLEN *is telling one of her favorite stories.)*

ELLEN. So I said to the girl seated next to me, I said Lorna there's nothing I hate more than a *soggy cake.* And what does the hostess come in with, right that very moment?

KATHY. A soggy cake!

DEAN. Right!

ELLEN. *(Mimicking the hostess entering proudly.)* *"Baba au Rhum."* This enormous rum-soaked thing. I was so embarrassed.

DEAN. So she ate every bite on her plate.

KATHY. Oh that's so funny. Isn't that funny, Ryu?

RYU. Does anyone need a refresher?

DEAN. You know what I'd love? A vodka rocks.

RYU. Grey Goose okay?

DEAN. Grey Goose, what's that?

RYU. Vodka, my friend.

ELLEN. No, he means: *What's that.*

RYU. Oh you mean—

KATHY. *(Suddenly sober.)* We're so sorry.

DEAN. That's all right, it happens to everyone.

KATHY. I'll pour it out.

DEAN. Gin will be fine, Ryu.

ELLEN. Smirnoff. That's a kind of Vodka we like. They've been making it such a long time.

    (Another cut. DEAN *and* ELLEN *are gone now.* KATHY *and* RYU *are splayed on the couch.)*

KATHY. Well that wasn't so bad, was it?

RYU. I don't know about Ellen.

KATHY. I think she's just shy.

    (They lock eyes for a moment. Then they burst into laughter.)

RYU. *(Furiously.)* "Four syllables!"

KATHY. Oh dear. Well, I think we're off the hook for a while. I better get to work on this.

RYU. Let me help you.

KATHY. Nonsense. That's my job.

    (She starts to clear the plates. RYU *lying on his back on the couch.)*

RYU. (*Content.*) I'm beat.

KATHY. You had a long day.

 (*She continues to clear.* RYU *sits up suddenly.*)

RYU. Kath.

KATHY. Mm?

RYU. "Hillary Rodham Clinton."

 (*Short pause.*)

KATHY. (*Sotto voce.*) Already?

RYU. I'm sorry.

KATHY. What is it?

RYU. I think I saw something tonight.

KATHY. You saw something?

RYU. It was Dean.

Outside.

3.

 Split scene. At the factory, RYU *assembles a box while* ROGER *times him.*

ROGER. Ready,

Set,

Go.

 (*At the same time,* KATHY *stands in the kitchen, squinting at an open cookbook.*)

KATHY. "Celery is often underrated, yet it can be the secret star of any dish. First, cut the stalks lengthwise. Then cut crosswise to dice. Try to make the dice as small and uniform as possible, both because it is aesthetically more pleasing and because the small pieces will cook more uniformly."

 (KATHY *starts to dice an onion, just as* RYU *finishes the box.*)

ROGER. Twenty-two seconds.

You sure you haven't made boxes before?

RYU. No. But I used to work with my hands.

ROGER. Thought you said you were a taxi driver.

 (*Short pause.*)

RYU. Oh, I mean back before.

ROGER. (*Nodding solemnly.*) Back in the old country…

RYU. I did *Ikebana.* You know what that is?

ROGER. Something with knives.

RYU. Flowers. Flower arranging. It's not so different really—the planes of the petals, the sort of minimalist thing.

ROGER. I gotta say, your English is—wow.

RYU. Thank you. I work hard.

ROGER. Make a better life for the Missus. I get it.

Hey, tell me something about her.

RYU. Well, she's um, she's pretty as a picture.

ROGER. (*Playful.*) Yeah, but can she cook.

RYU. She's getting there.

(*Light shifts to* KATHY, *who has returned to the cookbook.*)

KATHY. "Strain liquid through a fine mesh strainer into another large stockpot." (*Looking around.*) Fine mesh strainer…

(*And back to the factory.*)

ROGER. Tell me her name again?

RYU. Kathy.

ROGER. She must be something else.

(*Beat.*)

I mean, if you'd do all this for her.

(*Short pause. How much does* ROGER *know about them?*)

RYU. When we lived in the city, sometimes it was like I never saw her. Even when I was with her I never saw her. But here, it's like…

ROGER. You see her.

RYU. But you know how it is, you've got a wife.

(ROGER *smiles.*)

What about Madge, can she cook?

ROGER. Are you kidding? She *lives* to cook.

RYU. (*Tentative.*) Was it…her idea, to move here?

ROGER. (*With a rueful smile, not answering the question.*) It's always someone's idea, right?

RYU. I don't know.

ROGER. (*Coded.*) Sometimes, when people come here, it means making sacrifices, socially-speaking.

RYU. (*Coded.*) And does that work out…for people?

ROGER. I'll let you know when I find out.

(*The phone rings in* KATHY's *space. The factory light fades.*)

KATHY. Hello?

—

Ellen, hello!

—

No, no. Just wrestling with *mirepoix*.

—

Oh. Well, you're kind to think of me. I just hope I have something to wear.
Do you think gloves are too much?

—

To the wrist. Of course.

>   (RYU *comes in the door.* KATHY *laughs, scandalized by something* ELLEN
>   *says.*)

Opera length! In the afternoon?

—

No, no, thank *you*. To tell you the truth, it was getting a little quiet around here.

—

Perfect. 2 o'clock. Bye now.

>   (*She hangs up.*)

That was Ellen. I'm going to the committee with her tomorrow.

RYU. She finally wore you down, huh.

KATHY. I don't know, it might be fun. How was work?

RYU. I'm down to twenty-two seconds.

KATHY. That's wonderful.

RYU. But the boss...

KATHY. Did he ask you about the old country again?

RYU. Now I'm an Ikebana master. In addition to bonsai and karate.

>   (*Beat.*)

He said he'd never seen a foreigner learn so fast.

>   (KATHY *shakes her head, bemused.*)

RYU. Is it bad it feels kind of good?

KATHY. What.

RYU. Low expectations.

KATHY. I'll forgive you if you forgive me.

My main accomplishment today was learning the difference between chop
and dice.

RYU. And?

KATHY. Dice means I only cut off a small piece of my finger.

RYU. What did you make?

KATHY. Chicken stock.

> (*Beat.*)

It was amazing, Ryu. It took *seven hours.*
I had to chop, I had to dice, I boiled the water.
I skimmed, I strained. Things changed shape. Chemistry.
When it was done—there was something there that wasn't there before.

RYU. So we're having chicken stock for dinner.

KATHY. I made something. With my hands. I know it sounds small.

RYU. It doesn't.

> (*Beat.*)

KATHY. I think I might be a little happy.

4.

> KATHY *is having a dream.* JENNA *and* OMAR *sit in her living room. Suburban quiet now, in place of the din of the first sleeping scene.*

KATHY. [Kathy slept through the night now. There were crickets outside her window for lulling her to sleep.[2]]

Kathy had dreams every night now. But every night, she dreamed about the world she'd left behind.

JENNA. Fancy salad place?

OMAR. Always.

JENNA. I can never make up my mind. So many dressings.

OMAR. I know, right?

JENNA. I think I'll get the chipotle-balsamic.

OMAR. (*"It's your funeral."*) Indulge.

JENNA. (*Crestfallen.*) I thought it was low-fat.

OMAR. Not like the ginger-miso. You get the chipotle-balsamic, you might as well be having a whole focaccia.

JENNA. The focaccia's lower-cal than the ciabatta, right?

OMAR. Not like the parmesan flatbread.

So. I was eye-flirting with this guy at the gym—he was, *Oh.*

JENNA. "Oh." What's "oh"?

> (*He raises an eyebrow.*)

I mean I know what "oh" is but I want *details.*

---

2   Optional cut for production.

OMAR. Let's just say he's not having the ciabatta.

(DEAN *enters.*)

DEAN. Excuse me.

OMAR. Here he is now.

DEAN. Can you tell me where 200 Fifth Avenue is?

OMAR. You just found it, Mister.

DEAN. Oh. Thank you.

(OMAR *and* DEAN *start to neck.*)

JENNA. (*Faux-annoyed.*) You guys, we're right here.

KATHY. You're—in the wrong place.

(OMAR *and* DEAN *still necking, deeply. Shirts are coming off.*)

JENNA. Tell me about it. Like get a room, right?

KATHY. No, I mean—Everyone's in the wrong place.

JENNA. Kind of hot though. At least somebody's getting some.

(OMAR *starts to pull* DEAN *offstage.* JENNA *follows them.*)

You guys, where are you going?

OMAR. To get a room.

KATHY. Everyone's wrong.

Everyone's—

(KATHY *wakes with a start in the living room.* RYU *is standing next to her, his hand on her shoulder. The others are gone.*)

Wrong.

RYU. Shhh, you're okay. You were sleepwalking.

KATHY. Where are we?

RYU. Home.

KATHY. I mean—when?

RYU. 1955.

(*Beat.*)

Come back to bed.

KATHY. I'm going to sit up a little while.

RYU. You sure?

KATHY. Just until things settle.

Do you ever…forget?

RYU. Sometimes, when I first wake up.

But then there's the wallpaper.

(*She takes in the dark living room.*)

And you in your nightie.

(*He tugs at the hem of her nightie.*)

KATHY. My mind is racing.

RYU. I have an idea.

KATHY. Warm milk?

(*He lowers to his knees.*)

RYU. Close your eyes.

KATHY. (*She does.*) Why?

RYU. Just relax.

(*He starts to lift up her slip.*)

KATHY. What are you doing?

RYU. You know what.

KATHY. Baby, I don't think / we should—

RYU. What are you afraid of? The neighbors aren't watching.

KATHY. What if they are?

RYU. Close your eyes.

(*He starts to kiss her under her nightgown.*)

5.

ELLEN *speaks directly out. She is seated now, addressing an unseen circle of people.*

ELLEN. Well ladies. I wanted to talk today about a bit of a touchy subject. Contraception. As you know, we've been letting people determine their own boundaries. But it seems to me that the disruptions have become...rather disruptive.

For instance, when I go to the drug store, I'm just a bit surprised to see a long line of ladies getting their prescriptions filled for birth control. Or when we go to Mass, I'm surprised to see families, good Catholic families, with only a single child. And very recently a girlfriend of mine was bragging that her husband was positively cheerful in his attitude toward wearing a condom. Cheerful!

What's to be done? Well, there's the usual letters to the editor. But I think we should consider drafting a bill. The birth control pill wasn't in homes until 1960—as long as it remains available, people will continue to disrupt. Without the pill, it would be much easier to accurately portray a woman's role at the center of the family, financially dependent on her husband and rooted to the home.

Speaking of which, I want to officially welcome our newest homemaker on the committee, Kathy Nakata.

(KATHY *enters, wearing gloves to the wrist.*)

KATHY. Thank you. (*To the entire group.*) Thank you so much for having me.

ELLEN. Kathy and her husband have been with us a couple of months now. Right now it's just the two of them.

6.

KATHY *is reading a hardcover copy of* Peyton Place *while something simmers on the stove.* RYU *comes in the door, lunchbox in hand.*

RYU. Honey, I'm home.

KATHY. Hi.

RYU. Something smells good.

KATHY. Chicken à la King.

RYU. My favorite.

(*He plants a quick kiss on her.*)

KATHY. Should be just a few more minutes.

RYU. (*Re: the book.*) How is that, anyway?

KATHY. Well it isn't Tolstoy. But I think she has a real narrative gift. I mean, everyone on the block is reading it.

RYU. I know—even the boys at the factory are reading it.

KATHY. I bet they're flipping forward to the cheeky parts.

RYU. You think anyone's town is really that bad?

KATHY. I'm sure.

(*In another part of the stage, light on* DEAN *and* ROGER *lying in a park somewhere. Post-coitus.*)

DEAN. Fuck.

ROGER. Yeah. You can say that again.

(*Beat.*)

Change of pace, fucking when it's light outside. When everyone's just sitting down to supper.

(*In another part of the stage, light on* ELLEN *at the dinner table, alone. A casserole sits in front of her, growing cold. Light remains on her during the rest of the scene.*)

DEAN. You sure this is safe?

ROGER. Sure. Never seen anyone on this side of the pond.

(DEAN *starts to put his clothes on.*)

Same time next week?

DEAN. Too soon.

ROGER. Too soon?

DEAN. It has to get to the point where I'm so full of...

ROGER. Cum?

DEAN. (*Irritated at his coarseness.*) *Wanting.* So full of wanting that it... overcomes the guilt.

ROGER. Yeah, you're really good at the whole guilt thing.

Me, I like to think, after a long week of work, I deserve a little present.

(ROGER *watches as* DEAN *puts his pants on.*)

Just a little longer. Please.

DEAN. It's nearly suppertime.

ROGER. Let her wait an hour. I waited all week.

(*He pulls* DEAN *back down by his belt loops. They kiss, more tenderly now.*
Back to KATHY *and* RYU, *eating dinner now.*)

KATHY. I was at the committee today.

RYU. Again?

KATHY. There was a vote.

They voted to outlaw the Pill.

RYU. They can do that?

(*A slight nod from* KATHY.)

There are other options, right?

KATHY. Of course.

Or, I was thinking. Or. We could not worry about it.

RYU. Oh Kathy, do you mean it?

KATHY. Now that we're here. (*The hint of a contract in this:*) I can imagine having a baby...*here.*

(*Beat.*)

It's four months now.

RYU. I know.

KATHY. We have to decide sooner or later.

(*Back to* ROGER *and* DEAN.)

ROGER. Sometimes I wish we didn't have to hide. You know? Sometimes I wonder if there's a place like that. A place where it'd be you and me sitting down to dinner in one of those houses.

DEAN. You know, Roger. I'm not sure you understand.

We don't know each other.

ROGER. What?

DEAN. You and I—we don't *talk* to each other.

We got what we needed from each other, so.

(*He extends his hand for a handshake. It's a punch in the gut to* ROGER.)

ROGER. I wish you wouldn't—

(*Sotto voce.*)

I mean it's just the two of us here.

DEAN. I'll see you around.

ROGER. No you won't. You never see me, not really.

DEAN. What's going on?

ROGER. I've been thinking for once. Does that scare you?

DEAN. (*Putting on his hat.*) It was a mistake to stay. I've confused you.

ROGER. This is really enough for you. You don't ever think what if it was you and me in one of those houses?

DEAN. I have a house.

ROGER. Jason. I love you.

(DEAN *stops in his tracks.*)

DEAN. Don't—EVER—call me that.

(*Back to* KATHY *and* RYU.)

RYU. If we were to stay…what do we tell it?

KATHY. ?

RYU. I mean would the baby know…the things we know. (*Sotto voce.*) She could grow up thinking there isn't anywhere else.

KATHY. Maybe that's a gift.

(*Short pause.*)

RYU. We had a choice, to come here, but she

KATHY. "She."

(*He smiles, bashful.*)

I thought all fathers wanted boys.

RYU. I want a little girl to spoil. I just hope the rest of the world will spoil her too.

I don't want it to be…hard.

"Hillary Rodham Clinton."

KATHY. Please. You can do this.

(*Pause.*)

RYU. (*Grudgingly.*) Like Reiko.

(KATHY *nods.*)

I was almost out of high school when we went to the camp, but Reiko was only…

(*He seems not to remember.*)

KATHY. Seven.

RYU. Seven.

KATHY. God.

RYU. She was all right at the camp. She made friends so fast. It was when it was over, when we moved back home—I'll never forget watching my little sister learn she was different. The way the kids looked at her at school. The Evacuation Claims Act couldn't fix that. I don't want our little girl to go through that.

KATHY. It'll be different for her. The world is changing, one step at a time.

RYU. Is it?

KATHY. But it's 1955, not 1945. That's what I mean. We're right smack dab in the middle of things changing—and we're the ones helping people change their minds!

RYU. That's fine for us—but what I'm saying is maybe our *child* deserves to know there are fifty years of history / that she's—

KATHY. Will you please try not to / disrupt—

RYU. We have to TALK about this!

(KATHY *looks down at her plate.*)

I'm sorry.

KATHY. No, that was good.

RYU. What?

KATHY. You took charge. Remember you can do that.

You're the husband.

(ELLEN *stands up, hearing someone at the door.*)

ELLEN. Dean?

(DEAN *comes in.*)

DEAN. Darling I'm so sorry. I lost track of time.

ELLEN. Oh, that's all right. I'll put the casserole back in the oven. It'll warm right up.

DEAN. It looks delicious.

ELLEN. Oh, don't sit down. There's mud on your pants.

DEAN. Well look at that. It must've been that walk in the park.

(*Short pause.*)

ELLEN. Go put on a fresh pair, and I'll toss those right in the wash.

(He starts to go.)

DEAN. Ellen?

ELLEN. Yes?

DEAN. I'm a lucky man.

7.

At the factory. ROGER *and* RYU *with lunchboxes.*

RYU. Bologna and cheese.

ROGER. Turkey lettuce tomato.

RYU. Wanna trade?

ROGER. No deal.

RYU. I don't blame you.

ROGER. I mean, what *is* bologna anyway?

RYU. It's Italian. *(Playful.)* Very continental.

    (ROGER *leans over impulsively and takes a bite of* RYU*'s sandwich, looking at him the whole time.*)

RYU. Oh, hey, what are you, um—what do you think?

ROGER. *(Still looking at him, intense.)* Salty.

RYU. I better get back to work.

ROGER. Hey, we got five minutes. Stick around. I was just playing.

RYU. Sure, okay.

ROGER. You're a good worker, Ryu. *(He pronounces it* "Rye-You.") I like having you around.

RYU. Listen, Roger…

Kathy and I are thinking of starting a family.

ROGER. Congrats, Sport! It's about time.

RYU. Yeah, and I was wondering, maybe, I was wondering, if it might be time for me to have a raise.

    (Pause.)

ROGER. *(With some difficulty.)* I'm sorry, Sport.

RYU. Oh.

ROGER. You're one of the best on the floor, but standard raise is after half a year. You've barely been here, what is it?

RYU. Five months. Stuckey was only here three when he got his.

ROGER. Sorry.

(ROGER *starts to go.*)

RYU. Were you at my house, a few months ago?

(ROGER *stops.*)

ROGER. Was I at your house?

RYU. It's just that I thought I saw you, out my window.

ROGER. Why would I be at your house?

RYU. I guess it must have been someone else.

(ROGER *starts to go.*)

Whoever it was, it seems like a fellow could get into a heap of trouble if someone saw him.

(ROGER *stops again.*)

ROGER. Let me tell you about a heap of trouble, Ryu.

See, I know you're really a nice guy. And I know you wouldn't want to do something to mess up your prospects here. Because I've been giving you the good word. I've seen lots of people come through here and nobody does well without the good word from the floor manager. Especially the non-whites.

And if you think that it can't get worse for you than making a thousand boxes a day, then you better take a look at those poor suckers laying tar on the roads or putting spikes in the railroad tracks. Is all I'm saying.

Because I think you and the wife could do really well here, despite your being a little "different" and all, just as long as you have the good word. So why don't you keep your head down and do your work and eat your fucking bologna. See you later.

(*He leaves abruptly.*)

8.

KATHY *turns on a lamp. She has just gotten home, her coat still on. She sits on the arm of the sofa. She touches her stomach.*

RYU *comes in suddenly, startling her.*

KATHY. How was work?

RYU. Work was shit.

KATHY. Language.

RYU. You think I give a fuck?

(*Beat.*)

Why don't you have your apron on?

KATHY. I'm sorry, I was—

RYU. Great, that's just great—Work is shit and dinner isn't in the oven.

KATHY. My appointment was running late.

RYU. You're always at that damn committee.

KATHY. It wasn't the committee.

RYU. Well it sure seems like you're always there. I'm hungry.

KATHY. There are two TV dinners in the freezer. I thought we could heat them up and watch *Lucy*.

> (*Short pause.*)

RYU. What kind?

KATHY. (*Hopefully.*) Salisbury steak.

> (*Seeing how meekly she says this, something relaxes in* RYU.)

RYU. I'm sorry I was sore.

KATHY. What happened today?

RYU. I didn't get the raise

KATHY. Oh Ryu

RYU. And then Roger got angry.

KATHY. He got angry?

RYU. When he said no—I told him what I saw.

KATHY. That night.

RYU. I thought that might change his mind.

KATHY. You mean blackmail?

RYU. I don't know, I didn't think that far. I just thought maybe then he couldn't treat me like a second-class citizen. I'm faster than everyone on that floor. Roger included.

KATHY. You'll show him. Someday you'll be running that factory.

RYU. Damn right. Damn right I will.

KATHY. I'm glad you said it. Now he knows who he's dealing with.

> (*He takes her and kisses her. Suddenly heated.*)

RYU. Even when the neighbors aren't very…neighborly, it makes me feel closer to you.

> (*They continue to kiss—A kind of fire we haven't seen from them before.*)

KATHY. I have something to tell you.

RYU. Let me guess. Those ladies passed another bill.

KATHY. I told you, / it wasn't—

RYU. Oh right.

KATHY. I went to see Dr. Anderson.

RYU. —

KATHY. I'm pregnant.

RYU. Oh my god.

KATHY. You're not upset are you?

RYU. Upset? Are you kidding?
I'm thrilled!

(*He picks her up and whirls her around.*)

I'm fucking ecstatic!

KATHY. (*Amused.*) Language!

RYU. Why would I be upset?

KATHY. I just thought, if you still weren't sure, about staying…

RYU. Oh

KATHY. (*Not endorsing this.*) …then I imagine there are alternatives.

RYU. Alternatives.

(*Beat.*)

KATHY. "Hillary Rodham"—

RYU. No. We're going to have a baby, and we're going to love it.

(*He takes her hand.*)

What other choice is there?

KATHY. The ladies at the committee will be so excited. They were really rooting for us. I think they like me there, more than Ellen even. They were saying I could be a Vice President someday.

RYU. My wife, a woman of influence.

(*They kiss.*)

9.

KATHY *speaks out, seated.* ELLEN *is seated to her left.*

KATHY. Thank you. I wanted to speak today about tolerance. Since Ryu and I first moved here, so many of you have welcomed us with open arms. And while I admit that the hospitality feels wonderful, I worry that it may be jeopardizing the authenticity of our experience—and your own.

Many of you have asked me what it's like to have an Oriental as a husband. And I told you that Ryu is just like you. But that isn't altogether true, is it. He isn't like you. His eyes are a different shape. He was born in another country, a country where suicide is noble and gardens are made of rocks, not grass. A country that, in the very recent past, was at war with your own. I'm not like you either, if I would have him as my husband.

Yes, it's the North. Yes, it's 1955. There's a kind of kindness born out of guilt, about the camps. But that's not the same as tolerance, is it. We don't expect flaming crosses on our lawn. That would be out of proportion. But here are some ideas: You might stare at me in the supermarket line. You might tell Ryu how much you like Chinese food. Your teenage boys could bang trash can lids outside our house, late at night. These are just a few ideas.

I know, it's hard—We're all doing our best here, and I know that we'll be able to find even more ways to give each other an authentic experience. Thank you.

ELLEN. Thank you, Kathy.

Questions for Kathy Nakata.

10.

> KATHY *is asleep in bed with* RYU, *dreaming.*
>
> ELLEN *and* ROGER *sit at the foot of the bed. At least, it looks like* ELLEN *and* ROGER. *They wear '50s clothing, but they sound more like* JENNA *and* OMAR.

KATHY. Kathy still dreamed about the world she left behind.

ELLEN. (*To* ROGER.) So I tried the Master Cleanse?

ROGER. That's the one Beyoncé did.

KATHY. But tonight was different somehow...

> (KATHY *sits up in bed. She is visibly pregnant now.*)

ELLEN. I only lasted four days.

ROGER. It gets boring right?

ELLEN. Totally. Lemon juice and cayenne, it's just like...

ROGER. *Boring!*

ELLEN. *Boring!*

ROGER. Oh hi Katha.

KATHY. "Katha."

ELLEN. Can we do anything for you?

KATHY. I—forget what I came in here for.

ELLEN. White-out, maybe?

ROGER. Or a fax sheet?

ELLEN. Maybe if you go and come back, you'll remember.

KATHY. Maybe.

> (KATHY *starts to lie down again.*)

ROGER. (*Back to* ELLEN.) Okay whatever. So what's going on with you. Any new suitors?

ELLEN. Well there's Ben. And there's Jerry.

ROGER. What?

ELLEN. Oh I was joking, like, "Ben and Jerry's"?

ROGER. Oh. Ha.

ELLEN. Like Saturday nights at home with a pint?

ROGER. Look on the bright side. You could have an Oriental for a husband.

ELLEN. (*Delighted by the scandal.*) She's *right* over *there*.

KATHY. Ryu?

(ROGER *and* ELLEN *start to exit.*)

ROGER. You could be popping out Jap babies.

ELLEN. Ohmigod, totally.

KATHY. Ryu.

ELLEN. I feel bad. Maybe I should bake her some cookies.

ROGER. You never bake *me* anything.

KATHY. Ryu.

(RYU *touches her and she wakes up. The others are gone.*)

RYU. Are you okay?

KATHY. I was having a dream.

RYU. A nightmare?

KATHY. Not exactly. It was about now.

RYU. —

KATHY. I mean, the place we live now. Sort of. As opposed to where we used to live. I mean it was *about* there, but it looked like here.

RYU. (*Almost asleep, humoring her.*) Wow.

KATHY. Do you ever dream that way?

RYU. What way, Honey.

KATHY. About here?

I mean maybe it's like moving to a foreign country. For a while, you only dream in your own language. Your sleep takes you back home. So that's the sign of real fluency—when you start dreaming in the new language.

RYU. It's four in the morning.

KATHY. Sorry. I was just / thinking.

(*A brick crashes through the window and lands in the middle of the floor.*)

Oh my god.

(RYU *turns on the bedside lamp, gets up.*)

What was that?

RYU. There's a note.

(*He unwraps the paper from the brick.*)

KATHY. What does it say?

RYU. (*Baffled.*) It's just one word.

(KATHY *reads it too.*)

KATHY. What does it mean?

11.

DEAN *speaks out, with* ELLEN *looking on.*

DEAN. Thank you all for coming. It has come to our attention that a vandal, or possibly a coordinated team of vandals, has chosen to attack the public spaces of our community.

ELLEN. And private—

DEAN. And in some cases, the private spaces too.

(*Light rises on* ROGER, *elsewhere. He shakes a spray paint can and starts spraying a word onto a wall. We can make out the letter "G."*)

This person, or persons, is using a word designed to undermine our beloved town—And when I say undermine, I mean not only our morals and our civic beauty, but our authenticity.

(ROGER *has now spray-painted the letters, "G," "O," and "U."*)

This is, above all, an attack against our hard-won authenticity.

So, to the vandal, or vandals, I say, simply:

(*We can make out the entire spray-painted word now: "GOOGLE."*)

If this isn't the community for you, we ask you to leave peacefully at once, or face the consequences.

12.

DEAN *and* ELLEN *at home.*

ELLEN. I still don't understand, why would they paint our house and none of the others on the block?

DEAN. We're public figures, Ellen.

ELLEN. The windows of your car. The door to your office.

DEAN. Plainly we were targeted because of our position in the community.

ELLEN. You mean you. *You* were targeted.

DEAN. What are you suggesting?

ELLEN. Could it be someone you know.

Could it be—

DEAN. It could not.

> (*Pause.*
>
> *Grasping at straws:*)

What if it was the Communists?

ELLEN. Don't be ridiculous. This isn't about Communists.

DEAN. No, but could it be helpful if it was?

> (*She looks at him.*)

The whole community is rattled. We name a few names. Possible suspects...

ELLEN. Names like who?

> (*A cell phone rings. They freeze.*
>
> *It rings again—a terrible, unmistakably modern ring.*
>
> DEAN *takes keys out of his pocket. He goes to a drawer. It rings again.*)

It must be an emergency.

> (DEAN *has opened the drawer. The ring is louder now. He answers.*)

DEAN. Hello?

> (*Light on* ROGER, *elsewhere.*)

ROGER. I have to talk to you. I mean really talk.

> (DEAN *tries to sound as neutral as possible.*)

DEAN. We're talking.

> (*He moves farther from* ELLEN.)

ROGER. Didn't you get my messages?

DEAN. Messages. Is that what you call them?

ROGER. "Google." Our Safe Word.

> (*Short pause.*)

Why didn't I hear from you?

DEAN. I was...scared.

ROGER. Scared you feel the same way?

> (*Pause.*)

Is she there?

DEAN. Of course.

ROGER. I have to talk, like ourselves. I can't be this person any more. I feel ugly. All the time. It isn't worth it. I want to be with you. And I don't just mean fucking.

ELLEN. Who is it? /

DEAN. Headquarters.

ROGER. (*Overlapping at "/"*) For a while it worked. I'm not saying it didn't. But I wake up next to her and for the first second I'm awake I think I'm with you—and then it all comes back to me, and there's still a whole day of being someone else ahead of me.

DEAN. It's not someone else. It's you.

ROGER. If it's not someone else, why am I different in my dreams?

> (*Pause. ELLEN has moved to DEAN. Touching his shoulder supportively, possessively.*)

Jason, don't hang up. Jason? I'm sick for you. I was scared that if I didn't play along—but it's worse being here and not seeing you. Or seeing you at the store and you look like you don't even know me.

That used to be hard for you too.

> (*Short pause.*)

What if we just walked away?

> (*Short pause.*)

It would be so easy. We could just keep walking 'til there's highways and electric signs and Toyotas. I'll go without you if I have to. But what if we both just walked away.

DEAN. I'll have to call you back.

> (*DEAN flips the phone shut and ROGER's light goes out. He puts the phone in his pocket, not the drawer.*)

That was Headquarters. I have to go right away.

ELLEN. Where?

DEAN. To the city. It's an emergency.

ELLEN. What kind of emergency?

DEAN. I can't—.

ELLEN. Will the community need to know?

DEAN. That's what we'll have to decide.

ELLEN. How long will you be gone this time?

DEAN. As long as it takes.

ELLEN. A day? Two days?

DEAN. As long as it takes.

ELLEN. Why don't I come with you?

DEAN. The community is unsettled. They need you.

ELLEN. They're not so unsettled. *We're* unsettled!

> (*Beat.*)

I think I should go with you.

DEAN. You know you don't make sense out there, Darling. I love that about you.

(*He touches her face.*)

You're my best girl. You always were.

ELLEN. I wasn't always.

(*He kisses her on the cheek.*)

DEAN. I better be off.

ELLEN. Why don't I make you a sandwich?

DEAN. That's all right.

ELLEN. Dean.

You forgot your hat.

(*She holds the hat out to him. The stakes seem curiously high. He takes the hat.*)

DEAN. Well then. (*He's opened the door.*)

I'll bring you something back. Some new fabric, maybe.

ELLEN. (*A desperate outburst.*) Please don't leave me.

DEAN. I'll see you soon.

(*And he's gone.*)

13.

KATHY, *even more pregnant now, speaks to the seated circle.*

KATHY. As you know, we've had a flurry of questions in light of recent events. What is the most authentic way for us to respond to the graffiti? That word. Do we take it in as we would a racial slur? Or should it be nothing but a harmless, made-up word, a nonsense word? What about First Amendment rights? Property damage aside, is our vandal simply exercising free speech?

More importantly, though, it raises questions about what to do with our knowledge of the world outside. It's impossible to forget the things we know, after all. It's possible, I suppose, that when you try to forget something, it can get louder and louder until all you can do is say it out loud. If that's what happened to the vandal, could it happen to you or me? I just think we need to ask the big questions.

(*Pause.*)

I'm sorry, I know Ellen should really be leading us through this…complicated time. I'm sure she's going to be here soon. I know she would never willfully miss a meeting.

14.

KATHY *is visiting* ELLEN, *who looks a wreck.*

ELLEN. Five days.

KATHY. Have you called the police?

ELLEN. It's outside their jurisdiction.

KATHY. What do you mean?

ELLEN. I mean it's…outside.

KATHY. I see.

ELLEN. He's sometimes called away like this—but never this long.

KATHY. They must really need him there.

(*Pause.*)

Forgive me, but has it always been…happy between you two?

ELLEN. What do you mean?

KATHY. Forgive me if I'm being personal—

It's just, an attractive man like that, going off on the road…

ELLEN. You mean did he ever stray.

KATHY. Yes, thank you.

I don't mean to pry.

ELLEN. Oh Kathy, that's exactly what you mean to do.

KATHY. I'm sorry?

ELLEN. When you first moved here, we wondered if you'd mix with the community. "I don't want to be a *housewife.*" But you've really involved yourself, Kathy. You're so *involved.* You'd think you were after my job.

KATHY. I don't think I deserve that, Ellen.

ELLEN. Oh?

KATHY. You've been cooped up in this house all week, no one's seen hide nor hair of you, the girls at the Authenticity Committee are saying "Off with her head" but I stand up for you, Ellen, I say *Ellen is under a lot of stress, Ellen needs our love and support right now.*

ELLEN. They said "Off with her head"?

KATHY. Well, there was a little more decorum than that.

ELLEN. Look at you. You really think you can take over. And what exactly qualifies you to run a community? Is it your crab puff recipe? Or is it your miraculous fertility?

KATHY. You think I'm awfully naïve, don't you. You've always thought so. But I know some things you don't.

ELLEN. All you know is how to keep that Jap husband of yours on a short leash.

KATHY. *Ellen.*

ELLEN. Or don't you even know that much?

Maybe that's why you're always making eyes at my husband.

KATHY. DEAN IS A HOMOSEXUAL!

(*Short pause.*)

He and Roger. Ryu saw them together. Dean is a fucking homosexual.

(*Pause.* ELLEN *laughs to herself.*)

ELLEN. Don't you think I know that?

KATHY. What?

ELLEN. Dean and Roger have always been together.

Long before we came here, they were together.

KATHY. (*Sotto voce.*) Are we talking about?—

ELLEN. (*Not sotto voce.*) The real world, yes.

KATHY. Are you saying—what are you saying?

ELLEN. Jason and I first met in college.

KATHY. Jason?

ELLEN. Dean's real name.

We were class of '95 at Sarah Lawrence. We were roommates for two years. Then we moved to New York after graduation. That's where he met Roger. His first boyfriend. Roger moved in it seemed like overnight. Whenever they fought, Jason would come and talk to me. And I would listen.

KATHY. You were in love with him.

(*Short pause.*)

ELLEN. I was in love with him.

I'm still in love with him, God help me.

It's such a stupid old story, isn't it.

KATHY. It's not stupid.

ELLEN. Jason and Roger got jobs at start-ups. I got my Master's at NYU. We went to bars. Everything you're supposed to do. But it was too easy.

KATHY. Too easy?

ELLEN. That's what Jason said. When we were trying to figure out what was wrong with us.

KATHY. So it was Jason's idea?

ELLEN. You'd press a few buttons and a tub of Häagen-Dazs would come ten minutes later. DVDs. We put the trash at the end of the hall and someone made it disappear. I took a whole class online. I got an A. Easy. There was nothing in the way, nothing to—remind us… I'm not making sense.

KATHY. No, I think I—

ELLEN. And Jason and Roger, that was too easy too. Their families accepted them, they could walk down any block holding hands. There was no friction.

KATHY. What do you mean friction.

ELLEN. (*Searching for the words.*) No resistance. No…friction. (*Beat.*) And then Jason met a man from a place where it was different. A man with a hat and a briefcase. They thought it'd be an adventure.

KATHY. What about you?

ELLEN. Jason asked me to come with him. To be with him. He made it fun. He got down on one knee, he gave me a ring. We were laughing. Me and my gay husband. But the longer we were here, the less it was like pretend. I cooked, I cleaned, he supported me, he called me Darling—and once in a while, he would even—

KATHY. You don't have to tell me.

ELLEN. I don't see why not. He would fuck me, Kathy. Once in a while. *Quid pro quo.* But I never got pregnant, I couldn't get pregnant—like the universe knew it was pretend or something. But whenever I worried that it was all pretend, I'd look down at my ring and that was real. Even the feeling of not having a baby when everyone was supposed to be having them—that was real too, that was mine. That was something more than I had in the other world. Do you understand?

KATHY. Yes.

ELLEN. Dean carried out his homosexuality in a perfectly authentic way, with the right shame and secrecy. Of course I saw the clues—he'd say he couldn't sleep, he'd go out for night walks… And I'd suspect, the way a '50s wife would suspect. And I'd be grateful that I was the one he came home to. And it was harder than our old life, and it was better.

(*Pause.*)

KATHY. But, if you already know about Dean, then why are you…

ELLEN. Such a fucking mess?

KATHY. (*As in "I wasn't going to say it."*) Well.

ELLEN. Because I know he isn't coming back this time.

(*With sudden difficulty.*)

What am I going to do?

KATHY. I'm going to speak firmly for a moment, Ellen.

You have to bury your husband. You have to fit this into your Dossier.

ELLEN. —

KATHY. The key will be to make everything as true as possible.

ELLEN. How?

KATHY. Maybe we say that Dean and Roger *were* homosexuals, yes.
They both had wonderful wives, but their deepest desires were eating at them
from the inside.

ELLEN. But Dean, no one will believe that he would / just leave his—

KATHY. (*Placating.*) We'll say that Dean rejected that part of himself. He
cut things off with Roger, he prayed, he…killed the darkness in himself. But
Roger couldn't accept it. That's why he started terrorizing the community.
Finally he asked Dean to meet him in a park one night. And, when Dean
rejected him again…Roger shot him.

ELLEN. And himself. He killed himself too.

KATHY. Good.

> (*Pause.*)

The official story will be a little different, of course: We'll call it a mugging,
maybe…a tragic mugging. Dean couldn't sleep, he was out for one of his
night walks, maybe he ran into a vagrant.

> (*Pause.*)

We'll buy you a widow's dress. We'll have a beautiful funeral. Dean was so
important to this community.

ELLEN. And I'm supposed to just…be that forever? The widow everyone's
sorry for?

KATHY. Or you could leave.

> (*They lock eyes.*)

But think how rich it will be. How complicated. When you pass by, people will
whisper, why was Dean in that particular park, so far from his house? Some
people might even whisper that he ran off to be a homosexual in that other
world. People will whisper. What could be more authentic than that?

But everyone will be so moved by how you handle it. With your head held
high and proud through all the gossip.

ELLEN. Yes.

KATHY. And when you're ready, you'll come back to the committee.

> (*Short pause.*)

ELLEN. What about his responsibilities? Dean did more in that job than
anyone knows.

KATHY. Just leave that to me.

ELLEN. You're being so nice to me. Why do you even want me to stay?

KATHY. Because you're my neighbor.

> (*Beat.*)

You've been so helpful to me, Ellen. I'm so happy I can help you now.

15.

RYU speaks out. KATHY stands farther off, enormously pregnant now.

RYU. First of all, welcome. Welcome to the SDO.

I'm sure you all have a lot of questions.

"What do I wear?"

"How do I talk?"

"How do I explain this to the kids?"

Kathy and I will help you answer all of these perfectly normal questions.

KATHY. The most important thing to remember is that all of us were newcomers at one point. I mean gosh, we're *still* newcomers. Ryu and I have only been here, what

RYU. Fourteen months.

KATHY. Fourteen months. And Ryu's already the floor manager at the box factory. I'm so proud.

RYU. Honey...

KATHY. Now I'm embarrassing him, but I think it's important to know how life in 1955 can really focus you.

In the modern world, people are always talking about their problems. Always asking "How can I be happier?" Maybe if I had a different diet, maybe if I had a different therapist. A different childhood. In the '50s, you have to keep it together. You aren't just living for yourself. You have a responsibility to make life wonderful for your husband and your child and your community. (*Suddenly more personal.*) It's amazing how...healing that responsibility can be.

(*RYU comes forward to join KATHY.*)

RYU. We are not saying life is better in the 1950s. We are not saying people are happier necessarily. We are saying that they're more *present.*

KATHY. Thank you, yes.

RYU. We are not in pursuit of the past.

We are in pursuit of the present.

(*The baby kicks inside KATHY.*)

KATHY. Oh.

RYU. What is it?

KATHY. (*Hand to her belly.*) The present.

16.

KATHY *is asleep next to* RYU, *dreaming.*

DEAN *and* ELLEN *in the living room, still dressed in '50s clothing.*

KATHY. Kathy hardly ever dreamed of that other world any more. Most nights she dreamed a row of houses just like the ones at Maple and Vine.

DEAN. It was a lovely day, wasn't it.

ELLEN. It was. One of the loveliest I can remember.

DEAN. I'm a little hungry. Are you hungry, Darling?

ELLEN. Yes, a bit. I suppose I should get dinner on the table.

KATHY. But tonight her dream was different.

In this dream, everything was a little bit easier.

ELLEN. Were you thinking of something in particular?

DEAN. Oh anything, really. Whatever you can whip up.

KATHY. In this world, there was a button to call for everything.

(*There is a knock at the door.* ELLEN *opens the door and there is an entire Thanksgiving dinner sitting on the welcome mat.*)

DEAN. That looks wonderful.

ELLEN. It does, doesn't it.

DEAN. Well, what are you waiting for? Bring it in.

(*She does.*)

KATHY. There was a button for bringing the milk, and a button for crab puffs, and a button for soggy cake, God knows why.

(DEAN *starts to eat a turkey leg.*)

DEAN. This is excellent, Honey.

ELLEN. Thank you.

(*There is another knock at the door.*)

Who could that be now.

KATHY. There was even a button for bringing the things you most desire, so you didn't have to go looking for them in the night.

(ELLEN *opens the door and* ROGER *is there. He looks at* DEAN.)

DEAN. Well, what are you waiting for? Come on in.

ELLEN. Are you hungry, Roger?

ROGER. (*Looking at* DEAN.) Always.

KATHY. All of these buttons were part of a brand-new machine. And the genius of this machine was that it brought things to people, instead of bringing people to things.

ELLEN. I'll put a record on. It's so much nicer to eat with music.

DEAN. Something slow and pretty.

(ELLEN *doesn't lift a finger, but light rises on the hi-fi. A beautiful piece of night music starts to play.*)

ROGER. What is that? Brahms?

ELLEN. (*There is no album cover.*) I'm not sure, the album cover just says "Classical for Lovers."

KATHY. This worked with information too—so there was no more need to go to a library to learn the answer to something. Now you only had to wonder for a few moments.

DEAN. It's Chopin. The "Raindrop Prelude."

ROGER. Ah yes.

ELLEN. You could almost dance to it.

KATHY. And before long, there was no more need to go anywhere.

(ROGER *stands. He holds out his hand to* DEAN.)

ROGER. Well?

DEAN. I have two left feet.

ROGER. (*Gentle.*) I know.

KATHY. There was no longer anyone watching over you. No one to tell you what you could or couldn't do.

(DEAN *takes* ROGER's *hand. They start to slow dance to the music, very simply and beautifully.*)

The new machinery worked so smoothly and so well that people never sensed how it was changing them.

(ELLEN *watches them dancing while she eats. Content. The dream doesn't get scarier exactly, so much as it gets more hypnotically tranquil, more enveloping.*)

These warm and well-fed people didn't realize that they were dying inside.

(RYU *stirs in bed.*)

RYU. Kath.

KATHY. It was so easy to get what they wanted that they no longer wanted anything.

RYU. Kathy.

KATHY. It was so long since they'd had to go anywhere or talk to anyone, that they forgot who they even were. They thought they knew, but somehow, slowly, they'd forgotten.

RYU. Kathy.

(RYU *touches her and she wakes up.*)

KATHY. What?

(*The music goes out. The others are gone now.*
We hear the soft crying of a baby in a crib next to the bed.)

RYU. Shh, it's okay. You were talking in your sleep.

KATHY. What was I saying?

RYU. I couldn't make it out. But you sounded scared.

KATHY. I was having a dream.

RYU. A nightmare?

KATHY. Yes.

RYU. Well you're okay now.

(*He picks up the baby.*)

Shhh. Shhh.

(*He hands* KATHY *the baby.*)

We're here at Maple and Vine, and your daughter is almost sleeping through the night.

(*He holds* KATHY *as she rocks the baby.*)

It was all a bad dream.

KATHY. Yes. Yes it was, wasn't it.

End of Play

HYGIENE
by Gregory Hischak

Copyright © 2011 by Gregory Hischak. All rights reserved. CAUTION: Professionals and amateurs are hereby warned that *Hygiene* is subject to royalty. It is fully protected under the copyright laws of the United States of America and of all countries covered by the International Copyright Union (including the Dominion of Canada and the rest of the British Commonwealth), the Berne Convention, the Pan-American Copyright Convention and the Universal Copyright Convention, as well as all countries with which the United States has reciprocal copyright relations. All rights, including professional, amateur stage rights, motion picture, recitation, lecturing, public reading, radio broadcasting, television, video or sound recording, all other forms of mechanical or electronic reproduction, such as CD-ROM, CD-I, information storage and retrieval systems, and photocopying, and the rights of translation into foreign languages, are strictly reserved. Particular emphasis is laid upon the matter of readings, permission for which must be secured from the Author's agent in writing.

Required royalties must be paid every time this play is performed before any audience, whether or not it is presented for profit and whether or not admission is charged.

All inquiries concerning rights, including amateur rights, should be addressed to Gregory Hischak at alarmpup@verizon.net.

BIOGRAPHY

Gregory Hischak's full-length play *The Center of Gravity* won the 2009 Clauder Prize and received its world premiere at Portland Stage Company (Portland, ME). *Volcanic in Origin* was staged as part of the 2011 Source Festival (Washington, D.C.). His other full-lengths—he prefers not to talk about. His short works have been staged by Actors Theatre of Louisville (KY), City Theater (FL), Firehouse Theatre (MA), Pan Festival (CA) and the Boston Theatre Marathon (MA). *Poor Shem* and *Crows Over Wheatfield* are included in the Smith & Kraus anthology *Best Ten-Minute Plays of 2010*. Hischak is a 2011 Finalist with the Massachusetts Cultural Council (in Playwriting). He lives in South Yarmouth, Massachusetts.

ACKNOWLEDGMENTS

Hygiene premiered at the Humana Festival of New American Plays in March 2011. It was directed by Kent Nicholson with the following cast:

WENDY	Teresa Avia Lim
HOWARD	Daniel Pearce
RITA	Sara Surrey

and the following production staff:

Scenic Designer	Ryan Wineinger
Costume Designer	Lisa Weber
Lighting Designer	Nick Dent
Sound Designer	Paul Doyle
Properties Designers	Jay Tollefsen
Wig Designer	Heather Fleming
Media Designer	Philip Allgeier
Stage Manager	Kathy Preher
Dramaturg	Rachel Lerner-Ley
Casting	Zan Sawyer-Dailey

Hygiene was developed for Theatre Under The Influence's Radio Activity Series (Seattle, WA) and underwent additional shaping with the Northwest Playwrights Alliance (Olympia, WA). It was staged as part of the 2010 Boston Theater Marathon with Mary Callanan as Rita, Will McGarrahan as Howard, and Santina Umbach as Wendy. Directed by Jim Fagan.

CHARACTERS

WENDY, a seven- or eight-year-old girl.

HOWARD, her father.

RITA, her mother.

SETTING

Action unfolds in the present day in a—let's say, ranch-style—home.

Sara Surrey, Teresa Avia Lim and Daniel Pearce
in *Hygiene*

35th Annual Humana Festival of New American Plays
Actors Theatre of Louisville, 2011
Photo by Joe Geinert

Yes! 3 Copies (handwritten)

HYGIENE

The suggestion of a living room in a present day—le
center stage, a large chair that WENDY sits on. Po
table has been positioned close to the chair. What may
is that WENDY has a large human-like creature, i
shoulder-to-feet from the top of her head. Though awkward
the creature neither speaks nor causes anything but emotion

RITA. (*Into phone.*) No, I said— (*Beat.*) Howard, turn the rad___ ___wn. (*Beat.*) I said Wendy came home early from school today.

WENDY. Mommy, they told me to come home.

RITA. I know, dear. (*Into phone.*) St. Theresa's called me to say they were… what?

WENDY. I didn't do anything wrong, Mommy.

RITA. No honey. (*Into phone.*) They found something in her hair.

(WENDY *wipes her nose across her sleeve.*)

WENDY. Mr. Yampolski said—

RITA. I know, dear.

WENDY. He patted my head—

RITA. I know, dear.

WENDY. I didn't put anything in my hair…

RITA. Honey, I'm talking to your father. (*Quieter into phone.*) It's doubled in size since she got home. It…I don't know what it is. No, it's not lice. It's bigger than lice…no, bigger than a tick. What? (*Beat.*) No, bigger than that… Howard, I know what a Chihuahua looks like. It's bigger than that— (*Beat.*) A lot bigger than that. OK, I'll see you soon.

(RITA *hangs up phone, stooping down to examine* WENDY*'s hair.*)
Wendy, let me take another look at that.

(RITA *works her fingers through strands of* WENDY*'s hair.*)

WENDY. OK…ouch.

RITA. I'm sorry, hon.

WENDY. Ouch.

RITA. I'm sorry, hon.

WENDY. Ouch.

RITA. I'm sorry, hon.

WENDY. Ouch.

RITA. I'm sorry, hon.

WENDY. Ouch.

orry, hon.

Y. Ouch!

TA. Wendy, what I'm trying to do is find the head.

WENDY. The head?

RITA. Sometimes these things bury their heads…into…

(*Beat.*)

WENDY. Into what, Mommy?

RITA. Into things. Do you want any juice or something?

WENDY. It's getting heavier, Mommy.

RITA. It's growing, dear. (*Quietly grunting in revulsion.*) I'm going to the other room to get the book.

WENDY. The good book?

RITA. No, the medical book.

WENDY. The big book with the scab pictures?

RITA. Yes.

WENDY. That's the good book.

RITA. Will you be OK alone for a minute?

WENDY. Uh huh.

(RITA *exits upstage.*)

Mr. Yampolski patted me on the head in music class.

RITA. (*From offstage.*) I know, dear.

WENDY. I was riffing on "Wheels on the Bus." (*Sung.*) THHHHE—WHEELS ON THE BUS GO ROUND AND ROUND, ROUND AND ROUND, ROUND AND ROUND. THE WH—

(RITA *re-enters with book.*)

RITA. Wendy, why was Mr. Yampolski patting your head?

WENDY. He liked my riffing and he patted my head. He patted my head and then he jerked it away and got real strange—

RITA. Don't squirm, Wendy.

WENDY. I Didn't Put Anything In My Hair—it was just There.

RITA. It's something you picked up.

WENDY. What is it, Mommy?

RITA. Wait a minute, dear.

(RITA *compares several pages with the parasite on* WENDY'*s head.*)

WENDY. (*Sung.*) THHHHE—WHEELS ON THE BUS GO ROUND AND ROUND, ROUND AND ROUND—

RITA. Dear.

WENDY. (*Spoken.*) The wheels go round and round, Mommy.

RITA. I know they do, dear. Please stop singing for a moment. (*Reading from book.*) Dark blue turtleneck, black corduroys—(*Quiet shudder of revulsion.*)—black corduroys… Oh—My—God.

(RITA *shuts the book with grim finality.*)

WENDY. Did the big scab book tell you what it is?

(RITA *stoops down beside* WENDY.)

RITA. It did… Dear, I'm afraid you've picked up a minimalist composer somewhere.

WENDY. (*Frantic.*) Get it off me! Get it off me! Get it off me! (*Beat, then calmly.*) Mommy, what's a minimolic compaler?

RITA. A minimalist composer, dear. You probably picked it up in music class.

WENDY. Can you get it off me?

RITA. Well you see dear, the minimalist composer has buried its head deep into your scalp.

WENDY. What's it doing there?

RITA. It's feasting off your defenseless capillaries.

WENDY. Can you get it off me now, Mommy?

RITA. We have to remove it very carefully, dear. We have to make sure we remove the head. Otherwise a new minimalist composer will grow from the old head that's left in there—and you'll get infected.

WENDY. What do the heads of min-i-mal-ist composers look like, Mommy?

RITA. I can't really tell, dear.

WENDY. Can you please, please get it off me?

(*As* RITA *continues to pull at* WENDY'*s strands.*)

Ouch.

RITA. I'm sorry, hon.

WENDY. Ouch.

RITA. I'm sorry, hon.

WENDY. Ouch.

RITA. I'm sorry, hon.

WENDY. Ouch.

RITA. I'm sorry, hon.

(HOWARD *enters.*)

HOWARD. Rita?

RITA. Howard, thank god you're here.

HOWARD. Rita, I'm leaving you.

RITA. Howard, can it wait?

(HOWARD *pauses to notice the minimalist composer protruding from* WENDY*'s head.*)

HOWARD. Is that it?

RITA. What do you mean is that it?

HOWARD. That's not a Chihuahua?

RITA. Of course it's not a Chihuahua, Howard.

HOWARD. What in god's name is it?

WENDY. It's a minimolic compaler.

HOWARD. What in the world is that?

RITA. It's a minimalist composer.

HOWARD. What in the world is that?

RITA. It's what's growing out of your daughter's head. I looked it up in the book.

WENDY. The big scab book, Daddy.

HOWARD. The good book?

WENDY. Uh huh. I picked it up in music class.

(RITA *twists at the minimalist composer.*)

HOWARD. For all the money we spend sending her to St. Theresa's—

RITA. Well, you had us pull her out of Immaculate Conception.

HOWARD. They had folk singers at the youth mass.

RITA. And Lindey Elementary before that.

HOWARD. They were bringing poets into the school, Rita—Poets.

RITA. Well, this is the good it did us.

HOWARD. Did you try pliers? Did you try a match? A match, Rita—

WENDY. I'd like it off me now, please.

RITA. Mommy's trying, dear.

HOWARD. That's one persevering little blood-sucking parasite.

WENDY. Is it off now, Mommy?

RITA. Almost, dear. (*To* HOWARD.) Wendy was riffing in music class.

HOWARD. Riffing?

WENDY. I was riffing. (*Singing.*) THHHHE—WHEELS ON THE BUS GO ROUND AND ROUND—ROUND AND ROUND,

(*Song continues over* RITA *and* HOWARD*'s dialogue section below.*)

ROUND AND ROUND. THE WHEELS ON THE BUS GO ROUND AND ROUND ALL THROUGH THE TOWN.

HOWARD. Rita, there's something you need to know.

RITA. Not now, Howard.

HOWARD. There's something very important—

RITA. Not now, Howard.

HOWARD. That you need to know, Rita—

(WENDY *stops singing.*)

RITA. Howard. Your daughter has a minimalist composer growing out of her head.

HOWARD. I know the timing is bad.

WENDY. Is it off?

RITA. Almost, hon. (*To* HOWARD.) Will you comfort your daughter?

HOWARD. (*Stooping down beside* WENDY.) Wendy, I'm leaving your mother.

WENDY. Again?

HOWARD. (*Annoyed.*) Yes, again—(*Looking closely at the minimalist composer.*) Is that a turtleneck?

WENDY. Dark blue.

HOWARD. No, it's black.

WENDY. Mommy said dark blue.

RITA. It's dark blue.

HOWARD. Is it?

RITA. The corduroys are black—who is it, Howard?

HOWARD. (*Beat.*) Denise.

RITA & WENDY. Again?

HOWARD. (*Annoyed.*) Yes. Again.

WENDY. Is Denise going to be my new mommy again?

RITA. Howard, I think at this point we need to focus on our situation here.

HOWARD. I'm talking about our situation.

RITA. I'm talking about the bloodsucking parasite situation.

HOWARD. Always in denial, aren't you, Rita?

RITA. Howard, try to be of some help here.

(*While* RITA *continues tugging,* HOWARD *squats down beside* WENDY.)

HOWARD. Wendy? Do you remember last summer, at the lake, when we found that mime in your shoe?

WENDY. That was icky.

HOWARD. It was. And what did Daddy do…? Remember?

WENDY. You threw it on the fire and burned it.

HOWARD. That's right. I threw it on the fire and burned it and that nasty old mime never bothered anyone ever again, did it?

WENDY. Why does the milimedic cowholer stick itself into people's heads?

HOWARD. Ask your mother.

WENDY. Mommy, why does the—

RITA. The minimalist composer needs blood to live, dear.

WENDY. Doesn't it have its own blood?

RITA. Some creatures, like minimalist composers, and mimes, and glass-blowers—

HOWARD. And poets.

RITA. And poets—

HOWARD. And playwrights.

RITA. And playwrights are born without their own blood—and so they need to find a host creature in order to survive. You see, without its host, that minimalist composer on your head would die.

WENDY. (*Adamant.*) I want it to die!

HOWARD. (*Adamant.*) Dammit Rita, I want it to die too!

RITA. We all want the minimalist composer to die. Now hold still, for just a minute, dear.

(RITA *continues tugging during the following rhythmic exchange.*)

WENDY. (*Sung.*) THHHE WHEELS ON THE BUS GO ROUND AND ROUND.

HOWARD. Rita, we should talk about it.

RITA. (*Heavy exertion.*) Errrrghh.

WENDY. (*Sung.*) THHHE WHEELS ON THE BUS GO ROUND AND ROUND.

HOWARD. Rita, we should talk about it.

RITA. (*Heavy exertion.*) Errrrghh.

WENDY. (*Sung.*) THHHE WHEELS ON THE BUS GO ROUND AND ROUND.

HOWARD. Rita, we should talk about it.

RITA. (*Heavy exertion.*) Errrrghh.

WENDY. (*Sung.*) THHHE WHEELS ON THE BUS GO ROUND AND ROUND.

HOWARD. Rita, we should talk about it.

RITA. (*Up.*) What The Hell Is Happening To This Family?

HOWARD. I've been under a lot of stress, Rita.

WENDY. (*Sung.*) THHHE WHEELS ON THE BUS GO ROUND AND ROUND.

RITA. (*Annoyed.*) Wendy.

HOWARD. (*Urgent.*) Rita—

WENDY. Ouch.

RITA. I'm sorry, hon.

WENDY. Daddy, which one is Denise?

HOWARD. The redhead.

RITA. Auburn.

HOWARD. Redhead—is it auburn?

RITA. It is and this isn't the time.

HOWARD. When is it the time, Rita?

RITA. The next time, Howard. The next time around.

HOWARD. It's always the next time around, Rita.

RITA. It has to be, Howard. It always has to be the next time around.

HOWARD. Why not this time?

RITA. Because it would be the end.

HOWARD. (*Beat.*) Isn't it time?

WENDY. Are you two riffing?

HOWARD. Rita, there's no time li—

RITA. Like the next time.

HOWARD. (*Beat, then to* WENDY.) We're riffing, sweetie.

RITA. Mommy and Daddy are just riffing.

WENDY. OK, "Wheels on the Bus," everyone.

HOWARD. We're getting her out of that school.

WENDY. (*Sung.*) THHHHE—WHEELS ON THE BUS GO ROUND AND ROUND, ROUND AND ROUND, ROUND AND ROUND.

ALL. (*Sung.*) THE WHEELS ON THE BUS GO ROUND AND ROUND ALL THROUGH THE TOWN.

WENDY. (*Sung.*) THE MOMMY ON THE BUS SAYS

RITA. (*Sung.*) I-LOVE-YOU. I-LOVE-YOU. I-LOVE-YOU.

WENDY. (*Sung.*) THE DADDY ON THE BUS SAYS

HOWARD. (*Sung.*) I-LOVE-YOU-TOO—

ALL. (*Sung.*) ALL THROUGH THE TOWN.

WENDY. Again!

> (*Quick strike to black.*)

End of Play

CHICAGO, SUDAN
A choreopoem for too soon gone...
by Marc Bamuthi Joseph

Copyright © 2011 by Marc Bamuthi Joseph. All rights reserved. CAUTION: Professionals and amateurs are hereby warned that *Chicago, Sudan* is subject to royalty. It is fully protected under the copyright laws of the United States of America and of all countries covered by the International Copyright Union (including the Dominion of Canada and the rest of the British Commonwealth), the Berne Convention, the Pan-American Copyright Convention and the Universal Copyright Convention, as well as all countries with which the United States has reciprocal copyright relations. All rights, including professional, amateur stage rights, motion picture, recitation, lecturing, public reading, radio broadcasting, television, video or sound recording, all other forms of mechanical or electronic reproduction, such as CD-ROM, CD-I, information storage and retrieval systems, and photocopying, and the rights of translation into foreign languages, are strictly reserved. Particular emphasis is laid upon the matter of readings, permission for which must be secured from the Author's agent in writing.

Required royalties must be paid every time this play is performed before any audience, whether or not it is presented for profit and whether or not admission is charged.

All inquiries concerning rights, including amateur rights, should be addressed to: MAPP International Productions, 140 Second Avenue, Suite 502, New York, NY 10003, ATTN: Cathy Zimmerman.

BIOGRAPHY

Marc Bamuthi Joseph returned to Actors Theatre after premiering *the break/s* during the 2008 Humana Festival. He is the Artistic Director of the HBO documentary *Brave New Voices* and an inaugural recipient of the United States Artists Fellowship. Premiering at Yerba Buena Center and visiting the Walker Art Center and the Brooklyn Academy of Music, among other sites, his performance piece *red, black and GREEN: a blues* engages the eco-equity movement in Black neighborhoods across America. In 2011, he collaborated with Amy Seiwert and Daniel Bernard Roumain to premiere *Home in 7*, a commissioned libretto for the Atlanta Ballet. Bamuthi's *Word Becomes Flesh* was remounted in December 2010 as part of the National Endowment for the Arts' "American Masterpieces" series and will tour throughout North America and Hawaii through 2012. He is the 2011 Alpert Award winner in Theater.

ACKNOWLEDGMENTS

Chicago, Sudan premiered at the Humana Festival of New American Plays in March 2011. It was directed by Michael John Garcés and featured Marc Bamuthi Joseph, with the following production staff:

Scenic Designer	Ryan Wineinger
Costume Designer	Lisa Weber
Lighting Designer	Nick Dent
Sound Designer	Paul Doyle
Properties Designers	Mark Walston
Media Designer	Philip Allgeier
Stage Manager	Kathy Preher
Dramaturg	Rachel Lerner-Ley
Casting	Zan Sawyer-Dailey

Chicago, Sudan was commissioned by Actors Theatre of Louisville. It is part of *red, black, and GREEN: a blues*, co-commissioned by Yerba Buena Center for the Arts, Walker Art Center, Cynthia Woods Mitchell Center (University of Houston) and Lehigh University; and supported by The National Endowment for the Arts, New England Foundation for the Arts National Dance Project, The MAP Fund (a program of Creative Capital), Eastbay Commissioning Fund, United States Artists and The America Project, supported by Ford Foundation and Nathan Cummings Foundation.

PLAYERS

One in flesh, but the rest just as loud.

DG (the man), speaks for the voice.

TV (the voice), speaks to soothe the mom.

KASÉ, when the best way to speak is to move.

NOTE

You must understand that what you mean by play, and what I mean by play may be different. What follows is a slight structural stretch toward you. I welcome your similar stretch toward me.

Marc Bamuthi Joseph
in *Chicago, Sudan*

35th Annual Humana Festival of New American Plays
Actors Theatre of Louisville, 2011
Photo by Joe Geinert

CHICAGO, SUDAN

About a man. A mom. And a voice. Playing by the side of the road.

The sound of a marching band.
Silence.
A light up. A man (DG) is dancing (KASÉ). Somewhere in the movement
signature is a reference to the second of death. The first rising of ghost.

DG WITH KASÉ. The guy singing was my baby mama's last boyfriend
before me...
We've been dancing around my son, pretending that the boy isn't destiny...
The church you smell in his voice is grief...
He lost his mom while waiting to perform at a festival for life...
Somewhere between Sudan, and Chicago's south side...

DG. Me and the woman whose son just died are sitting on a bench
While a marching band goes by
Without turning
She offers me watermelon
Unripe fruit from a tree never grown

DG WITH KASÉ. See the warning
It is warming
And that's just the block
Feel the heat rising like ghosts of dead teens levitating among falling stocks
Feel the temperature rising
And that's just the block
Black boy angels flying up like summer raindrops

DG. About a year ago me and some other non-profit do-gooder types
threw an eco-party in the hood
Mos Def bustin in the park on a solar powered stage
Green the ghetto
Sustainable hip hop...
We produce these all over now...
Harlem
Houston
Oakland
Atlanta

DG. I meet her in Chicago
She offers me watermelon
And I hear this guy singing
Hear him moaning out molecules to river his mother's spirit down
like rapids raging

like injustice
and I know she's not from this country
cuz new world blacks always give each other a secret absolution handshake
before we offer each other watermelon
Sudan she says…
And I am awash in the iTunes ubiquity of the word Darfur which I know
George Clooney and Madonna really care about and I know lost boys and
genocide but I don't know why they're lost and I don't know who's killing
who. A Starbucks activist I know what I read between the door and my dirty
soy chai
But I do know that I found a clue in the shaking voice of a mother tongue
just now loosened in the still dark shadow of the loss of her son. Inner City
school kid // life violently left invalid. Gun blast. Book bag. Blood soaked.
Chicago Mourning.

DG. Me and my do-gooder friends are greening the ghetto
I ask a mother about environment
She responds in the language of disaster
The culture of hazard
Summer climax of climate
36 school kids gun-blasted to the hereafter
her son was a witness that got dealt with before he could even think to snitch
she spits out a seed
looks at me and asks the question…
I ask a mother about environment she tells me of guns
Of emotionally disabled boys
Whose green movement consists of recycling the sorry narrative of black on
black crime
If you brown you can't go green until you hold a respect for black life.
she spits out a seed like a wasted leaf of a tree never grown
looks at me and asks the question…

TV WITH KASÉ. She hands me his picture.
If you look real close
You can see he has about 21
Maybe 27 and a half hairs on his chin
At first you miss the hair
Because the FIRST thing you notice is his skin
If it were soil, his is the earth brown you'd want to sow in.
A Chicago sun
Hard times
He does not blink
So think of this brother brown
Now see this mother black

See how dark the day becomes when you bury the sun
How you set the future back
A mother inters a murdered teen

DG. I visited Sudan before it became two countries…
Me and the singing man…the mourning man…the moaning man…
Are among six who stand on a riverbank at an apex where the Blue Nile and
White Nile meet
All but me and the moaning man are Sudanese
Northern Sudan
we sharing rolled stems brown leaves and seeds

DG WITH KASÉ. The darkest among us is from Southern Sudan
he is the color of solar eclipse
his skin is crisp like the center of my heartbroken iris kissed
living placenta planted in Nile papyrus.
Just on the other side of blue Black. Sudan

DG. The Northern Sudanese dandelion blow their way through an explanation
of Darfur, blah blah blah displacement blah blah blah oil yada yada tribe
And I don't get it but I DON'T ask the question…
Looking around and gesturing the man who looks most like me says we are all
considered white here. Except him.
A storm of bashful ivory breaks the seal of the eclipse's lips
Miraculously, at the river there is a nigger among us, and I am closer to white
than I have ever been.

DG WITH KASÉ. I am prescribed to vision American diversity, I see the
chromatic logic of ethnic cleansing with untrained lens. My paradigm for race
is civil rights and apartheid-based.
us and them
There are two pandemics in American black life…
Fatherless sons and sons gone too soon…
And in between there's a motherless man-child moaning to make meaning
lending music to me a Sudanese woman and a marching band

DG WITH KASÉ. First time I threw this festival
me and my co-producer meet with
the program staff of this big eco-group in Oakland
swear to god they take us to a vegan Vietnamese restaurant for the meeting
where they LITERALLY pray over tofu for 10 minutes before we start talking
the purpose of the meeting is to articulate our desire to brown the green
movement
they say mmm mmm
yeah yeah a lot
but I'M not explaining myself right
cuz by the time the waitress clears the mock ginger chicken

I'm pretty sure that I've agreed to go to a composting sweat lodge to vision-
quest our idea, but they haven't helped me GREEN my BLACK eco festival...
And by the time I leave, I say to my co-producer, fuck green
I wanna throw a joint to celebrate LIFE...
And so we do...
Healthy living
Sustainable survival practices
Mourning...
DG. Over watermelon
On a bench in Chicago
I tell a mother about the man who was almost my son's father
The man who came with me to Sudan
Whose song I hear every time she opens her mouth.
He was born in this city
Will bury his mother here
The machines that were keeping her alive can't be buried
Their plastic bones won't decompose
Their plastic parts will move into another home
Where another family will spend all they have to give someone they love
another day
She spits out a seed
That won't grow in the desert she was born in...
Spits out a seed like a wasted leaf of a tree never grown
Looks at me...
Asks...
Young sir...
How much did the moaning man pay...
What was the cost of his mother's life, by the day?
     (*Lights out...*)

End of Play

ELEMENO PEA
by Molly Smith Metzler

Copyright © 2011 by Molly Smith Metzler. All rights reserved. CAUTION: Professionals and amateurs are hereby warned that *Elemeno Pea* is subject to royalty. It is fully protected under the copyright laws of the United States of America and of all countries covered by the International Copyright Union (including the Dominion of Canada and the rest of the British Commonwealth), the Berne Convention, the Pan-American Copyright Convention and the Universal Copyright Convention, as well as all countries with which the United States has reciprocal copyright relations. All rights, including professional, amateur stage rights, motion picture, recitation, lecturing, public reading, radio broadcasting, television, video or sound recording, all other forms of mechanical or electronic reproduction, such as CD-ROM, CD-I, information storage and retrieval systems, and photocopying, and the rights of translation into foreign languages, are strictly reserved. Particular emphasis is laid upon the matter of readings, permission for which must be secured from the Author's agent in writing.

Required royalties must be paid every time this play is performed before any audience, whether or not it is presented for profit and whether or not admission is charged.

All inquiries concerning rights, including amateur rights, should be addressed to: John Buzzetti and Derek Zasky, William Morris Endeavor Entertainment, 1325 Avenue of the Americas, New York, NY 10019.

ABOUT *ELEMENO PEA*

This article first ran in the January/February 2011 issue of Inside Actors, *and is based on conversations with the playwright before rehearsals for the Humana Festival production began.*

"This is where you live? THIS IS WHERE YOU FREAKING LIVE?!?!"

At the start of Molly Smith Metzler's keenly-observed, fiercely funny *Elemeno Pea*, Devon has landed in the rarefied world of Martha's Vineyard, just off the ferry to visit her younger sister Simone after a summer apart. She's amazed by what she finds: Simone's job as personal assistant to the wife of one of the island's elite means that her new home is a "ludicrous" beach estate; not only that, she's wearing a 268-dollar designer dress and dating a rich dude with a sailboat and pink pants (or rather, "dockside-sexy" Nantucket Reds, as Simone insists). It's a different planet from the blue-collar Buffalo where these women grew up—and also from Devon's current digs living in their mom's basement, after giving up her social work job on a bad romantic gamble. So when she sees her sister in this world of infinity pools and Bentleys, and how Simone embraces its pink pants and fine wines even after her employers have left for the season, Devon is aghast.

Even more surprising to Devon than her sister's lavish lifestyle is the dawning realization that Simone has refashioned herself to fit into it, absorbing the attributes and priorities that her wealthy new friends ascribe to her. She even bosses around Jos-B (the estate already had a José), the hilariously bitter caretaker. What's happened to the girl who tailgated in her Buffalo Bills jacket and was once an aspiring novelist? And in becoming this new Simone, Devon wonders, is her sister making a terrible mistake? When Simone's demanding employer, the mercurial Michaela Kell, unexpectedly crashes the sisters' reunion in the throes of her own crisis, the situation escalates. In a flash, this quick-witted comedy about class, ambition, and regret becomes a complex struggle among these three smart women—and a battle for Simone's soul.

"I've been thinking about the characters in *Elemeno Pea* for ten years," says the playwright, who had a Martha's Vineyard adventure of her own a decade ago after landing a job waiting tables at the Edgartown Yacht Club right out of college. In search of a "romantic writing summer" near the ocean, the upstate New Yorker, who'd worked her way through state school at Red Lobster, found herself observing America's gentry up-close. "I had my graduation money and my little car and a job at this unbelievably exclusive club, and I got to witness some amazing things," Metzler explains. "These are the people whose grandfather's grandfather's grandfather was a member of the yacht club—really old money."

At work, Metzler met a difficult, "absolute knockout" of a woman who was infamous for making the waitstaff pick all of the potatoes out of her New England Clam Chowder. "Everyone rolled their eyes and said, 'Get ready, you're going to have to deal with this woman all summer,'" she recalls. That fiery trophy wife—and Metzler's fascination and eventual empathy for the "craven drive" of the beautiful women who'd married into this class, rather than being born into it—would later become the inspiration for Michaela, Simone's boss. At the same time, the strange social mix of the über-wealthy and the workers who lived among them fueled the play's vividly-drawn class divides and aspirations. "I stole material from all the people I waited on that summer. So the moral of the story is, if I am your waitress, be careful of what you say!" Metzler laughs.

"I also wanted to write a play about women: complicated, funny, awesome women," the playwright notes. Her trio of female characters are all formidable personalities, all at different pivotal moments in navigating their choices. When the writer recalled her own middle-class family's wide-eyed visit to the Vineyard in the summer of 2000, and how they "reminded me of who I was," she began to imagine a play about a protective older sister who is watching her little sis get wrapped up in the allure and sparkle of that world. Metzler found the deep concern and conflict between sisters to be the perfect vehicle to explore "the nature of mistakes and choice, and the big right and left turns we take in life."

And so as Devon tries to wrest Simone from Michaela's clutches, the play unfolds quickly in real time, over the course of a late afternoon when each of the women has something huge on the line. That energetic momentum also feeds *Elemeno Pea*'s comedy: "Martha's Vineyard is absurd, when you have a bird's eye view; the island fills to capacity and then empties, and it all happens with hilarious speed," says Metzler. But that humor and drive also works in tandem with the play's desperate stakes. "I think you really can lose someone you love in an hour and a half," she argues. "Everything that happens in the play happens really quickly, but I find that tempo true to life. Our lives are a series of really fast choices that dramatically affect who we become."

—Amy Wegener

BIOGRAPHY

Molly Smith Metzler grew up in Kingston, New York. Her plays—including *Elemeno Pea, Close Up Space, Carve,* and *Training Wisteria*—have been produced by Manhattan Theatre Club, Actors Theatre of Louisville (Humana Festival), South Coast Repertory, SPF, Cherry Lane Mentor Project, Ars Nova, Tristan Bates Theatre (London), Boston Playwrights' Theatre, and The Kennedy Center, where she was the recipient of three KCACTF national playwriting awards. Her work has also been developed by The O'Neill Theater Center, Manhattan Theatre Club, Chautauqua Theatre Company, Williamstown Theatre Festival, Playwrights Horizons, The Lark, and more. Molly is a recent graduate of The Juilliard School and a member of the Ars Nova Play Group, Primary Stages writing group, and Ensemble Studio Theatre. She lives in Brooklyn with her husband and their awesome Boston terrier.

ACKNOWLEDGMENTS

Elemeno Pea premiered at the Humana Festival of New American Plays in March 2011. It was directed by Davis McCallum with the following cast:

Devon .... Cassie Beck
Simone .... Kimberly Parker Green
Ethan .... Daniel Pearce
Jos-B .... Gerardo Rodriguez
Michaela .... Sara Surrey

and the following production staff:

Scenic Designer .... Michael B. Raiford
Costume Designer .... Lorraine Venberg
Lighting Designer .... Brian J. Lilienthal
Sound Designer .... Matt Callahan
Properties Designer .... Mark Walston
Stage Manager .... Kathy Preher
Dramaturg .... Amy Wegener
Casting .... Calleri Casting

Directing Assistant .... Zach Chotzen-Freund
Scenic Design Assistant .... Ryan Wineinger
Assistant Costume Designer .... Amanda Sox
Assistant Lighting Designer .... John Juba Alexander
Production Assistant .... Jeremy Stamps
Assistant Dramaturg .... Jessica Reese

Elemeno Pea was developed for the Humana Festival of New American Plays by Actors Theatre of Louisville through a partnership with New York University.

CHARACTERS

MICHAELA, married to Peter Kell and the owner of this house

SIMONE, her assistant

DEVON, Simone's sister

ETHAN, a friend of Peter and Michaela's

JOS-B, the property caretaker

PLACE

A *ludicrous* beach estate located right on a bluff in Martha's Vineyard.

In real life, this house is on the same street as the Kennedy compound in Aquinnah.

TIME

This year, just after Labor Day. The island has started emptying out, but you can still smell suntan lotion (the expensive kind).

NOTE

This play occurs in real time with neither scene breaks nor an intermission.

Daniel Pearce, Cassie Beck and Sara Surrey
in *Elemeno Pea*

35th Annual Humana Festival of New American Plays
Actors Theatre of Louisville, 2011
Photo by Joe Geinert

ELEMENO PEA

Lights up on the beach estate in Martha's Vineyard, late afternoon (around 4 p.m.).

A fancy alarm system deactivates and SIMONE *enters. She is a natural beauty and is very tan, very poised, and dressed from head to toe in Lilly Pulitzer. The upstage curtains cover an entire wall of glass doors that open out onto a wrap-around deck and a *ridiculous* view of the ocean.*

DEVON *hovers by the door, mouth agape. She carries a tattered duffel bag and has absolutely never been anywhere this rich.*

SIMONE. Come on, come in! Make yourself at home.

DEVON. ....*holy*........................*shit*...................

SIMONE. I know, right?!

DEVON. Holy Shit!

SIMONE. I know, right?!

DEVON. Simone! This is where you *live?* THIS IS WHERE YOU FREAKING LIVE?!?!

SIMONE. I know right?! And Dev, look:

(Activating the automated curtains, which reveal:)

500 feet of private beach on the Nantucket Sound. It's *literally illegal* for anyone but us to walk on that beach.

DEVON. ....*shut*............*up*............

SIMONE. *(Pointing to something else.)* And see over there? Hot tub, infinity pool. And there's a pool-side fridge with a case of Cristal chilling for us.

DEVON. *Oh my God.* Your life's a J-Lo movie! I'm in a freakin' J-Lo movie for the weekend!

SIMONE. *(Showing off.)* What's that? You want to hear some J-Lo?!!

(To the ceiling.)

Disco, play "Jenny from the Block" by Jennifer Lopez.

(It plays, surround sound.)

DEVON. Wha... how did you do that?!

SIMONE. Voice-activated iTunes. It's in the ceiling. *(To ceiling.)* Disco, *stop!*

DEVON. JESUS CHRIST, ARE YOU KIDDING ME WITH THIS PLACE?!?! Who *are* these people, *Bill Gates?*

SIMONE. No, they're Peter and Michaela Kell. But Bill's stayed here a few times. Peter has some *very* fancy friends. He's the CEO of the Advertising Company that did the Budweiser Frog commercials. You know, "Bud...

Weis...Er"? Coca-Cola's his account, too.

DEVON. Oh I see, I see. So they've got *monies*.

SIMONE. What do you mean?

DEVON. *Monies.* Money plural. The rich people in movies are always talking about their monies; gotta move their *monies*; gotta check on their *monies*. Does he go down to the Caymans?

SIMONE. No, he doesn't *launder* money, Devon. He's hardworking and legit; that why he's this successful at 40.

DEVON. This pimp's only 40?

SIMONE. Yeah. And Michaela's just as young.

DEVON. Hooker.

SIMONE. *Devon.*

DEVON. Sorry. It just came out. Whore. See? Sorry. I just—it's like rich-people Tourette's.

SIMONE. Well, I hate to disappoint you, but they are super nice people. Especially Michaela.

DEVON. Oh yeah? What does she do?

SIMONE. (*Nothing.*) Well, she has a Yale law degree, but these days she's more focused on the charity circuit, she does a lot of volunteer/ work for—

DEVON. Bitch, ho.

SIMONE. Okay, that's enough of that subject. The point is: she's *really* good to me.

    (*Heading to the bar.*)

So what can I get you to drink? We have fresh squeezed juices, lemonade, iced tea?

DEVON. Look at you, all, "What can I get you to drink?"

SIMONE. What.

DEVON. Like it's your bar.

SIMONE. It *is* my bar.

DEVON. Yeah but not really. You know what I mean.

SIMONE. No, I don't know what you mean. What do you mean, Devon?

DEVON. I mean: you're the help. It's not really your bar because you're *the help*, right?

SIMONE. (*How hilarious.*) "The help"? I think the Flux Capacitor sent you to the wrong year, Dev.

DEVON. "Assistant" then. Potato, potahto. It's all a fancy way of saying you're their bitch.

SIMONE. I am not the Kells' "bitch," I'm like family here. I can touch, drink, eat, drive, play, wear, borrow, take anything I want to.

DEVON. Really?

SIMONE. Yes.

DEVON. Why?

SIMONE. What do you mean "why"?

DEVON. I mean "why."

SIMONE. Because that's how this thing goes. They're called perks and bennies.

DEVON. All of this shit is free.

SIMONE. Yes.

DEVON. Full-access pass.

SIMONE. Yes.

DEVON. Completely free of cost.

SIMONE. Yes.

DEVON. Price tag zero point zero/ zero dollars—

SIMONE. *Yes,* Devon. Perks and bennies.

> (*Beat.*)

DEVON. Well! …In that case, you can go fuck your iced tea! (*Pointing.*) I will have two fingers of that Lap-Hog 30 from the high shelf!

SIMONE. See? It's that easy. *That* is how it's done.

> (*During the following,* SIMONE *fixes* DEVON *her drink and something more fussy [with garnish] for herself.*)

So finish your story from before about Aunt Terry—she came to the party or no?

DEVON. Well, she said she *wasn't* going to come but then she made a *guest appearance.*

SIMONE. *Oh no.*

DEVON. *Yep,* and I have some updates for you regarding her gland problems: she's been experiencing constipation, weight gain, depression, hair loss, and bloating.

SIMONE. *God.* Who talks about their glands at a party?!

DEVON. And then, instead of singing me Happy Birthday, the Ter-ster announces to everyone that *I'm* gonna inherit her constipation, weight gain, depression and hair loss.

SIMONE. But not the bloating?

DEVON. Oh, yes, extra bloating. Thank you.

SIMONE. So, in other words, it was the best Bday ever.

DEVON. Yes. Between that and Dom getting laid off an hour before the party, it was a real rager.

SIMONE. (*Shaking her drink in a shaker.*) Dom got laid off?

DEVON. …Yeah. I told you this.

SIMONE. No, I thought you said it was Jeff.

DEVON. Yeah. Dom and Jeff got laid off within a week of each other. We officially have zero first cousins with employment.

SIMONE. God, that sucks. Are they really depressed?

DEVON. No, Simone, they're elated. They went to Sandals Jamaica to celebrate.

SIMONE. Well, they still should've sang you Happy Birthday, is all I'm saying. Speaking of…(*Handing her a glass, formally starting to toast.*) I'd like to propose a—

DEVON. N-n-n-no, we're drinking to *you*, Simone! To you hitting the jackpot! To you getting your ride pimped, Son! I don't care how bad the uniform is, you've got the motherflocking BEST GIG OF ALL TIME OUT HERE, babe. Cheers!

(DEVON *throws back the scotch. It burns her throat and she coughs.*)

SIMONE. It's not a uniform.

DEVON. (*Scotch.*) Ooo fuck me (*Cough cough.*) That's the/ stuff!—

SIMONE. I said it's not a uniform.

DEVON. (*Cough cough.*)…Hm?

SIMONE. This is not a uniform. This is a $268 cotton jacquard Betsey-Clare dress from *Lilly Pulitzer.*

(*Beat.*)

DEVON. …………………you're wearing that *voluntarily*?

SIMONE. Yes.

DEVON. You *want* to have that on your body?

SIMONE. *Yes, Devon.* And I have six others from her summer collection.

DEVON. ………Were they all on sale for one hundred percent off?

(*Beat. Glare.*)

No! Totally! I'm just kidding—it's a really perky dress. Plus, it's a good investment…

(*Trying to make a joke.*)

Because now you can match all the dudes out here in their *pink* pants.

SIMONE. See? I knew you were gonna be like this! They aren't *pink* pants, Devon, they're salmon!

DEVON. Those pants *be pink.*

SIMONE. They're not pink! Nantucket Reds happen to be enriched—

DEVON. *They have a name?*

SIMONE. —yes! And they happen to be enriched with nautical and historical significance and are considered dockside sexy!

DEVON. Wait hold up, hold up, hold up here a second. *Just hold the flipping phone.*

(*Dramatic beat.*)

............Does your new boyfriend wear pink pants?

SIMONE. No.

DEVON. Oh my God, he does? Ethan rocks the pinkies?

SIMONE. No.

DEVON. Simone! How can you be serious about someone who wears those puppies?! He'd look less ridiculous in assless leather chaps and bunny ears—

SIMONE. Well I *am* serious about him, Devon—*really serious*—and if you don't stop it I *will not* introduce you tonight, **do you hear me?!**

(*Beat.*)

DEVON. Jeez Simone, I'm just kidding. When'd you lose your sense of humor?

(*Not forgiven.*)

Okay fine, we'll do a do-over toast, okay? To my Old Ass. What do you say?—

SIMONE. I say you need to get a damn color wheel out Devon and *study the difference between* pink and salmon—

DEVON. Okay, Simone, fine: I was *really really* wrong about the pants, okay? Saying they were pink was cruel and unfair of me, and I'm sorry. I think I'm just jealous of them because they get to live here on Paradise Island, while I live in Mom's basement, where my bed is two beanbag chairs and my glandular problems are impending, okay? *Okay?* Now (*Toasting.*) would you freakin' cheers me already? Because your life is perfect and I'm honestly happy for you.

SIMONE. Fine, cheers. But you better be nice to Ethan, I mean it. He's the real deal.

DEVON. I see that. And I will be, I promise.

(*They clink, drink.*)

SIMONE. Wait, you're not *actually* sleeping on a bean bag chair, are you?

DEVON. No, I am. That is a true story.

SIMONE. Why aren't you staying up in the computer room on the futon?

DEVON. You mean Mom's "scrapbooking room"?

SIMONE. Oh my God, Dev, you gotta get out of there.

DEVON. No, I seriously do. Last weekend I played the Wii for 36 hours straight and when Mom finally came down and said I had to come eat dinner,

I said, "Can't you just bring me down a tray like they do in prison?"

SIMONE. Shit. I'm so sorry I haven't been able to come visit. I'm still bummed I couldn't make your party.

DEVON. Hey, you gotta work, you gotta work. I am very understanding about that.

(*Beat.*)

Except when it comes to Christmas. That was *bullshit* that you had to work last year. Mom drank too much boxed wine and like *caressed* your empty chair all night. Total shitshow.

SIMONE. Well, the Kells paid me *double-overtime*; what was I supposed to do?

DEVON. No, believe me: I know. You can't say no to that kinda cash. But for the record, if they try to make you work Christmas next year, I'm gonna call the Better Business Bureau/ and then face punch—

SIMONE. Would you calm down? I'll get it off. And besides…I've been thinking: wouldn't it be really fun if I flew you, Mark and Mom to New York for Xmas? Ethan's in the city that time of year, and you could meet Michaela! The Kells have an entire guest floor we could use. Can you say: Rockefeller Center, Christmas Spectacular?

DEVON. Yeah but Mom does the meatballs.

SIMONE. Ooooo, right. Because it would be so much more fun to cram around Mom's card table with our depressed cousins? It's a *four-story townhouse* on Central Park, Dev. They shot one of the scenes from *Gossip Girl* in their foyer.

DEVON. Yeah but/ it's not—

SIMONE. And it's not like Mom can't make her meatballs on Michaela's stainless steel range top; it has radiant heat—OH! Hey look!

(*Pointing out the window.*)

It's (*Pronounced Hose-Bee.*) Jos-B! You gotta meet him, he's the best.

DEVON. *What's* his name?

SIMONE. José, but the Kells already have a José—their long-time landscaper—so he's Jos-B.

(*Opening the door, shouting.*)

JOS-B, COME HERE FOR A SEC!

(*To* DEVON.)

He's the caretaker, lives here year-round. *Such* a sweetie.

(JOS-B *comes up to the glass and enters, grumpily. Loathes to speak.*)

Hey Jos-B!

JOS-B. (*I hate you.*) What do you need?

SIMONE. Hey! I wanted to introduce you to my sister! This is Devon, here from Buffalo for the weekend. Devon, this is Jos-B, caretaker extraordinaire. Michaela calls him her *life blood*.

DEVON. Hi, how's it going? Nice to meet you.

JOS-B. (*Fuck you.*) Yeah.

(*Beat.*)

SIMONE. (*Friendly.*) What are you up to out there, Jos-B? Were you doing a little rakin'?

JOS-B. Yep—rakin' the beach for you girls.

SIMONE. Oh! That was really sweet of you. You didn't have to do that.

JOS-B. Yes, I did. The bitch say I have to rake beach for you girls.

SIMONE. (*Laughing like he made a joke, to* DEVON.) Ha ha, Jos-B has a bit of a love-hate relationship with the Kells. That's what happens when you work for them so long, right Jos-B? How long's it been, eleven years?

JOS-B. Ten years, four months, thirteen days, five hours. Guess what stupid jackass left behind this year.

SIMONE. (*To* DEVON.) Ha ha, he's joking with the name-calling—every year Peter leaves something important behind when he goes back to New York, and it's become a lighthearted joke.

JOS-B. Dickhead left his golf clubs in Main House again. He send me a text message—all it says "Clubs." Now instead of relaxing, instead of ding dong the witch is dead, I ship two hundred pounds of "Clubs" to New York. I'm gonna text back SUCK MY BIG BALLS.

SIMONE. Well, great—I just wanted to introduce you to Devon, but we won't keep you.

DEVON. Um, did you say the "Main House"? Sorry—what's a "Main House"?

SIMONE. Oh my God. I'm the worst hostess ever!

(*Pointing out the window.*)

Okay, well see out there, across the lawn...*that's* the Main House. That's where Peter and Michaela stay when they're here.

DEVON. I thought that was the neighbors' house. Or a museum.

SIMONE. I know right?! And see (*Pointing in a different direction.*) that carriage house? Guess whose house that is?

DEVON. The Obamas'?

SIMONE. No silly, it's mine!

DEVON. I'm......gonna stab myself in the face.

SIMONE. I know, right?! I have my own carriage house!

JOS-B. (*Pointing.*) Yes and I live in studio apartment above garage that smell like cat piss.

SIMONE. (*Laughing.*) Aw! You're so funny Jos-B! (*To* DEVON.) He's just kidding, Dev/ his apartment doesn't—

JOS-B. *Stink like cat ass,* yes it does.

DEVON. Wait, sorry. I'm confused. If those are all *their* houses, then whose house is this?

SIMONE. This is their *guest house,* for guests. Ordinarily, as soon as the Kells leave, everything gets boarded up for the season. But Michaela had this house made up just for us.

JOS-B. Yeah. Me. Jos-B make guest house up for you. And why **the help** gets to vacation here is BIG MYSTERY QUESTION. But no, is okay. You have fun. (*In Spanish, exiting.*) *Me dan vacación? Na! He trabajado aquí catorce años, y a mi me dan vacaciones? Da que/ jode. Odio este trabajo—*

SIMONE. (*Punishment.*) Jos-B! *Before you go.* Michaela told me that—as her Guests—if we had any problems, we should be sure to let you know, and well, we have one. The water pressure in the outdoor shower. It's coming out like a drippy, unsatisfying mist.

JOS-B. Really.

SIMONE. Yes.

(*Beat.*)

I think you need to fix the water pressure.

JOS-B. Really.

SIMONE. Yes.

JOS-B. *You* think *I* need to fix water pressure.

SIMONE. Yes.

JOS-B. Of a shower that has grass growing in it.

SIMONE. Yes.

(*Beat.*)

And I think you should do it *rápido.*

JOS-B. (*Burning hatred.*) Did you just say *rápido?????*

DEVON. (*To the rescue.*) Um hey Simone? He doesn't have to do that—I kinda like a drippy shower!

SIMONE. Don't be ridiculous. He loves plumbing.

(*To* JOS-B, *brightly, goodbye.*)

Thank you, Jos-B. We'll let you know if we need anything further.

JOS-B. Yeah you do that. Also, the bitch left a gift basket in the kitchen for Danielle.

SIMONE. Who's Danielle?

JOS-B. (*Pointing at* DEVON.) Her. Whatever. Her fucking name.

(JOS-B *exits.*

SIMONE *promptly exits and returns with* DEVON'*s gift basket. An overly large, overly enthusiastic display of gifts.*)

SIMONE. *Oh my God.* She did way too much! Look at all this!

DEVON. Simone—what the hell was that? That guy *hates* your ass.

SIMONE. Who? Him? He just has an attitude. (*Re: gift basket.*) *Look!* She got you a Black Dog sweatshirt!

(*Holding the sweatshirt up against her.*)

AW! That's gonna look so cute on you! Now smile and give me like a thumbs up so I can text her a thank-you-so-much-you-love-it pic from my Berry.

DEVON. Your "Berry"?

SIMONE. (*Excited, directing.*) No! You know what? No. Let's do a video instead. Look over here and say, "THANKS MICHAELA!" and wave.

DEVON. Absolutely not.

SIMONE. Say "THANKS MICHAELA! YOUR HOME IS LOVELY! THANKS FOR HAVING ME AND FOR MY FERRY TICKET!"

DEVON. Wait, what?

(*Not okay.*)

She bought my ferry ticket?

SIMONE. Oh, no, it's not like that. She has endless ferry passes and frequent flier miles.

DEVON. Simone! She paid for my *flight* too? You said you had miles.

SIMONE. Yeah but she has like two hundred billion thousand miles, okay, I'm filming! Go! "Thanks Michaela for…"

DEVON. (*To* SIMONE'*s phone.*) Well gee hi and thanks Michaela for paying for all of my transportation this weekend, which is not humiliating at all. Also, a *special thanks* for the ginormous Black Dog sweatshirt. A black lab actually bit me in the face in fifth grade, so I can't tell you how excited I am to be wearing his doppleganger here on my chest. P.S.: *Getta job*!!!

SIMONE. (*Waving and smiling into camera herself.*) *Yay*!!! I'll just send it without sound. (*To* DEVON.) That'll make her day. She's been a little depressed this week—Labor Day itself, you know? Time passing. Kids going back to school. Sands through the hourglass. It's been a tough year for Michaela.

DEVON. Oh no, really? This rich bitch has problems?

(*To the ceiling.*)

Disco, play "Everybody Hurts" by REM.

(*It plays, surround sound.*)

SIMONE. You know, Devon. I think you should really try to have more *perspective* about people.

DEVON. Should I?

SIMONE. Yes! That's the biggest thing— (*To ceiling.*) Disco, *stop*! —I've learned this year with this job: that we should all try to have more *empathy* for each other because…there's more to people than meets the eye, Devon, that's all I'm gonna say.

DEVON. No, keep going, Obi-Wan: why should I have empathy for this lady?

SIMONE. Never mind. I didn't mean to get into this.

DEVON. Yes you did.

SIMONE. No I didn't.

DEVON. Yes you did.

SIMONE. *No* I didn't.

DEVON. Her husband's a douche? Is that it?

SIMONE. No.

DEVON. Then what?

SIMONE. Nothing.

DEVON. How's he a douche?

SIMONE. He's not.

DEVON. What's he do that's douchey?

SIMONE. Devon, seriously, never mind! I can't talk about this with you, okay? I signed a confidentiality agreement when I took this job.

DEVON. And I showed you how to use a tampon, Simone. I *showed* you.

(*Beat.*)

SIMONE. Okay. Just. I don't know, yes. He can be a little…meticulous.

DEVON. How so?

SIMONE. I don't know…like this morning. When they were leaving for the airport, Michaela was in the kitchen and had her compact out to pluck a super-quick eyebrow hair with a tweezer. One quick hair, you know how you do, real quick, when you don't think anyone's looking?

DEVON. Yeah.

SIMONE. And, he just made a comment. He said something like, "Don't forget the one on your chin."

(*Beat.*)

And… I think there's been other stuff like that. Like on a much larger scale.

(*Beat.*)

DEVON. What's her response when he says stuff like that?

SIMONE. I don't know. Nothing. Or like, she'll say thank you. Like it was nice of him to bring a chin pube to her attention. That's the thing about her, she just gives and gives. She's been so good to me this year.

DEVON. Yeah, you keep saying that; that she's *so* good to you. What does that mean, exactly?

SIMONE. I don't know, she's generous? And nice? We're sorta friends.

DEVON. You're sorta her *employee*, Simone.

SIMONE. See? This is why I don't tell you things, Devon. God! Because you become an interrogating freak and you get "crazy eyes" and everything's suspicious.

DEVON. I think it is suspicious that José calls her the wicked witch and you can't seem to give me one real, non-vague/ example of how she's—

SIMONE. (*Listing.*) She taught me how to play tennis.

She read my five hundred and ninety page novel.

She's been really cool about me dating Ethan. How are those?

DEVON. Why *wouldn't* she be cool with you dating whoever you want to date?

SIMONE. I don't know—he's her husband's friend. It could be weird if she were less awesome. She also *read my five hundred and ninety page novel*, Devon, in case you didn't hear me say that just now.

DEVON. I read your novel, Simone, I just haven't had a chance to tell you that I did.

SIMONE. Yeah? What's the title?

DEVON. Well, whatever. What does your new BFF pay you, huh? Cuz that's the true test of friendship

SIMONE. That's a very impolite quest—

DEVON. Look at you, all "That's a very impolite question." Girl, you are from Buffalo. I've seen you tailgating with a Boone's fruit punch, rocking your puffy Bills starter jacket—

SIMONE. She pays me generously, okay?

DEVON. I want a figure. 20? 25? 30?...35? You can't make/ more than 35—

SIMONE. Devon, there's a hostel in Oak Bluffs and I'll do it. I'll drop you there.

DEVON. Do it, bitch. I love hostels. 40? 45? Not 50. You do not make 50-fucking-K to babysit a rich lady with no kids and no job.

(*Beat.*)

Are you kidding me?! 51? 52? 53—

SIMONE. I make one hundred and four thousand dollars a year plus benefits, clothing allowance, room, board, *and* she paid off my student loans.

(*Beat.*)

DEVON. (*Genuinely alarmed.*) Simone, *what?* Why in God's name would anyone pay off your student loans? I'm gonna be paying off my MSW until 2065.

SIMONE. Maybe that's what I'm *worth.*

DEVON. That's your "worth"? According to who?

SIMONE. I'll tell you *whom:* my placement service. Ivy League degree. Bilingual. I know HTML, Outlook, and QuickBooks. I type 120 words a minute with 90 percent accuracy. I'm attractive. I'm/ able to—

DEVON. You're *attractive?*! Did you just say that?

SIMONE. So? It's a fact that when you're paid to be someone's public representative—like an executive assistant—being attractive ups your base salary.

DEVON. Like being a filthy prostitute?

SIMONE. Okay, I'm done. This is done. I knew I shouldn't have/ invited you out here—

DEVON. You're twenty-seven, Simone! You're supposed to be hitchhiking and seeing the world and having fun and sleeping with people named Skip, not making "monies" because you're attractive.

SIMONE. I'm *twenty-nine*, Devon.

DEVON. Well, whatever. Why can't you even take a day off? All year you were like, this summer we're doing a sisters' camping trip in the Berkshires and *all year* you put me off/ until finally I came to you—

SIMONE. Yes because I don't have any vacation days left, Devon! Because I used my *entire allotment of vacation time* to move you from New York to San Francisco, only to turn around three months later and fly out there to move you back!

DEVON. For which I've said *thank you* about three hundred times. But it's not like you gave me a kidney, Simone, you helped me move! Big whoop! I moved you to Boston!

SIMONE. You helped me move a *bed* to Boston, Devon. And you abandoned me halfway up the stairs because/ you had Celtics tickets—

DEVON. That is revisionist history! Revisionist hist—

SIMONE. Look, I have *empathy and perspective* about everything you've been through, okay? I'm sorry that you screwed the pooch with California. I'm sorry that you quit your entire life to get engaged to some dude you didn't know. But that doesn't mean you get to show up here with your crazy eyes and poop all over my great gig, especially when I have been *so there for you this year.*

DEVON. There for me?! I'm back at Mom's house! I'm basically in a van down by the river here and I haven't seen you in six months! Don't you give a shit about what's going on with me?!

SIMONE. Of course I do, Devon! Of course I do! That's why I invited you out here for a REALLY FUN BDAY WEEKEND!

DEVON. WELL MY FUCKING BDAY WAS THREE MONTHS AGO AND YOU DIDN'T BOTHER TO SHOW! AND YOU LOOK LIKE A RETARDED EASTER EGG IN THAT GETUP!

SIMONE. WELL EXCUSE ME FOR WANTING TO SHARE MY BEACHFRONT SUCCESS WITH YOUR BASEMENT-DWELLING FRAGGLE ROCK *ASS*—

DEVON. I CANNOT *BELIEVE* YOU LET SOME DUMB BITCH GET HER BLACK AMEX OUT AND PAY FOR ME TO COME HERE! I WOULD RATHER INHERIT AUNT TERRY'S GLANDS THAN DO THAT TO YOU, YOU MONKEY'S BUTT WHORE FACE J.CREW WANNA-BE SELLOUT—

SIMONE. YOU IMMATURE, UNGRACIOUS PERSON! GOD! YOU ARE JEALOUS OF EVERYTHING I DO! IT'S DISGUSTING! TO THINK I WAS *ACTUALLY* LOOKING FORWARD TO YOU COMING! I WANTED TO IMPRESS YOUR JUDGMENTAL, ALMOST-FORTY-YEAR-OLD ASS!—

(The sound of frantic knocking. They turn.

A woman is coming across the glass doors, waving at them. She is strikingly beautiful and impeccably groomed, even if she is windblown and red-faced.)

SIMONE. *Oh my god. It's Michaela.*

(Urgent.)

Devon, if you're not polite to Michaela, I will *never* forgive you.

DEVON. Why's she smiling? Didn't she hear me call her a/Black Amex slut whore?

SIMONE. It's soundproof glass—*do not embarrass me, Devon!!!!*

DEVON. I thought you said she was gone?!

SIMONE. I mean it, I will kill you dead—*do *not* embarrass me, Devon!!!!*

(SIMONE slides open the soundproof door.)

SIMONE. *(Dramatic tone shift.)* Michae-la! What a surprise, yay! Michaela, allow me to/ introduce my sist—

MICHAELA. I can't do that yet. Sorry. Could you grab me a water please?

SIMONE. Of course…hey, are you okay? Why/ are you all red?

MICHAELA. Phil wouldn't take the jet out until the fog cleared, and Peter got all *Peter* about it and said he would therefore *drive himself* back to the city in his stupid Jaguar to which I said, "Honey, the fog is supposed to clear in less than an hour, why don't we just go to Rafaella's for oysters and by the time we're done, it will be perfect" to which he said, "Why do you always try to take my balls?" and he slammed my car door shut and peeled out and left me standing there. I'm nauseated, can you get some ice for the back of my neck?

SIMONE. Wait…I don't understand, he?

MICHAELA. Yes! He left me at the airport. Just standing there on the tarmac with Phil and our packed jet. It was totally humiliating. I just turned around and started running—

SIMONE. (*Nothing about this lady is athletic.*) You *ran?*

MICHAELA. Along the beach! Can you believe it? I've only ever done Pilates but it was totally exhilarating. I went up to the top of that lighthouse and shouted FUCK YOU PETER!!!!!! And then I kept running—

SIMONE. You ran here *from the airport?* That's like six miles, Michaela.

MICHAELA. I know! I know! I didn't know where I was even running to. I just pounded the sand, you know? And then I got your video, and I couldn't tell what the video was saying without the sound, but it seemed like you were inviting me over and so I thought, yes, I'll pop by the guest house and I see now that it's a good thing that I did because I specifically DID NOT WANT WHITE.

SIMONE. Let's just slow down, okay? What's white?

MICHAELA. (*Pointing to the flowers.*) I asked for *blue! Blue hydrangea.* Labor Day's over! I said to the florist on the phone, I said, *No White!* If you give me white…if you *fucking give me white*…and did she listen Simone?!—

SIMONE. No?—

MICHAELA. I obviously should've done the flowers myself but for some *asinine reason*, I thought it was more important to accompany my husband back to New York because for some *asinine reason*, I actually thought I…I thought we…

(*Breaking.*)

…And he just…

SIMONE. Okay Michaela, let's take a big/ *big* deep breath—

MICHAELA. Why don't I have any shoes on? I'm losing my mind now…

SIMONE. You're not losing your mind, Michaela. Your shoes are on the floor by the door, see? You took them off/when you came in—

MICHAELA. (*Crying.*) And my makeup's a mess now and I don't even have my makeup bag! All my stuff is…who knows where. In the jet, I guess?/ I don't even…

SIMONE. You have extra makeup/ bags in all of the cars—

MICHAELA. We have to text him. Will you text him from your phone and tell him that you haven't seen me? I want him to worry about where I am—I want him to think I was abducted by sailors.

SIMONE. Absolutely, we can text him later. But right now you/ have to calm down—

MICHAELA. Who does that son of a bitch think he is to peel out and leave me standing there with our pilot?! I am *premium pussy!* Isn't that what that psychic told me, Simone?! Isn't that what she told me? She said, YOU ARE PREMIUM PUSSY, MICHAELA!

SIMONE. You *are* premium pussy, Michaela! *That is what you are!*

DEVON. Okay, Simone? I'm going to say something now. I.................. am in the room.

> (*Long beat.* MICHAELA *notices* DEVON *for the first time since she's entered.*
>
> *She composes herself.*)

MICHAELA. *Oh my God,* Devon. You must be Devon. Oh! I'm so terribly sorry!

SIMONE. Michaela, this is my sister, Devon. Devon, *this* is Michaela Kell.

MICHAELA. It is so nice to finally meet you, Devon. On behalf of Peter and I, welcome to Island Haven.

DEVON. Island Haven? I thought I was in Martha's Vineyard?

> (*Beat.*)

MICHAELA. I see what you mean, Simone! She's *very funny*. (*To* DEVON.) You are *very funny*, Devon!

SIMONE. Island Haven is the name of the *estate*, Dev. The property's called Island Haven.

MICHAELA. (*Warmly, to* DEVON.) Ugh, "Island Haven!" Isn't it the worst?! No, it is, you can say it. What kind of dumb tart names their island haven "Island Haven"?!

SIMONE. (*Explaining to* DEVON.) Peter's first wife named this place. Back before she became the ex-wife.

MICHAELA. Yes and she dabbled in interior design too, as you can see from the snaggletooth couch and *wall of mallards.*

> (SIMONE *and* MICHAELA *laugh hysterically.* DEVON *does not.*)

So Devon! When did you get in?

DEVON. Um, just now.

MICHAELA. Oh, that's terrific, that is terrific. And we have you here until when?

DEVON. Sunday.

MICHAELA. Oh wonderful, wonderful. And how'd you make out on the ferry, you poor thing? Simone says you tend to get seasick.

DEVON. Oh, that was nice of her to share with you. No, I was fine.

SIMONE. (*Explaining to* MICHAELA.) She yakked twice on the boat, once on the way home.

MICHAELA. Oh God! You poor thing. Well, you'd never guess you were sick by looking at you—and O! you *smell* terrific, too. What's that you're wearing?

DEVON. Um, I dunno… Barf?

(*Beat.*)

MICHAELA. God are you so *funny*! She is so *funny*! Yes, you are lots of fun! I like you!

(*Beat.*)

Seriously though, what's the perfume? I'm getting notes of gardenia (*Wafting.*) maybe sandalwood (*Wafting.*) some grassy herbs?

SIMONE. Oh, you know what I bet it is? She wears that roller ball stuff.

MICHAELA. What's a roller ball?

SIMONE. It's like a little vial, you know? With a roller ball on top? It's cheap stuff—like with greasy oil in it. What's yours called, Dev? Coriander something?

DEVON. Nope. Cheap 'n' Greezy.

MICHAELA. (*To* SIMONE.) *Coriander!* God, I forgot how much I *love* coriander. I want coriander soap in the Main House next season, Simone—can you make a note of that?!

(*To* DEVON.)

Soap is a bit of an obsession for me, Devon. I can't tell you how many times I've gone to wash my hands on this property only to find a cracked bar of Dial sitting in a tepid pool of sludge. That's what I get for having a male caretaker, I suppose!

(SIMONE *and* MICHAELA *laugh hysterically.*)

DEVON. Yeah, that's really outrageous. Hey Simone—can we talk alone for a minute?

MICHAELA. Wait, there was something else I wanted to say to you, Devon…what was it? Simone, what did I want to say to her…? Oh that's right: *Happy Birthday!* You turned thirty-five, right?

DEVON. Yes, that *is* the number.

MICHAELA. Well, I hope you liked everything in your gift basket. I didn't know what size you were so I just got an XL.

DEVON. The bigger the black lab the better! Excuse us for just a minute.

(DEVON *and* SIMONE *step out onto the patio and close the glass door. We can see [but not hear] them having a heated discussion with lots of pointing at* MICHAELA. *It comes to a climax and they reach some sort of agreement, though* DEVON *is not happy about it.*

Meanwhile, during the above, MICHAELA *is alone in the guest house. She throws herself on the couch and starts to cry.*)

MICHAELA. (*To the ceiling.*) Disco, play "Adia" by Sarah McLachlan.

(*It plays, surround sound. After a beat,* SIMONE *and* DEVON *reenter.*)

SIMONE. (*Emergency tone.*) Oh no!!!! Sarah McLachlan?!? (*To ceiling.*) Disco, *stop!* Michaela, what's wrong?

MICHAELA. (*Emotional.*) Sorry. I just. Seeing you two together—the little sister shorthand. The *warm bickering* between you. It was like watching fine art come to life, so beautiful. I don't have a sister, no women in my family at all, actually, except Peter's sister Jocelyn, who's feral. It's a terribly hard affair for me—not to have anyone to talk to.

(*Overly emotional.*)

I'm so glad you two have each other.

SIMONE. Aw, that's very sweet, Michaela, but you're not alone either.

MICHAELA. (*Openly crying.*) What a day! I was already very melancholy and angst-ridden. It's because we've closed the house down, and it's that time of year again, which always reminds me that time is passing…like sands through an hourglass… (*Crying.*)

DEVON. *Okay*, Simone, I'm gonna go execute the plan we discussed.

SIMONE. (*To* MICHAELA.) Devon's decided to take her book and go down to the hot tub for a little time-out for several hours.

MICHAELA. Oh? Well, that's a great use of your time, Devon. What are you reading?

DEVON. I don't know yet. I might, um, just like nap or hum.

MICHAELA. You know what you should read? Simone, go get her a copy of your novel from my office. It's a *stunning* work, Devon. My favorite of the four.

SIMONE. Yeah but Jos B already boarded up the main house; I don't think he'll let me in—

MICHAELA. Yes he will let you in. And then call Ethan and see if he's talked to Peter. And get me a makeup bag. Then call this florist and tell her that if she takes so much as a *watering can* to my property ever again, I'll have her injected with SARS. Thank you, Simone.

SIMONE. Sure thing.

(*Pointing.*)

Dev, you're at the end of the hallway on the left. And the sliding doors open directly onto the grounds, so you can go off on your own without having to come back this way.

DEVON. Awesome. See you kids later.

(SIMONE *exits and* DEVON *starts down the hallway.*

The moment the soundproof door is closed:)

MICHAELA. Ah actually Devon, I think you and I should talk for a moment. Why don't you sit down.

DEVON. Oh, no, that's, I'm really—

MICHAELA. You're my guest, I insist.

(*Grabbing her glass, heading to the bar.*)

What have you got there? I'll refresh your glass.

DEVON. Oh it's the eh Lap-Hog 30.

MICHAELA. You're drinking Peter's 30-year-old (*Pronounced La-froig.*) Laphroaig? Well, you don't mess around do you! A woman after my own heart! Come, let's "polish this bitch off" as your sister used to say. Please, sit down. Do you take rocks?

DEVON. No, no rocks. Just *extra.*

(MICHAELA *pours two scotches.*)

MICHAELA. So what do you do in Buffalo again? I can't remember now.

DEVON. I'm an alley coordinator at a chain restaurant.

MICHAELA. Oh, that's right, that's right. What's an alley coordinator?

DEVON. I stand in the kitchen alley and coordinate. When the pasta comes up, I take it out of its oily bag and put it in a bowl and then put cheese on it and say, "JANET OR A WALKER!" so that Janet or another server comes to walk it.

MICHAELA. I thought you were a social worker.

DEVON. Yeah, me too.

(*Beat.*)

MICHAELA. Well I think it's really admirable what you're doing.

DEVON. What am I doing?

MICHAELA. Saving up to get back on your feet. A lot of people I know— friends of mine, I dare say—would just ask someone for a bailout. It takes a real woman to admit her mistakes and live in her mother's basement and alley coordinate. We should celebrate women like you.

DEVON. Yeah I think a parade is in order.

(*Beat.*)

MICHAELA. So your goal is to get back to New York by the end of the year, isn't that right?

DEVON. Boy—Simone tells you stuff, huh.

MICHAELA. We do have a lot of down time in trains and planes and automobiles, yes. You know, I just…can I just take a moment to say how much I love your sister, Devon? Simone is…you know what she is? She is impossibly kind, and smart, and empathetic and *lovely.*

DEVON. Yeah, I know. Thank you.

MICHAELA. It's a compliment to your mother. She did a wonderful job raising her, especially as a single mother in that recessed armpit of a city. She should be very proud.

DEVON. Yeah, we're both very proud of Simone, but we worry about her, too. She's always been a little spineless.

MICHAELA. Simone? No.

DEVON. Simone Yes. And a touch superficial, which is a bad combo. She shaved the side of her head once because Bobby Bowen told her she had 'burns.

MICHAELA. (*Warm and full of laughter.*) Is that right? Ha! The things we do for men, am I right, Devon? Cheers by the way.

(*Smelling the scotch.*)

Wow......That's really special isn't it?

(*Wafting.*)

You get the peat and the smoke, but then some heather and wet moss and pepper. And what is that, chrysanthemum?

DEVON. ....yeah, I think so.

(DEVON *looks longingly at her duffle bag.*)

MICHAELA. So how much are you saving up anyway? To move back to New York. What's the going rate these days for first, last and security in Manhattan?

DEVON. Oh, I'm thinking more Brooklyn, actually. Deep Brooklyn. Like *airport* Brooklyn. But I'm on top of it, thanks. I've got a eh spreadsheet

MICHAELA. It can't be more than a few thousand dollars?

DEVON. ...I'm on top of it.

MICHAELA. Well, look at you. You *are* proud.

(*Beat.*)

I like your necklace.

DEVON. Sorry—is this—really what you wanted to talk to me about?

MICHAELA. No, this is called making conversation. I *noticed* your necklace earlier so now I'm mentioning that I like it. Whose is it?

DEVON. It's mine.

MICHAELA. No, I mean the designer—who's the designer?

DEVON. The Piercing Pagoda in the Tonawanda Mall.

MICHAELA. Oh it's *that* necklace. You melted down your engagement ring to make the charm, right?

(*Looking closer, reaching in.*)

Simone was worried about *the mall* doing it/ but it turned out just lovely, didn't it—

DEVON. Actually, I'd prefer if/ you didn't—

MICHAELA. (*Too late, manhandling it.*) Oh! Is there writing on the back?

DEVON. No.

MICHAELA. Yes, there is! It's so tiny. What does that say?

DEVON. It says, "Let go of my necklace."

MICHAELA. No! It says (*Pronouncing it el-lemon-o-pia.*) "elemeno pea"? What's that?

DEVON. Nothing, it's just nonsense.

MICHAELA. Oh! I get it! (*Pronouncing it l-m-n-o-p.*) Elemeno Pea, like from the alphabet?

DEVON. Yeah—it's an inside joke. A private inside joke I have with myself. Hence, my engraving it on the back, where no one would see it and ask me about it.

(*Beat.*)

So listen, I'd really like to unpack now and get the ferry barf out of my hair. So maybe you could just tell me what it is I can do for you, Michaela.

MICHAELA. Absolutely, I'll just get to the point:

(*Beat.*)

Is there any way I could pay you to leave?

(*Beat.*)

DEVON. I beg your pardon?

MICHAELA. I don't want to just uninvite you for the weekend because that would really upset Simone, so between us girls, how can I make you feel good about this?

DEVON. I'm sorry, *what?*

MICHAELA. Something's going down with my husband and I'm going to need some privacy and I'm going to need Simone so you're going to have an alley coordinating emergency.

DEVON. I'm sorry, *what is this?*

MICHAELA. Money. I'll pay you four thousand dollars to leave.

(*Beat.*)

DEVON. My sister *invited* me here.

MICHAELA. I know she did, and I feel really badly about that. That's why I was trying to be nice about it. But I need you to go, hon. I'll have Jos-B take you door to door in the Bentley.

DEVON. Look lady—I haven't seen Simone in six months and she's not on the clock.

MICHAELA. Simone's always on the clock.

DEVON. Yeah well not this weekend. This is *sisters'* weekend.

MICHAELA. You're right. Six thousand.

(*Beat.*)

Oh, please. You don't even read her novels, Devon.

And you let the poor thing waste all of her vacation days moving you back and forth across country so you could play house with some online boyfriend who turned out to be a raging porn addict.

(DEVON *is speechless.*

As MICHAELA *writes a check:*)

Let's call it ten thousand. And you're taking it.

You couldn't even afford the flight or ferry ride to come out here, am I right?

(*Beat.*)

Devon? Isn't it true that you could not afford the $45 ferry/ ticket to—

DEVON. I heard you and you're right, I couldn't.

MICHAELA. Here you go, sweetie.

(*Putting it in* DEVON'*s pocket.*)

It's a bailout and you're in worse shape than Wall Street.

(SIMONE *enters with a copy of her 590+ page novel and a makeup bag for* MICHAELA. *She sees* MICHAELA *and* DEVON *alone and is alarmed, but she's finishing up a phone call—she points to the phone and mouths "Ethan" so* MICHAELA *knows who she's talking to.*)

SIMONE. (*Into phone.*) Okay, great. Great. Yep, great, I'll tell her No, I think that's great. Awesome. I love you, too. No, I do. No, I do.

(*Something sexy.*)

Ooo! I do!

(*Beat.*)

Yep, byeeeeeee.

(*To* MICHAELA.)

Ethan's taking/ me to the—

MICHAELA. I don't care. Has he talked to Peter?

SIMONE. He's on his way over.

MICHAELA. (*Excited, hopeful.*) ....Peter's on his way over?!!!!

SIMONE. No, sorry, Ethan. Ethan's on his way over.

MICHAELA. *Simone, why*?? I don't need Ethan coming over here, I need Ethan *talking to Peter!* God! Someone needs to find out what the fuck is going/ on. Did you not make that clear?

SIMONE. I know, I told him, and he and Peter are just playing a little phone tag is all.

MICHAELA. WELL HE NEEDS TO CALL HIM BACK.

SIMONE. Okay, okay, he said he was gonna try him back right now on his hands-free. Hey Dev, did you get lost? Last door on the left? I thought you were going to go outside for a very long time.

DEVON. (*Still stunned.*) Yeah, I didn't make it.

MICHAELA. We got chatting about the architecture of the estate, you know how I can get going about antique wood panelling.

SIMONE. (*To* DEVON.) Oh cool. Did Michaela show you the original piece of wainscoting in the foyer?

(*Beat.*)

Hello?

DEVON. What?

MICHAELA. Yes I did show her and then we got talking about her necklace, which I love.

SIMONE. (*Uh-oh.*) Oh? Yeah, isn't it pretty? (*Trying to change subject.*) By the way, Ethan wants to/ know what he can bring—

MICHAELA. Simone, what's "Elemeno Pea"?

SIMONE. Um. What?

MICHAELA. Elemeno Pea. On her necklace.

SIMONE. (*Uh-oh.*) Oh. Um. D-did Dev tell you the story?

MICHAELA. (*Flirty.*) Noooo! There's a story?! Nooo, she didn't tell me!

DEVON. No, I didn't Simone.

SIMONE. Well, it's been 30 years, Dev—maybe we could all have a good laugh/ about it now?

DEVON. No I still think it's *aggressively* not funny, Simone—

MICHAELA. Ooo, Look at her face! This must be *really* embarrassing! What's the story, Simone?

SIMONE. Okay well…back when Dev was in what grade, Dev? First? She got it in her head that elemeno pea was one letter, not five. It's because of that damn song—abcdefghijklmnop. Anyway so she would like stubbornly cram all five letters into the little box on the workbook and then would like cry and cry when she failed Reading.

MICHAELA. And? So? What's so humiliating about that?

SIMONE. And, so…she like *couldn't* get it right, test after test, you know? So they finally held her back. *Twice.* And they um (*Trying to laugh.*) they actually sent her to the short bus wing of the school for a little while.

(*Beat.*)

But! The joke was on them because Devon turned out to be like *brilliant.* Tell Michaela what you got on your SATs.

DEVON. No.

SIMONE. 1580! And she took them one time. I took the Kaplan course and got a 40 the first time I took them. So yeah, Devon's a genius.

MICHAELA. Wow 1580 Devon! Way to show those crap New York public schools what you're made of. I barely made it out of there alive mys...

(*Beat, she did not mean to share that.*)

Simone, when's Ethan/ getting here, I—

DEVON. Wait Michaela, I didn't catch that last thing you said because you trailed off on purpose. You barely made it out of there alive *yourself*? Was that what you were going to say?

MICHAELA. No.

DEVON. You went to *public school*?

MICHAELA. No. Just K through 12.

DEVON. Oh yeah? Where'd you go?

MICHAELA. Smith, then Yale.

DEVON. No, for *public* school. Which New York State Public School System were you in?

SIMONE. (*Stop it.*) Devon.

MICHAELA. The Saratoga Springs area.

DEVON. Which town in Saratoga Springs?

MICHAELA. A teensy and affluent one you wouldn't know.

DEVON. Called what?

SIMONE. You've never heard of it so give it up, Dev. It's called Watervillay or something.

DEVON. (*Water-vill-eet, a total shithole near Albany.*) Watervliet?............. You're from *Watervliet*, Michaela?

MICHAELA. Did you *major* in New York geography, Devon?

DEVON. I went to SUNY Albany, babe, so I know my 'burbs, yes, yes I do.

(*Beat.*)

I actually have a friend from Watervliet, my college suitemate. Do you know Jessie Leiser?

MICHAELA. No.

DEVON. You sure? She has a *very* Watervliet look about her. Sides of her head razored into stripes?

MICHAELA. No.

DEVON. Rings on every finger?

MICHAELA. No.

DEVON. Little tear-shaped tattoo right here/ on her cheek?

MICHAELA. I don't know your friend, Devon, sorry.

DEVON. Well you guys should meet sometime. You'd really get along.

MICHAELA. Oh? That would be lovely!

DEVON. Then it's a date! We'll put some bulletproof vests on and go to Watervliet for a picnic.

MICHAELA. That *literally* could not sound better! Simone, could you go tell Jos-B to pull the Bentley around front please?

SIMONE. The Bentley! Oooooooo! Is Jos-B driving you back to the city?!?

MICHAELA. No, it's for Devon. She's decided that she is going to l—

DEVON. No no no, let me tell her, Michaela. I'd actually really prefer to tell her this myself.

(*Beat.*)

Simone, listen…as you know, I'm really broke these days and there aren't many shifts to pick up at the restaurant. And while you were at the Main House…I got a call from the manager saying they needed me to come work.

SIMONE. What?! But you just got here!?! Can't they get someone else to put cheese on the pasta?!

DEVON. I know which is why I said NO BITCH. That's not happening. I requested this weekend off two months ago cuz this is *sisters' weekend* and I'm not leaving this island for any reason.

SIMONE. Yeah, Dev, you go girl!—

DEVON. And Michaela was so impressed by my integrity, she offered me the Bentley for the evening so we can go to the Navigator in style.

SIMONE. No way!! We're getting to *drive* the Bentley?! Oh my God, Michaela! Thank you so much!

MICHAELA. No, of course! Of course! Go go go! It's my absolute pleasure—But she didn't say the Navigator, did she Simone? That's not really where you're taking your guest.

SIMONE. Yeah, Ethan and I have a whole plan. For dinner, we reserved a dockside table at the Navigator so Devon could see the must-see sunset, and then after dinner we're taking her out in his boat for mojitos.

MICHAELA. No, the Navigator is stupid. And I'm kinda off mint right now. We'll cook here instead. (*To* SIMONE.) Peter has a grill out there, doesn't he?

SIMONE. I think so?

MICHAELA. We'll get lobsters and corn and have a lobster bake.

DEVON. Yeah but you know what I'd really like to do for dinner, Simone? I'd really like to try that Navigator place.

SIMONE. Yeah but *lobster* Dev! Drawn butter! Yummy!

DEVON. Yeah but the Navigator was what we *discussed*, Simone.

SIMONE. Yeah but it's probably the last time to have lobster for like nine months, Dev!

DEVON. Yeah but *you* wanted to take *your* sister to *your* favorite restaurant with *your* boyfriend—

SIMONE. Yeah but lobster, Dev! Lobster in your tummy!

DEVON. Yeah but I wanted to see *you* execute *your* vision of *your* evening, Simone—

SIMONE. Yeah but visions change and we mortals adapt, Devon!

DEVON. Yeah but *I don't like* change, Simone and I'd really like to—

MICHAELA. Oh you two are adorable, but guess what? Ethan always votes lobster, we're three to one. Simone, where's Jos-B?

SIMONE. JOS-B!!!!!!!!!!!!!!!!!!!JOS-B!!!!!!!!!!!!!!!!!!!!JOS-BEEEF!!!!!!!!!!!!!!!!!!!!!!!!!!

JOS-B. (*Off at first, then entering.*) WHAT?! JESUS FUCKING CHRIST WHAT THE FU—

(*No idea she was there, big greeting.*)

Oooooo so happy!!!! Michaela!!!! Big surprise! Michaela in the guest house?!?!?

MICHAELA. Hi, Jos-B, you sweet thing.

JOS-B. Is the Peter with you?

MICHAELA. No! Why? Have you talked to him?

JOS-B. No.

MICHAELA. Hm. Why are you all wet, pumpkin pie?

JOS-B. I was fix the outdoor shower for the girls. (*To* SIMONE.) The water pressure is now like blast of little dumdum bullets.

MICHAELA. Oh, you are *a-mazing*, B! Jos-B can fix anything—he's my *life blood*. (*Baby voice.*) Aren't you my little Cuban *life blood*?

JOS-B. Yes, my love.

MICHAELA. I love this man. And this man loves me. Don't you, B? Tell them how much you love me.

JOS-B. Way much. Big, lots and lots.

MICHAELA. Lots more than who?

JOS-B. The first wife.

MICHAELA. And?

JOS-B. And the first wife get liposuction and pop laxatives like Tic Tacs.

MICHAELA. YES! Now say that Spanish love poem thing.

JOS-B. (*Sounds like "I love you."*) *Metete en la piscina "Infiniti" esa y sigue nadando, gringa de mierda, Michaela.*

MICHAELA. Aw! I love this man. You know just what to say to put a smile on my face, Jos-B. Now, listen, my sweet, I have a question for you: where does Patrice get lobster?

JOS-B. That would be Dawson's.

MICHAELA. What's that?

JOS-B. It's a grocery store about an eighth of a mile from here, my love.

SIMONE. She's asking because we're having a lobster bake here tonight. We are, just us.

JOS-B. (*To* MICHAELA.) I see. Well, Patrice is now gone for the season, like *most* of *the help*, but may I be of assistance to you, my delicious?

MICHAELA. Oh would you? You'd really be a little pot pie and help us? You are A-mazing, B. We'll have everything delivered, of course.

JOS-B. Dawson's does not deliver, my love.

MICHAELA. How about my sweet, sweet buttercup? Does he deliver?

JOS-B. For you? He does!

MICHAELA. Take a big gratuity for your trouble. How does *five* dollars sound?

JOS-B. *Wow.* Thank you, my extra generous love. *Okay!* Lobster. What else do we need here, you want corn? Simone, you want stinky cheese?

SIMONE. (*Utterly revolted.*) Stinky cheese?! With shellfish?!

MICHAELA. No! God no! NO! Just get four lobsters and four ears of corn.

JOS-B. Absolutely. I should take the Lexus?

MICHAELA. You should take the Ford Taurus. *And B*, text Peter and see if we should expect him for dinner this evening, thank you.

DEVON. Actually, Michaela—could we make it *five* lobsters?

MICHAELA. Hungry piggy?

DEVON. No, I just…I met someone today and he's a nice human being so I'd like to invite him.

SIMONE. HIM? YOU MET A GUY? HOW HAVE YOU NOT TOLD ME THIS! WHERE? ON THE FERRY!??

DEVON. Calm down, Simone. I don't think it's a romantic thing. Can I invite him, Michaela?

MICHAELA. I literally could not care less.

SIMONE. Yay! Tell him cocktails now, dinner at seven.

DEVON. Did you hear that José? Cocktails now, dinner at seven.

JOS-B. I'm not deaf.

DEVON. No, Sorry. I didn't make that clear. I was *asking you*. Would you like to be my date for cocktails now dinner at seven?

JOS-B. You? Me? (*Laughing.*) No *bueno*. I have wife.

DEVON. No, not like that, just as friends. Two friends dining the opposite of them.

JOS-B. No, I can't be friends with the, no.

DEVON. Come on, man. Do me a solid. I'm an alley coordinator at a chain restaurant.

JOS-B. Which one?

DEVON. The Olive Garden.

> (JOS-B *knows that alley coordinating at the Olive Garden is a fate far worse than hell.*)

JOS-B. OOOOOOOOOOOOOOFFFFFF! Shit. Okay, I come.

> (*To* MICHAELA.)

You say I can come, yes, my love?

MICHAELA. Well, you are *always* welcome, B—

JOS-B. Then I come—

MICHAELA. But I do wonder how the rest of the staff would feel if I were to play favorites like that. It could be bad for *morale* if word got out.

DEVON. I know! Why don't José and Simone just pinky promise they won't tell anyone.

MICHAELA. I don't know what that is, no.

SIMONE. Yeah, me neither Devon, no.

DEVON. No problem, we'll show you. Ready, José?

JOS-B. Ready!

> (*Pinky.*)

I, José Jos-B Gonzalez, pinky promise not to tell the other José, Patrice, Marika or Ricardo that this lobster shit's going down.

DEVON. (*Pinky.*) I, Simone Ashley DeWitt, promise to do the same. Also, while I have you here, I'd like to apologize for being a heinous crotch to you all the time.

JOS-B. Aw thanks a lot. Now we cool.

> (*They shake pinkies. Look at* SIMONE.)

DEVON. So did you guys get that? Awesome. So that'll be five lobsters, right? Awesome.

MICHAELA. Yes awesome but *before you go* bring up a case each of Schramsberg and Bourgogne-St-Germaine from the cellar, Jos-B.

> (*To* SIMONE.)

I'll have a glass of each.

DEVON. Here, let me give you a hand with those buddy.

JOS-B. Bitch, please! You no lift a case of wine!

DEVON. Playa, I can bench press a case of wine. Come on, we'll bang this out *rápido.*

JOS-B. Oh shit, stop. That's some funny shit...

(*They exit downstairs, laughing.* MICHAELA *and* SIMONE *alone.*)

MICHAELA. Oh, she's really nice, Simone. Really really nice.

SIMONE. Really? Thanks. I think she's having a good time here.

MICHAELA. Oh, good good good. Good. *That's good.*

(*Beat.*)

Now listen, I think you were lying to me before, so this time I want the truth: when you called Ethan, had he *really* not talked to Peter yet?

SIMONE. (*Confidential.*) Um, no, he had. I just figured I shouldn't air your dirty laundry in front of guests. I'm really sorry I lied though, it was just a/ white one to protect—

MICHAELA. I don't care. What'd Peter say to Ethan?

SIMONE. Um...I'm gonna let Ethan talk to you about that when he gets here.

MICHAELA. I will hear the exact conversation you had with Ethan right now.

SIMONE. Ethan specifically said—

MICHAELA. (*An order.*) The exact conversation, right now, no paraphrasing.

SIMONE. Okay, well, um, okay. First I said, "Hi honey, last night was really..." um and then we talked about that for a minute and then we got to the part when I asked Ethan if he'd talked to Peter yet and he said "Yes, I'm with him at the club right now." And then I said, "Well Michaela's really upset that he up and *left her* at an airport out of clear blue" and he said "It's *not* out of the clear blue." And I said, "Well, I love you and I don't want to disagree with you, honey, but it *feels* kinda outta the blue because Peter and Michaela have been doing better. Their therapy's been going well and I think they're getting past it," and he said, "Pete's not past it." And then I said, "Well, Michaela is here at the guest house and she doesn't have her things and she had to run home from the airport and she's hurt and embarrassed and crying and I think it would be very gentlemanly for one of you to come over and talk to her," and Ethan said, "It's you I want to talk to, and I'll be over after we tee off."

(*Beat. This is bad news for* MICHAELA. *She looks crestfallen.*

Long beat.)

Michaela? Are you okay?

MICHAELA. He's not past it.

SIMONE. (*Explaining.*) I think he was talking about how/ he's not over—

MICHAELA. *I know* what he's talking about, Simone, I'm just repeating it.

He's not past it.

(*Beat.*)

SIMONE. I guess I'm not that surprised? I mean, right? We kinda knew.

MICHAELA. No, I'm surprised. I *am* surprised. I thought things have been really good between us. And Date Night was a huge success last night! We went to L'Etoile and talked all about the Rodin exhibit coming to New York, and the renovations we were going to do in Aspen, and how we were going to spend Columbus Day weekend in St. Barths. We *synced our i-calendars*, Simone! And then I put that black lace thing on for him and worked his nipples.

(SIMONE *nods empathetically.*)

But today he's not past it.

(*Beat.*)

Today he's not past it and he's playing golf with Ethan and the boys at the club, talking about what a fucking victim he is.

(*Broken.*)

What a victim *he* is.........

(*Long beat.*)

SIMONE. Michaela, what can I do?

(*Beat.*)

You want me to hold your pressure points?

(MICHAELA *extends her hands, so* SIMONE *can hold the acupressure points on her wrists. She never looks at her, though.*)

We're just gonna take some big *big* deep breaths, okay? It's going to be okay...

(ETHAN *comes up on the patio. We see him through the sliding glass doors. He waves cheerily at them.* ETHAN *is as handsome and sun-kissed as* MICHAELA *is beautiful. He has three bouquets of flowers with him—one yellow, one pink, one red. Oh, and he's wearing bright pink Nantucket Reds. He slides open the door.*)

ETHAN. Mikki! What are you doing, you dumbass? You're not an athlete. You can't just *run six miles* without training. That's how people die and like poop their pants. Why didn't you call me? I woulda come for ya.

MICHAELA. I don't know, Ethan. Maybe I was afraid of interrupting mini putt-putt with Peter.

ETHAN. (*Lying.*) Peter? That shithead's playing golf?! He didn't invite me.

MICHAELA. (*Knows he's lying.*) No? You weren't *tee-ing off* with him just now?

ETHAN. Nope, haven't talked to him. But you should *always* call me when you need me, Mik. *Especially* when you're in a bad sitch.

MICHAELA. Well, I was in a bad "sitch," Ethan, but I was fine because I had Simone.

ETHAN. *Fine* and *Simone*! Those words *do* belong together. (*Presenting flowers to* SIMONE.) These are for you m'lady. Hi, by the way.

SIMONE. (*I love you.*) Oh they are *just beautiful,* Ethan.

ETHAN. (*Confidential.*) I need to talk to you.

> (*Crossing to* MICHAELA, *giving her flowers.*)

And these are for you, m'other lady. Yellow Friendship for Mik. Red Passion for Simone.

And Pink Whatever for the little sis, where is she?

SIMONE. Big sis, Ethan. She's my *big* sister.

ETHAN. (*Oops.*) Big sis, right. No, that's right. Cuz *you're* the little sis. Where's the big sis?

MICHAELA. She's in the basement playing with Jos-B.

ETHAN. What?

SIMONE. She's just helping him bring up some cases of wine.

ETHAN. She's what?

SIMONE. She's helping him bring up some cases of wine.

ETHAN. She's doing *what?*!

SIMONE. It's not a big deal, Ethan; she's really strong and/ she just wanted to—

ETHAN. Don't be *disgusting,* Simone!

> (ETHAN *exits immediately, hero cape flapping in the wind.*)

MICHAELA. Can you hand me my purse please?

> (SIMONE *hands* MICHAELA *her purse, and she starts digging through.*)

What time is it?

> (*Handing her stuff.*)

Okay here we go: take my phone and wallet and go call Susan Coletti and tell her I need to see her in New York first thing tomorrow morning. Tell her I'm sorry it's a Saturday, but remind her how many zeros were in that retainer.

SIMONE. Coletti? She's in your contacts?

MICHAELA. Yes but she's under Indian Takeout.

SIMONE. You…want Indian takeout?

MICHAELA. No, Simone. She's not Indian takeout, Simone! Peter just hates Indian food.

SIMONE. I'm totally lost…

MICHAELA. Tell her the fucker's gonna file and we need to move. I need to see her A-Sap.

SIMONE. Wait, who's gonna file?

MICHAELA. Peter! Did you see Ethan's poker face? Go! Then get Phil on the phone and tell him I need the jet *the moment* it can fly.

(SIMONE *exits to the deck to make the calls.*

ETHAN *enters carrying not one but two cases of wine.* JOS-B *and* DEVON *come in after him.* JOS-B *holds nothing;* DEVON *holds her flowers.*

ETHAN *makes a big production of putting them down, opening the boxes with his strong and tan muscles.*)

DEVON. Boy, thanks again, Ethan. You really didn't have to do that.

ETHAN. (*Biggie.*) It's no biggie, Devon. No biggie at all.

DEVON. Okay. Well…thanks again.

ETHAN. (*Biggie.*) Hey, no biggie. It was *not* a biggie. It really wasn't.

DEVON. Great. Thanks again.

JOS-B. Yo Dev, you wanna come to Dawson's?

DEVON. Yes but I think in light of our conversation, José, I'd better stay here.

JOS-B. Sweet. (*To all.*) Okay I go to Dawson's now, everyone.

(*A little louder because he needs money.*)

I said I go to Dawson's now. Where I will be buying The Food Items.

ETHAN. (*Psst.*) Mik! I think you need to pay your guy.

MICHAELA. (*To* JOS-B, *who she wasn't listening to.*) Oh, I'm sorry, B! Simone has my wallet—take what you need.

JOS-B. Thank you, my love. The first wife fart in pool. I see with my own eyes—fart bubble.

MICHAELA. *Not now*, B!

(JOS-B *exits. He goes to* SIMONE, *takes* MICHAELA'*s wallet, takes the money, goes off to the Ford Taurus.*)

ETHAN. (*To* MICHAELA.) Did your guy just say that Jessica used to fart in the pool?

MICHAELA. Yes. So?

ETHAN. So…that's a weird thing to say. Why's he such a weird little Mexican?

MICHAELA. (*Bites his head off.*) He's not, Ethan! And what exactly is so "weird" about saying that Jessica the Great is fallible, huh? Everyone talks about Peter's ex like she's the Baby Jesus! *Well, she wasn't the Baby Jesus!* And I've been here for four years now/ so it's about freaking time that she stops being a subject of conversation! She's gone!

ETHAN. Bored. This is boring. I'm so bored. Wow is this boring—

MICHAELA. STOP DOING YOUR BORING THING!

ETHAN. (*Really light.*) Well then pump the brakes, kid. All I said was that your guy is weird, *not* a biggie.

(*Noticing.*) Why's Simone out there?! I need to talk to her.

MICHAELA. (*Pointing at* SIMONE.) She's firing this florist for me.

ETHAN. Oh, really? Crap, now I have to fire her too, or it'll be all awkward between us. That sucks because I like that girl. She gets the best calla lilies from Holland—

> (*Noticing.*)

What? ...This is a '77?! Where'd you get a whole case of '77 Bourgogne-St-Germaine, Mik? This is *insane.*

MICHAELA. (*Hostile.*) I don't know, Ethan. Why don't you ask *Peter.*

ETHAN. Yeah, I totally will. I wonder if Don Griggs put it aside for him. He probably did, that lying sack of shit. Where do you want all this? It needs to come down another twenty, maybe twenty-two degrees. Should I stick it in the sub-zero?

MICHAELA. I don't care where you *stick it*, Ethan.

ETHAN. Hey are you okay over there, Mikaroni? Why you being all Sulky?

> (*Beat.*)

We've got some Schramsberg over here, your fav! Would you likey a glass?

MICHAELA. No I would not *likey.*

ETHAN. Okay, what's with you, hun? You need a Midol? You need a little tune?

> (*Sing-songy.*)

Hey Mikki you're so fine, you're so fine you blow my mind, hey Mikki! (*Clap clap clap clap.*) Hey Mikki—

MICHAELA. WILL YOU JUST *SHUT THE FUCK UP* ETHAN!

> (*Beat.*
>
> DEVON *looks outside at* SIMONE, *who is still on the phone, talking on her hands-free to someone who really doesn't want to work on a Saturday.*)

ETHAN. (*To* DEVON.) Okey-doke, here's what you and I are gonna do. We're gonna put that little *bitcharoo* on a toddler timeout over there, and we're going to have ourselves some Schramsberg. How does that sound to you... (*Searching for her name.*) Simone's older sister?

DEVON. Devon.

ETHAN. Devon. How does that sound to you, Devon? Does that sound like fun?

DEVON. Yeah.

ETHAN. Good because I would like to have some fun. I, for one, would like to have *thirty seconds of fun.*

> (*He pops the champagne.*)

Did I get to nap today? Did I get to have my hot stone massage? No! I've been driving around all day dealing with upset people and if I *wanted* to have stress, Mikki, if I wanted to get shouted at by ungrateful little *bitcharoos*, Mikki, then I would just join the workforce, Mikki.

(*Handing her a glass of champagne.*)

So Devon. Tell me about yourself. You're Simone's sister, that's all I got.

DEVON. Okay, Well. I—

ETHAN. Travelling is what makes me tick. What makes you tick?

DEVON. Actually, I—

ETHAN. Wait, I should qualify that. *International* travelling.

DEVON. Oh yeah? Excellent. I actually travel quite a bit too.

ETHAN. *You do*?! Well, all right! That's Fantastic! You're a traveller. (*To* MICHAELA.) She's a little traveller. Where've you been?!

DEVON. I don't know/ a lot of places—

ETHAN. Have you been to New Zealand?

DEVON. No.

ETHAN. How about shellfish. You like shellfish?

DEVON. ...Um—?

ETHAN. Shellfish, New Zealand. My two favorite things. I think we're gonna get along very well. (*Louder for* MICHAELA.) In fact, I'm *refreshed* right now. It's *refreshing* to have such a mature and dignified convo. (*Filling his glass back up.*) So keep going, Delia. Where else you been?

DEVON. It's Devon, um and let's see...before I was in California/ I went to—

ETHAN. (*Loves California.*) Ooo, you were in California?

DEVON. Yeah. I was a *resident* of California. Your girlfriend helped me move there. And back. While you were dating.

ETHAN. Have you been to Eritrea? That's the next trip I want to take.

DEVON. (*This man is a jackass.*) Wow.

ETHAN. Yep! I want to take Ethan II up the Red Sea to Eritrea and then hike over to Djibouti.

DEVON. Who's Ethan II?

ETHAN. She's my boat.

(MICHAELA *makes a pointed, loud, disapproving snort sound.*

ETHAN, *suddenly to* MICHAELA:)

Okay, that's it. You've ruined my Eritrea story and now you're snorting at the mention of the Ethan II. Are you trying to hurt my feelings?

MICHAELA. It's a really unoriginal name for a boat, Ethan.

ETHAN. You had a personalized vest made for me—you said you liked it!

MICHAELA. Well I lied! Who buys a cigarette boat at your age? Grow up! You have two hundred dollar highlights in your hair, you poser. You're not a mobster, Ethan! You're not gonna run drugs back and forth to South America in your cigarette boat!

ETHAN. And now you're making me self-conscious about my bronze highlights?

MICHAELA. Just tell me.

ETHAN. I don't know what/ you're talking about—

MICHAELA. JUST TELL ME, ETHAN!

ETHAN. Fine! You want the deets? I'll give you the deets. But I am sworn to secrecy, *so* I will only answer yes-no questions.

MICHAELA. Does he have a lawyer yet?

ETHAN. Yes.

MICHAELA. Have they met yet?

ETHAN. Yes.

MICHAELA. How much time do I have?

ETHAN. ...Pass.

MICHAELA. Do I have much time?

ETHAN. No.

MICHAELA. How long have you known?

ETHAN. That this day would come? Since you made your bed, kid.

MICHAELA. Well, I think you should've named your fucking boat PETER'S FRIEND.

ETHAN. Mikaroni! I will not tolerate your tantrums, do you hear me? I am friends with *both* of you. I am Switzerland. But if you wanna keep me from de-friending you on the FB, you will march/ over here and say you're sorry—

MICHAELA. JUDAS!!!

ETHAN. Really, Mikki? Really? Because if you're gonna be like *this*/ I'm just going to—

MICHAELA. *Of course I'm gonna be like this, Ethan!* Of course I'm like this! I have to be with him ten years to get my full settlement! Ten years! TEN YEARS! And you sat on this information all day?/ I could've been—

ETHAN. *I am not your spy, Michaela!* I don't *have* to come running over here to give you the deets and I'm only here to talk to Simone. But since I have not heard an *apology* for being called PETER'S JUDAS FRIEND WITH A DUMB BOAT, maybe I won't give you any more deets now!

MICHAELA. (*In a sudden hysterical burst of tears.*) WELL I DON'T WANT YOUR STUPID DEETS SO JUST GO, ETHAN! JUST GO TO PETER! GO HAVE VIGOROUS GAY SEX WITH PETER BECAUSE THAT'S

HOW FAR UP HIS ASS YOU BELONG! (*To* DEVON.) AND WOULD YOU *PLEASE* TAKE A SOCIAL CUE AND LEAVE!!!!

DEVON. (*Going to the door.*) I would love to. Absolutely, I'll just be leav—

ETHAN. NO, DARIA STAYS!

DEVON. Devon.

ETHAN. DEVON STAYS! Devon you stay. You know why, Mikki? Because she is the *older*—?

    (DEVON *nods.*)

ETHAN. —*sister of my girlfriend* and you do not get to treat Simone's sister like this! You're *not mad at us*, you're mad at the sitch! But what did you expect to happen after what you did, huh?

MICHAELA. (*Gasps.*) *Are you taking his side?*! You're taking his side?—

ETHAN. Hun! Of course I'm taking his side. That's always been my (*Position.*) posish. I was out there (*Pointing at the ocean.*) doing kiddie regatta with him when we were both in Pampers and you ripped the man's heart out.

MICHAELA. Oh, I love that. I love that I ripped *his* heart out now. This is something I did to poor Peter's heart. What about *my* heart, Ethan?!?

ETHAN. I just think your heart's a little less relevant in this sitch.

MICHAELA. Stop! Saying! SITCH!

ETHAN. I will say *sitch* as per (*Usual.*) usge and now I'm leaving. You're boring me and this is boring and I'll wait to talk to Simone elsewhere. Goodbye, (*Still can't remember* DEVON*'s name.*) you.

MICHAELA. (*Panic.*) Ethan, wait! Wait! I'm sorry! I'm really sorry. I didn't mean to take it out on you. I just…

    (*Beat.*)

…God, you know!? I've worked *so hard for this*. You know I have. And I…just don't understand what happened. Can you help me? Please? Can you please just tell me what happened that all of a sudden I get kicked out of his car?

ETHAN. I just think people hit walls with stuff, Mik, you know? The man hit a wall.

MICHAELA. *Why??*

ETHAN. I don't know; he just did. He said he saw you coming up from the beach this morning, and it's that time of year again so he was thinking about it all again…I don't know. He said he saw you and just realized he's not in love with you no mo'.

MICHAELA. But I'm telling you: we were *fine/* last night, Ethan!

ETHAN. And I'm telling you: no you weren't fine last night. Just cuz he let you blow him doesn't mean the man is fine. He hasn't been fine all year. He drunk dials me at 3 a.m. most nights blubbering about what you did.

(*Somewhere around here,* DEVON *gets sandwiched on the couch between these two, stuck hearing this.*)

MICHAELA. What else was I supposed to do Ethan?!

ETHAN. Don't ask me that, kid.

MICHAELA. He *would not* look at the screen. The doctor would point and he'd just turn his head the other way and smooth all of his arm hairs until they faced the same direction. He was in total denial. I thought he'd be relieved, that's what I honestly thought…

ETHAN. Well, that may be true, Mik, but you're the one who's out. Those are the deets, kid: you're out. (*Really bad news:*) You're o-u-t out.

(*Beat.*)

MICHAELA. *O-u-t out* or just out?

ETHAN. O-u-t out.

MICHAELA. Did he say it in his CEO voice?

ETHAN. Yep.

MICHAELA. What if I were to—

ETHAN. Nope.

MICHAELA. But I coul—

ETHAN. Nope.

MICHAELA. But if I—

ETHAN. Nope.

MICHAELA. But, if—

ETHAN. He's done, Mik. He's D-U-N done. You can stay at Island Haven tonight, but then you gotta make other arrangements.

MICHAELA. …he's gonna put me in a hotel?

ETHAN. He said you can pick which one. You want the Four Seasons, fine. But he doesn't want to see ya until he and his team have their ducks in a row.

(*Beat.*)

And between you and me, as a friend, you need to *put your game face on* because he's gonna come after you hard.

MICHAELA. How hard?

ETHAN. Hard. He's got his own Indian Takeout Mik, and that curry is *spicy.*

(*Beat.*)

MICHAELA. Excuse me.

(*She exits. We see her go to* SIMONE *and take the hands-free from her and put it in her own ears to start urgently talking to Susan Coletti.* SIMONE *stands nearby looking empathetic, maybe a little frightened.*

ETHAN *gets up and heads to the bar to refill his glass. He sees* DEVON *[who's been sitting right next to him this whole time] and is surprised.*)

ETHAN. Oh hey there...buddy. Sorry about that. We got a little wrapped up there, didn't we.

(*To* DEVON.)

More Schramsberg?

DEVON. No, I'm good. Who's she talking to?

ETHAN. Oh Coletti, I'm sure. Her prenup's a piece of shit. This house, the townhouse, all his beer frog monies—it's all protected assets. I told her not to sign that thing.

(*Handing champagne to* DEVON.)

It's so sad when marriages fall apart, isn't it? It's just a *huge bummer* is what it is. I need to stop being friends with people around here. It's like a revolving door.

DEVON. What about you? You ever been married, Ethan?

ETHAN. Nope. Not yet. (*Winks.*)

(ETHAN *drinks his champagne.*)

Speaking of, what the hell is she doing out there?

(*To* SIMONE, *shouting even though she hears nothing.*)

SIMONE!!!! COME BACK IN HERE!!!!!

DEVON. Hey Ethan, do you think I could ask you a question?

ETHAN. Totes.

DEVON. You said before that you do not belong to the workforce. Does that mean you don't work?

ETHAN. Yep.

DEVON. You don't work?

ETHAN. Nope.

DEVON. Must leave you with a lot of free time to get set up with the "hot help" around here.

ETHAN. What, you mean Simone? We weren't set up. I mean, I think Pete had mentioned Simone in a vague way—he said she went to Yale like we all did, blahdy blahdy blah—but I didn't pay it any mind until I met her on Xmas Eve.

DEVON. ...You met Simone last Christmas Eve?

ETHAN. Yeah. Pete and Mik do a little yuletide whatever—*shindig.* Tommy Keller does the food and those famous a capella people sing.

(*Beat.*)

DEVON. And, so, what? Simone came round the corner in a tuxedo jacket with a tray of pigs-in-a-blanket and it was love at first sight?

ETHAN. (*Laughing.*) Simone? (*More laughing.*) Sorry! That's really funny. (*Still laughing.*) Simone with a bow tie (*Laughing until ready to talk.*) No, Simone wasn't *working*, she was a guest. She came down their marble staircase in a red strapless Vera gown and knocked me right outta my chair.

DEVON. Really.

ETHAN. (*Admiration.*) Yeah. It was *quite* an entrance, believe you me. I teased her that she *must've* choreographed the whole thing—with the *descent* into the room, some strategically-placed tinsel caught in her hair. But now that I know her, I know it was just Simone being Simone. (*Genuine.*) She has no idea how people stare at her and want to be next to her. It's because she's so *good*. She's good and sweet and let me tell you something I've learned about myself, Dora...Derot... (*Still can't remember her name.*) FUCK! Why can't I get this?! Is it an unusual name?

DEVON. Nope. Devon. Just like Kevin.

ETHAN. Devon. Devon, Kevin, Devon, Kevin. Let me tell you something I've learned about myself, *Kevin:* I *want* good and sweet and innocent and kind. Women spend hundreds of thousands of dollars on plastic surgery trying to get what Simone has—but you can't buy what she's got. Because it like comes through her skin or something. I mean, look at her.

> (*They do, and for a moment, what he's saying is actually strikingly true. SIMONE is indeed patiently, lovingly, radiantly sitting beside MICHAELA, being supportive. And MICHAELA looks like a demonic monster who has grown fangs.*)

ETHAN. I was on my Berry when Simone came down those stairs and you know what, Devon?

DEVON. What.

ETHAN. I didn't even say goodbye to whoever I was talking to or anything. Just:

> (*Reenacting.*)

There's Simone. End call.

DEVON. (*Genuine.*) Well, that's actually a/ really nice—

ETHAN. Plus sexually?...*she blows my mind.*

> (*Beat.*)

DEVON. You know I'm *her sister*, right? We're sisters.

ETHAN. Sorry! I just can't help myself. (*Laughing.*) When you're in love, you have no filter.

> (*A potted plant, thrown by MICHAELA, hits the door frame and shatters, soil and flowers going everywhere.*)

Okey-doke. Excuse me just a sec. It's starting to look like a *Gladiator* casting call out there...

(ETHAN *crosses to the door and opens it. We get a blast of* MICHAELA's *screaming into the hands-free:*)

MICHAELA. THEN WHY DID I PAY TO RETAIN YOUR MOTHERFUCKING SERVICES/HM?! WHY???—

ETHAN. (*Sweetly, to* SIMONE.) ....Honey! Simone? Would you come in here please?

(SIMONE *comes right in and* ETHAN *closes the door.*)

Jesus, are you okay, honey?

(*Seeing she's not.*)

No! Tears? No tears! Why tears?/ No! Why?

SIMONE. Sorry—I just...she's o-u-t out, Ethan! He's already got her jewelry on lockdown and everything. I feel so badly for her.

ETHAN. *This has nothing to do with us.* We're gonna be like swans. Underneath the water? Kicking and seaweed and algae, but above water? Graceful, calm swans.

SIMONE. I know, Ethan, but—

ETHAN. Pete's gotta do what Pete's gotsta do, and we gotta do what we's gotsda do. Is there somewhere we could talk alone for a second?

SIMONE. (*Noticing* MICHAELA.) Uh-oh, is that expensive?

(MICHAELA's *beating the shit out of the extremely expensive grill. Her weapon is a golf club, which she's brandishing overhead, execution-style.*

SIMONE, *starting to exit:*)

Uh oh, I better—

ETHAN. (*Stopping her.*) No, Simone. *Absolutely not.* (*Hero cape.*) I'll handle this.

(*When he opens the door, we get another blast of* MICHAELA *screaming.*)

MICHAELA. NO, FUCK HIM! I WON'T DO IT! FUCK YOU! ARE YOU FUCKING KIDD—

ETHAN. Mikki, stop hitting the grill. Stop it. You are being a child. Stop hitting the gr—

(ETHAN *closes the door.*)

SIMONE. (*Looking out the window.*) Jesus! She is really strong, huh?

DEVON. Um. Simone?

SIMONE. (*Still looking.*) Look at Ethan! He's such a gentleman, sweetly coaxing that out/of her death grip—

DEVON. HEY!!!!!!!!!!!!! SIMONE!!!!!!!!!!!!!

(*Beat. The shout startles* SIMONE.)

SIMONE. *Jesus,* Devon. What?

DEVON. What are you doing?

SIMONE. ....I'm....looking out the window?

DEVON. No: what are you *doing?*

SIMONE. What am I doing *with what*, Dev? You're gonna have to be a little more specific.

DEVON. Okay: what *is* this place?

SIMONE. What? Island Haven?

DEVON. No. These people. Who are these *fucking* people?!

(*By now*, MICHAELA *has thrown the phone into the lawn and stomped off to the Main House.* ETHAN *knocks on the door and again shouts silently,* "SIMONE! COME OUT HERE!" SIMONE *gives him the "just a minute" finger. He scrolls through his Blackberry, waiting.*)

SIMONE. (*To* DEVON.) Look Dev, I know you're upset and you have every right to be: I promised you a restful sisters' beach weekend, and this has not gone/ according to plan.

DEVON. I don't care about any of that, Simone. I care about *what you're doing here.*

SIMONE. What I'm doing with what?! I'm working. I *work* here.

DEVON. You work here, you live here, you sleep here, you get dressed here, you seduce morons here, you go to Christmas here, you lie/ to me here.

SIMONE. I "seduce morons," is that what you just said?

DEVON. Yes that clown is a *retard.* I cannot believe you bailed on Christmas so you could snag him—snag Clown Tard.

SIMONE. What a terrible thing to say to me, Devon! I love Ethan. I am *in love* with him.

DEVON. Simone, he thinks my name is Kevin. And he doesn't even know you moved me to California!

SIMONE. Yes because there's more to me than *where I move you*, Devon. You ever think of that? That maybe there's more to me than how *I* relate to *Devon?* He happens to know me intimately.

DEVON. Oh please, no he doesn't.

SIMONE. Yes, he does!

(*Listing again.*)

He won't order anything with sun-dried tomatoes because they gross me out. He took me to a three hour Katy Perry unplugged concert and pretended to have fun.

And he tracked down Mom's cameo, Devon—the one Dad pawned? He outbid 14 other buyers for it on Ebay—

DEVON. Well... I'm sure those gifts were your reward for "blowing his mind" sexually. Because those words actually came out of his mouth, Simone.

SIMONE. (*Giggling.*) So? That's kinda nice.

DEVON. What? No! No that's not nice! What are you even talking about anymore?! This Michaela bitch has got her talons deep into your brain, you're drinking some fucked up Kool/ Aid out here.

SIMONE. Oh brother, have you been watching *Pelican Brief* again? We *gotta* get that/ off your queue.

DEVON. I am not joking, Simone! What's going on in this house?

SIMONE. What are you even…? Nothing!

DEVON. Then why's he leaving her?

SIMONE. What? Who?!

DEVON. Don't "What? Who?" me! *Peter!* Why's he leaving Michaela?

SIMONE. I don't know, why does anyone split up? Why did Mom leave Dad? Why did you leave Tim?

DEVON. Tim was addicted to titty websites. Dad fucked a bartender.

SIMONE. Well, I don't know, Devon, okay? But it's probably something private and complicated and my/ confidentiality agreement—

DEVON. I don't give a rat's ass about your confiden-whatever agreement, Simone. Do you hear me? *I am worried about you.* There is some DARK ASS SHIT going on in this house. Something about emotional abuse/ and a doctor—

SIMONE. And it's *none of your business*, Devon.

DEVON. It is my business! *You* are my business. Have you watched a single Bills game out here? Have you made any friends of your own? Have you worn sweatpants and done Sudoku? Have you written *a single word* since you took this job? You are *disappearing* here, Simone.

SIMONE. No, I'm not, and you sound/ like an idiot—

DEVON. Why are you a Rent-A-Friend to these icky people?

SIMONE. What icky people?!

DEVON. STOP IT, SIMONE!

SIMONE. NO *YOU* STOP DEVON! YOU STOP! You're not my mother and you have no idea what I do here and you *are not going to ruin this for me!* I didn't judge you when you dropped your job in New York like a hot potato. It took you two years to get a job in your field, Devon, *two years*. And you threw it all away for Tim. So you can stop. YOU STOP. You were calling her hooker and whore the minute you walked in here—

DEVON. No, I was—

SIMONE. YES YOU WERE! And she is none of those things. She's literally the nicest, most generous, most kind-hearted person I know and *she takes the time for me*. You have no idea how depressed I was back in Boston, Devon.

Temping, trying to write my stupid novels that no one reads, getting rejected from every M.F.A. program in the country for the *third* year in a row. My friend from Yale is a *senator*, Dev. A senator! So you can stop. You have no idea how much I *like it here*. HOW MUCH I LIKE WHO I AM HERE.

DEVON. Well I think who you are here *sucks*. I think *you suck*, Simone.

(*Beat.*)

SIMONE. Excuse me.

(SIMONE *exits to talk to* ETHAN, *who's so happy to have her alone for a moment. During all of the following, the two of them are up behind the soundproof glass, leaning over the banister with their backs to us, having a deep conversation. Beat.*

JOS-B *enters with lobster and corn. There's something different about him; like he has a secret or a joke.*)

JOS-B. Yo yo yo! Where are all the dickheads?

DEVON. Outside.

JOS-B. Sweet! I got two-pounders for you and me.

DEVON. Awesome.

JOS-B. (*Noticing.*) …Hey you okay over there, amiga?

DEVON. José, do you think you could give me the skinny on something?

JOS-B. Of course. But I drink this Schramsberg and take my boots off while we talk, is okay?

DEVON. Yeah. What's going on in this house? Simone won't tell me. It's something about a baby? Right?

JOS-B. Well. Okay. I can tell you, amiga, but it's some fucked-up shit. You sure you want to know?

DEVON. Yeah.

JOS-B. Okay. Well, this time last year Michaela was pregnant— (*Holding his arm out a small bit.*) about this big—and then suddenly she no pregnant. And the Peter was furious. Because he was saying is okay not perfect, and she was saying is no okay not perfect, so she go.

DEVON. Wait…what wasn't perfect? The baby?

JOS-B. Yes, baby was going to be, how you say? Dwarf. Little guy. And everything must be perfect at Island Haven—so she go take care of situation.

(*Beat.*

DEVON *looks out at* SIMONE, *talking to Clown Tard.*)

DEVON. That's who my sister's a Rent-A-Friend to? To someone *that* superficial?

JOS-B. Yep. She hire Simone a few days later.

(*Beat.*)

I tell you what, amiga, it's a funny place, this island. These people? They coming, going, coming, going, coming, going. Every year is same.

(MICHAELA *has arrived on the patio carrying things from the Main House and she now comes in, barking.* SIMONE *follows her in.* ETHAN *goes off.*)

MICHAELA. (*Entering.*) Okay we have to (*Seeing.*) Jos-B! Why are you on my couch and why are you barefoot?! Get your ass off my couch and go over to the garage and get the box that says "Indian Takeout Menus" and bring it over here.

(*To* SIMONE.)

He thinks he can put me in a hotel? He doesn't know what I've got up my sl—

(*To* JOS-B.)

Hello! (*Snapping.*) Jos-B! I said I need the box/ from the garage—

JOS-B. Yes I hear you, you bitch, and I busy drinking your shit.

(*Beat.*)

MICHAELA. *What* did you say?

JOS-B. I say BITCH. I say bitch. I say I hate you, you fucking bitch. I hated you every day for entire four years you been here. You tip like shit; your stupid face is like look at el diablo; your music is whiny woman whiny woman; your cookies taste like ass; your soaps is big *who cares* problem and I am *not from Cuba!!* I am from Puerto Rico. And when I say to you all these years "*Metete en la piscina 'Infiniti' esa y sigue nadando, gringa de mierda*" I am actually say *Go jump in infinity pool and KEEP ON SWIMMING, you horrible! White! Cunt! Bitch!* .

(*Beat.*)

MICHAELA. You are so fired, Jos-B. Go get your shit out of the studio apartment.

JOS-B. No, I no think that is the case, my love.

MICHAELA. Yes, that is the case, my love. You are fucking fired.

JOS-B. No because I work for the Peter, my love. So when I go to Dawson's, I just give the Peter quick call to check is he coming to dinner. And he say no, he is not coming to dinner. But he also say I am promoted because guess why.

MICHAELA. *Why.*

JOS-B. Because I tell him I see a box of deeds and legal documents labeled "Indian Takeout Menus" hiding in the garage. And he grateful that I put it through the shredder just now.

(*Beat.*)

MICHAELA. Simone, don't just stand there! Go get the Bentley and bring it around front. Then pull up the ferry schedule and see how soon we can get back to New York—

SIMONE. Um, actually Michaela, there's something I need to tell you.

MICHAELA. Can't it wait until after we?!—

SIMONE. No, it can't wait, it's important.

> (*Beat.*)

The thing is, Michaela…I'm *not* going home to New York with you.

MICHAELA. Oh—my bad. I thought I told you this. We're going to a hotel.

SIMONE. No, I know about the hotel. But the hotel is for you. Just you. I'm not going with you.

MICHAELA. Then…how are you getting there?

SIMONE. No. See, considering how things have panned out today, I think it would be best if I don't work here anymore.

> (*Beat.* DEVON *is ecstatic, makes "Yeah!" gesture.*)

MICHAELA. ….I'm sorry…*what?!* You're really going to drop this on me *today*, Simone?

SIMONE. I'm really sorry, Michaela. This has nothing to do with how I *feel* about you.

MICHAELA. Then what does it have to do with?! Money?! Because I'll find a way to/ pay you, Simone. I'll take a credit card advance—

SIMONE. This isn't about money, Michaela. This is just about me doing what's best for me.

DEVON. Yeah, she needs to focus on other things for a while.

MICHAELA. You need to focus on *what* exactly?

SIMONE. I don't know. Writing? Travelling?

> (*Beat.*)

It's not like I wanted to be an assistant forever. And this job has been really stressful recently. It's not the right place for me anymore.

DEVON. Well this has turned out to be a freaking awesome day. *Thank God!*

SIMONE. *Dev.*

DEVON. (*Handing* MICHAELA *a mallard.*) Don't forget your mallard, babe. C'mon Simone, let's get/ the fuck outta here—

MICHAELA. *Ugh, Devon, shut up!! Why are you still here!?*

DEVON. I dunno, Michaela. Maybe you should late-term abort me.

> (*Long beat.*)

SIMONE. It wasn't me, Michaela. I didn't tell her. It wasn't me.

JOS-B. No, it was me. I tell her.

MICHAELA. Well, so what. You know? So what? It's not like I give a shit what you think, Devon.

DEVON. I think that it's *revolting*, that's what I think. You make me want to throw up.

MICHAELA. Is that right?

DEVON. Yes, that's right.

MICHAELA. Well, go head, Devon, knock yourself out.

DEVON. You know what, I think I will! I THINK I WILL! You know I worked at a school in Bed Stuy with students who ate garbage for lunch, Michaela. *Garbage*. And you have so *much money*. Look at your house! *Look at it!* You could afford anything, everything; you have *so much money*. How are you a person *who does that?*

MICHAELA. How am I a person who does what, Devon? Who decides—at 23 weeks—that the best thing to do, the *kindest* thing to do, is to research what state I have to go to to get one? A person who gets a room at a Super 8 motel in Connecticut and who stays there—*by herself for 3 days*—so she can go to a *clinic* like the whore in *Dirty Dancing?* Is that what you're asking me? How I'm that person?

DEVON. Yep.

MICHAELA. Well, let me tell you something Devon, you have *no idea* how it feels to have to *be* this person. You think this sounds a certain way, so you have *all the answers*. But you cannot *imagine* the kinds of things that were coming out of my husband's mouth, Devon. Words like leg-stretching surgery. Words like steel plates and bolts and screws that would "fix him." You have *no idea* how excruciating that little boy's life would've been in this house, Devon, or down at the club, Devon, or in his father's office, Devon. You have *no idea* what his little heartbeat sounded like, or what his name was, Devon, or how wildly and completely in love with him I was. And you have *no idea* what kind of *terror* raced through me when I realized I had to *be this person*, Devon.

(*Long beat.*)

Simone…

(*Beat.*)

If you need to quit and go off to write somewhere, I completely support and understand that. But I need you to come to New York with me.

SIMONE. Michaela, I—

MICHAELA. Just for a few days. Just one day, tomorrow.

(*Beat.*)

Please, Simone. As a favor to a friend. *Please* don't make me go back there by myself.

SIMONE. I'm so very sorry, Michaela, but no. I can't.

MICHAELA. Jesus, Simone…

DEVON. That's a little a rough, babe. We can go to New York before we head to Buffalo, can't we?

SIMONE. Dev, I'm not going to Buffalo, I'm going sailing with Ethan.

(*Beat.*)

DEVON. *What?*

SIMONE. We're going to take the next year off and do some international travelling before we settle down. We set sail at 22:00 hours.

MICHAELA. Before you "settle down"? Honey, he's not gonna marry you. He's 42! He has a different girl under our mistletoe every year.

SIMONE. Well, he says I'm different and I believe him and I love him and I'm going with him.

DEVON. No! No no no no no. This is—no. That is a terrible idea.

SIMONE. What do you mean?! This is a great opportunity for me. I thought you'd be happy for me. He just asked me, guys. He took my hand and said he couldn't imagine travelling *without* me. That it would be a major bummer if I didn't come. He wants to show me his favorite places on the globe and wake up every morning in the middle of the sea, with nothing to look at but my face and miles of blue. We're going to pick out my diamond in the Congo.

MICHAELA. *Oh my God.*

(*Beat.*)

DEVON. Simone, you're really gonna do this?

SIMONE. Yes.

DEVON. You're gonna go on a love cruise with someone you barely know?

SIMONE. Yes, and I do know him. Well.

DEVON. You can't just quit your job and go off on a boat with some dude who's gonna bankroll you! Not when you have plans!

SIMONE. Oh yeah? Which plans are those? Huh? What "plans" do I have?

DEVON. Let's make some then! We'll make some right now! We'll move to New York together and get our own place! And then we'll make you a plan, one that's actually really good!

SIMONE. This is a really good plan.

(ETHAN *has appeared on the patio and now opens the door.*)

ETHAN. ...too soon?

SIMONE. Yes.

(ETHAN *closes the door. Beat.*)

DEVON. *No,* Simone. Trust me, as someone who just really knows...don't go.

SIMONE. I'm not you, Devon. I'm me.

DEVON. Yeah but......! As your older sister then, please don't go.

MICHAELA. (*From where she is.*) She's already gone, hun. Just wish her luck.

JOS-B. Yeah! *Rápido* you go, Simone! Bye-bye!

(*Beat.*)

SIMONE. (*Light.*) It's not such a big thing, Dev! It's not like you're not gonna see me in like no time. You'll be back in New York soon and Ethan and I will be there all the time. We'll have our engagement party there! And you and I can meet up and go to brunch and shows and museums and do all kinds of fun stuff together in the city! Okay, Dev?

(*Beat.*)

So come on. Ethan and I are going to drop you off at the ferry station on the way to the boat.

(*Beat.*)

Okay, Dev?

(*No answer.*)

JOS-B. Simone, you go. I'll take Devon to the ferry in the Bentley when she ready to go.

(*Beat.*)

SIMONE. Devon.

(*Beat.*)

You know what you could do? Instead of looking at the floor, and making me feel like shit, you could look at me and tell me that you love me and you understand.

(*Beat.*)

You could say you love me and you understand?

(*Beat.*)

Fine.

(SIMONE *starts to exit.*)

DEVON. Simone. I do love you. Please be careful.

SIMONE. Totes.

(ETHAN *opens the door for her and enters.*)

ETHAN. (*Twirling the keys, to* SIMONE.) The car's all packed. We all good in here?

SIMONE. Yep, let's go.

ETHAN. Listen Mik...

(*To* MICHAELA.)

You listen to me, okay, kid? I want you to know that this is *not* the end of us, Mikaroo. I still want to be *very* good friends with you, okay? I have unlimited international texting with my plan so you should feel free to text me anytime, okay? If you need anything, Mik, you let me know because I am *so* there for you.

(*To* DEVON.)

And....................you take care.

(ETHAN *exits, sunglasses back on, holding* SIMONE*'s hand.*

Long beat.)

JOS-B. Come amiga, we blow this joint. Let's get you on your ferry.

DEVON. Ah actually, can you give me just a second? (*Indicating* MICHAELA.) I'll be right out.

JOS-B. What you got to talk to her for?!

DEVON. Just...give me a sec, okay?

JOS-B. Fine. I do donuts with the Bentley.

(JOS-B *takes a few bottles of Schramsberg and exits.*

Long beat.

The air in the room empties and everything slows way down, with just MICHAELA *and* DEVON *in this space.*

Long beat.

MICHAELA *looks only at the ocean.*)

DEVON. I gotta say............ I *did not* see that coming. Did you, Michaela?

MICHAELA. ......No.

(*Beat.*)

DEVON. Though...I guess now that I think about it, it was pretty obvious. I don't know *why* I didn't see it.

MICHAELA. ....me neither.

(*Long beat.*)

DEVON. You think she's gonna be okay with that guy?

MICHAELA. No.

(*Beat.*)

But, maybe she will. Who knows. Her novel was pretty good.

DEVON. It was?! *Really?!* Cuz the last one? *My First Apartment* or whatever? Fuck me, I could not get/ through that one.

MICHAELA. Oh, I know! Me neither! It was like taking a Xanax, reading that thing.

No but the new one was much better. I saw some real potential there.

(*Beat.*)

DEVON. I'm sorry about what I said before, that you make me want to throw up. You don't, and I'm sorry.

MICHAELA. Oh, that's okay, Devon. You don't need to say that.

DEVON. ....Yeah, but I was wrong. I'm saying I was wrong.

MICHAELA. It really doesn't matter.

(*Beat.*)

DEVON. Do you want to tell me what his name was?

MICHAELA. (*Hard for her.*) ....it was Jonathan.

DEVON. Oh, that's a nice name. Jonathan Kell.

MICHAELA. Thank you, Devon.

(*Long beat.*)

DEVON. You know Tim? My porn addict?

MICHAELA. Yeah.

DEVON. I knew about his problem when I said I'd marry him. I had seen some files on his computer, I knew. But I moved all the way out there and wore that ring anyway because...I thought I could handle it.

MICHAELA. Yeah.

(*Beat.*)

DEVON. So what are you gonna do now? I mean—are you gonna be okay?

MICHAELA. What am I going to do now and am I going to be okay.

(*Beat.*)

Well.

(*Beat.*)

I'm going to watch the sunset from here, I think, and then I'm going to go for a walk along the beach, and then I'm going to eat a lobster, and then I'm going to go in the hot tub, and then I'm going to watch the flat screen, and then I'm going to leave this island on a Peter Pan bus, Devon. And no, I'm not going to be okay.

(*Beat.*)

MICHAELA. What about you? What are you gonna do?

DEVON. Well.......I think I'm gonna go cash your check, Michaela.

(MICHAELA *looks at* DEVON *and really sees her. She smiles at her for the first time in the play.*)

MICHAELA. (*Laughing.*) Well, I'd hurry up if I were you, babe. That check won't be good for long.

DEVON. Yeah—I think we passed a Chase Bank on Dock Street on the way in.

MICHAELA. Perfect. They're open till 8. Just tell Jos-B to take Water Street 'cause Route 3 will be a shit show.

DEVON. Okay cool, I'll tell him. Thanks.

MICHAELA. You're welcome.

(Beat.)

DEVON. I do have a couple minutes though, so maybe I'll…just sit for a second.

MICHAELA. Of course, be my guest.

(Long beat. DEVON sits on the other end of the couch. They both look at the ocean maybe.)

DEVON. So. Okay…

MICHAELA. Yeah, okay.

(DEVON *is going to leave in a few, but for just a moment, the two of them just sit there together—alone and very still—on the couch in this gigantic guest house.*

The sun has started setting by now, and the light is a deep golden.

It is *so* quiet.)

End of Play

BOB
A Life in Five Acts
by Peter Sinn Nachtrieb

Copyright © 2011 by Peter Sinn Nachtrieb. All rights reserved. CAUTION: Professionals and amateurs are hereby warned that *BOB* is subject to royalty. It is fully protected under the copyright laws of the United States of America and of all countries covered by the International Copyright Union (including the Dominion of Canada and the rest of the British Commonwealth), the Berne Convention, the Pan-American Copyright Convention and the Universal Copyright Convention, as well as all countries with which the United States has reciprocal copyright relations. All rights, including professional, amateur stage rights, motion picture, recitation, lecturing, public reading, radio broadcasting, television, video or sound recording, all other forms of mechanical or electronic reproduction, such as CD-ROM, CD-I, information storage and retrieval systems, and photocopying, and the rights of translation into foreign languages, are strictly reserved. Particular emphasis is laid upon the matter of readings, permission for which must be secured from the Author's agent in writing.

Required royalties must be paid every time this play is performed before any audience, whether or not it is presented for profit and whether or not admission is charged.

All inquiries concerning rights, including amateur rights, should be addressed to: Bret Adams Ltd., 448 West 44th St., New York, NY 10036, ATTN: Mark Orsini. (212) 765-5630.

ABOUT *BOB*

This article first ran in the January/February 2011 issue of Inside Actors, *and is based on conversations with the playwright before rehearsals for the Humana Festival production began.*

BOB is playwright Peter Sinn Nachtrieb's epic theatrical tale of the life of one man. The play's eponymous hero is born in a public bathroom to a mother who doesn't want him, rescued (read: kidnapped, kind of, but in a good way) by a woman who believes it's her destiny to mother a great man, raised on the road in a run-down Chevy Malibu, and ultimately left to fend for himself at a highway rest stop. Undeterred by these setbacks, Bob sets out on his own, determined to find his place in the whole hullabaloo of it all and, so help him, to get his name on a plaque.

BOB found its origin in Nachtrieb's fascination with American mythology— "the way we tell history, how often it's embellished or elevated to a scale that's larger-than-life"—and what strikes him as a particularly American obsession with "stories of great people and their great achievements." He wanted to write a play about the idea of greatness: where the notion comes from, and what it might mean in America today.

Inspiration can strike in the strangest places. In Nachtrieb's case, it happened at a White Castle. While in Louisville early in 2009 to attend the first rehearsals for *BRINK!* (a Humana Festival Apprentice show which he co-authored), he happened to walk by a downtown White Castle restaurant. As he passed the tiny-burger-peddling giant, two details captured his attention. The first was a message posted on the restaurant's marquee, which urged its patrons, in utterly un-ironic block letters, to RESERVE YOUR VALENTINE TABLE TODAY. The second was a "Safe Surrender" placard. Kentucky law allows desperate parents to anonymously place babies they cannot care for at selected "safe places." This particular White Castle, Nachtrieb realized, seemed to be an official drop-off point. He found the unlikely constellation of details strangely compelling. "I thought, there it is!" he says, recalling his "Ah-ha" moment with a laugh. "That's how the play begins. Someone is born on Valentine's Day and abandoned at a White Castle restaurant in Louisville, Kentucky."

Energized, Nachtrieb dreamed up his hero: a scrappy sort-of orphan who's long on dreams but short on bearings. As Bob traverses the country in pursuit of greatness, he encounters waitresses and truck drivers, tangles with policemen and baristas, and combats more than his fair share of fleas. He falls in love. He eats ham and cheese omelets. And he discovers an America that's wistful and more than a little weary, full of people with big souls and huge regrets. Their pain-filled pasts and half-cooked plans for the future are rendered in *BOB* with equal parts veneration and humor. The result, Nachtrieb hopes, feels something like a carnival ride.

In addition to offering Nachtrieb a chance to grapple with (and poke fun at) some of life's most urgent questions, *BOB* also represents a welcome opportunity to take up new dramaturgical challenges. Having recently written the successful comedy *boom*, a three-hander played on a unit set, Nachtrieb now finds himself attempting something on a much larger scale: a sprawling epic that spans a lifetime, occupies many locales, and is populated by a dizzying array of characters. He has risen to the challenge with gusto, drawing inspiration from diverse literary models. Voltaire and Ibsen provided classic examples of the "life of one man" narrative with *Candide* and *Peer Gynt*. Shakespeare showed up to lend a hand with his canny five-act plot structure. The Greeks had this idea for a chorus, which Nachtrieb happily appropriates in *BOB*, charging four actors with the considerable artistic (and aerobic) challenge of portraying the play's more than two dozen supporting roles. "The formal aspect of the chorus," Nachtrieb explains, "is fun and appeals to me. *BOB* is very much a play about storytelling. Part of the pleasure of the play, I hope, is watching four talented performers tell a story and jump back and forth between so many different characters."

Throughout the play, Nachtrieb negotiates a fine balance between satire and earnest, warm-hearted affection for his characters—and, by extension, America. He hopes the resulting portrait is one that his audiences will laugh at, but also one with which they can identify. "Ultimately," he says, "I don't think the play has an explicit message—or I hope it doesn't—but instead asks questions. How do we define success? Why are we happy, if we're happy, or else why are we not? Is there such a thing as destiny, or is everything that befalls us the result of accident and luck? What are our goals, as individuals and as a culture? What does it mean to be great?" Whether or not Bob achieves his aim shall not be revealed here. But in Peter Sinn Nachtrieb's joyous whirlwind of a play, Bob's life becomes a hilarious and moving parable about the choices we make as we journey through life, and the myriad ways we change, and are changed by, the people we meet along the way.

—Sarah Lunnie

BIOGRAPHY

Peter Sinn Nachtrieb is a San Francisco-based playwright whose works include *boom* (TCG's most produced play of the 2009-2010 season), *T.I.C. (Trenchcoat In Common)*, *Hunter Gatherers* (2007 ATCA/Steinberg New Play Award, 2007 Will Glickman Prize), *Colorado*, and *Multiplex*. His work has been seen Off-Broadway and across the country including at Ars Nova, SPF, Woolly Mammoth, Seattle Repertory Theatre, Actors Theatre of Louisville, San Diego Repertory, Kitchen Dog Theater, and in the Bay Area at American Conservatory Theatre, Encore Theatre, Killing My Lobster, Marin Theatre Company, Impact Theatre, and The Bay Area Playwrights Festival. His newest plays are *BOB* (2011 Humana Festival of New American Plays at Actors Theatre of Louisville) and *Litter: The True Story of the Framingham Dodecatuplets* (American Conservatory Theatre 2011). Currently he's working on a commission through the National New Play Network and New Dramatists Full Stage USA program, as well as an original musical. Peter holds degrees in theater and biology from Brown and an M.F.A. in creative writing from San Francisco State University. He is a member of New Dramatists, a resident playwright alum at the Playwrights Foundation, and often works at the Z Space Studio in San Francisco. He likes to promote himself online at www.peternachtrieb.com.

ACKNOWLEDGMENTS

BOB premiered at the Humana Festival of New American Plays in March 2011. It was directed by Sean Daniels with the following cast:

BOB	Jeffrey Binder
CHORUS 1	Aysan Celik
CHORUS 2	Polly Lee
CHORUS 3	Danny Scheie
CHORUS 4	Lou Sumrall

and the following production staff:

Scenic Designer	Michael B. Raiford
Costume Designer	Lorraine Venberg
Lighting Designer	Brian J. Lilienthal
Sound Designer	Matt Callahan
Properties Designer	Joe Cunningham
Media Designer	Philip Allgeier
Wig Designer	Heather Fleming
Production Stage Manager	Paul Mills Holmes
Dramaturg	Sarah Lunnie
Casting	Judy Bowman

Scenic Design Assistant.......................................Ryan Wineinger
Costume Design Assistant...................................... Amanda Sox
Lighting Design Assistant ....Rachel Fae Szymanski
Sound Design Assistant...Dan Cassin
Production Assistant...Katie Shade
Stage Management Intern................................... Rachel Enright
Assistant Dramaturg ....Jessica Reese

BOB was developed for the Humana Festival of New American Plays by Actors Theatre of Louisville through partnerships with Florida State University and The Nevada Conservatory Theatre at University of Nevada, Las Vegas. The play was originally commissioned and developed by South Coast Repertory. It was developed with the support of Playwrights Foundation, San Francisco, Amy L. Mueller, Artistic Director.

CHARACTERS

BOB, from infant to old man. Possibly of a multiracial background. If handsome, unconventionally so. If not handsome, his personality adds something charismatic. Energy, Optimism, Open, Active.

THE CHORUS, two men and two women. The chorus is, ideally, of unspecified but diverse cultural backgrounds. American. The chorus will play themselves as well as every character in the play, aside from Bob. The chorus is dispassionate (perhaps humorously grave) but eloquent. The characters they assume are vivid, bright, sharp, distinct. Even if they only have one line, there is pathos, history, pain.

SUGGESTED CAST BREAKDOWN

BOB, male

CHORUS ONE, female
    JEANINE
    CAITLYN
    WAITRESS ONE
    PROSTITUTE ONE
    DEBORAH
    VERA
    and others

CHORUS TWO, male
    CONNOR
    JAMES
    WAITRESS TWO
    BARISTA
    TONY
    LEO
    and others

CHORUS THREE, female
    HELEN
    BONNIE
    KIM
    AMELIA
    WAITRESS THREE
    PROSTITUTE THREE
    and others

CHORUS FOUR, male
    SETH
    SAGÉ
    WAITRESS FOUR
    PROSTITUTE FOUR
    GUNTHER ROY
    ROULETTE DEALER
    SVEN
    and others

SETTING

All over the United States of America, interiors and exteriors. Plus one scene in Mexico. The play often changes rapidly from location to location and the shifts are quick. The speed of the changes is important and part of the ride of the play. My hunch is that the stagecraft in the play is exposed for being what it is.

TIME

From the birth to the death of Bob.

THE ACTS

Act 1: How Bob is born, abandoned, raised by a fast food employee, discovers his dream, and almost dies.

Act 2: How Bob does not die, comes of age at a rest stop, pursues his dream, falls in love and has his heart broken.

Act 3: How Bob pursues his dream across America, gets chased out of many towns, meets an important man, and turns his back on everything he believes.

Act 4: How Bob has a turn of luck, becomes a new man, achieves a false dream, meets an important woman and is redeemed.

Act 5: The rest.

MUSIC

Yes. Underscoring. Maybe a live musician. Maybe the chorus plays music.
I think there are short interludes of music or dance, maybe live, in between each act.

MOOD

Epic, cinematic, a whirlwind, a ride.

THANKS TO

Sean Daniels; Ken Prestininzi, John Glore, Kelly Miller, Megan Monaghan, Sherri Butler-Hyner and everybody at South Coast Repertory; Marc Masterson, Sarah Lunnie and everybody at Actors Theatre of Louisville; Madeleine Oldham, Emily Schooltz and Ars Nova, Jonathan Spector, Amy Mueller, Lisa Steindler and the Z Space Studio, The National Theatre Conference, The Resident Playwrights of the Playwrights Foundation, New Dramatists, Mark Orsini and Bruce Ostler.

Kasey Mahaffy, Rob Nagle, Larry Bates, Angela Goethals, Blake Lindsley, Danny Wolohan, Arwen Anderson, Delia MacDougall, Nick Pelczar, Liam Vincent, Lance Gardner, Sally Dana, Matt Dellapina, Brett Robinson, David Turner, Jackie Viscusi, Joey DeChello, Ryan Barrentine, Brigette Davidovici, Lauren T. Mack, Dhyana Dahl, Kevin Tomlinson, Tyler Hastings; the Theatre departments at Florida State University and University of Nevada, Las Vegas; Jason Aaron Goldberg.

Jeff Binder, Aysan Celik, Polly Lee, Danny Scheie, and Lou Sumrall.

Aysan Celik and Jeffrey Binder
in *BOB*

35th Annual Humana Festival of New American Plays
Actors Theatre of Louisville, 2011
Photo by Alan Simons

BOB

ACT ONE

The CHORUS *enters.*

ALL CHORUS. Bob. A life in five acts.

CHORUS ONE. Act one.

CHORUS TWO. How Bob is born, abandoned, raised by a fast food employee, discovers his dream, and almost dies.

(*A sterile fast-food restaurant bathroom.* CHORUS THREE *assumes the character of* HELEN. *She is sweating, crying, breathing heavy, legs wide.*)

CHORUS ONE. It is said that Bob was born on Valentine's Day in the bathroom of a White Castle Restaurant in Louisville, Kentucky. It is said that Bob's birth mother, whose name was Helen, was feeling particularly lonely and depressed on this holiday and felt that only a certain cuisine would soothe her ache.

CHORUS TWO. It is said that Helen was unaware of the Valentine's Day tradition of the usually more subdued restaurant to adorn their tables with candles and cloths and other romantic miscellany and that the restaurant would be packed with couples flaunting their couple-hood.

CHORUS FOUR. Nor was Helen aware of how severe her physiological reaction would be to witnessing this vast scene of public love until, after eating much faster than she intended, she rushed into the bathroom, pushed to urinate and her wombic fluids erupted onto the bathroom floor.

(*Wombic fluids erupt out of* HELEN.)

CHORUS ONE. Nor was she aware how quickly labor could be sometimes until five minutes after her water broke, Bob would emerge quickly and fiercely from her magic chamber.

(*A pop.* BABY BOB *flies out of* HELEN, *umbilical cord attached.*)

CHORUS TWO. Nor did she expect the emotional response she would have to this birth...a progression from joy to relief to memories to regret to fear to terror to anger to hatred to wanting absolutely nothing to do with what had just emerged.

(HELEN *pulls out a knife.*)

CHORUS FOUR. She *did* remember the small sign posted outside the restaurant below the "Meal Deal" poster: the blue outline of a house, silhouette of an infant sitting in large comforting hands, "Safe Place" written in multiple languages below. At that moment, Helen made a decision that would ultimately affect thousands of lives.

(HELEN *takes the umbilical cord, cuts it with the knife.*)

CHORUS TWO. It is said that this was the only advice Helen could think to give her newborn son.

HELEN. Good luck.

(HELEN *runs off.*)

CHORUS FOUR. This is what Bob did when he was alone.

(BOB *assesses the situation.*)

BOB. BWAHHH!

(JEANINE, *a White Castle employee, enters the bathroom.*)

JEANINE (CHORUS ONE). Oh my.

CHORUS THREE. Her name was Jeanine. This is how Jeanine saved Bob.

(*Lights shift. By the counter.* JEANINE, *holding* BOB, *reads corporate instructions on a piece of paper.*)

JEANINE. (*Reading.*) Step one: Retrieve baby/child and take him/her/it to a neutral yet safe space behind the service counter.

(JEANINE *moves.*)

Do not stand near fryers.

(JEANINE *moves again.*)

Step two: Determine if parent or guardian is still on the property.

(JEANINE *pulls counter microphone.*)

Attention Valentine's Day guests. We hope you are all enjoying your romantic meals. If there is anyone in the restaurant who may have left a personal item in the bathroom, would you please come to the counter at this time?

(JEANINE *waits.*)

Step three: Should no one claim baby/child, immediately phone the police, child protective services, and the corporate legal crisis line. Under no circumstances should you look in to the baby's eyes and fall in love with it. Do not fall in love with the baby.

(JEANINE *lowers the paper.*

JEANINE *tries to not look at* BOB.

JEANINE *looks at* BOB.

JEANINE *falls in love with* BOB.)

CHORUS FOUR. This is why Jeanine decided to raise Bob as her own.

(JEANINE *driving,* BOB *in a bundle next to her.*)

JEANINE. I was finishing up my Sunday night dinner at the Bamboo Wok. I don't know how authentic or healthy it is but I like the flavors. I'd been working my way through the menu for about a year. Each week, I would have a new entrée in order of appearance. I'd finally made it to the "Noodles slash Rice" section after several months of Lamb and I felt like I was entering a new era in my life.

When the waiter delivered the check and cookie, the fortune inside seemed different. The paper looked shiny, almost golden, the ink darker, more insistent.

FORTUNE COOKIE VOICE (CHORUS TWO). "You will be the mother to a great great man."

JEANINE. The fortunes I usually get are a little more vague than that. But this felt intentional. Like someone was watching me. From inside the cookie.

FORTUNE COOKIE VOICE (CHORUS TWO). "You will be the mother to a great great man."

JEANINE. It made me smile. I thought "Well, cool, Jeanine, maybe the future isn't only selling tiny burgers and having Asian food once a week." And then my stomach started to twitch, felt like I was gonna be sick. I started sweating, breathing heavy. And I thought Oh my god, it's happening already. I stood up from my table and shouted "I'm gonna be the mother to a great great man!"

Next thing I knew I woke up in a hospital bed. At first I thought I'd conceived my great man immaculate till the nurse told me that I'd almost died at the restaurant. That I had a severe reaction to the gluten in Asian-noodles slash rice that messed up my insides so much that I would never be able to make a "Great Great Man" the regular way.

I don't really care for fortunes very much anymore. But, funny, you know, there you are. There you are.

I must be just a weird noise in your ear. You little moving thing.

I will give you food and shelter. I will educate you. I will make sure that becoming President of the United States remains a possibility.

Even if it kills me, I will make you a great great man.

(*Shift.*)

CHORUS FOUR. This is how Bob got his name.

(JEANINE's *house.* BONNIE, JEANINE's *friend, is there.* JEANINE *is playing with* BOB. BONNIE *stares at* JEANINE. BOB *is examining.*)

BONNIE (CHORUS THREE). You don't look exhausted.

JEANINE. I'm not exhausted, Bonnie.

BONNIE. Trust me. In a few days you will be exhausted for the rest of your life.

JEANINE. He sleeps through the night.

BONNIE. Since when?

JEANINE. Since I got him five days ago.

BONNIE. I read that babies who sleep through the night often have learning disabilities. It was in *Newsweek.*

BOB. Ghshablah.

JEANINE. What should I name him?

BONNIE. You don't have a name for him yet?

JEANINE. It's not like I got to plan ahead for this.

(BONNIE *starts to cry.*)

Bonnie?

BONNIE. Are you sure you can do this?

JEANINE. I think so.

BONNIE. The choices you make right now will determine a life of joy or a life of pain.

BOB. Ooo.

JEANINE. It's just a name, Bonnie.

BONNIE. THE NAME IS EVERYTHING, JEANINE!

First impressions, schoolyard happiness, entire futures depend on the name. I read that in *Newsweek* too.

This is a child's future. THINK OF THE FUTURE.

JEANINE. You're getting a little angry, Bonnie.

BONNIE. I was given the wrong name!

Someone asks "What's your name?" and I say "Bonnie" and people think something's wrong with me 'cause I don't seem very "Bonnie-like." I'm suspect from the get-go and that ripples and ripples, a chain reaction against my favor and look at me now.

If I wasn't "Bonnie" I'd be a different person. I'd have a better life. I wouldn't want to die.

Chester.

(BONNIE *does a flourish with her hands. Exits.*)

JEANINE. What do you think? If you could be called anything in the world, what would it be?

BOB. Bwahhhhhhhhhhhb.

(*Beat.*)

JEANINE. What was that?

BOB. Argh baplbbbtss urgglmmmmmmmm...*bwaahhbb.*

JEANINE. Did you just say—

BOB. Bwaahb.

JEANINE. Bob? Bob. Bob. Bob.

BOB. Bwahb.

(JEANINE *looks out—a thought to the future.*)

CHORUS. (*They each take alternating lines.*)

2. Welcome our newest student, Bob.

3. What a beautiful painting, Bob.

4. You were just incredible at recess, Bob.

2. Bob the way you play hockey, I don't know what to feel.

3. Kiss me Bob.

4. Here, take this special chair, Bob.

2. Bob you can be anything you want.

3. Be a historian, Bob.

4. Be an artist, Bob.

2. Cure, Bob. Cure the sick.

3. Kiss me again Bob.

4. Bob, kiss us both at the same time.

2. I love you Bob.

3. I love you Bob.

4. Bob must be stopped.

JEANINE. Bob. Your name is Bob.

BOB. Bwahb.

(*A banging on the door.*)

CONNOR (CHORUS TWO). Open up, Jeanine!

CHORUS FOUR. This is why Jeanine decided to leave town with Bob.

JEANINE. That's the police, Bob.

(*A bang.*)

CONNOR. Jeanine!

JEANINE. It's open! Stay quiet, Bob.

BOB. Bwahb.

JEANINE. Stay quiet.

(JEANINE *hides* BOB *in a grocery bag.* CONNOR, *a police officer, enters.*)

CONNOR. Jeanine.

JEANINE. Connor.

BOB. Bwahb.

CONNOR. Been a long time.

JEANINE. Seen you around.

CONNOR. It's been a long time.

(*The pain of their history is felt.*)

JEANINE. How can I help you, Connor?

CONNOR. You still working at the White Castle?

JEANINE. You know I still work there.

CONNOR. Anything weird happen the last few days?

JEANINE. Something weird happens every day. Our lighting has a way of pushing people over the edge.

CONNOR. We got a call at the station today.

JEANINE. Well, good for you.

CONNOR. Some woman.

JEANINE. Of course it was a woman.

CONNOR. Crying. Didn't say her name. Just asked if *"He* was OK."

JEANINE. Who?

CONNOR. She wouldn't say. Said she "had to do it," that "if I knew the whole story" blah de blah and I had to interrupt: "Ma'am, what you are talking about?" She said "White Castle" and hung up.

JEANINE. How odd.

CONNOR. Anyone leave an infant at the White Castle on Valentine's Day?

BOB. Bwahb.

JEANINE. Not to my recollection.

CONNOR. You've always had a great memory.

JEANINE. Don't butter me, Connor.

CONNOR. I'm just saying you have a tendency of not forgetting any and all things that happen.

JEANINE. I like to learn from my mistakes.

(*Beat.*)

CONNOR. I've seen you at the Bamboo Wok.

JEANINE. Don't.

CONNOR. Eating alone every week.

JEANINE. I enjoy self-dining.

CONNOR. Maybe I can join you sometime.

JEANINE. Connor, thank you for your diligent police work but alas, I do not recollect anyone leaving a Bob at my place of employment.

CONNOR. A what?

BOB. Bob.

JEANINE. A baby.

CONNOR. You said Bob.

JEANINE. I meant a Baby.

BOB. Bobby.

CONNOR. Who's Bob?

(BOB *pokes his head out.*)

JEANINE. It's someone I'm seeing. His name is Bob.

(*Beat.*)

CONNOR. I don't believe it.

JEANINE. I fell in love with him the moment I saw him.

CONNOR. What does Bob do?

BOB. Bob Do. Do Bob Bob.

JEANINE. He is a great great man.

BOB. Gray. Man.

CONNOR. I guess it was a mistake to come here.

(CONNOR *almost exits, turns.*)

I want you back Jeanine. I want another chance.

JEANINE. You had your chance, Connor.

(*Beat.*)

CONNOR. If you see anything at work—

JEANINE. Nothing would overjoy me more.

(CONNOR *almost exits, turns.*)

CONNOR. One day, Jeanine Bordeaux, I will prove myself to you.

(CONNOR *exits.*)

BOB. Bwahb. Proo Mah Salf.

JEANINE. We can't stay here, Bob.

CHORUS FOUR. It is said that Jeanine collected the few belongings she felt to be essential, including a pillowcase filled with her life savings and left her home forever to raise Bob in her beige Chevy Malibu.

This is the road trip of Bob and Jeanine.

(*A "road trip" that spans 12 years. The* CHORUS *assists.*)

JEANINE. That is the sky.

That's a tree. Black walnut.

That's a dead goat.

That's a fire. You'll want to be careful with that.

(*White Castle.*)

That's where I worked.

(*Las Vegas.*)

That's where they play roulette.

(*A religious sign asking where you will spend eternity.*)

That's a good question.

(*Bamboo Wok.*)

Don't eat there.

That's a farmer.

That's someone who delivers things to people.

That one's crazy.

And that one's evil.

> (*The Grand Canyon.*)

This is the Grand Canyon, Bob.

BOB. Woah.

JEANINE. It was carved by the Colorado River over millions of years. And it's still changing.

> (*The rest are shown as well.*)

As are those Rocky Mountains, those mesas, this coastline. The ground beneath us is undergoing constant change, Bob.

BOB. Erosion.

> (*A house in South Carolina.*)

JEANINE. And it was here that they would rest, but only for a few hours. Danger was always close. Nineteen times Ms. Tubman made this journey. That's what you do when things aren't right, Bob.

BOB. Railroad.

> (*New Mexico.*)

JEANINE. And it was here that Mr. Oppenheimer dropped his experiment from a wooden tower and fission ensued. One event can change the world, Bob.

BOB. Chain Reaction.

> (*The first Wal-Mart.*)

JEANINE. And it was here that Mr. Walton opened the first stores that ushered in a new type of shopping experience. But he still always drove the same old truck, Bob.

BOB. Entrepreneur.

> (*Mt. Rushmore.*)

JEANINE. And even though Lincoln was killed at a play, the decisions he made would change the course of our nation. One man can change everything.

BOB. So if I do something amazing, someone else will carve my face onto a mountain?

JEANINE. There are lots of factors involved when getting put on a mountain. Politics. Popularity. Your face. A lot of achievements go completely unrecognized, not even on a plaque.

BOB. What's a plaque?

(*They look at a plaque.*)

JEANINE. It's a marker, Bob. To pay tribute to some great act or person.

BOB. (*Rubbing fingers over letters.*) "In Memory of Great Sculptor Gutzon Borglum." It's beautiful.

JEANINE. And they last forever.

BOB. I want to be on a plaque someday.

JEANINE. Well, you can be, Bob.

BOB. In Memory of Bob, the man who rescued a town from destruction!

Bob, the great entertainer and tamer of beasts.

Bob, the man who invented a blanket you can wear!

JEANINE. You better keep a piece of paper handy to write all your ideas down.

BOB. I've got some paper in my pocket!

JEANINE. You can do anything you want with your life, Bob.

BOB. You should be on a plaque, Mom.

JEANINE. Oh, Bob, that's, well, that's the nicest thing anyone has ever—

BOB. Let's go.

JEANINE. We don't always have to be in such a rush.

BOB. But Mom, if I am to become great, there is so much I have to learn and see!

(*The montage goes into overdrive. BOB's energy remains high. The trip is killing* JEANINE.)

BOB & JEANINE.

    B. Birthplaces!

    J. Battlegrounds.

    B. Big Cities!

    J. Empty Stretches.

    B. Public Parks.

    J. Private Islands.

    B. Man-made Lakes.

    J. Hoover Dams.

    B. Holy Sites.

    J. Corn Palaces.

    B. Dinosaur Bones.

    J. Swinger Camps.

    B. Monuments.

    J. Junkyards.

B. Luxury Homes.

J. Trailer Parks.

B. Ham and Cheese Omelets.

J. Coffee.

B. More Ham and Cheese Omelets.

J. Indigestion.

B. Fudge.

J. Ibuprofen.

B. Art and Science.

J. Wow that is hurting—

B. History and Civics.

J. Can't quite—

B. Beauty and Truth—

J. —catch my breath—

BOB. Knowledge and Experience!

JEANINE. (*In pain.*) Too much to experience.

(*Chicago.* BOB *is 12.* JEANINE *is ill.*)

BOB. C'mon the museum closes at four so we need to—

JEANINE. I can't seem catch my breath, Bob.

BOB. They're not gonna let us in!

JEANINE. Maybe we can go tomorrow.

BOB. No, I want to see the canvases now. The brush strokes with which Grant Wood captured the gothic soul of an elderly couple, the splatters of Pollock that drip anguish and liquor, the flowers of O'Keefe that evoke the beauty of nature and vaginas at the same time.

JEANINE. My, Bob, you soak everything up like a roll of Bounty.

BOB. Moving from place to place, collecting visitor guides and souvenir spoons, learning trigonometry as we eat ham and cheese omelets…I love everything we do together, Mom.

JEANINE. I'm not your real mother, Bob.

BOB. What?

JEANINE. You were left at the White Castle. I wasn't supposed to take you. But then I looked into your eyes.

BOB. You did?

JEANINE. Most people don't grow up in Malibus. They don't drive around the country with all their money in a pillowcase.

BOB. That's because we're special.

JEANINE. You, Bob, are a special special boy.

BOB. You're making me blush.

(JEANINE *collapses.*)

Are you OK?

JEANINE. There's a bit of money left in the bag, Bob. You're going to have to use it wisely.

BOB. You're soaking wet.

JEANINE. Keep an eye out for danger and advantage-takers. Don't skimp on oil changes for the Malibu. And always wear your undies.

BOB. What is happening right now?

JEANINE. I'm dying, Bob.

BOB. No you're not.

JEANINE. My liver is pressing out, cracking my ribs. It's getting harder to breathe. I want to blame those Bamboo Wok noodles that combo-cursed-and-blessed me years ago but I think it just happened. You know how things just happen.

BOB. I'll call an ambulance.

JEANINE. Don't.

BOB. Ambulance!

JEANINE. It's too late, Bob.

BOB. Phineas Gage survived a Metal Rod through his head. Lance Armstrong survived cancer to win the Tour de France. Dean Martin Lived till he was 78.

JEANINE. Look at you trying to do something. You're twelve years old and you're already a man.

BOB. I don't want to be.

JEANINE. Well in a second, Bob, I'm going to breathe my last breath and then I'm going to slump over and my body may twitch but I'll be gone. My heat will drain, but if you hug me it'll drain into you. After that happens, I want you light me on fire. Gather some flammables, lay me on top, and set me on fire.

BOB. I'm going get on the plaque for the both of us, Mom.

JEANINE. It's Jeanine. I love you, Bob.

BOB. I love you too, Jeanine.

JEANINE. Good luck.

(BOB *hugs* JEANINE.

JEANINE *dies.*

BOB *puts* JEANINE down.

He gathers a few sticks and newspaper and other burning supplies, and puts them under JEANINE.

BOB *lights a match, drops it on the ground.*

A police siren.

BOB *and* CONNOR, *who is now a Chicago policeman, at an interrogation table.*)

CHORUS FOUR. This is how Bob avoided prison.

CONNOR. You do realize it's illegal to cremate someone on the steps of the Art Institute of Chicago.

BOB. It's what she wanted.

CONNOR. There are concerns. About pollution. Asthma.

BOB. I don't care so long as she's everywhere.

CONNOR. And now we can't do an autopsy. We'll never get to know what caused her death.

BOB. She said some things just happen.

CONNOR. That's not good enough for the paperwork. Was she dead before you lit her on fire?

BOB. YES!

CONNOR. OK OK. It's required we ask that.

BOB. I don't know what it's going to be like without her.

CONNOR. It's going to suck, probably.

There's going to be a lot of people you lose in your life. Some die. Some move away. Some you just say the wrong thing to. You'll have those days. When you'll be so sad, praying you could just see her even for an instant before she vanishes into a puff of smoke.

BOB. Do you have any more Kleenex?

(CONNOR *gives a Kleenex to* BOB.)

CONNOR. Well, since there's no one to claim you, we may have to put you in prison till this all gets straightened out.

BOB. No. I have to learn about airports tomorrow!

CONNOR. It's a prison for kids, so it's not so gloomy.

BOB. I have a lot of great things to do with my life!

CONNOR. Well, you're not allowed to do that. Not till you're eighteen, uh, what is your name?

BOB. Bob. My name is Bob.

OTHER CHORUS. (*Whisper.*) Bob!

CONNOR. Why does that name haunt me?

BOB. It was my first word.

CONNOR. Where were you born?

BOB. In a White Castle.

OTHER CHORUS. (*Whisper, unsuccessfully in unison.*) White Castle.

CONNOR. What was the name of the woman you just burnt?

BOB. Jeanine. Her name was Jeanine.

(CONNOR *drops his pen.*)

CONNOR. Oh my. Oh my oh my oh my.

BOB. You dropped your pen.

(CONNOR *gets on one knee, pulls out a ring.*)

CONNOR. I was going to give this to her the next time I saw her. I've had this in my pocket for 11 years. I said "Connor, even if you're in a bathroom stall mid-tinkle and you see her, get on your knees ASAP and beg her to come back."

(CONNOR *grabs* BOB*'s hand, perhaps kissing the soot of Jeanine in* BOB*'s hand.*)

Oh my sweet Slider Highness…I'm sorry for being selfish and stupid. I'm sorry for making you so sad on the day you looked the prettiest.

(CONNOR *gives* BOB *the ring.*)

BOB. This would have looked beautiful on her finger.

CONNOR. Keep it somewhere safe. It's a dangerous world out there. Keep it in your undies.

I think I'm going to go back to the museum and, just breathe awhile. Good luck, Bob.

(CONNOR *exits.* BOB *is alone.*)

BOB. Hello?

(BOB *looks at the ring. He puts it in his undies and steps outdoors into the cold Chicago air.*)

You're on your own, Bob.

On West Monroe St. Chicago.

(*A gust of wind.*)

The "Windy City."

Home of the White Sox, late night sketch comedy, and the *fresheezie:* a hot dog wrapped in bacon and filled with American cheese…a meal that is delightful and cruel at the same time.

At the Alamo, the Texans were outnumbered, but they were able to fight off the Mexican Army twice before they all got killed.

In the Sierra Nevada, trapped by snow and bad teamwork, the Donner Party withstood bitter cold and the sour taste of human flesh for seven of them to survive and reach the state of California.

"You can do anything you want with your life." So said Jeanine Bordeaux, the safest driver and best breakfast companion ever. And today I'm going to get in our Malibu that should be parked right here and…

(*A* CITIZEN *walks by.*)

Excuse me, Business Person, have you seen a Malibu that was parked here?

(*The* CITIZEN *ignores* BOB. *Another* CITIZEN *runs by, avoiding eye contact.*)

Hello there, Forlorn Woman, did you happen to see what happened to a Malibu that was here?

(*A* CITIZEN *walks by, the pillowcase slung over his/her back, and scurries off.*)

There was a pillowcase with wet kittens on tugboats under the passenger seat…

(BOB *takes a step. His shoe breaks.*)

My shoe.

(HELEN, BOB*'s birth mother and now a thief, runs in with her knife.*)

HELEN. Give me your shirt!

BOB. What?

HELEN. Give me your shirt before I cut your face! NOW!

(BOB *removes his shirt, gives it to* HELEN.)

BOB. What are you doing with my shirt?

HELEN. Are you wearing underwear?

BOB. That's private.

HELEN. ARE YOU WEARING UNDERWEAR?

BOB. I always do!

HELEN. Then give me your pants.

BOB. Jeanine bought me these pants at the Rock and Roll Hall of Fame. Please my name is Bob and—

HELEN. WELL MY NAME IS HELEN!

CHORUS. (*Whispering.*) Helen.

HELEN. GIVE ME YOUR ROCK AND ROLL PANTS AND YOU'LL LIVE ANOTHER DAY ON THIS CURS-ED EARTH.

(BOB *removes his pants, gives them to* HELEN.

HELEN *looks into* BOB*'s eyes. An echo.*)

HELEN. If only you knew what has driven me to this…

Good luck.

(HELEN *runs off.*)

BOB. Good luck.

(BOB *walks against the wind, exits. Blackout. End of Act One.*)

Interlude 1

Interlude: A dance about Hardship.

CHORUS THREE. This is my dance about Hardship.

(*A dance.*)

Thank you.

ACT TWO

ALL CHORUS. Bob. Act two.

CHORUS THREE. How Bob does not die, comes of age at a rest stop, pursues his dream, falls in love and has his heart broken.

> (*The sound of brakes and tires skidding.* BOB *is lying on the ground.* SETH, *a trucker, holds a bag of trash.* SETH *kicks* BOB.)

SETH (CHORUS FOUR). You need to move.

BOB. Wh-what?

SETH. You need-o to move-o your body-o.

BOB. Where am I?

SETH. Boy, you are face down in a "large vehicle parking spot." On the pavement. Where bodies should not lay.

BOB. Am I dead?

SETH. You're conscious you're talking so dead you are not. But I almost ran you over with my Rocky Mountain Double and if that'd happened, well, you'd be a flapjack and I'd be devastated.

> (SETH *dumps a plastic bag of trash into a trash can.*)

BOB. This scary woman named Helen stole my pants and I was crying and walking along the Interstate and I don't remember how—

SETH. "Just say no," boy.

BOB. No. What?

SETH. I quote you the immortal words of Nancy Reagan. I lost two children to the stuff. One's dead to me and the other one's dead.

Every part of my past hurts so I've turned to God and the road. A little prayer and air on my face and I'm just starting to enjoy the warmth of the sun and you almost bescuttled the whole effort so for the love of Jesus and Literal Seven Day Creation BE CAREFUL WHERE YOU SLEEP!

> (SETH *exits.*
>
> BOB *pulls himself up, sees a sign in the distance.*)

BOB. William Burroughs Memorial Rest Stop.

Mound City, Missouri. 550 miles from Chicago. How did I get here?

(*Perhaps accompanied with a flashback.*)

CHORUS ONE. It is said that Bob fell unconscious during his walk out of Chicago and fell into the back of a Honda Civic owned by Jeanine's friend Bonnie who had recently left her hometown in search of a new name. Bonnie had pulled to the side of the road and raised the trunk to prevent other drivers from seeing her urinate on her birth certificate in a ceremonial ritual of transition to a new life.

Bonnie discovered Bob when she re-opened her trunk at the William Burroughs Memorial Rest Stop where she pulled him out.

BOB. Jeanine used to pull out a Snickers from her purse every time we hit a snag, like when there was four hours of traffic to get to Hoover Dam, when I got a B on a Chemistry test, or when we got to the Michelle Kwan museum and it was closed for renovation.

I could really use a Snickers right now.

(BOB *walks to* SETH'*s trash bag and begins to look through it.*)

BOB. Water.

One-eighth of a Cheeseburger.

Seven Pringles.

This note is legal tender.

(*Turns it sideways, reading a scrawl.*)

Barry Metcalf is a slut.

Bloody Shirt. Rubber Gloves. Knife.

(*Condoms.*)

Balloons!

The Grapes of Wrath by John Steinbeck.

The Adventures of Huckleberry Finn by Mark Twain.

The Long Road Home by Danielle Steel.

(*Finds a Snickers wrapper.*)

Jackpot.

"Pick stuff up from the ground and make something." The great semi-accessible combinalist Robert Rauschenberg said that.

And be careful where you sleep.

(BOB *gets dressed in a bizarre outfit, each piece reflecting a different person's fashion.*)

CHORUS ONE. It is said that Bob built his shelter in a gulch behind the rest stop lavatories that nobody seemed to notice. He kept himself fed, clean, warm, and occupied himself with fitness, foraging, self-cleaning, reading, and writing.

BOB. Dear Bob's Diary: 4,023 people passed through the W.B.M.R.S. today. Of those travelers, four came up and talked to me.

(JAMES, *a middle-aged bear.*)

JAMES (CHORUS TWO). I'm James.

BOB. Today I met James. Brand new RV.

JAMES. I was living in Florida.

BOB. Oo the Everglades!

JAMES. Felt like a sticky bun whole time I was there. But Roberto, mi oso novio, he loved it. Met him at this very rest stop many years ago. Got so lost in his eyes the itchiness of the shrub we were under hardly made an impression. He's gone now. 'Gator caught my Bear skinny dipping. Roberto put up quite a fight but it'd been a while since he'd been to the gym.

I've come to spread his ashes on the bush where we met. I could mourn forever but 'Berto'd hate me for it so I've burnt our house down, used the insurance money to buy that RV, and I plan on having enough sex in public places for the both of us.

BOB. Lesson: Live for the dead. Don't mourn forever. Honor the bushes.

(CAITLYN, *sorority sister. INTENSE relief.*)

CAITLYN (CHORUS ONE). I almost didn't make it!

BOB. Caitlyn. Volkswagen Cabriolet.

CAITLYN. I've had to go for like a hundred miles!

BOB. Go where?

CAITLYN. Frikkin forty-eight ounce ice tea. Stupid, Caitlyn!

BOB. You are stupid, Caitlyn!

CAITLYN. But I made it. I breathed deep and I sang and I cried and I texted my friends and I clenched and I saw the darkness but I *made it I made it* and I was seriously peeing for like two minutes. Wooooooo! Wooooooooooo!

BOB. Lesson: You can make it if you clench.

(KIM, *little girl.*)

KIM (CHORUS THREE). Do you have a pencil?

BOB. Kim, 1988 windowless Dodge Van.

(BOB *gives* KIM *a pencil.*)

KIM. I met that damp man over there in the Rainforest Cafe parking lot a week ago. He said get in, and I got in. I realize now that was a mistake and now I understand why the rule my mom told me exists.

I s'pose I could just ask someone to help set me free, but then I wouldn't learn. As my daddy said when I spilt pudding on the floor: "You made the mess, you clean it up." So I'm waiting for the perfect moment to stab his neck with a pencil and get home to my mom and dad. Thank you.

BOB. Lesson: Always have a pencil.

(SAGÉ, *Burning Man hippie.*)

SAGÉ (CHORUS FOUR). We're like a thousand human fleas—

BOB. Sagé. Schoolbus covered with metal spirals and beach glass.

SAGÉ. And this rest stop is like a wolf. And we have all gathered in its fur to relax and share stories. A hundred million years from now, the world is going to be how it is because we were here. Hopping. And hopping. And—

BOB. Not everyone has a lesson. But everyone has a mission!

(CHORUS *as other travelers.*)

MERTLE (1). I'm bringin' pot roast to my son locked in prison.

VIJAY (2). I sell Indian food from the back of my Jeep.

SALMON (3). I'm raising awareness of the Prairie Mole Cricket.

WAYNE (4). I bring cocaine and cheap labor to greater Wisconsin.

BOB. Everyone has a hero!

CHORUS.

    1. I want to be like Michael Jordan.

    2. I want to be like Hillary Rodham Clinton.

    3. I want to be like Harvey Milk.

    4. I want to be like Joseph Smith.

    1. Hester Prynne.

    2. Jack Bauer.

    3. Holden Caulfield.

    4. Buffy the Vampire Slayer.

JAMES. Roberto.

KIM. My Daddy.

CAITLYN. My bladder.

SAGÉ. Hop hop.

BOB. I am going to be a hero for someone.

(BOB *shows his list.*)

My list of great ideas is growing longer and stronger every day. So much I can do and this is where it begins, Bob's diary. I can make this the greatest rest stop in the country.

I'll clean the bathrooms every other hour. I'll carve better trails into the hills and tidy the bushes where the men meet their soulmates. Late at night, using paint left by the trash, I will reconfigure the parking design to foster a greater sense of community amongst the travelers.

Bob, rest stop maverick. The Bob Memorial Rest Stop. Put it on a plaque.

Do you think when someone reads your name on a plaque hundreds of years after you're dead, for a brief instant, you exist again?

All of a sudden the patch of mushrooms, the bit of that tree, that soil or dust that were once your molecules suddenly experience a moment of connectedness, a memory of their past teamwork as being part of a human being that did something that was so important it had to be recognized. On a plaque.

CHORUS THREE. It is said that in the years that Bob lived at the William Burroughs Memorial Rest Stop near Mound City, Missouri it became the most cared for stop in the country.

CHORUS FOUR. It is said that the reputation of the facility spread among the traveling community, even gaining special mention in Lonely Planet Missouri.

CHORUS ONE. It is said that people who stopped in did indeed feel more rested.

CHORUS TWO. Six years passed.

CHORUS THREE. New chemicals began to course through Bob's body.

BOB. (*Slightly deeper voice.*) Hello there.

> (BOB's *body changes. More adult.*)

CHORUS FOUR. Bob's body began to change. Thicker, stronger.

BOB. Oh wow, new hair.

CHORUS FOUR. Bob became a man.

> (BOB *has a surprising orgasm.*)

BOB. I am a man!

CHORUS ONE. It is said that Bob felt love for this place.

BOB. I love this rest stop.

CHORUS TWO. Bob felt love for many things.

BOB. I love my shelter. I love this table. I love my books.

CHORUS TWO. But this is how Bob fell in love for the first and only time.

> (AMELIA, *radiant and urgent, walks in and kisses* BOB *on the lips. While they kiss, she takes a picture with a Polaroid.*
>
> AMELIA *exits.*
>
> AMELIA *returns.*)

AMELIA (CHORUS THREE). What's your name?

BOB. Bwahhh. Bob.

> (AMELIA *writes* BOB's *name down.*)

AMELIA. You're a good kisser, Bob.

BOB. I've never kissed anyone before.

AMELIA. Then you're a natural.

BOB. Oh well I don't know if I'mmrrfruhljsakj.

    (AMELIA *exits.*)

Hey!

    (AMELIA *returns.*)

What's *your* name?

AMELIA. Amelia.

BOB. Like the aviatrix?

AMELIA. That's who I was named after.

BOB. She broke barriers. She was a vanguard. And then she disappeared.

AMELIA. That's my favorite part about her. The mystery. She wanted to go where nobody would find her.

BOB. Into the ocean?

AMELIA. Or maybe she found a place she could hide.

    (AMELIA *almost exits.*)

BOB. Could we do that again?

AMELIA. Kiss?

BOB. I would like to very much.

AMELIA. That's not on the list.

BOB. You have a list?

AMELIA. "One kiss with a stranger at a rest stop." I've got a thousand things I have to do before I get home.

BOB. I've got a list too!

AMELIA. You do?

    (BOB *pulls out his list.*)

BOB. I write down every idea of what I'd like to accomplish with my life: Create defensive knives for children in danger.

Design ornaments that widows can hang on their lovers' bushes.

Cure diseases that suddenly kill people on steps of museums.

AMELIA. (*Pulling out her list.*) See an old growth Redwood forest in the nude. Do a shot of tequila with an on-duty policeman.

Fill a jar with water from the Pacific Ocean.

BOB. Your list is fun.

AMELIA. Yours is long.

BOB. I'm only 18.

AMELIA. Are you in high school or college?

BOB. Jeanine, who raised me but was my false mother, taught me a whole lot before I set her on fire. I made a promise that I'll become a great man.

AMELIA. You may need to go to college to do that.

BOB. Sean John Puffy Combs didn't finish college. Jimmy Dean, sausage king, didn't finish high school. Nor did Ansel Adams. Or Grover Cleveland. Or Walt Disney. Thomas Edison.

AMELIA. You have a point.

BOB. I like your hair.

> (*Beat.*)

AMELIA. I'm getting married this summer.

BOB. Oh. Congratulations.

AMELIA. My parents set it up. They're big into lineage, having a marriage "mean something" on a historical and financial level. And Chet, that's actually his name, is the perfect match. He's the son of a CEO, and I'm the daughter of a CEO, and our union will restore peace to the Corporate community. But I don't love him.

BOB. That doesn't sound like a very good marriage.

AMELIA. I told my parents that I would be miserable with Chet and they told me not to be selfish.

BOB. That's terrible.

AMELIA. I insisted that if I go ahead with it that I needed to leave town on my own for a trip around the country where I could celebrate my final moments of happiness.

I asked fifty friends and family to come up with a list of things they think I should do before the big day. They all came up with twenty. One thousand final acts.

I've got three months.

BOB. We don't have a lot of time.

AMELIA. Where are you heading?

BOB. Just collecting some trash for an evening fire.

AMELIA. You *live* here?

BOB. Mostly behind the bathrooms. Check out my flat!

> (*They walk to the shelter.*)

AMELIA. Oh my.

BOB. See all the neck pillows?

AMELIA. Your own little hideout.

BOB. And I have books!

AMELIA. You know I can give you a ride somewhere. Some money.

BOB. I don't want to leave.

AMELIA. You're happy.

BOB. I am right now.

Hey, I just remembered another idea from my list.

>   (*Reading list.*)

Get second kiss from girl soon to be married.

AMELIA. You just made that up.

BOB. Does that matter?

>   (AMELIA *smiles.* BOB *kisses* AMELIA. *It's really good.*)

AMELIA. You've never kissed anyone before?

BOB. No.

AMELIA. That could be your legacy.

BOB. People aren't celebrated for being great kissers.

AMELIA. Burt Lancaster. Clark Gable. Charo.

BOB. You're really pretty.

AMELIA. I've got to go.

BOB. You're the most beautiful girl with a list I've ever seen.

>   (AMELIA *cries.*)

I didn't mean to—

AMELIA. I just wish I could do what I want.

BOB. You can do anything you want with your life, Amelia.

AMELIA. That's a slogan for shoes, Bob.

We all have constraints. Limits to what we can do.

BOB. Some of the greatest people in our country fought limits. Helen Keller fought the limits of her senses. Madonna fought the limits of her voice.

AMELIA. I think that's why you're such a good kisser.

BOB. What?

AMELIA. I can taste the optimism on your lips.

BOB. You do?

AMELIA. In your spit. It's sweet.

BOB. Someone just left a whole chicken on a picnic table this morning. It still smells good. We can roast it over a trash fire and watch the sun set over the Interstate.

AMELIA. My list...

BOB. I have a really large bed made with Kleenex.

AMELIA. I can't ignore my life.

BOB. This can be your hideout. Amelia's Island.

>   (*Beat.*)

AMELIA. Would you make love to me?

BOB. With what?

AMELIA. You'll figure it out.

BOB. I've only heard it in the parking lot.

AMELIA. Just let me taste that hope again.

> (*They kiss and fall to the ground.*)

CHORUS ONE. It is said that Bob and Amelia made love for fourteen hours on Bob's bed made of Kleenex.

CHORUS FOUR. It is said that it was the best lovemaking Bob and Amelia would ever experience. Way better than Chet.

CHORUS ONE. Amelia stayed with Bob at the rest stop for two weeks, making love for most of the day, taking breaks to sleep, giggle or forage for food from the trash bins.

CHORUS FOUR. For a post-coital moment, Amelia thought she might like to stay there forever. Until in the middle of one night, Bob said this.

BOB. Stay with me forever.

AMELIA. Oh Bob.

BOB. I don't want this to end.

AMELIA. What about your list?

BOB. I only want to do things I can do with you. Bob and Amelia, the best trash chefs, the best Polaroid photographers, the best rest-stop love-makers in America.

AMELIA. I wish I could just tear up all the roots of my life and stay with you but it's not that simple.

BOB. Forget about Chet. I hate Chet!

AMELIA. I've got to finish my list, Bob. I have one patch of time to accomplish something on my own and it might be the only chance I have. I can't give it up.

BOB. Let me help you with it! I know an on-duty policeman in Chicago—

AMELIA. This is a solo flight, Bob.

Some great things aren't supposed to last forever. Like fruit.

BOB. We're more than a couple of fruits.

AMELIA. You've got your own list. And it is heartfelt and inspiring and overly ambitious. You need to pursue it. Forgive me.

BOB. I love you.

> (AMELIA *kisses* BOB. *She gives* BOB *the Polaroid picture of their kiss.*
> BOB *finds a glass jar and gives it to* AMELIA.)

Don't give up on yourself, Amelia.

AMELIA. Keep looking for what you're looking for, Bob.

BOB. Promise me you won't go home when your list is checked.

AMELIA. Oh, Bob you know I have to—

BOB. Promise me you won't stop your journey and I won't stop mine. And then, maybe at some other rest stop somewhere, we can meet again.

AMELIA. Maybe we will.

BOB. You deserve happiness.

AMELIA. Good luck, Bob.

    (AMELIA *runs off quickly.*)

BOB. YOU DESERVE HAPPINESS!

CHORUS TWO. It is said that Bob ran after Amelia's Lexus until she sped away, disappearing behind a school bus carrying a high school cheerleading squad to a regional competition.

Amelia had already stayed too long with Bob to ever return to her past life, Bob's words echoing in her ear. And upon completing her final task, the filling of a jar with water from the Pacific Ocean, she began to think of the future. She thought of her namesake, of the great Amelia Earhart, and suddenly she felt fearless, and hopeful. She gathered driftwood, plastic and neck pillows scattered on the sand, laid on top of her newly made raft and began to drift west from the beach towards the islands of the South Pacific until she disappeared as her list, fully checked, broke apart in the water behind her.

    (BOB *holding the Polaroid.*)

BOB. This is where she kissed me.

This is where she read me her list.

This is where she never walked.

This is where we…

I hate this rest stop.

I hate my shelter. I hate this table. I hate my books.

"There's a journey ahead of you, Bob. Keep looking for what you're looking for." The great love of my life, Amelia notEarhart, said that.

CHORUS FOUR. And with that Bob took the only things of value that he had, put them into his underwear, and slipped into the trunk of a Ford Focus.

    (BOB *hops into a trunk, his items collected in a blanket on a stick.*)

BOB. Good luck, Bob.

    (*End of Act Two.*)

Interlude 2

Interlude: A dance about love.

CHORUS TWO. This dance is about love.

(*A dance.*)

Thank you.

ACT THREE

ALL CHORUS. Bob. Act three.

(BOB *runs in with urinary urgency.*)

BOB. Clench clench clench.

CHORUS THREE. How Bob journeys across America, tries to do everything on his list, fails, meets an important man, and turns his back on everything he believes.

(BOB *finds a bush. Pees.*)

BOB. Thank you, Caitlyn.

CHORUS FOUR. It is said the Ford Focus Bob jumped into drove for seven hours without stopping. Bob slept little, sweat a lot, and cried for various reasons he couldn't put into words.

BOB. (*A wordless noise.*) Ohhhhhhhlilili.

CHORUS TWO. It is said that the driver of the car was once again Jeanine's friend Bonnie who in the past seven years had attempted fresh starts with four different names: Barbara, Hillary, Laura and Michelle.

(BONNIE *appears.*)

Seeing Bob in her trunk once again, Bonnie was reminded how little had changed in her life and what was it, really, that she needed to feel comfortable in her own skin.

(BONNIE *thinks very seriously about what she needs. Exits.*)

CHORUS ONE. This is how Bob journeyed across America.

(*Zips up and wanders into town.*)

BOB. (*Looking around while peeing.*) Main Street.

Maple Lane.

Spruce Alley.

Evergreen Boulevard.

Deciduous Way.

Washington, Madison, Franklin, Van Buren.

The Mesquite Grill, El Sombrero, Luigi's, The Bamboo Wok.

(*Darker versions of the road trip. A* FARMER *walks by with a Monsanto-like seed bag, spirit crushed.*)

Excuse me, hello there, Farmer, can you tell me where I am?

(*A* DELIVERY PERSON *walks by with a foreclosure notice or something dark.*)

Pardon me, Delivery Person, is there a good place to stay around here?

(*A* CRAZY PERSON *walks by.*)

And Ma'am, I recognize that you might be crazy, but can you tell me if this is a good place to live?

(*An* EVIL PERSON *walks by. Insert funny cultural icon of your choice here.*)

Or…

BOB. Never mind.

(*A diner table.* WAITRESS ONE *enters with a coffee mug and a pitcher.*)

WAITRESS ONE. New in town?

BOB. I am.

WAITRESS ONE. I can tell.

BOB. My clothes?

WAITRESS ONE. Just something wet about you.

BOB. I was in a car trunk so I might be a little damp—

WAITRESS ONE. Cream and sugar?

BOB. That's the only way I can drink it.

WAITRESS ONE. How sweet.

(WAITRESS TWO *brings in cream and sugar.*)

BOB. Could you tell me—

WAITRESS TWO. You want to hear the specials?

BOB. No. I'll have a ham and cheese omelet.

WAITRESS TWO. Oo, a man who knows what he wants.

BOB. My favorite breakfast. Been a long time since I've had a real one.

(WAITRESS THREE *brings in toast.*)

WAITRESS THREE. Bet you need some white toast too.

BOB. With extra butter.

WAITRESS THREE. Knew it in your eyes.

(WAITRESS FOUR *brings in extra butter.*)

WAITRESS FOUR. So…what brings you to Sioux Falls?

BOB. Oh is that where I—

WAITRESS ONE. And what brings you to Roanoke?

BOB. I thought I was in—

WAITRESS TWO. And to Aberdeen?

BOB. The birthplace of Kurt Cobain?

WAITRESS THREE. And South Padre Island?

WAITRESSES.

    1. Bloomington?

    2. Glendive?

    3. Montana?

    4. Lansing?

BOB. It's just where the trunk opened so I don't—

WAITRESSES. (*Overlapping.*)

    1. Bella Vista?

    2. Duluth?

    3. Naples?

    4. Waterloo?

    1. Middletown?

    2. Portland?

    3. Southampton?

    4. Las Cruces?

BOB. Well, I've spent the last bunch of years thinking of ideas. Stuff I could do that might make a difference. And I wrote them down on a list. And now I'm looking for a place where I can do…things. Solve problems. And maybe be recognized for it on a plaque or possibly a mountain.

WAITRESSES. Ohhhhhhh.

WAITRESS ONE. We got ourselves a dreamer.

WAITRESS TWO. Young blood.

WAITRESS THREE. Fresh meat.

WAITRESS FOUR. Your eyes haven't sunk into your skull yet.

BOB. Have you ever done anything great with your lives?

    (*The* WAITRESSES *think.*)

WAITRESS ONE. I can be the only waitress in this diner, have it be packed and not miss a single order, not a single coffee mug dry.

WAITRESS TWO. I'm pretty good at quilts, how to tell a story and evoke memories through fabric. I gave one to my grandmother and it made her cry, so I consider that an accomplishment.

WAITRESS THREE. I'm the emperor of an online kingdom.

WAITRESS FOUR. I can tie a cherry stem into a knot with my tongue.

BOB. Maybe you can teach me.

ONE, TWO & THREE. Maybe we can.

WAITRESS FOUR. It depends on your tongue.

(*Each* WAITRESS *puts a ham and cheese omelet in front of* BOB.)

BOB. Jeanine, who stole me loved me and died, taught me that you could tell a lot about a place from the type of omelet that they make. The amount of care in its creation, or the total disregard. Breakfast, unlike jazz, is America's gift to the world. Is this a place that honors that culinary legacy? Is it a place that would give someone a chance?

(BOB *takes a bite of each omelet.*)

WAITRESS ONE. Is it?

BOB. I, uh, I think I'm going to go.

WAITRESSES. No!

BOB. Sorry, Those omelets are not very good.

WAITRESSES. No!

BOB. Something doesn't feel right about this place!

WAITRESSES. (*Various simultaneous muttering.*)

1. Well, yeah we know.

2. That's for sure.

3. Don't even get me started.

4. That's 'cause we're situated on a hellmouth.

(*The* WAITRESSES *turn to* BOB *seductively.*)

WAITRESS ONE. We'd really love it if you stuck around for a score.

WAITRESS TWO. I could show you the new quilt cycle I'm working on.

WAITRESS THREE. And we really like having a fresh young face to look upon.

WAITRESS FOUR. I like the way your lips open and close.

BOB. You're all leaning so close to me.

WAITRESS ONE. You're exciting.

WAITRESS TWO. You have a mission.

WAITRESS THREE. Desire and passion.

WAITRESS FOUR. Is there anything we can do to convince you to stay?

(*Sexy pause.*)

BOB. Maybe a bad omelet is an opportunity. There is a reason that trunk opened here and now. Because it is my job to transform this place from a drug-infested cesspool of decay into a Jacuzzi of opportunity and hope. And with this list I will—

(WAITRESS ONE *kisses* BOB.)

WAITRESS ONE. Oh my.

BOB. That wasn't—

WAITRESS TWO. Bob.

BOB. I didn't mean to—

WAITRESS THREE. Bob Bob Bob.

BOB. I don't even remember telling you my name.

WAITRESS FOUR. You're a great kisser, Bob.

BOB. It could be my legacy.

> (*Beat.* BOB *kisses all of the waitresses. It becomes a group kiss and they fall to the ground. A bizarre lovemaking scene ensues.*)

WAITRESSES. Yes!

BOB. Yes.

WAITRESSES. Yes!

BOB. Yay.

WAITRESS ONE. You taste amazing, Bob! So fresh.

WAITRESS TWO. Like a lemon.

WAITRESS THREE. Fabric softener.

WAITRESS FOUR. Carbonation.

BOB. And you taste like peanut oil.

WAITRESSES. Mmmmm!

WAITRESS ONE. So passionate.

WAITRESS TWO. Hungry!

WAITRESS THREE. Strong!

WAITRESS FOUR. Moderately hairy.

BOB. So are you!

WAITRESS ONE. Let's get some of these clothes off, Bob.

BOB. Oh that tickles.

WAITRESS TWO. Let's get these undies off, Bob.

BOB. Wait. There are some things in my undies that I need to—

WAITRESS THREE. I really want to get those undies off, Bob.

BOB. No really hold on, I keep stuff in there that I—

WAITRESS FOUR. Here I go about to take off your undies!

BOB. NO! STOP! STOP STOP!

> (BOB *emerges from the sheet protecting his undies. The* WAITRESSES *remain in a pile.*)

I'm sorry.

WAITRESS ONE. I was on the cusp, Bob.

WAITRESS TWO. Your tenderness, Bob, you're really good at that.

WAITRESS THREE. Just feeling your weight, Bob, made me teeter.

WAITRESS FOUR. Where'd he go?

BOB. There are a lot of important things in my undies.

WAITRESS THREE. My petals were starting to open.

BOB. Lovemaking is only great with someone you love.

WAITRESS FOUR. (*Whispering to another* WAITRESS.) I don't know if that's true.

BOB. Can I…just show you my list?

(*A small* WAITRESS *groan.*)

Isn't it long? I've got a whole section on "ways to restore a dying town back to health." Tourism! We could work together. Some creative marketing and a fudge shoppe and—

WAITRESS ONE. Our husband's gonna be home soon.

BOB. You all have a husband.

WAITRESS TWO. He just doesn't scratch everything we need, you know.

BOB. Well then find someone who can scratch it all.

WAITRESS THREE. We've got a pretty complicated itch, Bob.

BOB. "When you give up, you drown."

The great escapist Harry Houdini said that.

(*Beat.*)

WAITRESS FOUR. If you don't mind, let yourself out the back? Neighbors.

BOB. I don't think you realize how much tourists really love fudge.

WAITRESSES. Good luck, Bob.

WAITRESS ONE. And here's your *change*.

(*Leaving a plastic change container with a dollar on it.* BOB *alone.*)

BOB. (*Reading the dollar.*) "Barry Metcalf is still is slut."

And what am I?

(BOB *journeys across America.*)

CHORUS TWO. 317 towns. 23 unopened fudge shoppes. 1,100 waitresses. And Bob was unable to accomplish anything on his list.

BOB. (*Crossing things off his list.*) Create new network of safe houses for people to escape the South.

Open school that educates students through cross-country road trips.

Teach the long lost art of compromise to members of the United States Congress.

Nobody will give me a chance.

CHORUS ONE. Bob was reduced to performing some of the worst jobs in the nation.

BOB. Ventino quadruple low-fat-half-caf mocha latte for Deborah.

CHORUS THREE. But, much like a Cubs fan, Bob would enter each new chapter with a small amount of hope.

(BOB *hands the drink to* DEBORAH, *grabs her arm.*)

BOB. This could be better than it is, Deborah. If they let me make it how it should be made, with a little pitcher for the milk and grace in the pour, it could change your life.

CHORUS THREE. And much like a Cubs fan, Bob's hope would quickly fade.

BARISTA (CHORUS TWO). Customers do not need to be made aware of the mediocrity.

BOB. This is an opportunity to affect another person on this planet.

BARISTA. You're a barista.

DEBORAH (CHORUS ONE). My arm.

BOB. There are great baristas out there.

BARISTA. I majored in literature. At Cornell.

BOB. They have barista competitions and their own dirty style!

BARISTA. I was going to be the cultural critic of *The New Yorker.*

BOB. That's amazing!

BARISTA. It would have been, if I was the cultural critic of *The New Yorker!* If life were actually fair, if the UPenn Mafia didn't control the publishing world, if Sybil hadn't called me promiscuous on every dollar she had… My dream is over, dude.

DEBORAH. Let go of my arm.

BOB. Start your own magazine. Host culture at the store. Make it a critical Mecca.

BARISTA. Dude dude dude, chill the 'bition. Don't you see what Deborah and I are doing? The whole suffering of life gets a little bit lighter when you just give up.

DEBORAH. He's right.

(BOB *punches* BARISTA.)

BARISTA. Why did you do that?

BOB. BECAUSE WE ARE ALL GOING TO DIE OR DISAPPEAR. Vanish into small little bits and break hearts. And before that happens, before it all gets taken away, I'm supposed to be great at something. Even if it's foam.

BARISTA. You just punched me.

BOB. I am Bob and I will be a great man.

BARISTA. You're delusional, Bob.

BOB. You're a slut, Barry Metcalf.

BARISTA. You're fired, Bob.

BOB. I fire you!

(BARISTA *punches* BOB.)

You are all fools!

(BARISTA *punches* BOB.)

YOU ARE DOOMING THIS NATION TO SMALL DREAMS.

(DEBORAH *punches* BOB.)

BARISTA. You're the dream.

(*Punches* BOB, *he falls to the ground.*)

I'm reality. Get it, dude?

DEBORAH. Don't make me feel bad for what I've settled for.

(DEBORAH *kicks* BOB.)

BARISTA. Now get the hell out of Poncha Springs!

(BARISTA *and* DEBORAH *walk off arm in arm on their way to have sex.*
BOB *crawls into the boxcar of a freight train, wipes his bloody face.*)

BOB. Create catharsis through artistically moving beverages. (*Crosses off his list.*)
What degrading act will I be forced to perform next?

I don't know what to do anymore.

GUNTHER (CHORUS FOUR). Sounds like you haven't found your
Ringertraum yet.

(*A match is struck and a lantern lit revealing* GUNTHER, *a roughly dressed
man who looks like he may have been strikingly handsome back in the day, but
now has some wreckage.*)

BOB. Sorry, I didn't realize this boxcar was taken.

GUNTHER. Trade you a drink for some food.

BOB. All I have are muffin wrappers.

GUNTHER. My favorite.

(BOB *gives* GUNTHER *a couple muffin wrappers.* GUNTHER *takes a
swig and passes flask to* BOB. GUNTHER *chews.*)

GUNTHER. Blueberry?

BOB. Reduced Fat Blueberry Bran.

GUNTHER. Pretty good buds you got.

BOB. I used to sell them. Took the wrappers out of the trash.

(BOB *takes a sip and coughs.*)

BOB. What is this?

GUNTHER. It's Whin.

BOB. Never heard of it.

GUNTHER. My own special blend of whiskey and gin. Bottom shelf.

BOB. Oh.

GUNTHER. I only have one flask.

BOB. It's awful.

GUNTHER. Give it a few years and it goes down smooth.

>   (BOB *gives back the flask.*)

Something gnawing on your bone, tiger?

BOB. It's my birthday.

GUNTHER. On Valentine's Day? How sweet.

BOB. I'm 30 years old.

GUNTHER. Young buck.

BOB. Before they turned 30, Bill Gates founded Microsoft, Carolyn Davidson designed the Nike Swoosh, and Jimi Hendrix already died.

My greatest achievement to date is survival.

GUNTHER. Don't knock survival. Not easy keeping the blood pumping, hoping the wolves don't get you along the way.

BOB. I need to be more than alive.

>   (*Beat.*)

GUNTHER. I used to be more than alive.

BOB. Yeah, I'm sure you were.

GUNTHER. Perhaps you would be illuminated by my life story.

BOB. Actually I was thinking I might close my—

GUNTHER. My name is Gunther Roy.

BOB. Hi. I'm—

GUNTHER. I used to be known as the greatest animal trainer of all time. Lions, tigers, llamas, anything with a compound eye.

BOB. Sorry, I've never heard of—

GUNTHER. I toured for thirty years with the largest circus in the country. I stuck my head into the mouth of a lion. I made tigers jump through flaming hoops. I made geese fly in formations that spelled letters of the alphabet. U.S.A.

BOB. That sounds pretty—

GUNTHER. My closing act was called the "CreatureMaker" where I would command a lion and a tiger to mate. No other trainer could do that.

But then one night changed everything.

Do you want to hear about the night that changed everything?

BOB. Maybe in an hour, I'm tired and still bleeding and I—

GUNTHER. This is Gunther's flashback!

BOB. OK.

(*At the circus.* HELEN *runs in.*)

HELEN. Mr. Roy, that was amazing!

GUNTHER. Why thank you, little fawn.

HELEN. A lion and a tiger! And they seemed to enjoy it!

GUNTHER. They don't.

HELEN. I'm an animal trainer too.

GUNTHER. Oh. How wonderful.

HELEN. Aspiring. I work at a pet store to pay the bills.

GUNTHER. What have you forced animals to do so far?

HELEN. Little stuff. Getting sheep into various shapes: pentagons, rhombuses and whatnot. Got a whole coop of chickens to play dead when I rang a gong. That sort of thing.

GUNTHER. Pretty impressive. For a lady.

HELEN. Helen. My name is Helen.

CHORUS ONE & TWO. (*Whisper.*) Helen.

BOB. Helen…

GUNTHER. You smell like celery, Helen.

HELEN. Animals have been more faithful and loving to me than any person. And training is my life.

GUNTHER. What is your Ringertraum, Helen?

HELEN. You want to know my Ringertraum?

BOB. What is a… Wait how do you even say—

GUNTHER. Every great animal trainer has a Ringertraum. The dream they have, standing in the center ring, performing the one seemingly impossible act they've dedicated their entire life to being able to achieve.

BOB. I need one of those. 'Cause I have this big list and it is not—

GUNTHER. (*To* BOB.) Quiet!

HELEN. I've never told anyone.

GUNTHER. It's the most important thing to know about you. What is Helen's Ringertraum?

HELEN. I call it the "Living Totem." A tribute to Nature and our Native American ancestors. A prairie dog sitting on top of a bald eagle perched on top of a beaver lying on a wolf standing on a mountain lion hunched on a grizzly bear that's got each paw on one of four buffalo.

After they stack up, the lights would dim, and I would ask the audience…

"What animal are you? Which one is your guide on the trail of life? You are not alone."

I want my act to cause inspiration, revelation and tears.

GUNTHER & BOB. (GUNTHER *threatened*.) That is the most impressive Ringertraum I have ever heard.

HELEN. That's nice of you to say.

GUNTHER. Helen, you have the potential to become the Greatest Animal Trainer of All Time.

HELEN. You don't really mean that.

GUNTHER. Unless someone can stop you.

HELEN. If I can't become a trainer my life will be nothing but misery.

GUNTHER. Well then you should join the circus, Helen.

BOB. Yes she should.

HELEN. Right now?

GUNTHER. You can be my assistant.

HELEN. You're joking.

GUNTHER. I can keep an eye on you.

HELEN. I was just hoping for an autograph and a photo.

GUNTHER. Is that a yes?

HELEN. Yes yes!

BOB. Yes!

GUNTHER. Then we must kiss!

HELEN. Mr. Roy?

GUNTHER. To be a great trainer and assistant team, the animals must sense that we are mates, that we have tasted of each other, our smells intertwined, that we would defend each other's life with brutal conviction.

HELEN. Can't we just rub handkerchiefs on each other?

GUNTHER. Animals could smell that lie.

Join me, Helen. Sow your talent. Kiss my lips.

HELEN. You better not be just saying things to seduce me.

GUNTHER. Are you scared, Helen?

HELEN. I am never scared Mr. Roy. Even if it kills me, I will do whatever it takes to be the greatest trainer that I can.

GUNTHER. Tonight, we begin the great collaboration of Helen and Gunther Roy.

HELEN. Helen and Gunther Roy.

GUNTHER. Who knows what we can create together?

(*Back to the freight train.*)

BOB. I bet you created something amazing.

GUNTHER. It was the most incredible night of hanky-panky I've ever known. Heaven and earth crashing together, lightning striking water making life.

BOB. That's the best kind.

GUNTHER. Well Gunther Roy, for the first time, got scared.

BOB. But you conquered your fears and together you were the greatest animal act team the world has ever seen!

GUNTHER. When Helen ran home to pack her toiletries and leotards, I told the circus that something happened between a child and a clown, and we quickly left town. I had Helen blacklisted from all the other circuses, the animal schools, PETA... I made sure she would never train again.

(HELEN *runs in with a packed bag. Looks around at an empty lot, spinning.*)

BOB. No. No no no.

GUNTHER. When she described the Ringertraum she had, I knew she would unseat my title as the Greatest Animal Trainer of All Time. And so, much like a baby elephant, her spirit had to be crushed.

BOB. That's...terrible!

GUNTHER. Of course it is.

BOB. You destroyed her dream.

GUNTHER. Forty weeks later a voicemail was left on my trailer phone.

(HELEN *appears, post-birth. A phone booth outside the White Castle.*)

HELEN. Dear Mr. Roy. I should have known by the way you whip goats how cruel you really are. Now I know. You have bound another soul, cue the music. I thought you should know that your act has resulted in a baby boy. He's got your frown. Something sparkly about him but one sight of his face makes me want to rob his clothes. And so I have left him in a White Castle to fend for himself. Somewhere in America, your firstborn son is living. If you want to go find him and tell him things are different than you've shown them to me to be, be my guest. Until you do, I curse you to live a life that befits the type of trainer that you are.

(*A distant lion's roar.*)

Good luck.

(HELEN *runs off crying.*)

BOB. You deserved that voicemail.

GUNTHER. The animals sensed it immediately. They began to lose their fear and one day, when I stuck my face into the mouth of Mary Jo Sabre, I felt her jaw close just enough that I couldn't remove my head. I think she would have closed all the way if I hadn't shot her in the head with my gun. And from that moment I have lived a curs-ed life, of sadness and suffering that not even a full jug of Whin can obscure.

BOB. You had the opportunity to create something amazing. And you didn't. You're not a great man at all!

GUNTHER. All I wish is to redeem my existence just a little. And so I tirelessly wander across this land, looking for that boy that's got a bit of me placed in him 30 years ago.

    (Beat.)

BOB. Thirty years ago.

GUNTHER. Yeah. Thirty years and nine months.

    (Beat.)

BOB. I'm 30 years old.

GUNTHER. Happy Birthday.

BOB. I was born in a White Castle.

GUNTHER. I've heard worse.

BOB. I've never met my birth parents.

GUNTHER. I'm searching for my boy.

BOB. I'm not a girl.

    (Beat.)

GUNTHER. Smile.

    (BOB *smiles.*)

That's her smile.

BOB. Frown.

    (GUNTHER *frowns.*)

I've got your frown.

GUNTHER. I thought it looked familiar.

BOB. Father?

GUNTHER. Son.

BOB. Out of all the boxcars on this train.

GUNTHER. What's your name, son?

BOB. Bob.

GUNTHER. That's a short name.

BOB. Until this moment, my history started on a floor. But now I know why. And it's a wild, awful, passionate reason.

GUNTHER. Can you forgive me?

BOB. Teach me to tame lions.

GUNTHER. Oh boy.

BOB. Teach me to be fearless in the face of peril. Teach me to perform incredible acts that make an audience cheer.

GUNTHER. I don't think I know how to do that anymore.

BOB. I could be your assistant. We can get some new animals, find a small circus. I could help you drink Whin at a more moderate level.

GUNTHER. Oh that sounds so scary. I'm so scared, Bob!

BOB. I am your son. Show me things are different than you showed them to Helen to be. And your curse will be lifted.

Be the trainer that you are.

    (Beat.)

GUNTHER. You have any pets?

BOB. Just some fleas.

GUNTHER. That's a start.

    (They hug.)

Now the first thing you need to know is—

    (The sound of Hungry and Vicious Wolves.)

BOB. What is that?

GUNTHER. That is the sound of Hungry and Vicious Wolves.

BOB. Oh no. We must have entered the Nevada Desert freight train yard!

GUNTHER. There!

    (A pack of wolves appears.)

BOB. So many of them!

GUNTHER. Thirsty for blood.

BOB. The train is slowing down!

GUNTHER. If they don't eat us first, the railroad guards will.

BOB. Don't be scared, Dad. We're together! We can fight 'em off. Father and Son!

GUNTHER. Wolves can't be fought.

BOB. Then we will run into the desert as fast as we can!

GUNTHER. I CAN'T RUN WITH THESE KNEES!

    (GUNTHER makes a decision.)

Oh, Bob—

BOB. Oh, no.

GUNTHER. I wish I could share with you all sorts of animal training lessons, my favorite hobo recipes, or how to survive in a desert.

BOB. Don't talk like this.

GUNTHER. If you need to you can drink your own pee.

BOB. I don't like it when people give me urgent final lessons.

GUNTHER. It's looking like my only gift to you is saving your life.

BOB. I want to hang out with you. Live in a trailer, cook omelets together and laugh about sad things. You were about to tell me the first thing I need to—

GUNTHER. THIS IS MY RINGERTRAUM, BOB! FIND YOUR OWN!

BOB. But I don't know how!

GUNTHER. Good luck, Bob. JUMP!

> (*They jump off the freight car.*)

BOB. AHHH!

GUNTHER. (*Running towards wolves.*) AHHHH!

> (*The dogs eat GUNTHER.*
>
> GUNTHER's *arm flies in.*)

BOB. (*An angry prayer.*) Are you listening, Barry Metcalf? Are you listening, Poncha Springs? I have a father, who lived hard, smelled rough, who has done some terrible things in his life and he's still a greater man than all of you!

And somewhere in America I have a mother who has the power to curse through voicemails. Who had a beautiful Ringertraum. And I have her smile. And they've ruined their lives for me.

You evil, selfish, despicable land. You eat my father, poison my Jeanine, steal my Amelia, and you have soiled every beautiful idea I've written on pieces of paper with your mediocre filth. YOU ARE KILLING EVERYTHING I LOVE!

Well I curse *you,* Barry Metcalf. I curse Sioux Falls, Roanoke, and Aberdeen. I curse this ENTIRE NATION to live a life that befits who they are!

No more fudge shops. No more lists. America does not deserve the love and passion of a dreamer.

But I do. I have a dream. And I will pursue it by any means necessary until there is justice, until the pain you have inflicted upon me is avenged. I have a RINGERTRAUM and BOB WILL NOT BE STOPPED.

Good luck, Bob. Good luck, indeed.

> (*He walks. Blackout. End of Act Three.*)

Intermission

Interlude 3

Interlude: A dance about luck.
CHORUS FOUR. This is a dance about luck.
(*A dance.*)
Thank you.

ACT FOUR

ALL CHORUS. Bob. Act four.
CHORUS FOUR. How Bob has a turn of luck, becomes a new man, achieves a false dream, meets an important woman and is redeemed.
CHORUS THREE. This is how Bob had a turn of luck.
(*A doorbell rings in a very large house.* TONY, *a butler, heads for the door.*)
BOB. No!
(BOB *enters, 50 years old, perhaps dressed like Hugh Hefner. Fancy pajamas. He holds two glasses of champagne.*)
I'll get it, Tony!
TONY (CHORUS TWO). Yes, Bob.
(TONY *exits.* BOB *opens the door.*)
BOB. Just in time! The Jacuzzi is at the perfect temperature for—oh.
VERA (CHORUS ONE). Hello!
BOB. You are not who I was expecting.
VERA. My name is Vera Ponchatraine and I am a member of Troupe 599: The greatest scouting troupe of any gender in the Nevada area!
BOB. What do you want?
VERA. Did you know that there are over 1.3 million homeless and abandoned youths in the United States?
BOB. Oh no.
VERA. Yes, it is sad. All of us in troupe 599 are blessed to come from loving families, except for Bernadette Winters, and we would like to share a small portion of our blessings with those who are cursed. So, our troupe is building a brand new shelter for abandoned children in the Nevada Desert area. Because everyone deserves a place they will not feel alone. Would you be interested in purchasing a box of cookies to support our cause?
BOB. Would I be interested?
VERA. If I sell the most cookies, I win tickets to Water Kingdom.
(*Beat.* BOB *laughs. It grows large and disturbing.*)

VERA. What's so funny?

BOB. I used to be like you. "Doing Good Deeds." "Save The World." "Thin Mints." Guess where that got me?

VERA. It looks like you're doing very—

BOB. It seems like only twenty minutes ago that I was in the middle of the desert, no food or water, everything I loved robbed from me except for a ring in my undies moist with scrotal dew.

For all practical purposes I should be dead.

You know what death is, little girl?

VERA. Yes, my brother—

BOB. The point is, I'm not dead. I'm here living richly in this huge house. Isn't my house amazing?

VERA. It's very large.

BOB. And my silk pajamas. Don't they look comfy?

VERA. They're kind of opening up at the—

BOB. How do you think I did it, Brownie?

VERA. Did you pray?

BOB. No, chica, I got my feet under myself, cursed the nation, picked a direction, and I walked.

(BOB's *flashback/story begins.*)

Across hot sand. Past nuclear testing sites, foreclosed homes, and a terrible "arts" festival that was lighting something stupid on fire. I hunted and ate beetles, threw sand at vultures that were bird-kissing my flanks with their sharp, hungry beaks, and I followed the only piece of advice my recently met and killed birthfather gave me and drank my own pee.

VERA. There's a lot of ammonia in—

BOB. And I kept yelling at myself, "Don't die, Bob! Keep crawling, Bob and prove Poncha Springs wrong!"

VERA. Who?

BOB. I crawled for 40 days and nights or thereabouts until one scorching day that hot sand became grass, and that grass became a fountain and that fountain had a pathway that led to the floor of this very building.

VERA. You just crawled into your house?

BOB. The Martin Luther Casino. The only Civil-Rights-themed casino and adult playground in the country. "Martin Luther Casino: What's Your Dream?" That was the message blinking above the door.

VERA. That sounds wrong.

BOB. But I had a dream. And, much like the creators of the greatest musical ever, *Mamma Mia,* I knew I had to risk everything I had.

(*A roulette wheel spins in a melancholy way.* A ONE-ARMED ROULETTE DEALER *stands by the wheel.* BOB *staggers towards it. There are two* ONLOOKERS *as the scene happens.*)

DEALER (CHORUS FOUR). Roulette Wheel.

Ye tired, ye poor, ye huddled. Come to my wheel and place your bets.

BOB. It's so beautiful.

DEALER. You look like Walt Whitman.

BOB. It's a sign.

DEALER. It's a wheel.

BOB. I want justice. I want a different life. Can I do that here?

DEALER. Depends on what you risk. The more it hurts, the bigger the win.

(*Shows stump.*)

What you gonna bet?

(BOB *pulls out the ring.*)

BOB. Everything I have.

DEALER. What a moist ring.

VERA. You shouldn't bet that. You should be saving that for someone special.

BOB. Saving it for me.

Roulette Dealer, if I win, I promise I will honor and avenge the deaths of all I have loved. I will never again be slave to fools. I promise I will not be the man I used to be.

DEALER. Deal.

BOB. Red. Red is blood. I bet this ring on red.

DEALER. No more bets at this table please, this gentleman has bet it all. What do the fates have in store for us tonight? A story of joy or a story to learn from? It all depends on this one little shiny…BALL!

(*We hear the ball rolling and rolling and finally the ball bounces and bounces and lands in a slot.*)

DEALER. (*Putting down the marker.*) 30. Red.

(VERA *stifles a clap.*)

BOB. Yes!

VERA. Yes!

BOB. This is my moment.

VERA. Yeah, that's, oo… Well done.

BOB. Double or nothing!

VERA. No!

BOB. And if I lose, kill me. On the casino floor. Drag me through the streets, place my head on a spire along I-15.

VERA. My brother doubled or nothing'd and they found him—

BOB. This is my flashback, Sashy! Red again!

(*A crowd gathers to watch.*)

DEALER. BALL!

(*We hear the ball rolling and rolling and finally the ball bounces and bounces and lands in a slot.*)

27. Red.

VERA. Amazing! Oh wow! That's amazing! Holy cow.

BOB. It's not enough.

DEALER & VERA. Enough for what?

BOB. Again!

DEALER. Red.

BOB. Again!

DEALER. Red.

BOB. Again! Again! Again!

VERA. My tummy hurts.

BOB. And I won again. And again and again and again and that wheel landed on red 17 times!

(*The DEALER fades out.*)

VERA. 131,000 times the value of the ring.

BOB. And I would have kept going if the Martin Luther Casino hadn't gone bankrupt and everyone lost their jobs and they had to turn their property over to me and is now my very home in which you solicit today.

VERA. Wow, sir, it sounds like you were very very lucky.

BOB. THERE IS NO SUCH THING AS LUCK, POLLYANNA!

When Rockefeller was born at the right place at the right time, he monopolized. When Judy Garland chanced the part of Dorothy, she knocked it out of the park. And when Lou Gehrig stumbled upon a disease, he made sure his name would last forever.

I risked my life for this. I crawled towards a window and I jumped. Don't tell me that's not work, girlfriend.

VERA. I don't want to be your girlfriend.

BOB. Tell your little homeless children buddies that maybe they should stop hoping for handouts from ugly girls who really just want free tickets to Water Kingdom.

VERA. It's true what they say about you.

BOB. What do they say about me?

VERA. That you are not a very nice man.

BOB. No. No, I am not a nice man.

Nothing great ever happens from being nice.

VERA. I told my pastor I was going to save you.

BOB. The only reason I answered the door is that I thought you were a prostitute!

VERA. Mom!

     (VERA *runs off.*)

BOB. Yeah run back to Mommy! Run back to the parent who's alive and loves you! Hug her tight, mommyhaver!

     (*Door slams.* BOB *alone.*)

CHORUS. (*Whisper.*) Bob.

     (BOB *looks around. Whisper.*)

Bob.

     (BOB *looks around.*)

BOB. Quiet.

CHORUS. (*Whisper.*) Not a nice man Bob.

BOB. Music!

     (*Music plays.*)

CHORUS THREE. It is said that in the 20 years since Bob had his "this is not luck I totally earned this" moment, Bob had become the three thousand, two-hundred-seventh richest person in America.

BOB. Champagne!

     (TONY *brings* BOB *a glass of champagne.*)

CHORUS FOUR. Bob bought new clothes, got a butler, and put his money into Goldman Sachs instead of pillowcases where he made tons of money gambling on the misfortune of others.

BOB. Cake!

     (TONY *enters with birthday cake.*)

CHORUS ONE. Bob's kisses tasted different, he drank espresso from a can and he would occasionally lock himself in hotel rooms and urinate in jars. Bob never left the Casino grounds, and his eyes, the ones that saved him, had sunk into his skull.

TONY. Happy fiftieth birthday, Bob.

BOB. She knew about me.

TONY. Who, Bob.

BOB. Apparently I have a reputation in the female scouting community for "not being nice."

TONY. You must feel proud, Bob.

BOB. The world that you live in is not nice, Vera!

TONY. I don't think she can hear you, Bob.

     (BOB *pees in a jar.*)

BOB. Whatever. I have everything I need. Money. A casino turned into a house. A butler.

TONY. That is the trifecta, Bob.

BOB. I don't need validation from "scouts." I don't need a "birthday party" with "guests." I think I'm going to lock myself in room 709.

TONY. Bob…

BOB. Please no lesson on my birthday, Tony.

TONY. Bob, I have been a butler for several hundred years as I possess both a tremendous ability to attend to people's whims and a rare genetic disease where I shall never age nor die. I've seen money transform some of the most decent people. My last employer, a successful and mediocre entertainer, insisted I put diamonds in her salad. She wanted to feel them pass through her abdomen and come out the back, after which she planned to sell them on her website. She would have done so if the diamonds had not sliced through her small intestine, bleeding her dead in less than two hours.

BOB. I don't really care for salad.

TONY. Unpack the parable, Bob.

BOB. Are you saying it was wrong to pursue my happiness?

TONY. Are you happy, Bob?

BOB. What makes you think I'm not happy?

TONY. You seem a little lonely, Bob.

BOB. You seem a little lonely, Tony.

TONY. You could be a great man, Bob.

BOB. I am a great man.

TONY. Prove it.

BOB. You prove it.

TONY. I asked first.

BOB. Let me eat my cake in peace.

TONY. Happy birthday, Bob.

     (TONY *exits.*)

BOB. Nobody knows what I've been through.

Nobody understands who I am.

CHORUS ONE (AS VERA?). (*Whisper.*) You are not a nice man, Bob.

BOB. Quiet.

CHORUS. (*Whisper.*) You're not a nice man, Bob.

BOB. Shhh!

CHORUS. (*Haunting.*)

> **1.** D minus again Bob.
>
> **2.** Bob the way you play hockey, I don't know what to feel.
>
> **3.** I don't want to stay over at Bob's.
>
> **4.** You were just awkward at recess, Bob.

BOB. Let me eat cake!

CHORUS.

> **1.** You're not even a historian, Bob.
>
> **2.** You're a terrible artist, Bob.
>
> **3.** Don't cure, Bob. Don't cure the sick.
>
> **4.** Bob you can't lead us.

BOB. I could if I wanted.

CHORUS.

> **1.** I raised you in my Malibu to be better than this, Bob.
>
> **2.** I thought you'd use my ring for goodness, Bob.
>
> **3.** You are not the man that I kissed, Bob.
>
> **4.** You are not a trainer's son, Bob.

BOB. Hey, that's not... Yes I am! I'm doing this for—

CHORUS.

> **1.** Who are you, Bob.
>
> **2 & 3.** Who are you Bob?
>
> **4.** Bob has been stopped.

BOB. No, no I have not been stopped! Maybe it's time I did prove it to you, Tony. Vera. I am capable of great things. I will create something amazing. Something that will take away breath. Something really really large. It's time to show this nation who *Bob* really is.

> (BOB *runs off.*)

CHORUS FOUR. It is said that Bob ran into the scene shop of the abandoned French Canadian civil rights Cirque Show, *Egalité*, and ordered thousands of products from the Home Depot. For years Bob worked every day, and Tony heard noises from various machines, materials, yells of triumph—

BOB. (*A yell of triumph.*)

CHORUS FOUR. Yells of despair.

BOB. (*A curse of despair.*)

CHORUS FOUR. And yells of ambiguity.

BOB. (*An ambiguous yell.*)

CHORUS FOUR. And then on Bob's fifty-fifth birthday—

BOB. (*Singing.*) It is finished!

CHORUS TWO. Under cover of night and a sheet, Bob packed his creation into an oversized trailer attached to an RV, and hired three prostitutes to join him and Tony on a road trip. In the Black Hills of South Dakota, Bob pulled off Interstate 90 and drove towards a national monument that was dear to his heart. However Bob's vehicle was too large for the windy mountain road to make it all the way.

BOB. (*Off?*) Shoot! Fine.

CHORUS THREE. And so Bob was forced to pull into an overflow parking lot eight miles away from the Mount Rushmore visitor center, where he pulled out his creation from his trailer, covered by a sheet where it sat in a large vehicle parking spot.

This is how Bob achieved a false dream.

> (BOB *stands next to a sheet covering something.* TONY *and* THREE PROSTITUTES *are a little bewildered.*)

BOB. This way, Tony, prostitutes. You are a witness to one of the greatest achievements ever performed by a single person in America. A testament to what one man can do by himself, if they are someone like me.

PROSTITUTE THREE. Is it a death ray?

PROSTITUTE FOUR. A time machine.

PROSTITUTE ONE. A portal to another dimension.

BOB. All those things and more, my hired friends.

TONY. Oh, Bob, this is so exciting. I am so excited right now.

BOB. Eight miles from this very spot a fire was lit inside my soul and started a lifelong dream.

We all have big dreams of what we hope to achieve in this world, and most of us are too stupid or lazy to achieve it. But I am not.

I am someone whose dream has come true.

> (BOB *rips off an unseen sheet. Everyone looks up.*)

PROSTITUTE ONE. What is it?

BOB. It's my face. Chiseled in granite. And if you stand over here, and if I blow up that big chunk of mountain in between, it's as though I'm next to Abe Lincoln himself. And the best part, underneath...

PROSTITUTE THREE. Ohh. It's a plaque in a boulder.

PROSTITUTE FOUR. A mountain with your face on it.

PROSTITUTE ONE. And a plaque.

TONY. Oh, Bob.

BOB. I had to make it over 50 times to get it right.

The bronze letters, the leathery background… And this boulder looks like it could last for millions of years.

(*He rubs his fingers across the plaque.*)

I like the sound that it makes when I rub my fingers across my name. Did you hear that?

(*He rubs it again, looks at it.*)

I can almost see my reflection in the letters. I see me in me. That's funny. Hello me.

(*He kisses the plaque.*)

PROSTITUTE ONE. Did you say there was cheese?

BOB. I hope a child eats lunch on this. And she'll wonder who she's sitting on. And for a moment, I will exist again under her shorts. And she'll wonder if one day, she could be me.

PROSTITUTE THREE. (*Halfhearted.*) Yay. She could be you! (*Bad clapping.*)

BOB. So? What do you think, Tony? Whores?

TONY. Oh, Bob.

PROSTITUTE FOUR. Is it wine time?

BOB. This is everything I've always wanted.

TONY. It's a very good plaque, Bob.

PROSTITUTE ONE. Yeah let's celebrate.

PROSTITUTE FOUR. Celebrate(!)

PROSTITUTE THREE. How about we go to the RV and—

BOB. I AM BOB AND I AM A GREAT MAN AND I AM ON A PLAQUE!

(*They stare at him.*)

IS THIS NOT ENOUGH FOR YOU?

PROSTITUTE ONE. Yes.

PROSTITUTE FOUR. No?

PROSTITUTE THREE. I don't think I understand the—

BOB. I WILL STAY BY MY PLAQUE AND BE PROUD. Leave me alone!

(*The* PROSTITUTES *leave.*)

TONY. Bob.

BOB. You're fired, Tony!

TONY. I fire you.

(*The sound of an RV driving away.* BOB, *alone by his plaque.*)

BOB. That didn't go how I thought it would.

Bob, would you pack your child into a car, drive thousands of miles to show her this plaque?

I'm sorry, Jeanine.

Amelia, Gunther, Connor, James the Bear...I'm sorry you believed in me.

> (*A long beat.* BOB *breaks down and cries. Music. It begins to snow.*
> *Days pass.* SVEN, *a wolf, enters.*)

And here comes the wolf.

Can you smell my weakness and failure? Have you come all the way from the freight train yard to find your next snack? Well, here I am. Take me. Thin out the human herd. Sink your teeth into my flesh and don't stop chomping till you get to my heart.

> (SVEN *licks* BOB*'s nose.*)

Hey.

> (SVEN *starts licking* BOB*'s face. Unseen,* HELEN *enters, wearing the pants she stole from* BOB *in Act One.*)

Hey, stop it!

HELEN. He's a licker.

BOB. What?

HELEN. Loves salt. You must have a lot on your skin.

BOB. He's tickling me. Hey!

HELEN. Sven! Off!

> (SVEN *stops licking, stares at* BOB.)

His tongue can be relentless.

BOB. I was hoping he'd put me out of my misery.

HELEN. He's only done that a couple times.

Wanna see a trick?

BOB. I'm not really in the mood for—

HELEN. Sven!

> (SVEN *gets alert.*)

Do Fosse.

> (SVEN *does a small four-legged Bob Fosse-esque dance.*)

BOB. That's pretty good.

HELEN. I'm teaching Sven to dance in all the great choreographer styles. You should see his Cunningham.

BOB. I like that trick.

HELEN. I call it "Helen and the Dancing Wolf."

OTHER CHORUS. Helen.

> (BOB *hears the whisper.*)

HELEN. I need to gloss up the act a bit. Maybe sequins. That was the feedback we got at our Vegas audition. In a few years, if I'm lucky, I'll have a whole menagerie of creatures and you won't believe what I'd like 'em to do. Shuffle off now, Sven.

(SVEN *tap-shuffles off.*)

BOB. He seems nice.

HELEN. Poor thing has so many fleas can't ever get rid of 'em. But the dancing makes him forget. You got any?

BOB. Fleas?

HELEN. I bet you're pretty great with animals.

BOB. I'm not great with anything.

HELEN. But it's in your blood, Bob.

OTHER CHORUS. (*Whisper.*) Bob.

(*Beat.*)

BOB. Something about your face.

HELEN. I don't think you'd remember my—

(BOB *sees* HELEN'*s pants.*)

BOB. Oh my goodness. You…you—

HELEN. That's right, Bob—

BOB. (*Simultaneous with* HELEN.)

YOU STOLE MY PANTS.   **HELEN.** I AM YOUR MOTHER.

(*Beat.*)

BOB. Wait.   Woah.

No.   Really?

You're my mother?   I stole your pants?

I don't believe it.

HELEN. How god-awful is that?

BOB. Helen.

HELEN. Bob.

BOB. How did you find me?

HELEN. Well you look like half of him and half of me.

BOB. Yeah but—

HELEN. And then Sven licked you. Only does that to kin.

BOB. What do you want from me?

HELEN. I don't want anything from you.

BOB. Come out of the woodwork to collect on the good fortune of your long-lost son.

HELEN. I want to help you.

BOB. I'm doing fine. I have this glorious monument constructed in my honor which is amazing and you are disturbing my celebration.

HELEN. Oh sweetie, hollow plaques never made anyone happy.

BOB. Well I am happy. Here's a hundred dollars for some sequins. I hope everything works out wonderfully for you and Sven and I hope you get all the animals you need for your Living Totem.

HELEN. You know about that?

BOB. It's amazing and beautiful. Now goodbye. And *good luck!*

(HELEN *starts to walk off. Stops.*)

HELEN. I'm sorry.

BOB. For dumping me in a bathroom?

HELEN. No, that was for the best. Stealing your pants, now that's just cruel.

BOB. They were my favorite pants.

HELEN. That day was my lowest after a terrible string of lows.

My parents died in a mining explosion, had my life-dream destroyed, a baby I hated and dumped (*A gesture to* BOB.), lost my drive, my confidence, my job, my home, some teeth, and got taken advantage of by a credit card company. Ever had a rough go like that?

BOB. Something like it.

HELEN. Things had gotten so desperate for me I had resorted to robbing clothes from children just to get by.

But that day, you, I can't believe it was you, something in the way you walked, the embarrassment of being in the middle of the street in your BVD's was the least of your worries… I knew I had just stolen from someone who had no home to run to.

BOB. But you did it anyway.

HELEN. Stealing from you devastated me. I was on my way to throwing myself into the lake when I walked by the Art Institute, and I saw this cop on the steps, crying ferociously.

BOB. I know that cop.

HELEN. I watched him put his palms all over the steps and then lick his hands.

BOB. I know what he was licking.

HELEN. And I thought, oh, there is someone else in the world with as much pain and regret as me. Something made we want to talk to him. He told me the story of the great mistake he made in his life. And I told him mine.

BOB. So many great mistakes.

HELEN. We got married. Almost 40 years. We were pretty happy. Connor passed away a few years ago. Shot in the liver by a deep-dish pizza maker.

BOB. He was a good man. He gave me this ring.

HELEN. As he filled with liquid in all the wrong places, we reminisced about how we met that day at the museum steps. He told me about the boy who told him where his first love was. "How sad for a son so young," I said, "to have his mother die in his arms."

(CONNOR *appears.*)

CONNOR. It wasn't her son.

HELEN. Who was he?

CONNOR. It was a boy she'd found as a baby in a White Castle on Valentine's Day.

(JEANINE *appears.*)

HELEN. My baby!

CONNOR. He said he had to be a great man for her. His name was...

CONNOR & BOB. ...Bob.

(CONNOR *dies as he says "Bob." He and* JEANINE *disappear.*)

HELEN. And are you a "great man," Bob?

BOB. I'm smart, I'm well-meaning, and I'm pretty good at making love.

HELEN. All good things.

BOB. But if I never existed, would anything be different?

HELEN. That's an unanswerable question, Bob.

BOB. I wanted to have an answer.

I guess sometimes we're not who we hope we are.

HELEN. Ain't that the truth.

(*Beat.*)

BOB. So what is the point of even trying?

HELEN. Well, Bob I'm here to tell you—

BOB. What is the purpose of moving forward when you know you'll fail?

HELEN. You don't know that, that's not the—

BOB. Why even live another day, breathe another breath on this planet when you—

(HELEN *slaps* BOB.)

BOB. Ow!

HELEN. Why you want to spend precious breaths of life on this little pity party you got going on here?

BOB. But I—

HELEN. Doesn't do anyone a lick of good!

BOB. But—

HELEN. Take what you got, 'cause there's stuff you got, Bob. We're all in this big tragedy of a life together so shove some timber up your chute, get some matches and let her rip!

BOB. OK. Fine. Sheesh. Fine.

HELEN. Sven!

(SVEN *returns.*)

Remember what we talked about, Sven?

(SVEN *nods.*)

Bob, I give you Sven, the most talented trained wolf in North America. He will be your faithful companion and lead you to the ends of the earth.

(SVEN *turns to* BOB.)

BOB. No.

HELEN. It's the least I can do.

BOB. But what about the Vegas show?

HELEN. All of a sudden that dream seems a little tacky.

BOB. Hi Sven.

HELEN. I'm sorry I stole your pants. I should never have done that. It was cruel. I am deeply sorry for what I did to you.

(SVEN *stands between them, watching.*)

BOB. I forgive you, Helen.

HELEN. You do?

BOB. I declare those pants to be your own.

(*Beat.* SVEN *sniffles.*)

HELEN. Well, I better be going on my way before I tear up.

BOB. Helen.

HELEN. What's that, Bob?

BOB. Before you… Would you do your Ringertraum for me?

HELEN. Oh Bob I've never shown it to—

BOB. I want to see it.

HELEN. It's silly without all the parts and—

BOB. We've got Sven and his fleas and we can imagine the rest…

HELEN. I can't.

BOB. Inspire me. Reveal me. Make me cry.

HELEN. I don't know if I should even—TOTEM!

(HELEN'*s Living Totem is created, but unseen. It is strangely beautiful.*)

BOB. Oh wow.

HELEN. Bob, What animal are you?

Which one is your guide on the trail of your life?

You are not alone.

BOB. I am not alone.

(*The 'traum ends. HELEN is winded.*)

HELEN. Hoo-ey! That felt amazing to finally share that with someone. Thank you, Bob.

BOB. It was the greatest animal act the world has ever seen.

HELEN. Goodbye Bob.

BOB. Good luck, Helen.

(BOB *and* HELEN *hug.*)

HELEN. Funny, I always say "good luck" to other people too. Never knew whether it actually brought it or not.

BOB. I think it's just a nice thing to say.

HELEN. Remember, Bob, you are not—

(*Before she says "alone,"* HELEN *dies in* BOB*'s arms.*)

BOB. "You are not." So said the great animal trainer Helen on this Valentine's Day.

Goodbye, Mom.

We get one chance.

And then we disappear.

One chance.

And you're in the middle of it.

(BOB *puts* HELEN *down over his plaque.* SVEN *licks* HELEN, *maybe eats a toe. Beat.*)

BOB. Tony?

(TONY *runs on.*)

TONY. Yes, Bob?

BOB. Will you rehire me?

TONY. What do you need, Bob?

BOB. We need to light my birth mother on fire.

TONY. Yes, Bob.

BOB. And after that, I would like to put my casinohouse up for sale.

TONY. OK.

BOB. Sell all of my assets and bring me cash if you wouldn't mind.

TONY. Bob.

BOB. Take a million dollars for yourself and give the rest to the Park Service.

TONY. Bob.

BOB. Just, please, do what I ask.

(TONY *exits.*)

Sven, look into my eyes.

Don't you worry, Sven.

You and your fleas won't be left behind.

A great future lies ahead for us.

(SVEN *nods. Scratches.* TONY *returns with the two Martin Luther Casino bags of money.*)

Have a glass of champagne with me, Tony?

TONY. Bob, what are you going to do?

(*Blackout. End of Act Four.*)

Interlude 4

Interlude: A dance about hope.
CHORUS ONE. This is a dance about hope.
(*A dance.*)
Thank you.

ACT FIVE

ALL CHORUS. Bob. Act five.
CHORUS THREE. The rest.
CHORUS ONE. It is said that after Bob left his plaque at Mount Rushmore overflow parking, he was never seen in this country again.
CHORUS TWO. It is said that Tony, who looks a lot like me, found himself in a greater amount of perplexed reflection than he had ever felt for a client and desired to learn more about Bob's past.
CHORUS THREE. Tony searched many pockets of the nation based on the stories Bob had shared.
A coffee shop owner recalled a bloody fight with Bob.
BARISTA. That fight we had. It finally turned my life around. Bob helped me find my passion again. I'm having less but more meaningful sex and my coffee shop has become the literary Mecca of Poncha Springs!
CHORUS FOUR. Tony found hundreds of people with an anecdote about Bob.
(*A wild flurry of characters past.*)
BONNIE. Bob showed me that my name wasn't the problem. Seeing him in my trunk all those times made me realize it was something deeper, something more profound I should change with my life. And I did. And I'm finally the person I should be.
Please, call me Chester.
VERA. Bob taught me what I don't want to be like when I'm grown up. When I am a successful businesswoman, I will always buy cookies for a good cause, I will not lock myself away in a Casino, and I will not count on luck to make me happy.
ROULETTE DEALER. Bob got me fired from my roulette job that I was too lazy to leave even though it took my arm. Got me thinking about my Master's in Social Justice and my old desire to spread the message of empowerment. So now I'm the owner of The Malcolm X Bowling Alley in Fresno, California. Get an "X" for Malcolm. That's our slogan.

WAITRESS ONE. Bob never really left my waitress bed in a way.

WAITRESS TWO. Nor mine!

WAITRESS THREE. Nor mine!

WAITRESS FOUR. Nor mine!

WAITRESS ONE. His energy was inspiring.

WAITRESS TWO. Such an amazing kisser.

WAITRESS THREE. Oh wow his lips.

WAITRESS FOUR. I wish'd I'd glued them to mine with cement.

WAITRESS ONE. Bob convinced me to leave my large husband and spearhead a movement to transform our dilapidated town into a historical and vacation paradise.

WAITRESS TWO. Me too!

WAITRESS THREE. Me too!

WAITRESS FOUR. Not me. But I believe, thanks to Bob, I make the greatest ham and cheese omelet in the tri-valley area.

JAMES. Bob looked after Roberto's bush for years. I think a lot of people fell in love underneath it because of that.

KIM. Bob gave me a pencil. And I made it home.

CAITLYN. Bob was the only one who cared that I didn't pee in my car.

SAGÉ. Bob was like a flea that I can't remember but I feel his bite.

CHORUS THREE. It is said that if Tony were able to speak to the dead, they would have had a lot to say.

CONNOR. Bob helped me grieve. Sometimes you get so tossed up in your own problems it's hard to see beyond your own salad. I think I finally peeked out of the bowl after the day I met him. I'm glad I gave him that ring. That's something I'm proud of.

AMELIA. Bob gave me the strength to pursue my own happiness. It was better to die of exposure and starvation on a raft made of beach trash in the middle of the Pacific Ocean than the slow and painful way my parents had arranged. I wish there was some way I could tell Bob, let him know I didn't stop my journey.

GUNTHER. Bob had a little less hair than I expected. But I could still see it, the animal trainer blood in him. Times two. There are not a lot of people I'd get eaten for, him and maybe Jimmy Buffett but that's it. I believe there is a beautiful Ringertraum inside of him.

HELEN. Bob allowed me to die in a loved one's arms. And he gave me these pants.

JEANINE. Bob burnt me and it's the best thing he could have done. I am everywhere now. A particle here, a molecule there. You wouldn't believe everything I've bumped against since then. I hope Bob burns himself when the time comes. And I hope he finds a bit of happiness before that. I think a lot of people might have loved him. If they'd given him the chance.

CHORUS TWO. It is said that Tony was so moved he felt compelled to write a short story about Bob and sent it to *Harper's* magazine, which got printed, which got Tony a book deal, which became hugely loved by Oprah Winfrey, which caused the story of Bob to seep into the National Consciousness and for Tony to live the immortal life of his dreams.

CHORUS THREE. Other books about Bob appeared, some accurate, some absurdly false, some by people who had never met him. His story was used as lessons for children, for clever bumper stickers, and to prove varying political points of view.

CHORUS ONE. It was hoped by millions that the great celebration and knowledge of Bob's life would compel Bob to appear again.

CHORUS FOUR. He did not.

CHORUS THREE. Most became convinced that Bob was dead. A few came to believe that Tony had invented the entire story, though those people were largely viewed as people not very fun to be around.

CHORUS FOUR. Bob became a legend.

Like John Muir.

CHORUS. (*Quickly.*)
>   **1.** Harriet Tubman.
>
>   **2.** Robert Oppenheimer.
>
>   **3.** Sam Walton.
>
>   **4.** Mark Twain.
>
>   **1.** Eleanor Roosevelt.
>
>   **2.** Billie Jean King.
>
>   **3.** Leonard Bernstein.
>
>   **4.** Marilyn Monroe.
>
>   **1.** Duke Kahanamoku.
>
>   **2.** Chief Seattle.
>
>   **3.** Bill Gates.
>
>   **4.** Cher.
>
>   **1.** Cesar Chavez.
>
>   **2.** Jody Williams.
>
>   **3.** The guy who landed that plane.
>
>   **4.** Cher.

CHORUS ONE. And Bob will never know.

(*Beat. The* CHORUS *walks away.*
CHORUS THREE *runs back.*)

CHORUS THREE. Bob was seen one more time.

CHORUS FOUR. It is said.

CHORUS THREE. No, he was.

Years ago a young man, Leo, who is a friend of a friend, traveled to Mexico on a backpacking trip to "find himself" and celebrate his sexual attraction to Latin people.

On a ride down from Puerto Vallarta to all points South, Leo's bus pulled off the highway to a small rest area known for being the worst in all of Mexico.

By a cliff overlooking the Pacific Ocean, Leo saw a small shelter and next to it, a beige Chevy Malibu.

This is how Leo met Bob.

(*A Chevy Malibu.* BOB*'s legs are sticking out.* LEO *enters.*)

BOB. (*Under car.*) C'mon you stupid nozzle.

(LEO *adjusts himself to look handsome and alluring. In American accent, trying to be seductive?*)

LEO (CHORUS TWO). Buenos días.

BOB. (*A grunt.*) Bwaaah.

LEO. Me llamo Leo.

BOB. Hold on a sec, Leo. Just need to twist this one...

LEO. You speak English.

BOB. Correctamundo.

LEO. Are you American?

(BOB *emerges from under the Malibu. He is very old, big white beard and wild hair. Maybe dressed in a wolf hide.*)

BOB. Yes I am.

LEO. (*Disappointed.*) Great.

BOB. You here for the show?

LEO. I'm just going to head back to the—

BOB. No no! "Whenever someone is in need, put on your shoes!" The great entertainer Shirley Temple said that.

(*Over the course of the dialogue,* BOB *begins to set up little footlights around the Malibu trunk. He wheels out a box on a stand covered by a sheet.* BOB *changes into a slightly snazzy showman outfit.*)

LEO. I don't really need a—

BOB. Where you from, whippersnapper?

LEO. Small town you've never heard of.

BOB. Try me.

LEO. Mulberry.

BOB. Indiana.

LEO. How did you know?

BOB. One of the best community libraries in the state.

LEO. It's not worth staying in Mulberry for it.

BOB. Great waitresses in Mulberry.

LEO. People think I'm weird there.

BOB. You look a little weird.

LEO. I've known I've been weird since I was nine. I'm OK with it but doesn't seem like Mulberry is. And there's not enough Latin people there.

BOB. So you've set to the road to find your place in the whole hullabaloo of it all.

LEO. I've got a lot of cool ideas, things I could do that could be pretty awesome. I write them down in my journal and translate them into Spanish. I want to be someplace that will believe in me. Chiapas, Maybe.

I'm a little lost.

BOB. I've felt weird, lost and alone for most of my life. Used to look back at my history and all I'd see are dark moments of failure that stayed vivid and strong. A few little spots poking through like dim little stars that seemed so far away.

But, then one day, after years of traveling the continent, I pulled off to this very spot, walked to this very cliff when my trusty dancing wolf began shimmying towards the shore.

And there it was: a rectangle of driftwood and plastic and neck pillows all cinched together. On one side, tied to a rope made from a Snickers wrapper, was a glass jar. Filled with water. Its lid shut tight.

And I felt Amelia breathing inside of me. And Jeanine next to her. And Connor and Helen and Gunther Roy.

LEO. I don't know those—

BOB. I felt threads coming out of each memory, connecting everything to one another, a bunch of junk from all over the place, bound together into a single raft, keeping me floating above the deep. I felt connected to everything, everywhere, and everyone at the same time.

I wanted to capture that. In a case. And never forget that feeling. And I knew what I could do.

LEO. What can you do?

BOB. It'll cost you 500 pesos.

LEO. That's a lot.

BOB. Leo, you are at the strangest, weirdest attraction at the worst rest stop in all of Mexico. It could change your life. And it includes a shot of Whin.

LEO. I have no idea what that is.

BOB. Only one way to find out, Leo.

> (LEO *gives* BOB *the money.* BOB *gives* LEO *the shot.* BOB *jumps up on the trunk behind the green-sheeted object. He wears his ringmaster outfit. The lights change to show lights, bright around the trunk and* BOB. *Maybe his voice amplified. Music accompanies.*)

Ladies, Gentlemen, Boys, Girls, young "weird" Mulberrian lover of the Latinos before me.

> (*A lick of music,* BOB *does a small dance move.*)

It has taken me a very long time to build the stamina and strength to perform the act you are about to witness. It may shock you. Thrill and delight you. It may make you cry. Are you willing to accept these risks?

LEO. Uh, yeah?

BOB. Are you ready?

LEO. I don't really know—

BOB. That doesn't sound like ready. Are you ready?

LEO. Yes! Yes I am ready. I am FRIKKIN ready!

> (BOB *pulls off the sheet revealing a flea circus model shaped like the United States of America. There is something about it that seems pretty great.*)

BOB. It's Bob's Adventures Across America Flea Circus Spectacular! See my incredible troupe of trained pests reenact one of the wildest collections of life stories ever told.

SEE how a fast food employee saves a baby from certain death! SEE how a hobo takes on a savage pack of wolves! Experience The Journey of The Ring, The Curse of the Dollar Bill, The Polaroid Kiss that Changed It All.

SEE a flea dance about hardship, love, luck, and hope.

> (BOB *picks a flea out of* LEO's *hair.*)

AND SEE the tender story of a young man who bravely travels thousands of miles so that he can feel less weird and touch the flesh of a culture he loves.

> (BOB *places the flea into the case.*)

SEE that no matter how far away you feel on the inside, no matter how dark your days can get, you can always take a big step back, look at all those fleas hopping next to you and see that you are NOT ALONE!

> (BOB *looks down and commands the fleas, or just stands by his circus. Perhaps he silently narrates.*)

CHORUS ONE. It is said that Leo stayed at Bob's for a week, and watched Bob's show several hundred times, and Bob charged him five 500 pesos every time.

(*Beat.*)

CHORUS THREE. It is said we like this added conclusion.

This final tale of Bob.

CHORUS FOUR. It is said we all like Bob, we think about him a lot, not just because Oprah loved him, but, 'cause, I don't know, we just do.

CHORUS ONE. It is said there are many of us who like uttering those words. We say it to ourselves as we go to sleep in our beds, words that give us comfort and hope in the face of all the discomfort and hopelessness.

That we are not alone.

CHORUS TWO. We are not alone.

CHORUS THREE. We are not alone.

CHORUS FOUR. We are not alone.

(BOB *with his fleas, content.*)

BOB. I am not alone.

I am not alone.

I am not alone.

(*Blackout.*)

End of Play

EDITH CAN SHOOT THINGS AND HIT THEM
by A. Rey Pamatmat

Copyright © 2011 by A. Rey Pamatmat. All rights reserved. CAUTION: Professionals and amateurs are hereby warned that *Edith Can Shoot Things and Hit Them* is subject to royalty. It is fully protected under the copyright laws of the United States of America and of all countries covered by the International Copyright Union (including the Dominion of Canada and the rest of the British Commonwealth), the Berne Convention, the Pan-American Copyright Convention and the Universal Copyright Convention, as well as all countries with which the United States has reciprocal copyright relations. All rights, including professional, amateur stage rights, motion picture, recitation, lecturing, public reading, radio broadcasting, television, video or sound recording, all other forms of mechanical or electronic reproduction, such as CD-ROM, CD-I, information storage and retrieval systems, and photocopying, and the rights of translation into foreign languages, are strictly reserved. Particular emphasis is laid upon the matter of readings, permission for which must be secured from the Author's agent in writing.

Required royalties must be paid every time this play is performed before any audience, whether or not it is presented for profit and whether or not admission is charged.

All inquiries concerning rights, including amateur rights, should be addressed to: Samuel French, Inc., 45 West 25th Street, New York, NY 10010, www.samuelfrench. com. All other inquiries should be addressed to: Abrams Artists Agency, 275 Seventh Ave., 26th Floor, New York, NY 10001, ATTN: Beth Blickers & Polly Hubbard.

227

ABOUT *EDITH CAN SHOOT THINGS AND HIT THEM*

This article first ran in the January/February 2011 issue of Inside Actors, *and is based on conversations with the playwright before rehearsals for the Humana Festival production began.*

Edith is twelve. She's Kenny's little sister. He's sixteen, living with Edith 45 minutes from the nearest town, grocery store, or hospital. Their mother is dead and their father is almost entirely absent, save his intermittent ATM deposits and phone calls to make sure there's no reason for him to show up at the house. But Kenny's got his routine, and he's got it down: feed Edith, make sure she's doing her homework, budget food and gas for the week, keep up with his chemistry homework. As Kenny holds the household together, Edith prowls the perimeter with her air rifle and stuffed frog. Enter Benji, the only other sophomore in pre-calculus; he's Kenny's best friend and soon his first love. When their relationship is discovered, Benji is thrown into the siblings' household, sending Edith's protective instinct into overdrive. And when Edith gets the chance to show just how well she can shoot—and hit—things, Kenny's left with a situation his routine can't begin to handle.

Playwright A. Rey Pamatmat writes these characters with wit, insight, and a matter-of-factness that extends to his treatment of their sexuality—the play is far more about being a good boyfriend than the shock of coming out—as well as ethnicity. Kenny and Edith are Filipino-Midwesterners, and this part of their culture shows itself in the food they crave (chicken afritada as well as frozen French-bread pizza) and the stories their mother told them. Their background is as central and invisible to their lives as Benji's culture as a white Midwesterner, with a mom who still makes his lunches and tries to keep him away from his boyfriend's house.

Edith Can Shoot Things and Hit Them is set in the early 1990s on "a remote nonworking farm outside of a remote town in remotest Middle America." It's a setting that Pamatmat is familiar with. "I was a latchkey kid on a farm in rural Michigan," he explains. "My situation was very different, and the play's certainly exaggerated, but I'm interested in the dynamic between these siblings, and how responsibility works when a parent isn't around—how well Kenny and Edith really could take care of themselves in the middle of nowhere. But I also wanted to explore the limits, and the cost, of taking on that responsibility."

Pamatmat theatricalizes their isolation directly. For all the power that the over- and under-involved adults exert over the kids of the play, they never appear on stage. Dad comes through the telephone, Benji watches his mother keep tabs on him from her living room window, and the concerned/nosy mom of Edith's friend calls in to make sure that Edith hasn't gone completely feral. Yet none of these grownups are directly seen. This wasn't Pamatmat's initial plan for the play. "I fully intended for the father to appear at the end of the first act," he says. "It just never happened. I am fascinated by powerful unseen characters, though. When a character doesn't have the opportunity to confront someone, this absence becomes one of the play's obstacles, and it gives us a chance to see the onstage character a lot more clearly."

While the adults' influence looms over these kids, the play itself centers on the makeshift but resilient family that the three teens create, in near isolation from everything that would tell them who to be. Kenny and Benji look to dictionaries and comic books for images of other men in love, and the chance to stake their own claims in undiscovered romantic territory ultimately leads them to form a relationship that best suits them. Kenny and Edith are more loving and functional than any of the other sibling pairs the play mentions, and their isolation feeds their imaginations and ingenuity. Their isolation also forces them to draw lines about how to provide for the family they've created: Kenny's impulse is to manage situations while Edith's is to change them, which by the end of the play involves not only her BB gun and a quiver of arrows, but also bribery, manipulation, petty theft, and arson. "The things you do have consequences," Kenny tries to reason. "The things you don't do have consequences, too," Edith retorts.

And the solutions they hit on, as Pamatmat reveals with humor and honesty, live somewhere between the two points of view. Faced with a situation he can no longer manage his way out of, Kenny has to consider depending on others, just as Benji is given a chance to build a little independence for himself, and Edith is thrown into a world where she can't always hold the gun.

—Adrien-Alice Hansel

BIOGRAPHY

A. Rey Pamatmat recently received the 2011-12 Playwright of New York Fellowship from the Lark Play Development Center. His play *Edith Can Shoot Things and Hit Them* began its rolling world premiere at the 2011 Humana Festival of New American Plays before playing at New Theatre, Actor's Express, Mu Performing Arts, B Street Theatre, and Manbites Dog in the 2011-12 season. His plays have been produced Off-Off Broadway by Second Generation (*Thunder Above, Deeps Below*), the Vortex Theater (*DEVIANT*), HERE (*High/Limbo/High*), and Vampire Cowboys (*Red Rover*). Both *Edith Can Shoot Things and Hit Them* and *Thunder Above, Deeps Below* will be published by Samuel French in 2012. Rey's work has been developed nationwide at The Public, Playwrights Horizons, Ma-Yi, the O'Neill, Victory Gardens, The Magic, Curious Theatre, American Theater Company, Ars Nova, Rattlestick Playwrights Theater, Ensemble Studio Theatre, New Dramatists, and The Lark. He was a recipient of the Princess Grace Fellowship for Playwriting, a New York Foundation for the Arts Playwriting Fellowship, an Ensemble Studio Theatre/Alfred P. Sloan Foundation commission, and is a proud member of the Ma-Yi Writer's Lab. B.F.A.: New York University, M.F.A.: Yale School of Drama.

ACKNOWLEDGMENTS

Edith Can Shoot Things and Hit Them premiered at the Humana Festival of New American Plays in March 2011. It was directed by May Adrales with the following cast:

EDITH	Teresa Avia Lim
KENNY	John Norman Schneider
BENJI	Cory Michael Smith

and the following production staff:

Scenic Designer	Brian Sidney Bembridge
Costume Designer	Connie Furr-Soloman
Lighting Designer	Jeff Nellis
Sound Designer	Benjamin Marcum
Properties Designer	Joe Cunningham
Media Designer	Philip Allgeier
Fight Director	Drew Fracher
Stage Manager	Kimberly J. First
Dramaturg	Michael Bigelow Dixon
Casting	Zan Sawyer-Dailey

Directing Assistant .... Rachel Paul
Scenic Design Assistant .... Ryan Wineinger
Costume Design Assistant .... Lisa Weber
Lighting Design Assistant .... Rachel Fae Szymanski
Sound Design Assistant .... Dan Cassin
Production Assistant .... Lizzy Lee
Assistant Dramaturg .... Mik Mroczynski

Edith Can Shoot Things and Hit Them was produced at the Humana Festival of New American Plays as part of a National New Play Network Rolling World Premiere. The play was first developed in the Ma-Yi Writers Lab and read as part of the Public Theater's 2010 New Work Now! series. It was originally presented by Victory Gardens Theater, Chicago, Illinois, Dennis Zaceck, Artistic Director, Jan Kallish, Executive Director, as part of IGNITION 2010.

CHARACTERS

EDITH, 12, Filipino-American, a girl, KENNY's sister.
KENNY, 16, Filipino-American, a young man, EDITH's brother.
BENJI, 16, any race, a friend.

SETTING

A remote non-working farm outside of a remote town in remotest Middle America.

TIME

The early '90s.

PLAYWRIGHT'S NOTE

Edith Can Shoot Things and Hit Them should be performed by young-looking adult actors, not actual teenagers. The shadows in "For Mother" can be done with puppets, projections, or something else non-human. Please do not use actual people—NO GROWN-UPS!

Teresa Avia Lim
in *Edith Can Shoot Things and Hit Them*

35th Annual Humana Festival of New American Plays
Actors Theatre of Louisville, 2011
Photo by Michael Brosilow

EDITH CAN SHOOT THINGS AND HIT THEM

ACT I

Everyone Says So

In darkness a girl's voice hums "Ein Männlein steht im Walde" from Engelbert Humperdinck's Hansel und Gretel.

Lights rise on a barn with a rafter that intersects with a cross support firmly rooted in the dirt. There are a couple bales of hay and a haystack at its base.

EDITH *sits on the rafter, 10-12 feet above the ground. She is 12 and wears a stained T-shirt, ratty shorts, and is barefoot. She holds a giant stuffed frog to which she is too old to be talking, but she does exactly that.*

EDITH. I am very mature for my age. It's true, Fergie, I am. I look twelve, but I'm really much, much older. Everyone says so.

(EDITH *looks at the frog as though listening to her, pauses, and then punches her in the face.*)

Who cares what you believe? The truth is true. Our kind mature at a different speed than stupid, little human girls. On my planet, I'm a full-grown grown-up, and I have my own apartment where I live without my twenty parents. Who needs them?

(*Pause.*)

Yeah! Twenty people to build one baby, and they all get together to help the baby grow. Feed her and make her clothes and paint her bedroom a different color every month no matter how expensive it is. There's always someone around, because everyone has twenty parents.

But that was when I was small. Now I'm stuck here, alone on this planet as a test. To see—well, I don't know, but it's a test. THAT'S the test: for me to figure out what the test is. And I've got to do it fast, before the evil shape-changing aliens from an enemy planet take over our world!

And Kenny waits to see if I complete the test, which is how he'll know I'm ready to fight in the war. And when I am, I'll sprout wings and fly away! My kind have wings when they grow up.

(*Pause.*)

Well, I mean, I'm grown up now, but when I grow up more, I'll fly away and return to my planet, shoot those aliens in their faces, save Kenny's life, and rescue my twenty parents, who are really, actually helpless without me. And I'm going to do it all by myself.

And when I do, Kenny will stay home because he'll be so proud of me. For being such a big girl. A big, grown-up girl. With wings.

(*End of scene.*)

Liar

Moments later. KENNY *enters and looks up to the rafter, where* EDITH *sits.* KENNY *is 16, a fairly average guy. The most outstanding thing about* KENNY *is the masterful degree to which he doesn't stand out. He's dressed to leave home.*

KENNY. You shouldn't be up there.

EDITH. When is he coming home?

KENNY. How should I know?

EDITH. He tells you.

KENNY. Not always.

EDITH. When I look out the barn door from here, I can see past the hay all the way into the orchard.

KENNY. Will you get down?

EDITH. Last time he was here, it was so annoying. I was practicing my song for choir, but he needed to sleep. He yelled at me, and I was all, "This is homework!" So I came out here, because he's a jerk.

KENNY. He didn't mean it. To yell.

EDITH. Yes, he did.

KENNY. Only because he was tired.

EDITH. So I came out here and sang and sang and sang until my head exploded. And it made me want to fly, so that's when I figured out I could get up here.

KENNY. Don't ever go up there when I'm not home.

EDITH. I'm not going to fall.

KENNY. But what if you do? You shouldn't even be up there now.

(EDITH *tumbles like she's going to fall, but wraps her legs around the support so she just dangles upside down.*)

EDITH!

(EDITH *laughs.*)

If you fall—

EDITH. I WON'T.

KENNY. Accidents aren't on purpose, that's why they're accidents, and if you have one, it'll take the police or an ambulance an hour or more to get here.

EDITH. Forty-five minutes. They'll do the sirens.

KENNY. Forty-five minutes is still too long if your head is cracked open.

(EDITH *makes a siren noise.*)

Get down.

EDITH. He was home anyway.

KENNY. Like that matters. He wouldn't have done anything. When you were little—when we were both little, there were termites in this barn.

EDITH. There were?

KENNY. An infestation of termites that ate through everything, and even though the wood looks fine, the barn isn't. It could fall. That rafter could break. You could fall. At any time.

EDITH. When we were little?

KENNY. Yeah. Yes.

EDITH. We didn't live here. When we were little we didn't even live here.

KENNY. They told us when we got the house.

EDITH. You're such a liar.

KENNY. Can you please come down?

EDITH. What do you think happens when you go out?

KENNY. What do you mean?

EDITH. Why won't your friend come here?

KENNY. We already have plans. I'm going to his—

EDITH. Benji's.

KENNY. His mom would freak.

EDITH. Why?

KENNY. No proper supervision here.

EDITH. He's sixteen. You're sixteen.

KENNY. She's over-protective.

EDITH. And we're under-protected.

KENNY. I protect you.

EDITH. I can protect you, too—

KENNY. Which is why I want you to get down. Because I'm being over-protective.

EDITH. You just want to leave. And you don't want Benji to come over here, that's why you're leaving. And when you do, I'll just be here by myself and anything could happen.

KENNY. But it won't.

EDITH. You don't know.

KENNY. But I trust you.

EDITH. Make him come over. Stay here. There's nobody here.

KENNY. Ed…

EDITH. Kenny…

KENNY. Next time, I'll. I'll try to figure out something next time, if you climb down now.

EDITH. GET down. You can only climb up.

KENNY. I'll ask Benji. Get down.

(EDITH *considers. She gets down.*)

EDITH. What's for dinner?

KENNY. Spaghetti?

EDITH. Pizza. The long ones in the oven, not the microwave ones.

KENNY. We don't have any.

EDITH. Take me to the store.

KENNY. Okay, but we're walking.

EDITH. Why?

KENNY. We're almost out of money.

EDITH. He didn't put any in the bank?

KENNY. Don't worry. He will. He just hasn't yet.

EDITH. Drive me to the store, and I'll walk back by myself. And then you can just go on to Benji's from there. Or I can go with you.

KENNY. You're not walking at night for half an hour by yourself. We'll get you pizza and walk home together. Then I'll go. By myself. And you won't climb up there while I'm gone.

EDITH. Okay, but the long kind. On bread.

KENNY. Get your shoes on.

EDITH. Maybe you should call him.

KENNY. I left him a message.

EDITH. What if he doesn't call back?

KENNY. He will. And if he doesn't, I'll figure it out. I always figure it out, right?

EDITH. Mostly.

KENNY. There will be money in the account tomorrow.

EDITH. He'll forget. Just call. Call Dad.

(*End of scene.*)

Hunting for Gnomes

EDITH *sits on the couch. The TV is on playing a movie like* The Gnomemobile *on VHS. In her lap is sixth grade math homework. Next to her is a partly eaten French bread pizza. Next to that are a remote control, a cordless phone handset, and her stuffed frog. The couch seems huge with her on it all by herself.*

She watches TV. Does a math problem. Eats some pizza. Again.

Time passes. She's completely alone.

The phone rings. EDITH *pauses the movie and answers.*

EDITH. Hello?

Hey. I'm doing it now.

Invert and multiply.

You flip the numerator and the denominator. INVERT.

Dina, this is so basic. This is the review lesson before the actual lesson. This isn't even the sixth grade math part of sixth grade math.

I don't know why it works, it just does. Just do it.

No, I don't want to talk to your mom. Don't. Don't put her—

Hiiiiiii… I'm okay, Mrs. Osheyack.

My dad's at work.

My brother's in the bathroom

Pizza.

Okay, we'll eat healthy tomorrow.

I'm going to bed soon.

He's here; he's just in the bathroom. I'm completely safe. I can take care of myself.

Could you put Dina on?

I hate you.

I'll hang up next time. Tell her to worry about you. You're the one who can't remember fractions.

Invert. Multiply. Reduce. Then you're done.

Yeah, I'm going to bed now.

Okay. See you tomorrow.

> (EDITH *hangs up. She looks around the room, pensively, and then turns to the frog.*)

We're completely safe.

> (EDITH *re-starts the movie, turns up the volume, looks around again, and then exits.*)

TV. OH, WE'LL HUNT FOR GNOMES IN THE COUNTRYSIDE,
OVER HILL AND DALE, BOTH FAR AND WIDE.
AND WE WILL NOT REST TILL WE'VE FOUND A BRIDE,
A GNOME WHO WILL STAND AT CASPER'S SIDE.

IS THAT A GNOME HERE? OR THAT A GNOME THERE?
AND WHEN WE FIND HER WILL SHE CARE,
THAT CASPER IS HANDSOME AND TRUE AND FAIR,
SO SHE'LL HAPPILY BE HALF OF OUR MARRIED PAIR?

> (*As the TV plays, there is noise offstage. A door opening, some rummaging, maybe a trunk opening or a step stool unfolding.*
>
> EDITH *re-enters. In one hand she holds a hand-pumped air rifle; in the other, a hunting bow and some arrows. She uses the remote to turn off the TV and exits the opposite side of the stage [and the house]. End of scene.*)

Changing

> *The next evening. The same couch.* BENJI *stands next to one end, clutching his gigantic book bag.* EDITH *sits on the other end scrambling a Rubik's Cube.* BENJI *will one day go to MIT to become a civil engineer or to RISD to become an architect. Right now, though, he is too thin and too hunched over with hair that's a bit too long, clothes that are too starched, and aviator glasses that are too big for his face. He's 16. A classmate of Kenny's.*

EDITH. Is it a sleepover?

BENJI. Just hanging out.

EDITH. No one's here.

BENJI. Why?

EDITH. No one's ever here but us. You could sleep over, and no one would care.

BENJI. There's school tomorrow.

EDITH. We go to school, too.

BENJI. My mom would worry.

EDITH. Tell her not to. It's safe here. I can shoot things. You're totally safe. I can hit stuff.

BENJI. Why would I…would you do that?

EDITH. Because it's true. We're well-supervised and protected.

> (KENNY *enters with a stack of comic books.*)

KENNY. (*To* EDITH.) Do your homework.

> (EDITH *holds out the Cube.*)

EDITH. Do it.

KENNY. I'm not doing your homework.

EDITH. No this.

KENNY. (*To* BENJI.) You can sit.

(BENJI *does.*)

EDITH. Fix it.

KENNY. You mixed it up, you do it.

EDITH. I can't. Fix it.

BENJI. You can? Let me see.

(KENNY *hands* BENJI *the comics and takes the Cube.*)

KENNY. I'll do it, and then you'll go in the kitchen and do your homework.

EDITH. Okay, okay.

(KENNY *starts solving the Cube.*)

He's not really figuring it out. He uses algorithms. Do you know what that is?

BENJI. That is—they are set series of steps.

EDITH. Right. So if the cube looks one way, he does these steps. If it looks a different way, he does different steps. He doesn't know why he twists one side or the other. He just knows what will happen in the end once he completes the steps.

BENJI. That's still figuring it out.

EDITH. It's like, "If this, then that. If this, then that." Over and over till it's done. Like a computer following a program. He's like a robot. He doesn't even need to think sometimes. He just knows what to do and does it. Barely thinking. Just doing.

BENJI. How did you learn?

KENNY. I got this book and one weekend I just learned how.

EDITH. We didn't have gas, and there was no money left in the bank, so we were trying not to go anywhere.

(KENNY *has finished the first two layers by now.*)

BENJI. Wait. Is it done?

KENNY. Almost.

(KENNY *finishes the last layer as* BENJI *watches, fascinated.*)

There.

BENJI. Wow.

EDITH. Again! One more time.

KENNY. I'm not your monkey. Do your homework.

(EDITH *huffs and goes off.*)

BENJI. That's so rad.

KENNY. You could learn, too. She's right: I'm not thinking, just doing. (*Holds up a comic.*) This is it. Issue 20.

BENJI. Does it hint or does it show it?

KENNY. Actual, full on, lesbian kissing. There are these girls—Kathy and Lenny—and they're traveling across America with this alien guy, Shade. And Kathy's in love with Shade but also feels like she doesn't get him, because, you know—

BENJI. He's an alien.

KENNY. So she ends up hooking up with Lenny. Total girl on girl.

BENJI. You said kissing.

KENNY. Well, they show kissing, but they definitely do more. I mean, there's even an issue where Shade changes into a blanket.

BENJI. What do you mean?

KENNY. That's his power. He changes into things or people. So he changes into a blanket and Kathy and Lenny don't know, and they do it on top of him.

BENJI. Girl on girl.

KENNY. Yeah.

BENJI. Lesbian stuff?

KENNY. Yeah.

BENJI. Wow, that's so—

KENNY. YEAH. And there's one where—

(EDITH *comes in carrying her homework.*)

Kitchen.

EDITH. It's boring in there. I'm doing my homework. I'm just doing it here.

KENNY. (*To* BENJI.) Let's go to my room.

EDITH. NO. Stay here.

KENNY. We're having a private conversation. (*To* BENJI.) Or we could go to the barn.

EDITH. No. You're here, so stay here. I'll go to the kitchen. Just don't leave the house.

KENNY. Okay. We'll be there soon to make dinner.

(EDITH *gets up and goes back into the kitchen.*)

BENJI. You can cook?

KENNY. Yeah. Okay, so there's this other issue where Shade changes into a woman. His power is out of control. And while he's a she, he has sex with this gardener.

BENJI. Who's a guy, I assume?

KENNY. Yup.

BENJI. So, it's like, gay.

KENNY. Not really, because Shade's a woman. But mentally he's a man, and he talks about how it feels having someone inside him instead of being inside someone else.

BENJI. Your dad lets you read this?

KENNY. He doesn't know.

BENJI. Can I read them?

KENNY. Yeah. Take them. I've read all of them.

BENJI. No. Can I read them here? My mom will freak if she sees them. She goes through my stuff, and if she misses stuff, my brother tells her.

KENNY. What a tool.

BENJI. That's what older brothers are like.

KENNY. I'm not.

BENJI. Not in general. But you are to Ed. A little.

KENNY. You said you brought something?

BENJI. I'll show you later. In the barn.

KENNY. No one's here.

BENJI. Ed.

KENNY. Ed doesn't care.

BENJI. I do.

KENNY. We can just go in my bedroom. She's not allowed in there. She knows I'd kill her if—

(BENJI *kisses* KENNY. *It's sudden but seductive.*)

BENJI. I'd rather go out back to the barn. Okay?

(BENJI *kisses him again.*)

KENNY. Okay.

(*End of scene.*)

Interruption

A rotary phone. It rings. KENNY *goes to it.* BENJI *reads comics.* KENNY *pauses, readies himself, and then answers.*

KENNY. Hello?

We're fine. We're about to make dinner. You know how Ed likes that Hamburger Helper with the macaroni and cheese? I figured there must be a way to do it with real cheese and—

Oh, sorry. You tired?

We will.

Wait. Did you put money in the bank last week? It didn't go through if you did. Mostly gas, so we need food.

> (EDITH *pokes her head in the room and watches* KENNY *on the phone, intently.*)

(*In phone.*) Well, I have to pick Ed up from extracurricular stuff. Choir. And there's driving her to practice and voice lessons.

You got two months, after that I used the money in the bank. And we need food.

I will, but you missed a week.

Yes, you did, and we need food.

What should I do? Send her to Mrs. Osheyack's for the weekend again?

> (*Yelling comes from the phone.* KENNY *takes it from his ear and holds it against his chest to quiet the yelling.*)

EDITH. What are you doing?

KENNY. Shhh. Wait one sec.

> (KENNY *puts the phone to his ear again.*)

Sorry. I won't…sorry for my tone.

I'll budget better this week. I will. But we still need something.

Okay. How much?

> (KENNY *gives a thumbs up.* EDITH *is relieved.*)

Okay. Ed's here, so—

Oh. All right. I'll tell her. Thanks.

Bye.

> (KENNY *hangs up.*)

He's busy.

EDITH. Is he at work?

KENNY. No, Chloë's. But he has to rest so he can—

EDITH. I don't care. He paid for six months. Of voice lessons.

KENNY. He doesn't remember. He doesn't really know how much each month cost.

EDITH. Because you got them, right? You told him what to get me for Christmas, and you got them, right?

KENNY. Yeah. Anyway, now he'll put extra money in the bank, and we'll save it in case he forgets again.

EDITH. And now you don't have to tell him you used up gas driving to Benji's every night.

KENNY. We need the money.

EDITH. And now he's here, and you'll have to use more gas driving him home.

KENNY. You wanted me to bring him over, and I did.

EDITH. I know. I don't care.

BENJI. Um...Kenny?

(KENNY *realizes* BENJI *has overheard their conversation.*)

KENNY. Let's start dinner.

BENJI. Should I do something?

EDITH. Can you cook?

BENJI. No. I can...set the table.

EDITH. Table? We eat in the living room with the TV.

BENJI. Only barbarians watch TV while they eat.

EDITH. What?

BENJI. That's what my mom says.

EDITH. Barbarians don't even have TV. Where'd you find this guy?

KENNY. We're the only sophomores in Pre-calc. Go in the kitchen and do your homework. (*To* BENJI.) Could you put those comics in my room?

(EDITH *and* BENJI *go.*

KENNY *looks at the phone. He hates it. He picks up the receiver, pauses, then puts it back down off the cradle.*

He disconnects the phone from the wall. End of scene.)

Science

KENNY *and* BENJI *in the barn, sitting in the hay.* BENJI *pulls a dictionary out of his book bag.*

KENNY. That's what you brought?

BENJI. Yes.

KENNY. I have a dictionary. You didn't have to carry that in your bag all day.

BENJI. But I marked pages.

(BENJI *shows him strips of paper that he's inserted between pages.*)

Pages with key words. Because they exist. Words...for what we do. Are doing.

KENNY. Doing when?

BENJI. You know when.

KENNY. But I want you to say it.

BENJI. Words like, fellatio.

KENNY. "Fellatio?"

(BENJI *turns to the page in the dictionary.*)

BENJI. (*Reading.*) "Fellatio. Noun. Oral stimulation of the penis."

KENNY. I already have a word for that. BJ. Blowjob. A word and an abbreviation.

BENJI. I know what a BJ is, thank you.

KENNY. Exactly. So why do we need a dictionary?

BENJI. Why do we need a comic book with lesbian kissing in it?

KENNY. Because it means that this stuff happens. People kiss people. Not just boys kissing girls or girls kissing boys. People just kiss people. And give them BJs.

BENJI. That's what I mean. There are words for it. And not just crass words or the words they use at my mother's church. These words…"fellatio" is scientific. It's not—there's no. It's not condemning people who do it, and it's not glorifying them either. No bias. There's a scientific word for it, because it is a scientific fact that it happens. And since it happens it needs to be named. And so it is.

(KENNY *kisses* BENJI.)

KENNY. What's the word for that?

BENJI. That's just a kiss.

KENNY. Just?

BENJI. How come we go to my house?

KENNY. I…don't know.

BENJI. Is your dad ever home?

KENNY. Not really.

BENJI. Where is he?

KENNY. Work. Or his girlfriend's. Chloë.

BENJI. So…

KENNY. It's embarrassing. He's never here.

BENJI. That's a good thing. I mean, no interruptions.

KENNY. Most of the time. But then he'll just suddenly show up. We'll come home from school and there he'll be, or he'll get off a late shift at the hospital and just show up here in the middle of the night.

BENJI. But most of the time—

KENNY. Sometimes I just. I want to leave here. That's all.

BENJI. Have you ever run out of money?

KENNY. A couple times. I just send Edith to Dina Osheyack's, and then all I have to do is fend for myself.

BENJI. How come your dad's never here?

KENNY. Look: can I fellatio you now?

BENJI. It's not a verb.

KENNY. So can I give you a fellatio now?

BENJI. It's an act, not an object. Were you even listening to me?

KENNY. Yes.

BENJI. You're making fun of me.

KENNY. Not really. A little.

BENJI. You will not be getting any fellatio today.

KENNY. Oh, really?

(KENNY *starts to rub* BENJI *through his pants.* BENJI *tries to stare at him, stonily, but is failing.*)

BENJI. There are...words. Other words.

KENNY. Like what?

BENJI. Homosexual. That's a scientific word. Not faggot—like burn the faggots. Or gay—like we're carefree and happy and gay. "Adjective. Of, relating to, or having a sexual orientation to persons of the same sex." No judgment. Just a fact. Homo-homosexual.

(KENNY *keeps rubbing, leaning in closer.*)

KENNY. Mm-hmm.

BENJI. And mutual masturbation. Frottage.

KENNY. What else?

BENJI. A...uh. There's, uh...

KENNY. What?

BENJI. Anal. Anal intercourse.

(KENNY *stops.*)

KENNY. Oh.

BENJI. Um, you know what that—?

KENNY. Of course, I do. It's fucking, but... I mean, yeah. It's fucking butt.

BENJI. Right.

KENNY. Have you ever?

BENJI. No. I've never anything. Except.

KENNY. Fellatio.

BENJI. Blowjobs. Yeah. Have you?

KENNY. No. How could I have...?

BENJI. I don't know. I was just asking.

(They *sit quietly not knowing what to do with themselves.*)

KENNY. (*Indicating the dictionary.*) Is there. Is it in there? Anal intercourse.

BENJI. No. But I found a medical book.

(BENJI *takes out a scrap of paper that he scribbled on.*)

(*Reading.*) "Anal intercourse: the sex act involving insertion of the penis into the anus."

KENNY. That sounds. I mean.

BENJI. What?

KENNY. Pretty easy.

BENJI. Yeah. It also…it sounds. Very scientific. We could. Be like scientists.

KENNY. What do you mean?

BENJI. I did research, and we could be like scientists. We could do an experiment.

(BENJI *pulls a bottle of lotion out of his bag.*)

KENNY. Oh, an experiment…?

(BENJI *kisses* KENNY.)

BENJI. Only if you want to. You don't want to?

KENNY. I don't…know if I want to.

BENJI. Oh.

KENNY. But I want…

(KENNY *kisses* BENJI. *He takes off* BENJI'*s glasses and takes* BENJI'*s head in his hands, staring into his eyes.*

20 seconds.)

Okay.

BENJI. Are you sure?

KENNY. Yeah. Okay.

(*They start to make out.*)

BENJI. (*Backing away.*) If you were running out of money, why did you use up gas to come get me?

(KENNY *reaches for* BENJI *and kisses him again. End of scene.*)

Keeping Watch

Outside the barn. EDITH *drags a metal bucket onstage. In her other hand her air rifle and bow. Under her arm is her giant stuffed frog. She flips the bucket upside down and sits.*

EDITH. I don't know what's better, Fergie. Back to back? If we sit right up against the barn, we can sit next to each other and still have a good view of the surrounding area.

(EDITH *pulls the bucket further upstage and then sits on it facing slightly to the left. She positions Fergie next to her facing slightly to the right.*)

This is a very important mission, okay? Keep the intruder inside the barn, by any means necessary. Kill, don't capture, capice?

It won't be hard. Did you see that guy? He's the kind of guy who's allergic to something stupid like peanuts or corn or air or something. He would lose a fight with a mosquito. But that's no excuse to be lazy. He could be a shape-changer—part of the test to see if I'm ready for war! And even if he's not, we've got to be sure he doesn't make trouble. You know what happens when outsiders come here, right?

It's a good thing we're so good at this, Fergie. Because Kenny really isn't. He gets in a tough spot and he won't blast his way through, guns blazing. He doesn't even get himself into tough spots. He just walks around them. But to execute this mission—our mission—you have to stand up and face things and say:

(EDITH *bolts upright and points the rifle at someone.*)

"Hey! Who goes there?"

(EDITH's *eagle eyes pierce through the night. After a moment, she relaxes and lowers the gun.*)

False alarm. Thanks for backing me up, though.

Hey, watch this. See the hay bale?

(EDITH *pumps the rifle and shoots. Sound of a pellet getting swallowed up by straw.*)

Pretty good, right? Okay, okay. Watch this. See the trash can?

(EDITH *pumps. Shoots. Sound of a pellet hitting plastic.*)

One more, one more. That leaf.

(*Pumps. Shoots. No sound.*)

Okay, well. I'm still good, though. I just need more practice.

Anyway, I don't know what Benji's deal is. So till we figure it out we have to keep a close eye on him. This is a very, very important mission, Fergie. Very important.

(EDITH *keeps watch.*

10 seconds.

Lights change, indicating the passage of time. EDITH *has fallen asleep on the ground in front of the bucket. She hugs Fergie to her.* KENNY *and* BENJI *enter, holding hands, and see* EDITH. KENNY *nods to* BENJI *who exits.* KENNY *wakes her.*)

KENNY. Hey. Ed. Eddie.

EDITH. (*Sitting up quickly.*) The mission!

KENNY. Edith.

(EDITH *sees* KENNY.)

Go in the house. I'm going to drive Benji home.

EDITH. I'll come with you. I have to keep an eye on him.

KENNY. He'll get home safe, I promise. Go to bed.

(KENNY *starts to walk off.*)

EDITH. I'm tired of being here by myself. You get to leave, but I'm stuck here.

(*A beat.*)

KENNY. Bring a pillow. Lay down in the back seat and go right to sleep, okay? You can't be falling asleep in school tomorrow. You need to be well-rested, okay?

EDITH. I'll use Fergie as a pillow.

KENNY. Okay.

(EDITH *tries groggily to stand. After a moment,* KENNY *picks her up.* EDITH *wraps her arms around* KENNY*'s neck as he carries her to the car. End of scene.*)

Cleaning the House

The living room. BENJI *sits on the floor in front of the couch doing Pre-calc homework.* KENNY*'s book is next to him, but* KENNY *is not there.* EDITH, *however, is. She watches him, her arms hiding something behind her back. After a few seconds,* BENJI *feels her eyes on him. He looks up at her.*

EDITH. You again.

BENJI. ...Hi.

EDITH. Mm-hmm. You're always here.

BENJI. Studying.

EDITH. Why do you have to study so much?

BENJI. It's an accelerated class. We cover Algebra II and Trig in one class instead of two.

EDITH. It's still a lot of studying. You stupid?

BENJI. Is your brother stupid?

EDITH. No. He's almost as smart as me.

BENJI. Well, we're in the same class, so I guess I must be almost as smart as you, too. That's why we're study buddies.

EDITH. Is that all you are?

BENJI. I… I don't…what do you mean?

EDITH. He's never needed a study buddy before.

(EDITH *takes her arms from behind her back. She holds her bow in them, trained on* BENJI, *who freezes.*)

BENJI. What's that for?

EDITH. Nothing. Do you know Mrs. Osheyack?

BENJI. Mrs.….what?

EDITH. Or Dina Osheyack? Her brother goes to your school.

BENJI. Tom Osheyack? He stuffed me in a locker when I was a freshman, because I wouldn't trade it for his. I hate that guy.

EDITH. Tommy did? Oh… So you aren't friends?

BENJI. Definitely not. Is that okay?

EDITH. I'm friends with Dina, and one time her mom drives me home from choir. And Dina's mom has to pee so bad, she comes in the house. I don't want her to, but she does.

And the house is a mess. She asks, "Is anyone here?" Dad is at work. Kenny is still at yearbook. She gets all weird about it. I show her how when I'm home I microwave food for dinner. Or, if I know Kenny is coming home fast, how I start the rice cooker. But it makes her even more upset, so she plants herself in the living room and waits till Kenny gets home. She even cleans the living room a little bit.

And then she keeps calling, for weeks after that, asking for my dad. And, finally, they talk. And then he yells at Kenny for not keeping the house clean, and then he yells at me for letting someone inside.

BENJI. Your dad sounds—that sucks.

EDITH. So Kenny doesn't really let anyone in the house anymore. And he cleans a lot.

BENJI. It is, yeah, really clean.

EDITH. But he let you in.

BENJI. Oh.

EDITH. Did Mrs. Osheyack hire you to spy on us?

BENJI. No!

EDITH. She's always in our business now.

BENJI. I don't even know her.

EDITH. Maybe Tommy paid you to trick Kenny, so you could—

BENJI. Tommy—Tom wouldn't be caught dead talking to me.

EDITH. Then why are you here?

BENJI. Because Kenny falls asleep in class.

EDITH. No, he doesn't.

BENJI. Yeah. Kenny missed the assignment one day and asked me what pages we were supposed to do for homework. Because he was sleeping.

EDITH. Doesn't he get in trouble?

BENJI. He did once. But he said to Mr. Eaton, "When I stop getting straight A's in Pre-calc, then you can tell me to stop sleeping. But right now, my method is working fine."

EDITH. WHAT?

BENJI. I know. I was amazed. Your brother doesn't like adults that much.

EDITH. I don't, either.

BENJI. So anyway, we kept talking to each other when we didn't get stuff, and then we'd sit together, and then we were friends.

EDITH. You're hiding something. He talks about you all the time.

BENJI. No, I'm... Oh. He does? Good stuff?

EDITH. Yeah. Ever since Mrs. Osheyack, Kenny says no one can know Dad's not here, because they'll split us up. But here you are and you know. It's like you cast an evil spell on him. Or tricked him.

BENJI. Well, I didn't. I just... I'm studying. I wouldn't do anything to...get Kenny in trouble. Or you. Trust me. It's the last thing I'd ever want.

(*10 seconds.* EDITH *lowers her bow.*)

EDITH. Okay.

BENJI. Okay?

EDITH. Yeah. I believe you.

BENJI. Good.

EDITH. Does Kenny talk about me?

BENJI. Yeah.

EDITH. All the time?

BENJI. He said you could sing really well. And he said you like ice cream. Butter pecan.

EDITH. And French Vanilla. But not regular vanilla. I don't know why.

(KENNY *enters with some snacks.*)

KENNY. Dad just called. He wants to know if you learned your music for tomorrow.

EDITH. Liar.

KENNY. Okay, I want to know.

EDITH. Yup. I did.

KENNY. So sing.

(*A beat.* EDITH *considers making something up and then relents.*)

Go learn your music.

(EDITH *sighs and exits.*)

Didn't mean to make you babysit.

BENJI. No, it's cool. Edith's all right.

KENNY. Oh. Okay.

BENJI. Don't worry. I still like you more. I talk about you all the time.

KENNY. Shut up. I don't care.

(KENNY *picks up his book and starts studying, as* BENJI *watches him, smiling.* BENJI *resumes studying, too. End of scene.*)

Showdown

KENNY *wears an open button-down.* EDITH *wears her usual stained, ratty clothes. The rotary phone is between them.* KENNY *puts his hands on his hips.*

KENNY. You cannot wear that outside this house.

EDITH. I can do whatever. I. Want.

KENNY. Change. Your. Clothes.

EDITH. Make me.

KENNY. You really want that? Because I will force a dress on you.

EDITH. I'll tear it off.

KENNY. I'll glue it on you.

EDITH. You can't do that!

KENNY. I have this special glue that will keep a dress stuck on you for a week, and if you try to take it off, it will rip off your skin. So either put one on for a couple of hours, or plan on having one stuck to you for days.

EDITH. You're all talk.

(KENNY *jumps at* EDITH *and chases her around the living room, but she's far too fast.*)

I'll call the police! I'll tell them you touched me in an area covered by a bathing suit!

KENNY. Do it and you'll starve.

EDITH. I'll make pizza. I can walk to the store. I have the other ATM card.

KENNY. Ed, get dressed right now.

EDITH. I don't have to do anything you say. You're not Dad!

KENNY. And it's a good thing, because Dad wouldn't take you to your recital or talk to you at all and you'd just be stuck here by yourself, all the time.

(EDITH *is fuming—she's about to explode.* KENNY *backs off. He starts to button his shirt, tuck it in, and so on.*)

You have to look nice for your recital. There will be pictures. You have your own solo. I'm trying to look nice. See? For you.

EDITH. You need me, too. Don't forget.

KENNY. I know.

EDITH. Without me, he'd leave you here all alone, too. Benji can't replace me.

KENNY. I don't want Benji to replace you.

EDITH. I'm wearing pants. The nice black ones, but pants. No dress.

KENNY. Okay. And brush your hair.

EDITH. I'll put it in a ponytail.

KENNY. Good.

(*A beat.*)

EDITH. Does he even know about my recital?

KENNY. I'm sure he has a good reason for not coming.

EDITH. Like what?

KENNY. It isn't easy for him to get time off work.

EDITH. Max's dad came to parent-teacher conferences, and he's a doctor, too. Dad has to get time off. It's the law. He took time off before Mom.

KENNY. Get changed.

EDITH. He doesn't deserve your loyalty.

KENNY. He's our father.

EDITH. Don't remind me. Remind him that we're his kids.

KENNY. He hasn't forgotten.

EDITH. DON'T DEFEND HIM.

KENNY. We're going to be late for your recital. We'll talk later.

EDITH. I'll be the only one without a parent there.

KENNY. Mom will be there. She's always there.

EDITH. She doesn't count, because she's not really there, is she?

KENNY. Yeah, she is, Eddie. How do you think we've made it this long? Mom's here. And when you sing your solo, she'll be so proud of you.

(EDITH *can't argue with that. She almost goes, but then…*)

EDITH. Can Benji come?

KENNY. You want… Why do you…?

EDITH. Everyone will have a mom and a dad. So I'll have a you and a Benji. It'll be more fun.

KENNY. It'll be fun whether he goes or not. But...I'll ask him. If you want me to. If you want him to come. Do you want him to come?

EDITH. Whatever.

> (EDITH *goes, at last.* KENNY *looks at the phone. He's nervous. He plugs the phone back into the wall and dials. As the rotary dial click-click-clicks,* BENJI *enters. The electronic ring of a phone.* BENJI *takes out a cordless and answers.*)

BENJI. I know it's you.

KENNY. Do you just say that every time you answer the phone?

BENJI. No, I know. The phone rings differently.

KENNY. Do birds suddenly appear?

BENJI. No. Stars light up in the sky.

KENNY. What are you doing tonight?

BENJI. An essay. Position paper.

KENNY. What position?

BENJI. Missionary. Con.

KENNY. Con?

BENJI. Pro doggy-style.

KENNY. It's all you ever think about, isn't it?

BENJI. And getting into a good school.
Hey, did you know that "boondocks" comes from a Filipino word?

KENNY. Okay...

BENJI. Like when you say someone lives in the boondocks. In the sticks. It's because *bundok* is the Filipino word for mountain and the mountains are in the middle of nowhere. American soldiers brought the word over.

KENNY. How do you—why do you know this?

BENJI. I was just reading some stuff. I thought it was cool. You're Filipino, and you live in the boondocks. And...

KENNY. Uh-huh.

BENJI. So...uh, what are you doing tonight?

KENNY. Ed has a thing. A recital. She wants to know if you want to go.

BENJI. *She* wants to know?

KENNY. Yeah. She said, "Is Benji going?"

BENJI. That's weird.

KENNY. Not really. Ed's weird.

BENJI. I know but...wait. Are you asking me out?

KENNY. WHAT? No, I'm not... Ed asked me if—

BENJI. Do you not want to ask me out?

KENNY. No, I just. It sounds weird: "Asking out."

BENJI. It's not any weirder than what we did under the bleachers yesterday.

KENNY. Come to the recital with us tonight.

BENJI. Us?

KENNY. Me.

BENJI. On a date.

KENNY. I... I guess. Really? A "date." Like, two guys on a date?

BENJI. All right. If it's too weird to take me to your sister's recital on a date, then I guess it's too weird for me to give you a hand job under the bleachers tomorrow.

(KENNY *pauses.*)

KENNY. You're like a prostitute.

BENJI. Shut up.

KENNY. You're a hooker.

BENJI. Bye.

KENNY. No, no, no, no. Wait. Okay.

BENJI. Date or hand job?

KENNY. Well, both. I mean, clearly I don't get one without the other. So I'm asking you on a date, to go with me to my sister's recital.

BENJI. Okay. I'd like that. To go on a date. But that doesn't mean I have to give you a hand job in exchange. If I do, it's because I want to. Not because I'm a hooker.

KENNY. Okay, whore. Whatever you need to tell yourself.

BENJI. Jerk.

KENNY. Bye, whore. I'll pick you up in twenty minutes, whore.

(KENNY *hangs up the phone.* BENJI *disappears.* EDITH *enters, half-dressed.*)

EDITH. Did you ask him out?

KENNY. Did I...? Yes. We have to pick him up.

EDITH. Good. It's a date.

(EDITH *grins at him. End of scene.*)

Space is Infinite

The front seat of a car, late at night. KENNY *drives* BENJI *home from* EDITH's *recital.*

BENJI. Space is infinitely divisible. Say, for example, you have Point A and

Point B, and they're ten centimeters apart, and you're going to bring them together by halves.

KENNY. Okay.

BENJI. So do it.

KENNY. So…five centimeters, two-point-five centimeters—or, I guess, twenty-five millimeters. One hundred twenty-five micrometers. Sixty-two-point-five micrometers?

BENJI. Or six hundred twenty-five nanometers.

KENNY. And on and on.

BENJI. Exactly: and on and on. Forever. When will you get to an order of magnitude, a unit of distance, of space that cannot be split?

KENNY. Theoretically, never.

BENJI. Because space is not particulate. There is no elementary particle for space. The distance by halves will never be completely traversed. A and B in theory will never come together, because space is infinite. Theoretically, moving by halves—by any fraction—nothing can touch. They can only connect if they go all the way. Isn't that mind-blowing? That's so cool. See? If you stayed awake in class, you'd know this stuff.

KENNY. Oh, my god. You're ridiculous.

BENJI. It is cool, though.

(KENNY *pats* BENJI's *thigh.*)

KENNY. Okay, okay.

(KENNY *leaves his hand where it is, and* BENJI—*let's face it—is 16 and in love for the first time, so…insta-boner.*)

BENJI. What are… What are you doing?

KENNY. You're such a nerd.

BENJI. No, I'm not.

KENNY. You've tried to seduce me with dictionary definitions, research about the Philippines, and theoretical calculus.

BENJI. Successfully, by the way.

KENNY. I'm not complaining. But don't kid yourself. You're in Band. You play clarinet.

(BENJI *lightly punches* KENNY's *shoulder.*)

Ow!

BENJI. I'm not a nerd.

KENNY. You hit me.

BENJI. Oh, sorry. Just testing the theory.

KENNY. Your theory is stupid.

(KENNY *reaches for* BENJI, *who tries to get away but is, of course, trapped by the car.* KENNY *pulls* BENJI's *head onto his shoulder and kisses it. He leaves his hand in* BENJI's *hair, stroking it gently.* BENJI *stops struggling.*)

You feel that?

BENJI. You didn't traverse the distance by halves. You went all the way.

KENNY. Is that okay?

BENJI. Yeah.

(BENJI *closes his eyes. They drive in silence.*)

KENNY. Huh.

BENJI. What?

KENNY. I told Edith that Mom would be watching her recital, and, in a way, I guess she really was there. Because if the distance between A and B and me and you and everything and everything else is infinitely divisible, then really my mom's only as far from me as you are now. Infinity.

BENJI. What happened to your mom?

KENNY. She left.

BENJI. I thought she died.

KENNY. She did. She loved us all very much. And if it were possible, she would have stayed with us forever. She never would have left any of us.

BENJI. You tell it like it's a story.

KENNY. It is. It's the first lie I ever told Edith. The biggest one.

BENJI. She's not dead?

KENNY. Of course she is. She…left. She… My mom and dad met in med school. Got married. Had us. And then Mom. She felt like my dad was not with her or us. Like he was distant, which he is. If you want proof that space cannot be traversed he's it, and eventually she got tired of it.

BENJI. And she just left.

KENNY. She cheated on him. With my fourth grade teacher.

BENJI. Whoa.

KENNY. And she moved away—Ed doesn't remember this. She was leaving him. She was going to get a place with Mr. Simons. Bill. And then when they were set up, she was going to come get us. But then, a month later, she got her diagnosis.

A brain tumor. And she knew it would be too confusing for Ed and me, both things at once. So she left Mr. Simons and came back to my dad. But only for us. And only to die. She left him. She came back. She left us all. And then he left Edith and me.

(BENJI *takes one of* KENNY's *hands off the wheel and holds it close to him.* KENNY *is uncomfortable.* KENNY *shrugs his shoulder and takes back his hand.* BENJI *sits up on his side of the car.*)

Now you think I'm some kind of freak. Some mopey... I'm not.

BENJI. Okay.

KENNY. And you can't tell Eddie.

BENJI. I won't.

KENNY. You can't tell anyone.

BENJI. Who have you told?

KENNY. No one.

BENJI. Why? You can't just deal with everything all by yourself.

KENNY. Except I do. Most of the time.

BENJI. You don't have to. I could... I don't know.

KENNY. You could what?

BENJI. I...don't know. I.

> (BENJI *stares out the passenger side window. Silence.*)

KENNY. Edith needs Mom to be perfect, you know? To think that she's always watching over her and caring for her. To know that Mom didn't abandon her. Especially since my dad is...my dad.

BENJI. You're not a freak, Kenny. It's okay to miss your mom. If my mom were gone or left... I mean, I can't even imagine life without my mom. And your mom didn't leave you. She was going to come get you. She loved you.

KENNY. Not enough to keep our family together. Edith needs to believe that our family is worth keeping together.

BENJI. She does or you do?

> (*A beat.* BENJI *takes* KENNY's *hand. This time,* KENNY *doesn't pull away.*)

KENNY. I ruined our date.

BENJI. No, you... You told me something you've never told anyone. This is the best date I've ever had.

KENNY. This is the only date you've ever had.

BENJI. Yeah, well, you, too.

> (KENNY *turns the wheel, pulling into* BENJI's *driveway.*)

KENNY. So...here we are.

BENJI. So.

KENNY. Okay, well. I guess... I'll see you tomorrow.

BENJI. Yeah. So...

> (KENNY *leans in.* BENJI *looks panicked, and shrinks back.*)

KENNY. What? I...

BENJI. No, it's. I'm sorry.

KENNY. See? You don't. GOD—I shouldn't—

BENJI. NO. It's... My mom. She watches. Behind the curtain in the front window. She spies.

Last week, Stacy Stroud drove me home from practice, and when I went inside, my mom was like, "Why did Stacy take you home? Is she your girlfriend?" Not only did she see it was a she, she could see who it was.

I really want to kiss you, Kenny. Because of what you told me. But I can't.

(KENNY *turns away from him and stares out the window.*)

KENNY. She's watching.

BENJI. Yeah.

KENNY. Yeah.

BENJI. So I... Tell Edith I said she was great again.

KENNY. I will.

BENJI. First date. No kiss.

KENNY. It's fine.

BENJI. No, it's—

KENNY. I get it. Go. She's watching.

BENJI. Just...go?

KENNY. Go.

BENJI. Okay. I'll just. See you. Tomorrow.

KENNY. Okay. See you tomorrow.

(KENNY *continues to look away, unresponsive.* BENJI *quietly opens the door. He steps out. He's barely holding it together.* BENJI *shuts the door and runs off.* KENNY *puts the car in reverse and pulls away. End of scene.*)

Faith

BENJI *in his bedroom with his Pre-calc text and bag. He listens to a Walkman while writing in his notebook.*

BENJI. (*Singing quietly to himself.*) BUT I GOT TO THINK TWICE,
BEFORE I GIVE MY HEART AWAY.
AND I KNOW ALL THE GAMES YOU PLAY,
BECAUSE I PLAY THEM, TOO.

(BENJI *pushes his book aside and re-reads what he's written.*)

(*Singing, still quietly.*) OH, BUT I
NEED SOME TIME OFF FROM THAT EMOTION,

TIME TO PICK MY HEART UP OFF THE FLOOR.

AND WHEN THAT
LOVE COMES DOWN WITHOUT DEVOTION,
WELL, IT TAKES A STRONG MAN, BABY, BUT I'M SHOWING YOU
THE DOOR.

> (*Singing, getting louder.*)

'CAUSE I GOT TO HAVE FAITH.
I GOT TO HAVE FAITH.
'CAUSE I GOT TO HAVE FAITH FAITH FAITH.
I GOT TO HAVE FAITH FAITH FAITH.

> (BENJI *tears the page out of his notebook and starts to fold it, origami-like, for easy passing in class. Singing, full voice.*)

BABY,
I KNOW YOU'RE ASKING ME TO STAY,
SAYING PLEASE, PLEASE, PLEASE DON'T GO AWAY,
YOU SAY I'M GIVING YOU THE BLUES.

MAYBE
YOU MEAN EVERY WORD YOU SAY,
CAN'T HELP BUT THINK OF YESTERDAY,
AND ANOTHER WHO TIED ME DOWN TO LOVERBOY RULES.

BEFORE THIS RIVER,
BECOMES AN OCEAN,
BEFORE YOU THROW MY HEART BACK ON THE FLOOR…

> (BENJI *has finished folding. He takes the tape out of the Walkman and puts it together with the now folded note. Singing to the note and tape.*)

OH, BABY, I,
RECONSIDER MY FOOLISH NOTION,
WELL, I NEED SOMEONE TO HOLD ME,
BUT I'LL WAIT FOR SOMETHING MORE…

> (BENJI *kisses the note. Singing.*)

'CAUSE I GOT TO HAVE FAITH.
I GOT TO HAVE FAITH.
'CAUSE I GOT TO HAVE FAITH FAITH FAITH.
I GOT TO HAVE FAITH FAITH FAITH.

> (*He closes them into his book and stuffs them into his book bag. When they're safely put away,* BENJI *suddenly breaks out his George-Michael-dancing-with-acoustic-air-guitar moves. Singing and dancing.*)

DOO, doo, DOO, doo, DOO,
DOO, doo, DOO, doo, DOO,
DOO, doo, DOO, doo, DOO,

Duhn, d-duhn, d-duhn, d-duhn duhn...

(BENJI *dances offstage. End of scene.*)

Budgeting Better

KENNY *and* EDITH *in the living room.* KENNY *writes on a tablet.*
EDITH *is playing with her bow throughout. The air rifle lies on the floor.*

KENNY. Do you like school lunch?

EDITH. It's gross. The pizza is like paper and ketchup with dried glue on top, and the fries are raw inside. But I like on Friday when they get fish sandwiches from McDonald's. I like the tartar sauce.

KENNY. What if we made one big thing of food and kept that for lunch all week? Like mongo. Or a big pot of spaghetti.

EDITH. No, the baked kind.

KENNY. Ziti.

EDITH. Yeah! With the cheese on top. I like when you make that. And you know what I can make?

KENNY. What?

EDITH. Tuna salad. I was at Dina Osheyack's house and her mom made it, and it's SO EASY. You cut a celery into little squares, then an onion into littler squares, then you mix it with tuna, mayo, salt, and pepper, and lemon juice if you want. Then you make sandwiches.

KENNY. That's a great idea. So you're okay with packing lunches? It will save us money.

EDITH. Yeah, okay. Why do we need to save money?

KENNY. Same as before. In case he misses a week.

(*Pause.*)

EDITH. And...?

KENNY. Benji's dad is driving him over. He's going to stay with us. For a little while.

EDITH. How come?

KENNY. Because his mother is sick.

EDITH. I know when you're lying now.

KENNY. It's not a lie. She is a sick person.

(*The doorbell rings.*)

I'll be right back.

(KENNY *exits to answer the door.* EDITH *looks at the tablet he's left behind.*)

EDITH. I'll write a grocery list for my sandwiches. Tuna. Onion. Celery. Mayonnaise.

I know what else will save money.

Can you hear me?

It will be automatic, because if Benji stays here, you won't have to use any gas driving to his house.

(KENNY *enters with* BENJI, *holding his hand.* BENJI *looks the worse for wear. His clothes have been thrown on—perhaps his shirt buttons are one buttonhole off. His too-long hair is unkempt. He has been or perhaps still is crying. His backpack is stuffed to overflowing with unfolded clothes.*)

Is your mom that sick?

BENJI. What?

KENNY. Never mind.

EDITH. What happened to you?

KENNY. Ed. Back off. He's a guest.

EDITH. He's staying here now. (*To* BENJI.) You live here now, and you'll be safe, okay? Don't be scared.

(BENJI *sets down his backpack.* KENNY *sits on the couch and pats a spot for* BENJI *to sit.* BENJI *does.* EDITH *perches on the arm of the couch.*)

BENJI. I made a mix tape. (*To* KENNY.) For you. Some songs that made me think of you.

KENNY. Oh. Thanks.

BENJI. I put it in my schoolbag. And I wrote a note to give you with it. To pass to you in Pre-calc tomorrow.

KENNY. And she found it.

BENJI. I'm doing my chores—washing dinner dishes. I go in my room when I'm done, and she's sitting there holding the tape and the note. Her face is all twisted. Disgusted. And then she yells for my dad and brother, and when they come in, she shoves the note at me and goes:

"Read it. Aloud. To your father."

And I read. And she shakes and cries. And my brother swears. And my dad just stands there. I get to the end and I hear this…this crack sound. And she snapped it in half. Your tape.

(BENJI *goes to his bag and pulls out the ruined cassette and the note.*)

I snatched it from her. I don't know why. It's useless now. She tried to take the note, too, but I held onto it, because I had to give it to you.

And then things are so messed up. She tells my brother to take me outside. And he just picks me up and she yells and yells as he takes me out front and throws me out of the house. He actually threw me off the porch. And they go back in, and I don't know what to do, so I just sit there on the front lawn too scared to go back in. And I hear more yelling, until eventually my dad comes out with a bunch of my stuff. He puts me in the car and says he'll talk to her, and if that doesn't work maybe his sister can take care of me for a little while, but is there somewhere I can stay right now? I'm sorry I told him to call you. I don't mean to—

KENNY. Don't be sorry.

BENJI. My dad goes, "I'm going to make sure Mom talks to you tomorrow." But I don't want to talk to her. I don't want to go home, to…with her. I want her to leave me alone.

EDITH. Read the note.

BENJI. Huh?

EDITH. Just do it. Kenny's here now. Read it to him.

BENJI. I don't—

KENNY. It's okay, you don't. Ed…

EDITH. Just read it. It's right there. Just read it.

(BENJI, *still a bit stunned, starts to read the note.*)

BENJI. "Dear Kenny, I don't know if you like all these songs, but they're mostly about not knowing how someone feels. So I really relate to them a lot, because sometimes I wonder what we're doing.

"If you relate, too, then I just want to tell you that you don't have to wonder about how I feel. You should have faith in me, and I hope hope hope that you want me to have faith in you.

"I can't dress stuff up with words like you do. Mostly, what I think or feel just comes out, so here it is. You make me feel really good. I'm happy when we're together. It's hard to concentrate on Pre-calc homework, because you're in that class with me, and college and differential equations just can't compete. I hope you feel the same way. I have a feeling you do. Even if you don't, I hope you at least like the tape.

"Love, Benji."

(BENJI *lowers the note. Silence.* KENNY *stands up and kisses* BENJI.)

EDITH. See? Look what happened. Did anyone throw you out? Or cry? Or anything?

BENJI. No.

EDITH. You read the note, and you're going to stay right here. And Kenny's going to take care of you, like he takes care of me. And I'm going to make sure your mother doesn't come by here and talk to you until you want her to. I'm going to protect you.

(EDITH *puts the bow down and picks up the air rifle.*)

You're safe here. I'm going to secure the perimeter.

    (EDITH *marches out the front door. KENNY picks up* BENJI's *bag.*)

KENNY. We can put your stuff in my room. Come on.

    (BENJI *doesn't move.* KENNY *holds out his hand.*)

Hey.

BENJI. Is it okay that I…what will your dad say?

KENNY. I…don't really care. Now, come on.

    (*End of scene.*)

For Mother

    The next night. EDITH *drags her bucket into the living room along with her frog and air rifle. She keeps watch. She sings "Ein Männlein steht im Walde" to herself.*

EDITH. (*Singing.*)
EIN MÄNNLEIN STEHT IM WALDE GANZ STILL UND STUMM,
ES HAT VON LAUTER PURPUR EIN MÄNTLEIN UM.
SAGT, WER MAG DAS MÄNNLEIN SEIN,
DAS DA STEHT IM WALD ALLEIN
MIT DEM PURPURROTEN MÄNTELEIN.

DAS MÄNNLEIN STEHT IM WALDE AUF EINEM BEIN
UND HAT AUF SEINEM HAUPTE SCHWARZ KÄPPLEIN KLEIN,
SAGT, WER MAG DAS MÄNNLEIN SEIN,
DAS DA STEHT IM WALD ALLEIN
MIT DEM KLEINEN SCHWARZEN KÄPPELEIN?

    (*She sits on the bucket.* BENJI *enters from the bedroom, partly undressed, perhaps an undershirt and pants.*)

BENJI. Where's Kenny?

EDITH. Laundry room. Getting towels.

BENJI. What are you doing?

EDITH. Keeping watch.

BENJI. Is that your job?

EDITH. It's not a job. I just do it. Someone has to keep us safe. What are you doing?

BENJI. I just wanted to… May I have a glass of milk?

EDITH. You don't have to ask permission.

BENJI. My mom usually brings me milk, a glass of milk, when I'm not sleepy.

EDITH. So go get some milk.

(BENJI *considers this and stands a moment uncertainly.*)

BENJI. I thought when I got up this morning or when we got back from school that your dad would be here. When is your dad going to be here?

EDITH. Doesn't matter. He wouldn't get you milk either. You need to take care of yourself.

BENJI. I know, but how do you know how to...to do that?

EDITH. I just do.

Sometimes I go to Dina Osheyack's house, and her mom is always there. She teaches us how to do stuff, helps us do our homework. And it's fun, even though Mrs. Osheyack can be really annoying. She wants to see Dina all the time and hear all about school and stuff.

But Mrs. Osheyack? She's always telling Dina what to do—pick this up and throw this out and show Tom some respect, he has cross-country tomorrow! And, it's like, when she's around, Dina is actually dumber. Dina needs to be told what to do. Dina's mom wants her to be dumb, and Dina wants to be dumb for her mom. Well, I mean, Dina's a little dumb, anyway. But not that dumb.

And your mom? She wants to worry about you, to see and hear you, but only if you're dumb, too. Only if you do the things she wants to see and hear. So she kicked you out, and you're practically a baby. Do you want to be a baby forever?

BENJI. No.

EDITH. Right. You're almost as smart as me, and I don't need anyone. So just do what I do, and you'll be fine. Show her you're fine. Live here and be like me.

(KENNY *enters with some fresh dish towels, as* EDITH *positions herself, sniper-like, on the couch.*)

KENNY. I thought you were going to bed.

BENJI. I'm just going to get myself some milk.

KENNY. Oh, okay. I need to finish in the kitchen, and then I'll come to bed, too.

BENJI. I can help. At home, I usually do the dinner dishes.

KENNY. You don't have to.

BENJI. No, it'll be... It'll feel normal. It'll make me feel normal.

KENNY. It's nice to feel normal sometimes.

EDITH. SHHHHHHHHHH...

(EDITH *raises a hand overhead, commandingly. They freeze. A tense moment, then she lowers her hand.*)

As you were.

KENNY. Ed, don't stay up too late playing.

EDITH. I'm not playing.

KENNY. Whatever you're doing. What do you want for breakfast tomorrow?

EDITH. Fried rice.

BENJI. You eat fried rice for breakfast?

KENNY. Our mom used to make it. (*To* EDITH.) Okay, fried rice. Not too late. You have to catch the bus tomorrow. I'm not driving you.

EDITH. Okay, okay.

(KENNY *and* BENJI *head for the kitchen.* BENJI *lingers.*)

BENJI. Thanks, Ed.

EDITH. For what?

(BENJI *goes.* EDITH *keeps her sights trained on the door. 5 seconds.*)

Fergie. I wish Mom was here.

(*Silence.*)

Now you sound like Kenny. I know she's here, like that. But I wish she was here here. Like, not dead. So she could protect us, instead of me.

(*Lights change, indicating the passage of time. Once again,* EDITH *has fallen asleep by the bucket.*

The sound of a door opening slowly as a shaft of light expands over EDITH's *prone body. Cutting across the light is the shadow of a person. The shadow is huge at first. It hesitates and then, with the accompanying sound of footsteps, it shrinks as the person casting it steps closer and closer to* EDITH.

Suddenly, EDITH *bolts up and grabs the gun. She aims it at the person casting the shadow, who backs up, causing the shadow to grow again.*)

HEY! WHO GOES THERE?

(*The shadow stops.*)

Just back away, lady. Just turn around and go right out the door. NOW.

(*The shadow shrinks, coming closer.* EDITH *pumps the rifle.*)

I said turn around. I'M NOT AFRAID TO USE THIS! I've got a bullet in here just for you...

(*Pumps. The shadow freezes.*)

I SAID GO AWAY. I—we're not defenseless. ARE YOU HIS MOM? Benji doesn't want to talk to you, okay?

(*Pump pump pump! The shadow shrinks more.*)

Go away.

GO AWAY!

I said...

(EDITH *shoots. She hits. The person casting the shadow collapses.* BENJI *enters from the bedroom in only a pair of briefs.*)

Go back in the room.

BENJI. What? Why?

EDITH. Just go…

(BENJI *sees the shot person.*)

BENJI. Ed? What is—? What…happened? What…?

EDITH. KENNY! KENNY!!!

(KENNY *enters, also in briefs, and sees the shot person.*)

KENNY. Ed! What did you do?

EDITH. I shot Benji's mom.

BENJI. What?

EDITH. I did. She wouldn't back away. I shot… And I shot. Her.

KENNY. Give me the rifle.

EDITH. NO!!!

BENJI. Kenny…

EDITH. I told her you didn't want to talk to her, but she just—

BENJI. That's not. I mean.

KENNY. Oh, my god.

BENJI. That's not my mom. That's not her. Not my mom.

EDITH. Then who did I shoot? Why is she here?

KENNY. Oh, my god. That's. That's Chloë, Edith. Remember from dinner? She and Dad—that's Chloë. That's Dad's—

EDITH. SHE WOULDN'T BACK AWAY. It's…her? It is?

(KENNY *stops as another shadow fills the shaft of light.* EDITH *screams, startled.* BENJI *jumps for* KENNY, *half clutching him, half covering them both up.* KENNY *pulls* EDITH *toward them. They all cower fearfully.*)

Daddy?

(*End of scene. End of Act One.*)

ACT II

Scared Robot

KENNY, EDITH, *and* BENJI *sit at a round table in an ice cream parlor. They eat ice cream cups in silence—Rocky Road, Butter Pecan, and Strawberry Cheesecake respectively. They look very, very tired.*

EDITH. Can you have butter pecan ice cream without the ice cream?

KENNY. Yeah. They're called wet nuts.

EDITH. Wet nuts? That doesn't sound all that good.

BENJI. I love wet nuts.

KENNY. Even now, that's all you can think about.

BENJI. Especially now.

EDITH. What is?

KENNY. What is what?

EDITH. All he can think about.

BENJI. Wet nuts.

KENNY. Stop it.

BENJI. Even dry nuts would be nice.

EDITH. You mean dry roasted?

BENJI. Hey, Kenny, let's get our nuts.

(KENNY *slams down his ice cream and walks away, exiting the parlor.* EDITH *and* BENJI *each eat a spoonful.*)

EDITH. I wouldn't have shot her if I knew who she was.

BENJI. He's mad at me, not you.

EDITH. He's mad at me, and you're standing in the way.
If he stood up to things, I wouldn't have to. And then I wouldn't mess things up. If he had his way, we'd just be quiet and alone on that farm. Till we died. Surrounded by hay and grass and nothing.

BENJI. He's trying. To take care of you.

EDITH. I can take care of myself.

BENJI. Ed, you shot your future stepmother. She went to the hospital to get a pellet removed from her shoulder.

EDITH. She should have backed away. And she's basically a stranger. He should have called us and told us she was coming.

BENJI. He said he tried, but the phone was unplugged.

EDITH. And anyway I didn't mean it; I was protecting you.

BENJI. Except you didn't shoot—she wasn't even my—

EDITH. I thought I was protecting you, okay? You should be thankful. That's what I'd do for you. Kenny would just slither away, like he did just now.

BENJI. I don't really want you to shoot people for me. Not even my mom.

EDITH. Why? You want to shoot her yourself?

BENJI. No.

EDITH. What if she were going to shoot you?

BENJI. She would never do that. She's my mom.

EDITH. She's sitting at home right now with no idea whether you're eating, whether there's a roof over your head, whether you're even alive. You think someone capable of that could never shoot you, just because she gave birth to you?

BENJI. Stop it.

EDITH. Even if she loves you, her love doesn't mean anything. When it matters, it doesn't mean a thing.

> (KENNY *re-enters.* EDITH *and* BENJI *clam up.* KENNY *walks deliberately to the table and sits. Without a word, he starts eating his ice cream again.* EDITH *stares angrily at* BENJI *as she rapidly shovels the rest of her ice cream into her mouth. When she finishes, she turns to* KENNY.)

I'm cold. I left my coat in the car.

> (KENNY *hands her the keys.* EDITH *exits.*)

BENJI. I'm sorry. I was trying to make you laugh.

KENNY. No, it's… I'm sorry. It's hard to laugh right now.

BENJI. Okay, so what should we do next?

KENNY. I don't know. I wasn't thinking. She shot Chloë and I switched into automatic. I thought, while he brings Chloë to the hospital, get Edith in the car and out of there as fast as possible. But that… That was all. It's just…the way he screamed at her. And the way she screamed back. And the rifle, still in her hands. I was like, "She's going to shoot him. Ed'll shoot him, too." Which is ridiculous.

BENJI. I can see why you would have thought that.

KENNY. But now, we've been sleeping in the car for two days, we can't keep skipping school, and we only have money for a week, at most. And I don't… It's like I got us in even deeper trouble than we were. I'm such a. GOD— WHAT A FUCKING LOSER. I'm such a fucking idiot.

BENJI. You're not an—

KENNY. We don't have anywhere to live. I don't make any money. I can't take care of us. Of her. I don't know how. I look like I've got it together, but Ed's right: I'm a robot who learned a program. If this, then that. But I'm not programmed for this. We're trapped in that house, and now that I got us out,

I don't know what to do or where to go.

(*A beat.*)

BENJI. You know the first thing Ed said to me?

KENNY. What?

BENJI. She walked right up to me and went, "I can shoot things. I can hit stuff."

KENNY. Well, she wasn't lying.

BENJI. Totally. I could never shoot someone.

KENNY. I'm glad. I don't want you to shoot anyone.

BENJI. And, like, when you're planning what groceries to get so you can make dinner and lunch and all the food for the week? I can't do that. I couldn't take Ed to school and extracurriculars and still get straight A's in Pre-calc and Chem.

KENNY. I got a B in Chem.

BENJI. I couldn't do half the stuff you can do. My mom tells me what to wear, and when kids used to be, like, "Your mom dresses you. Loser!" I didn't know why that was an insult, because I didn't really know that other people could do stuff. The only food I can make is a bowl of cereal. I still have my learner's permit. My mom does everything for me. Did.

KENNY. Do you miss her?

BENJI. No. Not…not really.

KENNY. Then why are you telling me this?

BENJI. Because you're not a loser.

You and Edith. You're all alone in that house and sometimes it's creepy and sometimes you're running out of money, but you can take care of yourselves. I would just be helpless. Or scared.

KENNY. But I am. I'm really scared, Benji. What have I gotten us into? Fine. Edith can shoot things and hit them. But she shouldn't have to shoot things. And I'm not a robot. I should be allowed to be scared sometimes instead of always fixing things. I just want to sit and be scared and for things to be okay.

(BENJI *brushes his fingers against* KENNY's *hand.*)

BENJI. Okay.

(BENJI *slips his hand under the table.* KENNY *does, too, so they can hold hands.*)

KENNY. What if people see?

BENJI. The only person I care about now is you. So don't look at anyone but me. Just be scared for a minute. Okay? Be scared. And then we'll figure out what to do. And I'll help. I can help. You won't have to do it by yourself.

KENNY. Okay.

(*10 seconds.* KENNY *really does look terrified.* BENJI *squeezes his hand, and after a moment the fear starts to fade.*)

SHE SHOT HER.

(*They both start to laugh, uncontrollably.*)

BENJI. Edith shot your stepmother.

KENNY. Potential stepmother. Or, I mean, formerly potential stepmother. I can't imagine she'll want anything to do with us now.

BENJI. Why, because she walked into the house and got shot in the shoulder with a BB?

KENNY. And the part where she walked in on my boyfriend and I in our undies.

BENJI. Maybe that'll be a plus in the whole, "Should I be a stepmother?" debate. Con: stepdaughter with air rifle. Pro: stepson who looks good in undies.

KENNY. That's just…EW.

(*A beat.*)

I should take you home.

BENJI. What?

KENNY. To your dad. You should go home, Benji. It's our mess.

BENJI. I don't want to. I'm going to help. You'll see.

(EDITH *enters, wearing her coat, looking utterly defeated. She's been crying.*)

EDITH. He's standing at the car.

He says you have one chance to walk out on your own, bring me with you, and drive back home.

He says if you don't, he'll tell the police that you kidnapped me and stole the car. He said Benji's mom wants to tell the police that we kidnapped Benji.

(*Silence.*)

KENNY. We're trapped.

(KENNY *stands up.*)

EDITH. Don't do it, Kenny, please. Let's sneak out the back or something. Don't.

(KENNY *heads for the door.*)

Don't, Kenny. PLEASE. PLEASE!!!

KENNY. We're going back. If the police get involved and catch us, they could take you away from me.

EDITH. They won't catch us. Let's run. Let's fly away.

KENNY. Edith, we're kids. We're just kids.

(KENNY *takes* EDITH*'s hand.* EDITH *reaches out to* BENJI, *who takes her other hand. All three look petrified as they exit the ice cream parlor. End of scene.*)

Uniform

(EDITH *stands in the living room.* KENNY *enters with a girl's school uniform, which he helps her into. It's like a Catholic school uniform, but even more drab, sexless, and depressing.*)

EDITH. Where is he?

KENNY. He'll be here tomorrow morning to drive you to the school. Are you packed?

EDITH. Yes. What about you?

KENNY. He wants me to stay here. Or, I mean, at my school. Now you get to leave, but I'm stuck here.

EDITH. I hate him, Kenny.

KENNY. Don't say that, Ed. You can't hate him.

EDITH. He's splitting us up.

KENNY. He can't split us up.

EDITH. He is.

(EDITH *is now dressed. She looks ridiculous, like a wild animal on a leash.*)

KENNY. It looks...all right.

EDITH. It looks stupid.

KENNY. It looks stupid.

EDITH. Let's get out of here. We'll get in the car, but we'll do it right this time. We'll drive and drive and drive until we never have to see him again.

KENNY. I'm going to tell you a story.

EDITH. I don't want any more of your stupid stories.

KENNY. It's Mom's story. She told it to us when we were little. You're too young to remember.

There's this turtle and this monkey, who is always trying to trick the turtle but never quite manages to, because he's too clever and patient. Like this one day, they fight over who gets to keep a banana plant they found. The monkey threatens to take the whole tree, but the turtle says, "Let's split it in half. Pick the half you want." So the monkey chops off the top of the tree, runs home, eats all the bananas, and thinks, "That stupid turtle. Hungry and sitting in the sun."

But the next time the monkey sees the turtle, he's napping under a beautiful banana plant with lots of fruit and foliage, because the turtle was clever.

EDITH. He kept the bottom of the tree and planted it.

KENNY. And patiently waited for it to grow. Right. So, envious of the new tree, the monkey scrambles up its trunk and eats all of the turtle's bananas and then falls asleep.

Finally, the turtle decides to teach him a lesson. He surrounds the tree with thorny branches and yells, "Crocodile! Crocodile!" until the startled monkey bolts awake, runs down, and gets stuck with thorns. In a fury, the monkey snatches up the turtle and says, "For that, I'm going to kill you!"

"Please don't!" says the turtle.

EDITH. I don't like this monkey.

KENNY. "I could smash you on the rocks or rake you over hot coals! Or I could drown you in the ocean!" The turtle knows he's too slow to run away, so he begs, "Don't drown me! Smash me or throw me in the coals—just don't drown me!"

And with that, the monkey bolts for the ocean, tosses the turtle in, and sits back to laugh as he drowns. But, of course—

EDITH. The turtle swims away.

KENNY. Because he's a slow turtle, too little to break free. But he's clever and patient, so he just waits for the monkey to set him free. You see?

EDITH. Yeah. Better than you do.

Mom is dead, Kenny. You can't just pull her out when you want me to feel better.

KENNY. I'm not. I don't do that.

EDITH. Yes, you do! When I won't do what you say, you make it what she says to get your way. She's not one of your lies. She's our mom. And she can't help us anymore.

KENNY. She is helping us. And this time you better let me get my way.

Dad could do a lot worse than this school, and he still might. You shot someone. You could be locked up in juvie or drugged up in some hospital for crazy kids. We can't let this get any worse.

So you do what I tell you and lay low. Go to this school. They'll try to tell you what to do: what to wear, how to eat, when to get up, and when to go to bed. Let them. Hide. Be patient, like the turtle. Just be a little bit like me.

EDITH. Clever. And patient. Maybe you have to be a little bit like me. To stop him. You cannot let him kick me out of this house.

KENNY. He's Dad.

EDITH. If you don't do something, I will.

KENNY. No. The things you do have consequences.

EDITH. The things you don't do have consequences, too.

KENNY. We didn't get into this mess because of something I didn't do. Wait until I figure this out, or he comes to his senses.

EDITH. WHAT? He's not going to just wake up and say, "I made a big mistake!"

KENNY. We don't know that.

EDITH. You're glad he's getting rid of me.

KENNY. SHUT UP.

EDITH. You leave all the time. To go to Benji's. To get away when he comes home. You don't want me here. You're just like him.

KENNY. I am your brother, and I love you.

EDITH. SO HELP ME. Help me or you're going to be stuck here by yourself all the time and—

KENNY. How am I supposed to help you, when I can't even help myself? I'm sixteen, Ed! And he's Dad. I can't fight him. I can't keep you out of trouble or stay awake in class or stop Benji's mom. I can't even make you catch the bus. I can't!

EDITH. I catch the bus. Most of the time.

I wish Mom was here to tell us stories or to teach us how to make tuna fish sandwiches or to worry about me staying out too late. Or sometimes I wish Dad would do those things. But they won't. They're not here.

You are. And I am. And one of us has to stop him.

(KENNY *is silent, helpless before her.*)

Forget it. I don't need you.

KENNY. Eddie.

EDITH. Let him send me to that school, and I'll get out before you know it. That's how clever I'll be.

(*End of scene.*)

Fixing It

The living room a week later. KENNY *does Pre-calc homework. The cordless phone is nearby. There's no sound other than his pencil on paper.*

KENNY *stops and looks around as if there should be someone there, but there isn't. No one is there. Time passes. He's completely alone.*

He takes something out from under the front cover of his textbook. A worn piece of paper, BENJI*'s note.*

KENNY. (*Singing.*) WELL, I GUESS IT WOULD BE NICE,
IF I COULD TOUCH YOUR BODY.

(KENNY *sets the book aside and dials the phone. Into the phone.*)

Hi. Is Benji there? I mean, Ben. It's Kenny.

Oh.

Okay. He can call back after dinner, I'll be home.

Oh.

Okay. Thanks, Mrs.—

(KENNY *is hung up on before he can finish. He leans back on the couch and starts to read the note.*

Suddenly, the TV flips on.)

TV. IS THAT A GNOME HERE? OR THAT A GNOME THERE? AND WHEN WE FIND HER WILL SHE CARE…

(KENNY *sits up, stuffs his hands between the cushions, and pulls out the remote control and the scrambled Rubik's Cube. He flips off the TV. A beat.* KENNY *picks up the phone again. Dials.*)

KENNY. (*Into the phone.*) Hi. Ed Tolen—Edith Tolentino, please.

Her brother. Kenny.

Oh. When can she receive phone calls?

Okay. Thanks.

(KENNY *hangs up and looks at the Rubik's Cube.*)

Fix it.

(*With several deft moves,* KENNY *solves the Cube. He stares into space. He stares. And stares. And stares. End of scene.*)

Making Passes

The sound of a school bell ringing. KENNY *and* BENJI *on opposite sides of the stage.* BENJI *pulls out a note folded like a football. As he opens it and starts to read,* KENNY *speaks its contents aloud.*

KENNY. Benji—Since when does Tom Osheyack care if we're hanging out? I can only surmise that Tom has a deep, unrequited (question mark) crush on you. The sight of me talking to you fills his spleen with jealous bile that courses through his veins and drips out of his every pore.

Meet me in the parking lot after school, and I'll give you a ride. I'll drive you home, too. —Kenny

(*School bell. They take a step closer to each other.* KENNY *pulls out a note folded like a ninja star. As he opens it and starts to read,* BENJI *speaks its contents aloud.*)

BENJI. Ken—My brother is on wrestling and cross-country with Tom. My mom doesn't want me talking to you, and he told his friends to help keep us separated. I was home when you called last night, too, but she wouldn't let me have the phone.

Believe me, the only thing boner-inducing about Tom Doucheyack is the idea of you punching him, so his love will have to stay unrequited.

Also, my brother is driving me home. We're going to have to be even sneakier than usual. —Ben

(*School bell. Step.* BENJI *reads the note in his hands;* KENNY *speaks its contents.*)

KENNY. B—Your mom sucks. And I refuse to believe that you and your brother are actually related. Although it's kind of sexy all this sneaking around, don't you think? —K

(*School bell. Step.* KENNY *reads;* BENJI *speaks.*)

BENJI. Ken doll—Not as sexy as me doing this to you.

(BENJI *draws a lewd picture in the air.* KENNY'*s eyes bug out of his head.*)

As you can surmise, I need to see you and not just in Pre-calc. What do we do? —Big Ben

(*School bell. Step.* BENJI *reads;* KENNY *speaks.*)

KENNY. Benjamin—We can meet up sixth period away from prying eyes. Ask Ms. Olds if you can spend study hall doing research in the library. She'll let you—you're too sweet to be untrustworthy. I'll get out of Comp by saying that I want to go to guidance. With everything that happened to Edith, there's no way Ms. Seaver will say no. I'll meet you in the library by the science books. Biology. Barely anyone goes to that back table.

No one will keep us apart. They can try all they want. But Edith's gone, and you're all I've got. She's really gone. —Kenneth.

(*School bell. Step. They now stand next to each other. Pre-calc. They stow their notes and then* BENJI *pulls out a new note folded into a heart. They hold their arms out,* BENJI *drops the note, and it lands in* KENNY'*s hand.* KENNY *reads;* BENJI *speaks.*)

BENJI. Kenny—Good plan. I don't know how you come up with this stuff. Have you ever lied to me?

(KENNY *looks up at* BENJI.)

And they are keeping us apart, aren't they? Why? We aren't hurting anyone.

See you in the library. I will now spend the rest of Pre-calc trying not to look like I'm gazing longingly at you. —Benji

(KENNY *stows the heart note, writes in his notebook, and turns it to* BENJI. BENJI *reads;* KENNY *speaks.*)

KENNY. I have never lied to you. I never will. Can't wait for the library. I'm going to gaze longingly at you right now.

(BENJI *looks up at* KENNY. *End of scene.*)

Going Solo

(EDITH *in a schoolyard. She's dressed to leave and talking to the frog.*)

EDITH. Okay, Fergie. This is probably our biggest mission ever, and it's not that I think you can't handle it… But we have to execute every stage with utmost precision, or it's over before it even starts. It's just me and you now. You're all I have.

You.

A stuffed frog.

From my mom. My mommy.

Let's review the mission parameters. To blow this joint, what we have to do is—I mean, what you have to do. I don't know what you have to do. What I have to do is…

Stop talking to a stupid stuffed frog who never really did anything.

Maybe, Fergie, it's time for me to go it alone. I don't think Mom really gave you to me anymore, and that when I talk to you I'm talking to her. I'm not talking to anyone.

Because Kenny is a liar. He lies, and it's not funny anymore. He tells stories, like that Mom got us all Christmas presents before she died. And that Dad asks about me when he calls. And that he's going to come and get me. Because Kenny's not going to come and get me. The only person who can take care of me is me. I've got to do this all by myself, like I have to do everything. No Kenny, no Mom, and no you. I'm going solo.

I don't need you, frog.

(EDITH *puts the frog on the ground and turns away.*

10 seconds.

EDITH *turns back to the frog, snatches her up and holds her at arm's length.*)

It's just… I. I'm alone now, Fergie. And I had to. It was a test. Because what we're doing is dangerous and important and probably illegal. So I had to know I could trust you. Because it's hard to know who to trust now that we're all alone. Because this…this is the test. THE test. Kenny can't come, because I have to prove to him that I'm a grown-up. That it's time to grow my wings and fly away. Fergie, we have to get rid of any parts of us that are still little girls. No more useless, weak, little girls. I'm going to take care of everyone. You. Kenny.

Even Benji.

But first we have to make sure that he's taken care of. Permanently. Make sure he can never leave us in a place like this again. Never, ever again. So I had to be sure that we were in this together no matter what.

> (EDITH *takes some matches out of her pocket, strikes one, and watches it burn.*)

Here we go.

> (*End of scene.*)

Curly Fries

> KENNY *and* BENJI *sitting at a table in the school library.* KENNY *has a few books.* BENJI *has his usual gigantic, overstuffed backpack.*

KENNY. Come over.

BENJI. I'm not supposed to.

KENNY. I liked it better when she'd given up on you.

BENJI. Me, too. At least we were getting laid.

Dad says it's not punishment; I'm just not allowed to leave because we all need to spend more time together. But when he goes to work, Mom barely speaks to me, because to her it IS punishment. And my stupid brother is just a dick. He tries to push or kick or hit me, and then he says something lame to piss me off like, "Fag!" or "Pussy!" or "Jesus saves!" And she lets him. So I tell him to quit touching me or he'll get my gay cooties. And then he walks around like some big stud being all, "I'm not queer. I screwed Jemma Lieber." And I actually think, as of two days ago, he is screwing Jemma. But my Mom won't say a word, because it comforts her. Like her oldest son is more of a man because he's boning a brainless perpetual shopping machine.

KENNY. God.

BENJI. So then I go, "You know what makes you a man? Taking it up the butt—if you can do that, you can do ANYTHING."

KENNY. WHAT?!

BENJI. Yeah. And then my brother punched me in the gut. And my mom locked me in my room. My mom will never let me go to your house again.

> (BENJI *takes the sleeve of* KENNY'*s shirt between his fingers, trying to look casual.*)

But we'll always have Pre-calc.

KENNY. So romantic.

BENJI. And maybe... My dad. He's taking me to dinner on Thursday. Just me and him. To A&W. I like the curly fries.

Do you want to come?

KENNY. With your dad?

BENJI. Yeah. He…wants to meet you. "He's your boyfriend. Shouldn't I meet your boyfriend?"

KENNY. Are you serious?

BENJI. You called me your boyfriend. When we got ice cream. I didn't—you said it, and I…

KENNY. Oh.

BENJI. I shouldn't have taken it so seriously. You were freaking out, but I…

KENNY. Okay.

BENJI. Yeah?

KENNY. Thursday. A&W. Will you pick me up, or should I drive?

BENJI. We'll pick you up. And he'll probably pay for everything, so…

KENNY. So…another date.

BENJI. Yeah. Sort of. With a chaperone.

What did your dad say? He saw us that night, so he knows.

KENNY. Yeah. He asked who you were. I told him. And he just…stared at me. Blankly. Like he…he didn't care.

BENJI. He's such a jerk.

KENNY. He's my dad.

BENJI. Can't you just say he's a jerk? Why do you defend him?

KENNY. Now you sound like Ed. Whatever. I don't care what he thinks. It's better if he doesn't care. If he leaves us alone.

BENJI. Your dad doesn't care enough. My mom cares too much.

KENNY. Yeah, right? Anyway, what's important now is Ed. I need to get her out of there, but I don't know how.

I used to leave her alone, Benji. And now I'm there alone, and it's so quiet. Edith used to watch the same stupid movies over and over again—like this gnome musical thing. And I never knew why. But now I know. Without her there's nothing there.

But what can I tell my dad so he'll take Edith out of that school? Nothing I come up with seems good enough to do the job.

BENJI. That's your answer. There's nothing to come up with. There's no story to tell.

KENNY. I can't just leave her there.

BENJI. Don't. Tell him that he can't leave her, because…he can't. You need to help your sister. And you need to stop telling stories to pretend your dad's not a jerk or to avoid confronting people or just to get your way.

KENNY. No, I have to at least… I can't stop—

BENJI. Kenny, if you don't, then you will one day, eventually, lie to me.

KENNY. No, I won't.

(*Pause.*)

I won't!

BENJI. Tell him the truth, Kenny.

KENNY. I…I don't know how to do that.

BENJI. You'll figure it out. You take it up the butt, remember? You can do anything.

(BENJI *tugs at* KENNY's *shirt again.*)

KENNY. I think about how you smell. Is that weird?

BENJI. How do I smell?

KENNY. Like Ivory soap. And dryer sheets.

BENJI. I think about your hand on the back of my head. Your fingers in my hair. I really want to kiss you, Kenny.

KENNY. Your brother might see. He'll tell your mom.

BENJI. She can't treat me any worse than she's already treating me.

KENNY. Benji, let's at least—we'll go somewhere, or—

(BENJI *kisses* KENNY.)

BENJI. I don't want us to hide. I don't want you to hide.

Tell him the truth. They threw us out, or threw us away. They have no right anymore to tell us what to do.

(*End of scene.*)

Wild and Free

KENNY *and the phone. He reconnects it to the wall. It starts to ring immediately. Surprised,* KENNY *waits a moment and then answers.*

KENNY. Eddie?

Oh. Hi. I was just about to call you. We need to—NO. Wait!

(*Yelling from the phone.* KENNY *takes it away from his ear, steels himself, and then brings the phone back in.*)

LISTEN TO ME. IF YOU WON'T TELL US WHAT TO DO SO THINGS GO RIGHT, THEN YOU CANNOT TELL US WHAT TO DO WHEN THINGS GO WRONG.

You have to take Edith out of that whatever you've sent her to. I mean, reform school? She has perfect grades, she sings choir. She has good friends. You put me in charge, so I'm in charge. Understand? You aren't a parent. You're an interruption. I take care of this house and of Edith, so I decide whether she lives here and how. So before this goes too far, bring her back here or you will never see her again.

That's not a threat.

You made us. You raised us to need nothing except the money in the bank. We used to want you to come back. But now when you're here all we want is for you to leave. I took what you left us and made a home. Our home. We don't need your supervision or your new girlfriend or your decisions about reform school. I can get us everything we need. Without you. You left us wild and free. You can't cage us now.

So if you don't want to lose us forever, call that school and bring Edith home. Now. She doesn't need to be reformed. She's Edith. And she's twelve years old. She needs to come back to her home.

(KENNY *listens.*)

What?

That school is supposed to be a prison.

(KENNY *listens.*)

Wait.

Don't worry. I'll find her. You don't even know where to look.

(KENNY *hangs up the phone. End of scene.*)

Fly High As the Sky

The barn. KENNY *stands next to the haystack at the foot of the rafter and its support. In his hand is a plate with a tuna salad sandwich on it.*

KENNY. How long have you been here?

(*The sound of a match being struck. A lit match flies from behind the rafter onto the floor of the barn.* KENNY *stomps it out.*)

Eddie.

(EDITH *appears from behind the cross support. She perches on the rafter.*)

EDITH. Is he home?

KENNY. No.

(EDITH *lights a match and throws it to the ground.* KENNY *stomps it out.*)

Stop it.

EDITH. That school was like a prison, except no one did anything cool like rob someone or kill someone or something. They just beat up a third grader or flashed their panties at the wrong person. And the other girls there are retarded. Does he think I'm retarded?

KENNY. Of course not. And you shouldn't say that. They're troubled.

EDITH. I'd be troubled, too, if I was retarded. Some of them can't even read or spell. They're the same age as me, but they can't. And some of them just stare like zombies, until you tell them what to do, and then they do as they're told. And the other ones are big, brutish, ogre girls. They're loud and stand up for themselves, but they're too dumb to know what they're standing up for.

I can do fractions and decimals and negative numbers. I learned all that German for my choir solo. I can shoot an aluminum can from fifty feet away.

Is that what he thinks I am: troubled?

KENNY. You shot Chloë.

EDITH. I tried your way the first couple of days. And it worked: they trusted me. But I couldn't take those other girls and all the adults kept telling me what to do. They were easy to trick, because they're used to matching wits with those troubled girls. Not with me.

One girl was there for setting stuff on fire. She hid all these boxes of matches in her rolled up socks. So I stole a box and, before she could see any were missing, I reported her to the teachers. The next day, I packed a bag and set the trash behind the kitchen on fire. They went after the other girl, and I walked right out of there.

KENNY. How'd you get home?

EDITH. I hitchhiked to the bus station. Then I used the other ATM card to get money, buy a ticket, and pay Dina Osheyack's brother so he would pick me up at the station.

Is he here? Did they call him?

KENNY. Yes. But he doesn't know you're here.

EDITH. Where else would I go? I don't know how to go anywhere else. But you know what I realized? I shouldn't have to.

KENNY. You want to see him?

EDITH. I hate him. I'm going to surprise him. This is our house, Kenny. He can't kick me out. He's never here. I'm going to kick him out.

KENNY. That will definitely be a surprise.

(EDITH *starts to light another match.*)

(*Stopping her.*) Ed, I have a sandwich for you. I made tuna salad this morning.

EDITH. You did?

KENNY. Yeah. Your recipe. I wanted to get it right for when you came back.

You want it?

EDITH. When he gets home, I'm going to set his room on fire. And if he won't leave, then you and me can just get in the car and fly on out of here.

KENNY. I don't think that's what you really want, Ed.

EDITH. Sure it is. I'm not going back there.

KENNY. You don't have to. I told you to wait till I took care of everything, and I have.

EDITH. Liar.

KENNY. You can tell when I'm lying, right? So listen to me now: I told him I won't let him do this to you. To us. You're not going anywhere and you don't have to run away, okay?

Now just get down, eat this sandwich, come into the house, and then watch some TV while I make dinner.

EDITH. He sent me to that place. That's what he thinks I am. That's probably what he thinks you are. That's why he never comes here.

Three hours in that car with him, the most time we've been together in years, and then he just leaves me there. Drops me off, like he's taking out the trash.

(EDITH *stands on the rafter.*)

He'll never do that to me again. I'm a big girl. I am out of his reach. I am free as a bird. I am high as the sky!

KENNY. Ed, come down.

EDITH. He thinks we're troubled.

KENNY. Please.

EDITH. Retarded.

KENNY. Please, Ed.

EDITH. Worthless. We're nothing to him.

KENNY. We're everything to him, and he can't stand it.

(*A beat.*)

You look like her. And now, you've started sounding like her. That's why he can't talk to you. Or see you. Us. You look like her, and I act like her. Dressing you up, fried rice for breakfast, telling her stories. In some ways I am her.

EDITH. But she's dead.

KENNY. Yeah.

EDITH. Does he want us to die, too?

KENNY. I don't know.

EDITH. That's not an excuse, Kenny. He's the grown-up.

KENNY. I'm just explaining.

EDITH. He's abandoned us. And if you keep defending him, then, in some part of you, you think he's right to just leave us here. Is he right?

KENNY. No.

EDITH. Are you sure?

KENNY. Yes.

EDITH. Are. You. Sure?

KENNY. Yes, Edith. He's a jerk, okay? A jerk. He's a jerk, and I hate him. I hate him, too. And that's the truth.

But you can't keep this up. You're going to hurt yourself.

EDITH. I told you. I'm going to fly out of here. Fly high as the sky. I'm going to take care of everything. I'll get us all out of here.

KENNY. But Benji and I need to stay here. And we both need you. To stay with us. Dad may not need you, but we do. You were gone, and then he told me you were missing, and I was so worried. What would I do without you? I need you.

EDITH. But I can't keep you safe.

KENNY. You don't have to. Don't be a big girl yet. Just come down, eat this sandwich, play with Fergie, and watch TV with me. That's all I need you to do. We don't need you to protect us anymore. You just have to be a little girl. Be a little girl for me for a little while longer.

EDITH. You need me. To be a little girl?

KENNY. Yeah, I'll be the big one now. I promise. One that you can count on. Now come down. Don't fly away from me. Please. Please, just come on down.

(EDITH, *still standing on the rafter, starts to cry.*)

EDITH. I'm really hungry, Kenny.

KENNY. I know.

EDITH. I've been waiting up here for so long. For him to come back. But he never comes back. I just wait and wait and wait.

KENNY. So stop waiting. We don't...we don't need him. This is all you need right now: a sandwich. Okay?

EDITH. Okay.

(EDITH *balls up her hands into fists and wipes away her tears. She crouches down on the rafter, shaking with emotion. As she puts her hands down on the wood... She loses her footing. Her hands, wet with tears, slip.* EDITH *falls behind the haystack.*

THUD.

KENNY *gasps. Silence.*)

KENNY. ...Edith? (*He drops the plate and sandwich.*) EDITH?!

(*He runs behind the haystack. The sound of a siren, which gets louder and louder. End of scene.*)

Homecoming

BENJI *in the living room.* KENNY *sits on the couch listening to him with the cordless phone in his lap.*

BENJI. So I'm just there with my mom. And she has the phone in her hand. And she threatens me. She actually says she'll kill me. Or if I call you, it will kill her. And all I'm thinking is, "Edith escaped. She stole matches, lied to the authorities, committed arson, went A.W.O.L., hitchhiked, stole money from your dad's bank account, hopped on a bus, bribed Tom Osheyack, and hid in the barn for a whole day before anyone found her."

Edith is twelve years old.

I'm sixteen, and all I want to do is call my boyfriend. And so I hold out my hand and say, "Give. Me. The phone."

And my mom hangs onto it with this fierce, angry terror. So I just snatch it from her, and I wait for her to scream or to hit me or to turn hysterical. But instead she just stands there like she's hiding in the corner. She's right in the middle of the room, but her face is like she's hiding in the corner.

And I call you. And we talk. And then I tell her I'm going to your place and don't wait up, because I'm spending the night.

Because Edith tried to fly, you know? And I thought, "She tried." And maybe she didn't make it, but she tried.

KENNY. I can't believe you talked to her like that.

BENJI. Me, either.

KENNY. Or that she went along with it.

BENJI. I've never actually stood up to her. It caught her off guard.

But she's been kind of leaving me alone, and I like it. I like picking my clothes. I'm going to pick my classes next semester. I'm going to take Art. And I made scrambled eggs for myself, and she was shocked. She was like, "How did you learn to do that?"

KENNY. And you said, "My boyfriend taught me," like a silly little girl.

BENJI. You're a girl.

KENNY. You wouldn't be here if I was a girl.

BENJI. Maybe I would. And you'd be pregnant like Jemma Lieber.

KENNY. Your brother's an idiot.

BENJI. So's my mom. She wanted a studly, super-hetero son, and she got one. And now she'll be a grandma before the age of forty. Or stud son will have caused an abortion—I don't know which is worse to her. I was all, "Be careful what you wish for," and, "At least I can guarantee that Kenny'll never get pregnant."

My problems are nothing ever since Jemma's love-child. My dad was all, "Ben is getting good grades. He takes care of himself. He would never do anything as irresponsible as this. Back off of him. And this Kenneth is a stand-up fellow."

KENNY. I'm a what? "Kenneth"?

BENJI. Yeah, I think my dad has a crush on you or something.

KENNY. You're sick.

BENJI. You're a stand-up fellow.

(*The sound of the oven timer going off in the kitchen. KENNY starts to get up.*)

No, I'll get it.

KENNY. Come on, don't—

BENJI. No, I will. I just have to put the potatoes in, right?

KENNY. And then stir.

BENJI. Potatoes and stir. I can do it. Just…sit.

(KENNY *does.* BENJI *smiles and then exits.* KENNY *grabs the phone and wills it to ring. Nothing happens. He checks his watch and then sighs, heavily.* BENJI *re-enters, wearing oven mitts.*)

Maybe we should do homework or something.

KENNY. I can't—couldn't concentrate.

BENJI. Just to occupy yourself. You should occupy yourself.

KENNY. It's so late.

BENJI. There would have been a call if something happened.

KENNY. God, I can't believe she—

BENJI. Hey.

(BENJI *sits next to him on the couch. He takes* KENNY'*s head into his oven mitt hands and kisses him.*)

KENNY. What are you doing?

BENJI. Distracting you.

KENNY. What are the mitts for?

BENJI. I put the potatoes in the pot like you said.

KENNY. With the mitts on?

BENJI. The lid was hot.

KENNY. You're hilarious.

BENJI. It's okay if I stay tonight, right?

KENNY. Oh…yeah. Um. Of course.

BENJI. It'll be a little embarrassing now. If I go home.

KENNY. No, I want you to stay. But my dad will be here.

BENJI. Really?

KENNY. He's on his way right now.

BENJI. Right.

KENNY. But I want you to stay. You're staying. Yeah. And if he says something, I'll just tell him again: this is my house, right?

BENJI. Right. Your house. Yours and—

(*The sound of a car pulling up into the driveway.*)

KENNY. Oh, thank god.

(KENNY *runs offstage.* BENJI *waits, expectantly.* KENNY *re-enters with* EDITH *who wears a cast on her right arm.* BENJI *claps the oven mitts together.*)

BENJI. Welcome home, Edith!

(EDITH *curtsies.*)

EDITH. Are you throwing me a party?

KENNY. A small one. You'll have a real one this weekend. I asked Dina Osheyack who to invite.

EDITH. They have to sign my cast. You have to sign my cast.

KENNY. We will.

BENJI. After dinner.

EDITH. What are you cooking?

KENNY. Chicken.

EDITH. Like Mom made?

KENNY. Yeah. Chicken afritada. Just for you, because we're so happy to have you back.

EDITH. I'm happy to be back. The hospital was better than the school, but I still didn't like it. Everyone was really nice, and I couldn't figure out why. I go, "I just broke my arm. You don't have to keep me here." And then I realized: they thought I tried to kill myself. So I said, "Why would I come all this way just to off myself? I'm trying to kill my dad!"

KENNY. You did not say that.

EDITH. No. Of course not.

KENNY. Did you?

EDITH. Yeah. Okay, yeah, I did. But then I laughed so they would think I was joking. But I saw his face. And he knows. Even though I'd never really do it, he knows that what I said was partly real.

He said he's going to stay here tonight.

KENNY. He said he'd probably stay through the weekend. He wants to make sure you're okay.

EDITH. He won't be here all the time now, will he?

KENNY. No, he won't. You know he won't.

EDITH. Good.

> (*To* BENJI.)

Is it a sleepover?

BENJI. Yeah.

EDITH. Good. Where's my gun?

> (KENNY *and* BENJI *are quiet.*)

Did he throw it out?

KENNY. No.

BENJI. Why do you want it?

EDITH. Just give it to me.

> (KENNY *exits.*)

BENJI. Where's your dad?

EDITH. In the car. I'm not going to shoot him.

BENJI. How do I know that?

EDITH. Because I'm telling you. I'm not going to shoot him.

BENJI. Don't shoot my mom, either.

EDITH. I won't.

> (KENNY *returns with the gun.*)

KENNY. Don't shoot Dad.

EDITH. I'm not going to shoot Dad!

> (EDITH *takes the gun. She holds it out to* BENJI.
>
> BENJI *stares. She insists.* BENJI *takes the gun.*)

I can't fire it when my arm is in this thing. So you have to learn how to use it.

BENJI. Oh.

EDITH. You have to protect us now. I know you can do it.

BENJI. Okay.

EDITH. Will you take off those stupid mitts, you doofus? You can't shoot it with those mitts on.

> (BENJI *puts the gun down, takes off the oven mitts, and then bends down hesitantly to pick it up again. Just before he can…*)

BANG! BANG!

> (BENJI *jumps back.*)

BENJI. I don't really want to shoot it. I don't–

EDITH. Well, someone has to. Even when they take this thing off…I'm too young to be playing with firearms. You have to do it. Grown-ups have to do all kinds of things they may not want to do.

BENJI. Okay. Yes, ma'am.

(BENJI *picks up the gun.*)

EDITH. Good. We'll go in the back and shoot some pop cans after dinner. Thanks.

BENJI. You're welcome.

EDITH. You're going to learn how to take care of yourself. Even if you're not kicked out anymore I don't think you can count on your mom, Benji. Not all the time.

BENJI. I think you might be right.

KENNY. Why is Dad still in the car?

EDITH. He said he needed a minute.

KENNY. Go fetch him. Dinner's almost ready.

EDITH. Okay.

(EDITH *goes.*)

BENJI. She seems fine.

KENNY. Does she?

BENJI. Yeah. And she's going to teach me how to shoot.

KENNY. You don't have to.

BENJI. It's okay. It'll be fun. Besides, I have to learn to take care of myself.

KENNY. When we were in the hospital the other day. Me and Dad. He kept getting up—to get coffee or to call Chloë or to just go somewhere else. But I just planted myself and waited. And I watched him. I saw him. And he looked…so small. I mean, he's still taller than me, but he's not that much taller. Not anymore. And he just kept getting up, like he wanted to go—like he needed to. And I felt so bad for him.

I mean, Edith and I are here every day. And things go wrong all the time. But all you have to do is take a little time, deal with a little stress, and then fix things. But it's like he made all these mistakes, and he just left them there. And they got bigger. And if he had taken care of them while they were small, maybe he would have realized it wasn't so bad, making mistakes. But now they were so big. And I just felt so bad for him. He didn't know it was possible to just go home, and that there would be people there, and it would be okay. You could just fix it. And then you could feel good about it again. Even the part that was a mistake.

But why am I still scared, Benji?

BENJI. I don't think we'll ever stop being scared. I don't think we have to stop.

(BENJI *holds* KENNY. *They kiss.* EDITH *re-enters, shaken.* KENNY *sees her.*)

KENNY. Ed?

EDITH. He's…

KENNY. What?

EDITH. Dad's in the car. He's crying. He said… He said to start dinner without him.

KENNY. Oh.

EDITH. He's just sitting there. Crying.

KENNY. Okay. Well…okay. We'll start dinner without him.

BENJI. I'll go set the table.

(BENJI *exits.*)

EDITH. Did I make him cry?

KENNY. I don't know.

EDITH. Should we wait?

KENNY. He said not to. He'll come in, eventually. Let's not wait. Let's just start without him.

(KENNY *holds out a hand.*)

Welcome home, Edith.

(EDITH *gives him her hand. They exit to the kitchen.*)

End of Play

THE EDGE OF OUR BODIES
by Adam Rapp

Copyright © 2011 by Adam Rapp. All rights reserved. CAUTION: Professionals and amateurs are hereby warned that *The Edge of Our Bodies* is subject to royalty. It is fully protected under the copyright laws of the United States of America and of all countries covered by the International Copyright Union (including the Dominion of Canada and the rest of the British Commonwealth), the Berne Convention, the Pan-American Copyright Convention and the Universal Copyright Convention, as well as all countries with which the United States has reciprocal copyright relations. All rights, including professional, amateur stage rights, motion picture, recitation, lecturing, public reading, radio broadcasting, television, video or sound recording, all other forms of mechanical or electronic reproduction, such as CD-ROM, CD-I, information storage and retrieval systems, and photocopying, and the rights of translation into foreign languages, are strictly reserved. Particular emphasis is laid upon the matter of readings, permission for which must be secured from the Author's agent in writing.

Required royalties must be paid every time this play is performed before any audience, whether or not it is presented for profit and whether or not admission is charged.

All inquiries concerning rights, including amateur rights, should be addressed to: Subias Literary Agency, One Union Square West, No. 913, New York, NY 10003, ATTN: Mark Subias.

291

ABOUT *THE EDGE OF OUR BODIES*

This article first ran in the January/February 2011 issue of Inside Actors, *and is based on conversations with the playwright before rehearsals for the Humana Festival production began.*

Bernadette boards a Metro-North train at the New Haven station. Over-caffeinated and under-slept, she's traveling from her New England prep school to New York City to share some news with her boyfriend, Michael. Bernadette is 16 but precociously articulate, innocent but discerning, and over the course of a night in the city, she begins to grasp the stark realities of adulthood. With startling intimacy, *The Edge of Our Bodies* captures the vulnerability and endurance of a teenager at the threshold of adult experience and insight.

When he began *The Edge of Our Bodies*, Adam Rapp was teaching at Yale, taking that very train ride twice a week. "Metro-North can be pretty brutal," he recalls. "There's a real harsh light and a deeply impersonal feeling—it feels like this strange conduit for lonely people." For several years, Rapp had been haunted by a story from a friend's adolescence about an excursion from her secluded school to the city. "It was an adventure, one of the first things she did in her life that was a bit illicit," he recounts. "She took a journey from Brooklyn all the way back to Connecticut on that train. I remember her talking about the cost of that experience and how alone she felt. I thought about a young girl who had been cloistered off in prep school, on a train, on the precipice of adulthood." The playwright was also reminded of his teenage years in military prep school and the many trips home to Chicago from Milwaukee: "You're caught in this little aquarium at school—and then there's the real world. I remember trains and buses being the things that take you to where the real world is."

Those memories and a year's worth of commuting crystallized for Rapp in the image of Bernadette, whom he began to see talking to him as he wrote. The unadorned intimacy of a single actor onstage appealed to the playwright and fueled the writing process. "One of the most underrated things I love in the theatre is the simple ease of gazing at a human being for an extended period of time," he explains, "the simplicity of someone sitting in a chair, or looking out a window, the story of somebody's face, their body, the way they use their hands." Rapp was drawn to the intrinsic theatricality of a lone storyteller. "The luxury of being with a narrator onstage is unique to the theatre. When a performer speaks directly to the audience, there is an incredible kind of listening that has to happen; we become a part of the scene—we collaborate on the journey."

That journey, for Bernadette, entails a series of encounters with men—all older, each somehow adrift and ailing. Her seatmate on the train is an old man, frail and near death. Looking for Michael at his apartment, Bernadette instead finds her boyfriend's father, who, battling cancer and withered by chemotherapy, describes feeling like he can "get outside" his body, "just beyond the edge of what we know. Where the skin…contains us." Bernadette herself is undergoing what Rapp calls the "hormonal apocalypse" of adolescence, and so the body—in states of transformation, revolt, and decay—becomes the vehicle through which Bernadette makes crucial discoveries about herself and the world. "There's a dream world that exists just beyond our skin," the playwright describes, "when we're drifting away from ourselves, when we become alien to ourselves." Alone and in control of where she goes and what she does for one night in a vast city, Bernadette feels at once invincible and powerless. She experiences the indifference of the world, but locates the possibility of compassion in small gestures. "My plays have to be as tender as they are brutal, as funny as they are awful, as cruel as they are sweet," Rapp says of the play's emotional landscape, "and the theme of the body has to be as painfully visceral as it is dreamlike." Confronted with her existential isolation, Bernadette perceives the beauty and cruelty of human frailty with new clarity.

With piercing insight, this coming-of-age narrative ultimately asks us to consider the nature of experience itself—and how it transforms us. "I'm interested in authentic experience," Rapp says. "I think there comes a point in our lives when we strive for a more magnified, intense appreciation for being alive, healthy, vital. There are moments when we actually realize that we are going to die, that our bodies break down and decay. Bernadette ingests a bit of the ugliness in the world and from the cost of that, she gains a purer understanding of being alive in the moment, and finds her legs under her are a little bit stronger. At the end of this story, her bones are going to feel different."

—Lila Neugebauer

BIOGRAPHY

Adam Rapp is an Obie Award-winning playwright and director. He is the author of numerous plays, which include *Nocturne* (American Repertory Theater, New York Theatre Workshop), *Faster* (Rattlestick Playwrights Theater), *Animals & Plants* (American Repertory Theater), *Finer Noble Gases* (26th Humana Festival of New American Plays, Rattlestick), *Stone Cold Dead Serious* (American Repertory Theater, Edge Theatre), *Blackbird* (The Bush, London; Edge Theatre), *Gompers* (Pittsburgh City Theatre), *Essential Self-Defense* (Playwrights Horizons/Edge Theatre), *American Sligo* (Rattlestick), *Bingo With the Indians* (The Flea Theater), *Kindness* (Playwrights Horizons), and *Red Light Winter* (Steppenwolf, Scott Rudin Productions at Barrow Street Theatre), which won Chicago's Jeff Award for Best New Work and was named a finalist for the 2006 Pulitzer Prize. Recent world premieres include *The Metal Children* (The Vineyard Theatre), *The Hallway Trilogy* (Rattlestick), and *Dreams of Flying Dreams of Falling* (Atlantic Theater Company). He has published seven novels for young adults, including *The Buffalo Tree* (Front Street Books, 1997), *Under the Wolf, Under the Dog* (Candlewick Press, 2006), which was a finalist for the *L.A. Times* Book Prize, and *Punkzilla* (Candlewick Press, 2009), which was named a 2010 Michael L. Printz Honor Book. He is also the author of the adult novel, *The Year Of Endless Sorrows* (Farrar, Strauss & Giroux, 2006), and the graphic novel, *Ball-Peen Hammer* (First Second Books, 2009). He also wrote and directed the feature films *Winter Passing* and *Blackbird*, which he adapted from his play. Most recently, he directed the New York premiere of his play, *Animals & Plants*, for the Amoralists Theatre Company, as well as Karen O's psycho opera *Stop the Virgens* for The Creators Project at St. Ann's Warehouse. After the New Year he will direct the film version of *Red Light Winter*, which he adapted from his play, for Scott Rudin and Parts and Labor Productions. His new novel, *The Children and the Wolves*, is forthcoming from Candlewick Press in February. His playwriting honors include Boston's Elliot Norton Award, The Helen Merrill Prize, The 2006 Princess Grace Statue, a Lucille Lortel Playwrights' Fellowship, and The Benjamin H. Danks Award from the American Academy of Arts and Letters.

ACKNOWLEDGMENTS

The Edge of Our Bodies premiered at the Humana Festival of New American Plays in March 2011. It was directed by Adam Rapp with the following cast:

BERNADETTE ....Catherine Combs
MAINTENANCE MAN ....Michael J. Burmester

and the following production staff:

Scenic Designer ....Tom Tutino
Costume Designer..Kristopher Castle
Lighting Designer.. Keith Parham
Original Music..........Christian Frederickson and Ryan Rumery
Properties Designer.. Mark Walston
Stage Manager...CJ LaRoche
Assistant Director/Dramaturg..........................Lila Neugebauer

Directing Assistant...John Rooney
Production Assistant...Leslie Cobb
Assistant Dramaturg ....Jessica Reese

The Edge of Our Bodies was developed for the Humana Festival of New American Plays by Actors Theatre of Louisville through a partnership with Louisiana State University.

CHARACTERS

BERNADETTE
a MAINTENANCE MAN

Catherine Combs
in *The Edge of Our Bodies*

35th Annual Humana Festival of New American Plays
Actors Theatre of Louisville, 2011
Photo by Alan Simons

THE EDGE OF OUR BODIES

The Blackbox Theater at Whitney Academy, a prep school in the Northeast. The set of Genet's The Maids. *A small platform stage that appears to be floating in darkness. A rococo dressing table with small colorful containers of perfumes, a glass jar of mimosa, a nice comb and hand mirror, a silver teapot. A small, richly upholstered stool. Upstage of the stool and table, a bench containing a silver tea set, an old-fashioned, arched radio, a fancy telephone, a bouquet of gladioli. Downstage left, a pouf, a teacup and saucer centered on the pouf. Above the table, an ornate chandelier.*

BERNADETTE, *16, sits on the upstage bench. She wears a tartan skirt, white shirt, a tie, white knee socks, proper shoes. She wears a gray wool trench coat. Her hair is tied back with ribbon. Her face looks freshly scrubbed, without makeup. She sits very still, clutching a black Moleskine notebook.*

The theater is empty.

After a long moment, she opens the notebook, begins reading.

1
The Train.

BERNADETTE. (*Reading from the notebook.*) I'm on the New Haven platform for the train to New York. There are three men who are taking turns staring at me. Though I repeatedly try and drift away from them we somehow enter the same car. They politely let me board first, as men who are pretending to be gentlemen will do. After I find a two-seater safely near the doors, whether they realize it or not, they wind up surrounding me. I feel like I've been thrown into the deep end of a public pool and they are treading water, waiting for me to resurface with tubes of sunblock clenched between their teeth. Two of them wear dark business suits and I am paranoid that the one in front of me—the mono-browed Israeli—is going to whirl around and hit on me. Recently I have perfected the art of keeping to myself and I believe that I can make myself smaller; my face, my arms, yes even my breasts, though I can't afford to lose much in that area or I would be mistaken for a boy. At times I believe I can shrink down to the size of a rabbit. When I'm feeling witchy, I even entertain the possibility of willing invisibility.

Only a few hours ago I was on the southbound Vermonter. I was supposed to board a connecting Amtrak train to Penn Station but I got nauseous and took too much time in the bathroom at New Haven and had to wait another twenty

297

minutes for the Metro-North, which is always a sketchy prospect when it comes to a young woman traveling alone to New York City. It's been rumored that recently a man was murdered on the New Haven-bound train, just north of the Bridgeport stop.

It's late Friday afternoon and the light in my car is typically harsh and makes my three travel mates look green and middle-aged. I'm sure I don't look much better. I am desperately trying to seem older and with all the concealer covering my pimples I look more like a fledgling female news anchor than a junior running away from boarding school. The guy to my left—the one who isn't wearing a suit, but a large thick hooded sweatshirt with UCONN across the chest—has a face like lunch meat and he's staring out his window as if the years have suddenly tripled on him and he's just realized it. It's as if he's searching for a lost coat in the trees that are flying by. The third man is sitting a few seats behind me and within minutes he's fallen asleep on his shoulder. He's almost completely bald, a former redhead, and has a face like a fat sick baby. My roommate Briel always talks about how men just get sexier as they get older—she would know because she's having an affair with our field hockey coach, Mr. Katagas, whose dark, Mediterranean chest hair can always be seen creeping through the neckline of his V-neck T-shirts in simian tufts—but I'm at a loss, always searching for this mysterious older-man magnetism on trains, at airport gates, and at the small café not far from campus where I eat two-dollar bowls of clam chowder and drink bad drip coffee. I mostly encounter men with jowly faces, potbellies, dyed, thinning hair, baggy, alcoholic eyes, arthritic limps, and an unfortunate phenomenon I've come to call middle-aged male asslessness.

It's early November and that troubling, pre-winter grayness that's capable of dulling even the most promising sunny morning has taken over. It's a week before Thanksgiving; that part of the late fall when the days seem to be cut in half and the nights are long and dank and fraught with the anticipation of a numbing winter. I'm on my way to New York to see Michael, who doesn't know I'm coming…or that I'm pregnant. Michael is 19 and hasn't yet started at Brown because he's living with his dad, who is undergoing chemotherapy treatments for prostate cancer. When Michael and I kiss our teeth lightly clink together like champagne flutes and he never has bad breath and possesses a perfect, hairless chest. Michael can also quote Shakespeare and Pablo Neruda poems. In the past year he's turned me on to Truffaut films and Frederick Exley and The Beatles, though I resisted all of it at first, especially the Beatles, not wanting to get caught up in a band whose two remaining members are older than my grandfather. Michael works at a small Carroll Gardens coffee shop and I resist using my cell phone to text or call because I want the pleasant surprise to buffer any complications that might arise once the cat is out of the bag. We spoke last night and I wasn't able to tell him the news and I stayed up till dawn, tossing and turning and clawing at the backs of my hands.

We fell in love during the spring semester of his senior year while working on the third act of *Hamlet* for his senior thesis project. Of course, he played Hamlet and I was Ophelia and we went crazy for each other in about two days.

I spent most of this past summer in New York, taking an acting class at a private studio in the West Village. I've gotten pretty close with Michael's father, Wayne, a retired history professor who taught at Brooklyn College. Their Carroll Gardens apartment smells like hemorrhoidal ointment and stale cigarettes and the recent disappearance of Michael's mother looms over everything like a dinner plate glued to the wall.

Michael came back to campus for Homecoming weekend and that's when it happened. We don't like using condoms. Michael has somehow convinced himself that he's perfected a "natural contraceptive" technique, meaning that he pulls out at the last possible moment and comes on my breasts and stomach.

My sister Ellen had an abortion in the spring and never seemed to care much about it one way or the other. She lives with her boyfriend in Cambridge, Massachusetts, where she's in grad school at Harvard. I've thought of calling her but I'm afraid she'd tell our mother who has enough problems lately. She's convinced that my father is having an affair with an airline stewardess and spends most of her free time watching the Home Shopping Network and popping Xanax.

At this point the only person who knows is Briel, who found my over-the-counter test on the top of the toilet tank in our dorm room. Not a smart move on my part. I saw the little blue line and slid down the bathroom wall and sat there for what seemed like hours. I woke up in bed and Briel was standing over me, clutching the evidence. We hardly talked about it but I did manage to swear her to secrecy. For some reason I trust Briel. She's Jewish, after all, and the Jews seem to be the only trustworthy people at boarding school (my three fellow Unitarian students are perhaps the most conniving). Plus, I recently wrote an English paper for her comparing *The Bell Jar* to *Geek Love* of all things. Briel owes me.

Before New Haven, on the Vermonter train, there was a group of students from Loomis Chafee who were tripping on mushrooms. Three jock boys and a freshman girl with dyed black hair who kept climbing over the backs of seats and sitting in their laps. Things got strange when they all started making out with each other; even two of the jocks started going at it. At one point they offered me a stem but I said no thank you and opened the Edith Wharton novel that I'm supposed to be reading for my American Lit class. I'm not afraid of drugs. I've done my share of cocaine at Whitney—cocaine and Vivarin, mostly. Briel and I crush it up and snort it and play an old Talking Heads CD and take most of our clothes off and dance to "Once in A Lifetime." *Dun dundundun. Dun dundundun. Letting the days go by, let the water...* I have nothing against a good time; I'm just not into shrooming with the kind of strangers who travel with lacrosse sticks.

At the New Haven station, after getting sick and missing my train, I had about a twenty-minute wait for Metro-North. I got a coffee at the Dunkin Donuts and headed to the platform.

(*Out.*) I should tell you that I've been drinking way too much coffee in recent weeks.

I should also tell you that I haven't slept in three days.

(*Back to notebook.*) Outside my window the sky is like mop water and by the Milford stop it starts to rain. Even in the dim reflection I can see that my skin looks terrible—I've been breaking out like crazy. I'm also starting to feel sick again. I've already thrown up twice today and the coffee isn't helping the nausea. The only relief is the trees, whose leaves are still colorful despite it being late fall. Growing up in northwest Connecticut, the sight of the trees changing is the one thing I always look forward to.

At Stamford the train starts to fill up and an old man sits next to me. He wears soft, puffy clothes and a wool coat and carries a small suitcase. I pull out the Edith Wharton novel and start re-reading the section I couldn't get through on the Vermonter train.

The old man seems sad, lost even, and I worry that he's senile and has gotten on the wrong train. After a few minutes he catches my eye and points to my book. He asks if it's any good. He doesn't sound at all like I thought he might. I expected a thin, dry voice but he's loud and hard of hearing. I tell him parts of it are good. The truth is that the book is depressing and long and in my opinion Lily Bart is a fool. I have to admit that the man who loves her, Selden, is the first fictional character I have ever fantasized about and there are times when I wished Michael was more like him. Quieter. More polite. Less concerned with his perfect chest.

The old man says, "*The House of Mirth.* House of Happy, I guess."

He takes an apple out of his pocket, considers it and then puts it back. A few minutes later he tells me he's on his way to New York to visit his grandson who is going to meet him at Grand Central Station.

"We're gonna see the Knicks play Orlando," he says, "Amar'e Stoudemire."

His grandson's name is Paul and he's just moved to the city where he has a job on Wall Street.

The old man says, "Handsome kid. Movie star looks. Smarter than most…"

And then he asks me if I have a boyfriend.

I tell him I'm on my way to see him. He asks me his name and what he does and I tell him and that he's about to start at Brown, but has deferred a year.

He says, "Ivy Leaguer, huh?"

I nod.

The old man has a face like wet Kleenex, with little broken blood vessels on his nose.

He says, "Well, Michael's a lucky man. You're very pretty."

I tell him thanks and then he asks me how old I am. For some reason I tell him the truth.

"I'm sixteen," I say.

He says, "Do your parents know you're going into the city to meet a boy?"

"Of course," I lie.

Then he asks me what school I go to and I tell him Loomis Chaffee even though I'm at Whitney. I left Whitney without permission, so I am most likely returning to face probation or a suspension.

The old man says, "Sixteen's a great age. What do you want to be when you grow up?"

"I want to write short stories," I answer.

"What kind of stories?" he asks.

"The good kind," I say. "Sometimes I get in trouble for using too many similes."

He says, "You could write a story about a young girl who meets an old man on a train."

"I could," I say.

He says, "They could talk about things. Have a chat."

"What do you think they would talk about?" I ask.

"Oh, I don't know," he says. "The important stuff. Life. Football... Sandwiches. Just make sure it has a happy ending."

Then he asks me what my parents do and I tell him that my dad's a rocket scientist and my mom's a dwarf in the circus. This confuses him and I can't tell whether he's disappointed because he somehow knows that I've started lying or if he's working out the physics of a dwarf giving birth to a normal-sized girl.

He says, "She's little, huh?"

I nod.

Lying always makes me feel like my hair is falling out.

As far as I know my dad is still directing a bad TV show in Los Angeles and in addition to the Xanax my mom is mostly taking anti-depressants and trying to bait her South American massage therapist into having an affair with her.

Then the old man points to my raincoat and asks me if I'm going to be warm enough.

He says, "It's sposed to get pretty cold tonight. It might snow."

"Oh, good," I tell him. "I like the snow."

We're quiet for the rest of the trip. The three men who've been on the train since New Haven are all asleep now, their heads seemingly too heavy for their shoulders. They appear to have somehow aged in unison with our increased proximity to New York. By a Hundred and Twenty-fifth Street they are old withered men.

> (*She turns the page. She sets the book on the bench, stands, starts to unbutton her trench coat when the radio snaps on. The chandelier lights goes out and she is in total darkness, save for the light coming through the radio. From the radio she hears her own voice and a scene partner performing a violent section of* The Maids, *during which a tea tray is thrown. She quickly crosses to the radio, turns it off. The chandelier light snaps back on. She stares up at it, confused, looks to a vom.*)

Hello?

> (*No response.*
>
> *She eyes the chandelier suspiciously, looks up to the stage management booth, then*

carefully finishes removing her trench coat, places it on the bench, picks up her notebook, crosses stage right, staring up at the chandelier again, plants her feet, briefly looks at the radio, then begins from where she left off…)

II
Michael's House.

BERNADETTE. At Grand Central Station I say good-bye to Paul's grandfather and walk as fast as I can through the concourse. I'm feeling queasy again but I don't want to throw up in a public bathroom or in my mouth for that matter, so I swallow hard and head for the subway.

I take the Four Train one stop uptown to Fifty-First Street and then transfer to the downtown F and arrive in Carroll Gardens at dusk. It seems like there are far fewer trees since the middle of August. Everything appears wan and withered. That mop water sky seems to have followed me from New Haven.

I walk over to Michael's coffee shop and nervously linger around the corner before going in. A guy with tattoos on his forearms and earrings the size of doorknobs tells me Michael isn't on the schedule and after buying a cappuccino I leave and spend several minutes entertaining the horrible possibility of him cheating on me; his beautiful chest poised over some Brooklyn girl, an Italian with olive skin and dark, smoldering eyes. I throw up most of my cappuccino on the street so I go to a deli and buy some gum and head over to Michael's dad's apartment on Third Place.

I am immediately buzzed in and Wayne, Michael's father, answers the door. Wayne is large and heavy like a football coach but much quieter and the cancer seems to have done more to his spirit than his body. He wears a light blue terrycloth robe, gray sweatpants, and a white T-shirt and slippers. His skin is waxy and he smells sickly sweet, of chemicals and perspiration.

He says Hello to me. His voice is dehydrated and one of his eyes seems like it's closing on its own.

He says, "What a surprise."

I ask him if Michael's around and he says he doesn't know where he is and asks me if I'd gone by the coffee shop. I tell him I just came from there and then he asks me to sit down, so we both sit at the kitchen table.

He pours me a ginger ale and sets the can next to my glass. He looks around confused for a moment and then tries to get up but something doesn't seem to be working—his knee or his hip maybe—so he remains seated.

I ask him if he's okay and he says, "I'm fine… Is it Friday?"

I tell him that it is and he points to a spool of coaxial cable in the corner. He says the cable guy was there earlier and has to come back Monday to finish the job.

"Finally switching to broadband," he says. "After all these years."

He is holding the metal ice tray from which he has forgotten to remove ice cubes. I ask him if I can take that from him and he says, "Oh, sure. Ice."

As I'm placing ice cubes in my glass he says, "So it's Friday then."

"It is," I say. "Friday the twenty-first."

He says that this must mean Thanksgiving is right around the corner.

I tell him it's next Thursday and he asks me if I'm doing anything special.

I mention the usual dinner in Connecticut and that my sister and her boyfriend will be coming down from Cambridge and how we'll most likely wind up playing Scrabble and watching *Planes, Trains, and Automobiles* for the ninety-seventh time. And then my mom will pull out the old photo albums and start talking about how fat everyone's getting.

Then Wayne tells me I'm welcome to join him and Michael. He says that his brother Ed and his daughter Chrissy might be coming too.

He adds, "Someone's bound to cook something halfway decent. A celebratory fowl."

I say, "Thanks, Dr. Fitzgerald."

The truth is that Michael hasn't mentioned anything about Thanksgiving. I can feel my stomach again. Like I've swallowed potting soil.

I ask Wayne how he's feeling.

He says, "Oh, not so great. My hip's really bothering me. I have a cane but I keep losing it in the house."

He says that he's about had it with all the treatments. The headaches. The nausea. How everything tastes funny.

Then he says, "What about you, Bernie? How's school?"

I tell him school's good.

He says that Mike just told him that I might be doing a play. I tell Wayne that I just auditioned for Genet's *The Maids* and that I'm waiting to hear.

He says, "Solange or Claire?"

"Claire," I say, and I do a little for him.

(*With flair, quoting* The Maids.)"Lay out my things. The white charmeuse slip. The fan. The emeralds."

He laughs and says, "Susannah York played her in the film. God was she beautiful. When they get it right it's a helluva play."

(*Quoting* The Maids.)"Lay out my things. The white charmeuse slip. The fan. The emeralds."

"Very well, Madame. All Madame's jewels?"

> (BERNADETTE *touches the silver teapot on top of the dressing table, then sets it on the tea set on top of the bench, then continues.*)

I tell him that I'm not getting my hopes up, that there are five girls vying for three parts.

He says, "Sixty percent. There are worse odds."

The kitchen light buzzes above us. I can see dead bugs in the fixture.

Wayne says, "Mike probably went into the city. You should give him a call."

I say, "I was sort of hoping to surprise him."

He says, "Well, surprises are always nice."

I tell Wayne how I'd just spoken to Michael the day before and how he'd told me he would be at work.

"They must have changed the schedule," Wayne offers.

I can hear the TV in the living room. It's CNN and someone is complaining about people who complain about the war.

Then Wayne asks me if I have any bags and I tell him I just have my purse.

He says, "What about a toothbrush? We got extras. Dozens of them. Never been taken out of the plastic. Mike's mother was always paranoid about losing the damn things. Her and her obsession with hygiene."

I tell him I have a toothbrush and then I ask him if he's heard from his wife.

"I'm afraid we haven't," he says.

I say, "I don't mean to pry, Dr. Fitzgerald."

He says, "You're not prying at all, Bernie. Hopefully Diana will show her face again at some point. Before the inevitable…"

The TV in the living room and the light buzzing above us seem to be enacting a conspiracy against peace of mind.

I ask Wayne when he'd last heard from his wife.

"Second week of September," he says. "Right smack dab in the middle of my last round of chemo."

I say, "She didn't leave a note?"

"No note," he says. "Not a single clue."

I say, "I'm so sorry, Dr. Fitzgerald."

He says, "Bernie, call me Wayne. My students don't even call me Dr. Fitzgerald."

"Wayne," I say.

After a pause during which I think I can feel my heart tightening, Wayne says, "Mike thinks she's in Central America."

I ask him why she would go there and he says, "Who knows? Mike seems to believe she has this fascination with Costa Rica, though I've never heard a peep about it."

"That must be really hard," I hear myself say.

"Yeah, the not knowing," he replies.

Then I tell him I hope she comes back and he says Me too and then he looks at his hand…

(*Looking at her hand.*) The front…the back. He looks at it for a long time.

"Is something wrong?" I ask.

He says, "Lately…"

"Lately what?" I say.

He says, "Lately I feel like I can get outside my body. Barely outside of it. Just beyond the edge of what we know. Where the skin…contains us I guess would be the best way to describe it. Just past that limit…I can get to that place and just sort of float there."

(BERNADETTE *breaks from looking at her hand. The lights shift and it is obvious that the audience has arrived. She speaks directly to us now, not needing the notebook.*)

His face is suddenly gray and corpse-like. The last thing in the world I want is to cry in front of him. Their cat, Nelson, darts into the room and grazes my calf. He is black with white paws and more stuck up than most of the seniors at Whitney.

Wayne says, "Probably sounds like a bunch of cockamamie."

"Not at all," I say.

He says, "This is what happens when you spend too much time with yourself. You start getting all metaphysical and boring."

I tell him that it's not boring and then he asks me how my parents are.

He says, "Last time I saw your dad he was about to head back to L.A. He still working on that TV show?"

I tell him that he's directing half the season now and Wayne says, "Good for him. It's a good show."

And then he asks me if I watch it.

"No," I say, "I don't."

"Oh, you should watch it," he says. "It really is good."

And then he asks me how my mom is and I tell him she's fine and he asks me if she goes out to L.A. with my dad.

"She mostly stays at home," I tell him. "I think she and my dad hate each other."

He asks me why I would say that and I tell him because my dad's fucking a stewardess.

I've never used this kind of language in front of Wayne. It just comes out of my mouth like water through your nose.

I say, "Her name is Candi. She has fake tits and lip implants and she's like six-two."

He tells me that he's sorry to hear about that and he hopes my parents will work things out.

I tell him that I doubt they will; that my dad hasn't been home in over a month.

Then Wayne tells me that these things happen; that the people we love the most are capable of unspeakable cruelties. He says it hurts more than anything else because of this profound love. He says that he still doesn't understand why his wife left; that they'd been married for twenty-three years.

I ask him if he thinks she's seeing someone else and then he looks at his hand again and asks if we can change the subject.

So we talk about my train ride: how I was on Amtrak but switched to Metro-North at New Haven. We talk about how uncomfortable the seats are and the strange smells.

Then he offers me something to eat. He says that there's sandwich meat in the fridge but I tell him that I haven't been feeling so well and pat my stomach.

He says, "There's plenty of Maalox on the premises."

I tell him I'm fine; that more than anything it's probably the result of a not-so-great week.

He asks me if it's anything I'd like to talk about and I tell him I'm late on an essay and I reference the Genet audition.

"Well, I'm sure everything will work out," he offers.

"I hope it does," I say.

He adds, "Stuff usually does when you're young…"

And then he suddenly goes blank. It's as if someone has flipped a switch. His body's machinery stalls for a moment. A terrible smell materializes. Something worse than human waste. I have to lean away and hold my breath. And then, just like that, he's back.

He says, "Well, I spose I should go rest. Feel free to stick around and wait for Mike if you'd like. You know you're always welcome here."

I tell him thanks and ask him if he needs anything and he gracefully declines my offer.

When he pushes away from the table, he almost falls. I move to help him but he holds up his hand to stop me. He then pushes off the table again and starts to exit toward his bedroom.

Just before he opens his door I call his name and ask him if Michael has said anything to him.

He says, "Said anything about what?"

"Our relationship," I say.

Wayne tells me that all Michael ever talks about is how madly in love he is. Bernie this, Bernie that. He says that if it'll put my mind at ease I can take comfort in the fact that I'm the subject of fervent hyperbole.

Bernie this, Bernie that.

Then I ask him if Mike has ever mentioned anyone else and Wayne tells me that as far as he can tell, the only competition I have for Mike's attention is Mike himself. He says that his son is a tenacious narcissist but that I probably already knew that. He says Mike takes after his mother in this regard.

And then he reaches into the pocket of his robe and produces a pocketknife.

He says, "Oh, by the way, you want this?"

I say, "Um. Sure."

And then he asks me if I have a penny.

I say, "I think I do. Why?"

He tells me that when someone gives you a knife, you're supposed to give them a penny in return. That it's good luck.

So I give him a penny and he gives me the pocketknife. It's much heavier than it looks. I slip it into my purse, and he says, "Those things always come in handy."

Then Wayne exits toward his bedroom, leaving the TV on in the living room.

After I put the ice tray back in the freezer I go into the living room and watch CNN. I think Wayne has gone to bed but he's stopped at the threshold of his room and he's just standing there, confused, his hand outstretched in front of him as if he's reaching toward a boyhood tree. He stays there for a long moment and then goes into his bedroom, leaving the door open.

On TV there is stuff about the war and stuff about the economy and stuff about women and men and how impossible everything is and I wind up falling asleep on the sofa.

I wake up a little after nine and turn the TV off.

I can hear Wayne snoring. It sounds like there's a stone lodged in his throat. I cross to his room and watch him sleep. His body reveals nothing more than it did when he was sitting with me in the kitchen. I figure that's what it's like with cancer: everything seems normal for a while and then there's one disastrous night when half of your mass digests itself or you wake up and all of your hair is lying next to you on your pillow. It's like a frost or a terrible lightning storm that destroys half a forest.

I close his door and go down the hall into Michael's room. He has recently bought a pair of circular mounts that are supposed to help you execute the perfect push-up, for the perfect chest. On his cluttered desk is a volume of plays by Edward Bond, half-opened to *Saved*, about three dollars in loose change, and a fresh pack of Camel Lights. His bed is half-made and there are clothes strewn everywhere.

> (*She sits at the dressing table. She opens a drawer, removes a silver cigarette case and a matching lighter.*)

I remove a cigarette and light it with a Bic lighter that's sitting next to a take-away coffee cup. I remove my cell phone from my purse and dial Michael's number but hang up as soon as I hear his outgoing voicemail message.

His room smells like him—like his deodorant and his unwashed hair—and I'm almost sickened by its immediate effect on me. I open the window above his desk and the cold November air floods in. I look for any evidence of our relationship among his scattered things: a letter; a ticket stub; one of my hair elastics, but there is nothing.

I smoke in his chair and cry as quietly as I can while in the other room his father drifts somewhere outside the edge of his body.

> (*She opens the cigarette case, removes a cigarette, lights it, smokes. After a moment, she stands, looks at the audience, and then slowly, teasingly, approaches the radio, turns it on. Some industrial punk music issues forth. She removes her school jacket, her tie, her hair ribbon, lets her hair down, rolls her sleeves up. The music gets louder and louder. She crosses to the pouf, grabs the teacup and saucer, ashes into it defiantly, turns, sets it on the dressing table, then sits on the corner of the dressing table, very much in control. The music ceases. She looks out at the audience, smiles, smokes, continues...*)

III
Marc.

BERNADETTE. I leave Michael's father's house around ten o'clock and get back on the F Train and head into Manhattan. I get out at the West 4th stop and just walk for a while. The temperature has dropped considerably so I button my raincoat all the way to the top.

I call Michael again and get his voicemail. I leave a message asking him to please call me. I tell him I have something important to talk about. I don't tell him that I'm in New York.

I find a small dive bar on Greenwich Avenue where I figure I can get served and the bartender, an actress named Tanya, doesn't even card me. Tanya wears black jeans and no makeup. She has beautiful light green eyes and a smoker's voice and for a moment I wish I could have her life: a bartender-actress with pretty eyes who fears nothing.

The place is surprisingly empty for a Friday night. The jukebox plays Radiohead and Nina Simone and Otis Redding and a Hispanic barback mouths the words to "Creep" while clearing booths.

Tanya tells me she likes my raincoat and asks if it's vintage. I tell her it is and she says something about how she can never find anything like it that fits her. I tell her about the vintage place I bought it from near Cape Cod and she asks me if that's where I'm from and I tell her that my family has a summer home there.

She eventually asks me what I'd like to drink and I order a Stella. She pours me a pint and lips a verse of some Van Morrison song in which he sounds like he's suffering on the toilet.

Part of me wishes I would see Michael pass by the window of the bar. I can feel myself willing his dark hair on the head of every young man who walks by. That summer, after the first time we made love, Michael laid his head on my stomach and I thought running my fingers through his thick dark hair represented the moment I had become a woman.

Tanya asks me if I'm new to the city and I tell her that I'm an NYU student. She asks me what I'm studying and I say Anthropology because I think it sounds good. She tells me she left SUNY Purchase after her sophomore year and that she came to the city to act and to sing in a chick band. To raise hell.

I ask her what her band is called and she says Tokyo Stunt Pussy. She says they mostly shout a lot and take their clothes off.

"Cool," I say. "That sounds cool."

Then Tanya pours herself a shot and says, "Here's to raising a little hell."

We clink glasses and drink and then Tanya moves away.

I am nursing my Stella when a man at the other end of the bar starts making eyes at me. He is barely handsome the way certain Southern U.S. Senators are barely alive.

He says, "I'm Marc."

I tell him my name is Diana and he comes and sits beside me. He tells me it's nice to meet me and that he's in town on business. Which probably means he has no business being in town.

Up close he's better looking, but just slightly, and I find that I like his teeth. They are chipped and one is a little discolored.

He buys me another Stella and himself a bourbon on the rocks. After Tanya slides us our drinks we talk about my adopted name.

He says, "Diana. Like the princess."

"Exactly," I reply.

He tells me his name is Marc with a C not with a K. I tell him that I'll keep this in mind. He tells me that that's good because people always get it wrong.

Then the music changes to Nina Simone and he asks me if I live in the city. I tell him I live in Brooklyn. He asks me what part and I tell him Carroll Gardens.

"That's nice," he says.

"It is," I say.

He says, "The fucking trees there."

And then he asks me if I'm originally from New York or if I'm a transplant. I tell him I'm from here and he says, "That's rare, you know. Practically everyone I meet is from somewhere else. Lots of Midwesterners. People from Kansas, Iowa, Ohio, Pennsylvania."

I tell him that Pennsylvania's not the Midwest.

He says, "Really? I thought it was."

Tanya comes over and tells him that I'm right; that she should know because she's from Pittsburgh.

Then she walks away and I ask him where he's from and he says New Jersey. The nice part of New Jersey, where they have steeplechases, shit like that.

I ask him what a steeplechase is and he tells me it's a horse race.

"They have to jump over hurdles," he says. "Hurdles and puddles."

Then he asks me if I like horses and I tell him I do.

He says, "Grace, power, speed. The ultimate animal."

After a silence Marc with a C looks at me and says, "Diana, can I tell you something?"

I say sure and he tells me that I'm the prettiest girl he's seen in a long time.

I say, "Oh, yeah? How long?"

He says, "Several months at least. Maybe even a year. And I travel."

His comment about traveling has not a shred of irony and I have an urge to tell him I have vaginal warts.

But instead I ask him if he ever travels to the Midwest.

He says, "Oh sure. The Midwest, the South, the West Coast. Europe."

I say, "Europe. Wow."

Then he asks me what I do and Tanya swoops back in and tells him that I go to NYU and that I'm probably young enough to be his daughter.

To Tanya he says, "Hey, back off, Xena."

And then he asks me my major and I tell him Anthropology.

He says, "That's like human beings and shit."

"It is," I confirm for him.

He says, "And animals too, right?"

I say, "If you count humans as animals."

And he says, "Humans as animals? Definitely. I would definitely, definitely say that's true. I mean look at us. We're disgusting creatures. Animals all the way."

And then he sort of jiggles on his stool and says, "I'm 34 in case you were wondering."

I say, "Really?"

He says, "Yeah, why, you thought I was younger?"

I say, "Thirty-four's old, Marc."

He says, "Old. These days you're not old till you're 50. I'm still just a kid in his prime…"

He shifts a bit on his barstool again and says, "What does one do with a degree in Anthropology, anyway?"

I say, "You learn how to read minds."

"Come on," he says.

I say, "No, you really can."

He says, "So you're saying you can read my mind?"

I say, "I can, yes."

He says, "What am I thinking, then—don't answer that."

I ask him what he does and he tells me he's in Home Furnishings.

I say, "Is that like interior design?"

He says, "Sort of, yeah. Carpets. Countertops. Wallpaper. All that pretty stuff that makes people feel better about their lives."

He watches me intensely for a moment. I feel like it's the first time someone's really looked at me in weeks.

He says, "So can I ask you a question, Diana?"

Before I can answer he asks me if I'm happy.

I say, "Happy meaning what?"

He says, "Happy meaning with your life."

I say, "Like on a scale from one to 10?" and he tells me it's a yes or no answer.

I say, "I'm happy," and he asks me if I'm sure about that.

"Yes," I say, "I'm sure."

He says, "Totally sure?"

I say, "Totally sure, yes."

He says, "Completely, like one hundred percent?"

I say, "I'm fucking happy, okay?"

And he says, "Then why are you crying?"

I feel my face and it's true. My cheeks are wet and I had no idea.

He says, "Rough day?"

I say, "Sort of," and he asks me if I want to tell him about it.

I tell him not especially and then he says, "That's some impressive thing you got going."

I say, "What thing?"

And he says, "Being pretty when you cry. That's not easy."

Then he says, "Come here," and I move to him and we hug.

Somehow the hug passes for the best thing that's happened to me in weeks. I collapse in his arms and it feels like all my bones have disappeared. His cologne smells peppery and somehow nauseatingly South American and I love it.

(She moves off the dressing table, standing now.)

We take a cab to the Chinatown Holiday Inn and Marc buys a scotch on the rocks from an Asian woman wearing a tuxedo and white gloves, tending a little bar near the front desk.

(Invaded.) "Those gloves! Those eternal gloves! I've told you time and time again to leave them in the kitchen. You probably hope to seduce the milkman with them. No, no, don't lie; that won't get you anywhere! Hang them over the sink. When will you understand that this room is not to be sullied, my little pigeon."

In the elevator we hardly speak and twenty minutes later we're in the room, simply staring at each other. He is lying in the queen-sized bed, on top of the covers, with his shirt off, still in his jeans, and I am sitting in a chair, still wearing my raincoat. He sips his scotch. We don't take our eyes off each other and I take strange comfort in this. I find his half-nudity somehow relaxing. Marc is at once flabby and muscular, thick around the middle, doughy even, and I can see that he shaves part of his chest, which I imagine will leave red marks on my breasts.

From the bed he asks me if I'd like to try his scotch.

(*She crosses to the pouf, sits on it, her legs tucked under her knees.*)

I cross to him and take his glass and drink. Up close his cologne is overwhelming. I can almost feel it coating the back of my tongue. I tell him the scotch tastes like an old tweed coat. I tell him that my father drinks Dewars neat.

He says, "Dewars. That's like drinking Budweiser."

Then he stares at me and starts to sing a Bruce Springsteen song.

(*Singing.*) *Hey little girl is your daddy home? Did he go and leave you all alone? Um hm. I got a bad desire. Oh ohoh I'm on fire...*

"Bruce," he says. "The Boss."

"The Boss," I say.

"He's the greatest," Marc with a C adds.

I hand the glass back to him and say, "So aren't you gonna try and fuck me?"

He says, "Diana, believe me, I would love to, but I can't."

I say, "Why not?"

He says, "Because of a slightly embarrassing situation that's not so easy to talk about."

I say, "What, you can't get it up?"

He tells me that that's far from the problem.

Then he drinks more scotch and tells me he has herpes.

I say, "Oh."

He tells me yeah, that it sucks pretty bad and that he takes medication for it, which makes everything basically normal, but that he's in the middle of an episode and he wouldn't want to pass it on.

I tell him that he's thoughtful.

He tells me he likes me.

"I like you," he says.

I ask him why he brought me to a hotel and he tells me because he enjoys my company.

"You're a beautiful girl, Diana. Plus you're nice. Most girls like you aren't nice."

Then I tell him my name's not Diana.

"It's not?" he says.

"No."

"Well, what is it?" he asks.

"Bernadette."

He says, "No shit? Bernadette? That's like French, right?"

"It is French, but I'm not French."

"What are you?" he asks.

"I'm just a little lost girl from the Northeast Seaboard," I reply.

Then he asks me if I would mind if he looked at me and relieved himself.

He says, "I'll totally understand if you say no."

"It's fine," I hear myself say.

He says, "Cool," and then he asks me if I wouldn't mind taking my shirt off.

So I remove my raincoat, and my sweater. I unbutton my blouse and undo my bra so I can show him my breasts.

He tells me I'm perfect. And then he reaches into his pants, pulls his cock out, and starts to masturbate. His penis is oddly dark. It looks poisonous and yet I find it comforting.

He tells me I have great tits. And that I'm so beautiful and that he wishes he could fuck me. He accidentally calls me Diana.

"It's Bernadette," I say.

He says, "I really wish I could fuck you, Bernadette."

I say, "You are fucking me, Marc."

He says, "Am I?"

I say, "You're fucking me so hard you're practically splitting me in half. Can't you feel it?"

He says, "Yes, yes, I can feel it."

I say, "And your cock is so big and hard."

He says, "I know. It's fucking huge, right?"

I say, "It is so huge. It's like a car."

He says, "It is like a car. It's like a Cadillac, right?"

I say, "It is a Cadillac."

He says, "It's the 2011 Escalade, right?"

I say, "It's the 2011 Escalade."

He says, "Black with smoked windows! Jesus, I'm gonna come!"

"Do it," I say. "Come inside me."

He tells me Holy shit, I'm coming.

He comes on his stomach in little grayish-white arcs. I can smell it from where I'm sitting. It smells gamey and chemical.

I hand him some tissues from the bedside stand. He wipes himself and hands them back. Like I'm a waitress. I cross to the bathroom and drop the tissues in the trash.

(*Directly to someone in the audience.*) "You hate me, don't you? You crush me with your attentions and your humbleness; you smother me with gladioli and mimosa."

When I come back out Marc has fallen asleep. His head has lolled back against the headboard, slightly tilted to the left. His mouth hangs open. It looks like he's been pulled from a car crash.

As I sit there watching him sleep I can feel myself outside of my own body, as if the thing that my skin was containing is now a slow, thick vapor drifting toward the small, inoperable window overlooking Lafayette Street. I'm not even aware of the sensation of breathing; I am simply vapor.

I am living someone else's life...the life of some stupid, desperate girl in a raincoat who likes to tease and lie to strangers.

I go into the bathroom and take a shower and wash my hair with the cheap shampoo sample and sit on the lid of the toilet and smoke another of Michael's cigarettes—the ones I had stolen from his bedroom. There's a silver handicap rail next to the sink and I briefly imagine myself with a broken leg, always lurching toward such things.

After I come out of the bathroom I take a twenty-dollar bill out of Marc's wallet. He does indeed have a New Jersey driver's license, but it says he is forty-four years old and that Marc with a C's name is actually Richard Romero. There's a small picture of a little girl, maybe six or seven, who I assume to be his daughter. She has his dark hair and big brown eyes. On the back of the photo it says "Angelface."

Before I leave I try to make myself cry again; I'm not sure why; maybe it's because I know Michael and I are over, or maybe it's because nothing really came of my little rendezvous with this strange man who is asleep in exactly the same position? Or maybe it's the simple fact that, at this late hour, my life isn't being witnessed by anyone; that this night hasn't ended in the disaster that part of me hoped it would.

It's the actress in me attempting to leave something behind; a few tears shed on the floor like rare coins to be found and cherished.

I even cross to the window and am nearly moved to feel something because of the sudden, surprising snow, but when I get right down to it there is nothing inside me so I let the drapes fall, pour the rest of his scotch on the phone, and leave.

(*She rises off the pouf, paces, seething. She crosses to the desk and hurls all the objects off it. It makes a loud crash against the upstage wall.*

A MAINTENANCE MAN enters. The theater work lights snap on.)

MAN. You okay?

BERNADETTE. I'm fine.

MAN. You sure?

(*The MAINTENANCE MAN exits briefly, re-enters with a cart. From the cart he unloads a black, two-step stair unit. He sets it in front of the platform, on the upstage right side, uses it to join BERNADETTE onstage, where he begins to strike the set. He strikes the table, carefully steps down the stair unit, sets it on the cart, returns for the stool, strikes that as well, sets it on the cart, then returns again for the pouf. He lifts it, faces BERNADETTE.*)

MAN. Is anybody else back there?

BERNADETTE. It's just me.

(*She rolls her sleeves down. He exits the stage with the pouf, sets it on the cart. He strikes the silver tea set, places it on the cart. He strikes the phone, starts to set it on the cart, stops. Picking up the receiver, playfully.*)

MAN. Mission Control? Looks like we got a live one.

(*He hangs up the phone, sets it on the cart. He sets the radio on the cart. From the cart he produces a cardboard box, begins to pick the scattered objects up off the floor.)*

BERNADETTE. Sorry.

MAN. Ain't no nothin', not at all. That's life, man.

(He continues picking up the objects, whistling now. He picks up her notebook.)

BERNADETTE. That's mine.

(He hands her the notebook. Referring to the deck of the set, the chandelier, etc.)

MAN. All this is gonna be gone tomorrow.

(He crosses to the cart, sets the box on it, starts to push it out of the theater, exits, returns moments later with a ghost light, sets it at the corner of the stage, unfurls the power cord, plugs it into the wall. The light is illuminated.)

I gotta lock up soon.

(She nods. He exits. Moments later, the work lights snap off.

BERNADETTE *is left in darkness, the ghost light the only source of light now. She crosses to the light, sits under it, opens her notebook, begins reading...)*

IV
Home.

BERNADETTE. *(Reading from notebook.)* I catch a cab to Grand Central Station and board the last train to Connecticut. The snow seems to thicken with every stop and by Stamford it's nearly a blizzard. I don't have enough money to go further than New Haven but my mom drives the ninety minutes south and picks me up at the train station. We barely speak in the car. I ask her if Michael has called but he hasn't. She seems bothered by something and it's obvious that we are both content with silence.

When I get home I finally sleep—nearly all weekend—and hide my morning sickness from her with a tenacity that I've not since mustered. My father's on set in Los Angeles and won't be coming home, so that makes things a little easier.

On Sunday morning I take a long walk down the two-lane road that runs in front of our house, treading through several inches of fresh snow in a pair of old rain boots, hoping that the trees will somehow make me feel better, but their leaves are all but gone now and they seem arthritic and withered.

That night my mother and I eat dinner in front of the fireplace. She makes a roast chicken with broccoli and we drink red wine because my parents allow that. Although I feel nauseous I force myself to eat my entire plate so as not to warrant any suspicion. I hadn't noticed it in the car a few days before but my mother has just dyed her hair a strange fiery auburn and I keep thinking she's wearing a wig.

After her first glass of wine she tells me that Dean Fessenden had called to tell her that I cut my afternoon classes on Friday without a permission slip. She asks me if it's true and I say, "Yeah. You gonna ground me?"

She doesn't answer.

I hadn't realized it but my mother has put on a Carpenters record. She loves to listen to the Carpenters and feel sorry for herself. She can spend entire weekends listening to the Carpenters and painting her dreary watercolors.

A few minutes later I take my dishes to the sink and come back with another bottle of wine and start to uncork it.

My mom tells me that my father wants a divorce.

"He emailed me last night," she says.

I ask her if it's because of the stewardess. She says that he didn't mention her in the email but that's her guess. My mom says that she thinks he cast her on the TV show.

I say, "So she's an actress?"

My mom says, "She is now."

I ask my mom if she's going to fight him and she says, "Tooth and nail."

And then she says, "Whatever you do, Bernie, don't let your ass get bad. A good ass will add years to your marriage."

While I'm drying dishes the phone rings. It's Michael. His voice sounds small and far away. When he says my name I feel myself turn to powder. I have to grip the countertop to keep my balance.

(*Looking up now.*) He tells me that his dad has just killed himself; that he came home and he was hanging from a hook in the ceiling in the living room where a light fixture used to be. He says Wayne had reinforced the hook with Gorilla Glue. Michael can't stop crying. He tells me his father used extra coaxial cable that the cable company had left when they came to install their high-speed internet. I ask if he wants me to come to Brooklyn and he says No. I ask if there's anything I can do and he says No again. I ask if he still loves me and he says he has to go; that there are all these people in his apartment—cops and EMT professionals and his Uncle Ed and that he'll call me later. I wait for his call all night but it never comes.

(*Reading from the notebook again.*) That Monday, my mother drives me back to school and I get off with a warning from Dean Fessenden, whose recent dramatic weight loss makes me think of Michael's father. He possesses a long, unfortunate horsey face but beautiful hazel eyes.

At the end of the meeting I ask him if he is okay. He tells me he's fine. I tell him he looks thin and he says something about his new diet; how's he's been eating mostly oatmeal and presses his own juices. He tells me he still eats the occasional steak and smiles on the word "steak" in a way that almost makes it seem as if his face will get stuck that way.

As I'm about to leave he asks me what I want to do with my life.

He says, "What are your plans, Bernie?"

"I want to write short stories," I tell him.

"You want to or you're going to?" he asks.

"I'm going to," I answer.

"It takes great discipline to be a writer," he adds. "Self-discipline."

(*Looking up from notebook.*) Two weeks later I get an abortion at a small Planned Parenthood in Bennington, Vermont. Briel drives me there in her day-student-boyfriend's Saab and waits for me while I take the mifepristone pill, which is large and white and tastes like a warm bitter spoon.

After speaking with the doctors about what to expect and how to deal with what's to come, Briel and I go eat pancakes at a diner near the Bennington campus. She tells me she's thinking about going to school here. We talk about the Donna Tartt novel in which all those college kids kill two of their classmates. She asks me where I want to go and I tell her I haven't really thought about it much. I tell her that my mom wants me to go to Mount Holyoke. Briel says that it's full of lesbians. I tell her she's confusing it with Smith and she says, "No, it's totally Mount Holyoke too. It's like the Lesbian Olympics there."

I can feel a new distance between us. It's as if I've acquired a permanent fishhook in my lip and there are those with fishhooks and those without.

Then Briel tells me that it's really fucked up about Michael's dad. She says he must have been in so much pain.

I tell her that I think he was.

She says that Michael must be so sad and asks me if we're officially over.

Then I reach into my pocket and give her the pocketknife.

She says, "What's that?"

I say, "A pocketknife."

She says, "What are you doing with it?"

I say, "I'm giving it to you."

She says, "Oh. Why?"

I tell her it's a token of my thanks for driving me up here.

She tells me that it's really no problem.

"So I skipped a few classes," she adds. "You'd do it for me, right?"

"Of course," I say.

She says, "That's what friends are for."

Then I ask her if she has a penny. She asks why and I tell her that when someone gives you a knife you have to give them a penny; that it's good luck.

She asks me where I'd learned that and I tell her I'd read about it.

"Who gets the luck?" she asks.

I say, "We both do."

Briel reaches into her pocket and produces some change. She tells me all she has is a nickel. I tell her that that'll do and she pushes the nickel toward me and takes the pocketknife.

We drive back to Whitney in relative silence. The radio plays classic rock and Briel sings along to a rockblock of the Rolling Stones. At school I wind up getting cast as Claire in Jean Genet's *The Maids*, which is directed by my drama teacher, Mr. Chubb, who as a person is droopy and listless but occasionally seems delighted with my capacity to role-play with Solange at murdering Madame.

One day after rehearsal he tells me that I'm a natural talent and that I should seriously consider pursuing acting.

> (*She rises, closing the notebook. She crosses to the other side of the stage, inhabited. From here on, the notebook remains closed.*)

"I know. You'd go through fire for me... Fasten it. Don't pull so hard. Don't try to bind me... Avoid pawing me. You smell like an animal. You've brought those odors from some foul attic, where the lackeys visit us at night. The maids' room! The garret! (*Graciously.*) Claire, if I speak of the smell of garrets, it is for memory's sake. And of the twin beds where two sisters fall asleep, dreaming of one another. There, (*She points to a spot in the room.*) there, the two iron beds with the night table between them. There, (*She points to a spot opposite.*) the pinewood dresser with the little altar to the Holy Virgin! That's right, isn't it?"

After I take the follow-up pill, I wait for the miscarriage the way you wait for a mysterious package to arrive from the post office. When it finally happens it is more painful than the Planned Parenthood doctor said it would be and I have to leave a Great Books class feigning low blood sugar at the infirmary, where they give me vanilla wafers and let me take a nap.

I manage to get through the next few days by sheer will and as much pot as I can get my hands on.

A few weeks later *The Maids* is thought to be a great success by students and faculty alike.

> (BERNADETTE *crosses to the upstage bench, opens it, removes a gold box, she sits, opens the box, removes emerald earrings, a hairclip, puts on the earrings, puts her hair up over the following.*)

"The orchestra is playing brilliantly. The attendant is raising the red velvet curtain. He bows. Madame is descending the stairs. Her furs brush against the green plants. Madame steps into the car. Monsieur is whispering sweet nothings in her ear. She would like to smile, but she is dead. [She is dead. She is dead. She is dead. She is dead...] She rings the bell. The porter yawns. He opens the door. Madame goes up the stairs. She enters her apartment—but, Madame is dead.

> (BERNADETTE *sheds her skirt and white shirt, removing her shoes, her socks, only in Madame's white charmeuse slip now. She rises, crosses to the downstage corner. It is clear now that she is also wearing an emerald necklace.*)

"Her two maids are alive; they've just risen up, free, from Madame's icy form. All the maids were present at her side—not they themselves, but rather the hellish agony of their names. And all that remains of them to float about Madame's airy corpse is the delicate perfume of the holy maidens which they were in secret. We are beautiful, joyous, drunk, and free!"

After the play opens, I try Michael every day for two weeks but he never calls back. With regard to his father dying I guess he's had a lot to deal with. Michael's way of breaking up with me was by becoming nothing, pollen, mist, perhaps something even finer.

It has been snowing a lot lately. The trees at Whitney are blanketed white and the occasional sound of a branch cracking can shatter even the most persistent campus silence.

(*Upstage of the platform, against the back wall of the theater, it starts to snow.*)

In my American Escapes class we read Jonathan Safran Foer's *Extremely Loud and Incredibly Close* and talk about how it relates to the endless war in the Middle East and all the problems in Egypt and our own small lives and I am mostly sad and bored.

(*She turns and faces the snow, crosses to her trench coat, puts it on over her slip, turns and faces the audience.*)

Long walks through the snow at dusk are the one thing I look forward to.

The snow and the trees and the slow, unbearable silence of winter.

(*She exits the stage with her notebook, faces the back wall, crosses to the door in the wall of the theater, opens it, passes through and into the snow.*)

End of Play

A DEVIL AT NOON
A PLAY ABOUT INNER SPACE
by Anne Washburn

Copyright © 2011 by Anne Washburn. All rights reserved. CAUTION: Professionals and amateurs are hereby warned that *A Devil at Noon* is subject to royalty. It is fully protected under the copyright laws of the United States of America and of all countries covered by the International Copyright Union (including the Dominion of Canada and the rest of the British Commonwealth), the Berne Convention, the Pan-American Copyright Convention and the Universal Copyright Convention, as well as all countries with which the United States has reciprocal copyright relations. All rights, including professional, amateur stage rights, motion picture, recitation, lecturing, public reading, radio broadcasting, television, video or sound recording, all other forms of mechanical or electronic reproduction, such as CD-ROM, CD-I, information storage and retrieval systems, and photocopying, and the rights of translation into foreign languages, are strictly reserved. Particular emphasis is laid upon the matter of readings, permission for which must be secured from the Author's agent in writing.

Required royalties must be paid every time this play is performed before any audience, whether or not it is presented for profit and whether or not admission is charged.

All inquiries concerning rights, including amateur rights, should be addressed to: Val Day, ICM, 730 Fifth Avenue, New York, NY 10019.

ABOUT *A DEVIL AT NOON*

This article first ran in the January/February 2011 issue of Inside Actors, and is based on conversations with the playwright before rehearsals for the Humana Festival production began.

Chet Ellis is a science fiction writer in a slightly imaginary 1981. His new book is going well—he's in a familiar zone of obsession, drugs, and efficiency, intrigued by every splendid contour of his characters' personalities and needs. But outside of his work, things are getting…a little odd. Ants are overrunning his apartment. His magnets are de-magnetizing. A woman he just met in an addiction meeting has popped up on his doorstep.

The inspiration for Anne Washburn's *A Devil at Noon: a play about inner space* was surprisingly personal. Washburn grew up in the Bay Area, and while on a visit, she realized how much of her experience of her hometown is drawn from an alternate universe—her past. "I was walking somewhere and having this odd train of thought about how well I know Berkeley," Washburn says. "I felt like every block had a thousand memories from all the different mini eras of my life but in the middle of this…smug, really, thought about how intimate I am with the place, I suddenly realized that the city I'm so familiar with is a Berkeley that doesn't exist anymore. People I half expected to run into were long dead, or moved away; places I assumed I could just turn the corner and walk into were actually gone. I realized that my reality wasn't a fully functional one. And then I thought, oh, that seems like a Philip K. Dick kind of thought."

Bay Area writer Philip K. Dick (1928-1982) serves more as a philosophical touchstone than the basis for the plot or even quite the characters of *A Devil at Noon*. Prolific and much awarded in the science fiction world (he even has an award named after him), Dick's work has also been adapted into several major movies, including *Blade Runner, Minority Report, Total Recall,* and *A Scanner Darkly.* His stories frequently focus on moments when reality turns inside out—a man's girlfriend is revealed to be a sophisticated android, a television actor wakes up to find he's suddenly completely unknown, a seemingly ordinary person realizes that his memories of his life were only recently implanted and that he's someone else altogether. "I'd been interested in doing something with Dick's late work for a while, and had just read a book of interviews he gave right before his death," says Washburn of the writer's influence on her early thinking about the play. "Those last books are peculiar and fragmenting; he's written himself directly into them. In one there's a character named Philip K. Dick who thinks the FBI is breaking into his house and taking drafts of his novel, his bank records—something he thought was happening in his own life. In another he appears as a character named Philip K. Dick *and* as an alias who is *also* clearly himself. They're fascinating books, more evidence than literature. It feels like his mind was breaking apart and he was trying to write himself into a powerful clarity. I was curious about that mixture of narrative and character, and how it could work theatrically."

Critic Laura Miller describes Dick's particular genius as being able to evoke the "vertiginous sensation of reality disintegrating underfoot." Likewise, Washburn's play theatricalizes a world that feels so convincingly familiar that its shifts, when they come, are all the more unsettling. To give away much more would rob *Devil* of its peculiar mix of incongruity and cheeky humor, but in a play about the addiction, power, and danger of dwelling in your imagination, Washburn has placed real demands on the imagination of the audience, and the actors. "It's so engaging to watch actors rise to ridiculous demands when they're performing," Washburn says. "It's immensely pleasurable, watching people pull off hard things; it makes you proud to be human. And I always enjoy, as an audience member, having to work as well, participating in the creation of the play, the reality of the world."

"My plays often come to the question of how difficult it is to know things, how difficult it is to know other people, or ourselves," Washburn continues. "It's a super complex world, so we have to make up stories to stay confident and sane." The play, as its subtitle suggests, considers what happens when these stories start to disintegrate. At its core, *A Devil at Noon* is a play about the fictions of our inner lives, the utterly surreal experience of building our reality on our own unstable perceptions—whether of the streets of Berkeley, of a friend's casual desire, or of the complexities that drive our understandings of our own inner space.

—Adrien-Alice Hansel

BIOGRAPHY

Anne Washburn's plays include *A Devil at Noon*, *Apparition*, *The Communist Dracula Pageant*, *I Have Loved Strangers*, *The Ladies*, *Mr. Burns*, *The Small* and a transadaptation of Euripides' *Orestes*. Her work has been produced by Actors Theatre of Louisville, American Repertory Theater, Cherry Lane Theatre, Clubbed Thumb, The Civilians, Dixon Place, Ensemble Studio Theatre, The Folger, London's Gate Theater, New York City's Soho Rep, D.C.'s Studio Theatre, Two River Theater Company, New York City's Vineyard Theatre, and Woolly Mammoth Theatre Company. Awards include a Guggenheim, a NYFA Fellowship, a Time Warner Fellowship, residencies at MacDowell and Yaddo, and an Artslink travel grant to Hungary; *Mr. Burns* was a finalist for the 2011 Susan Smith Blackburn Prize. She is a member of 13P, an associated artist with The Civilians and New Georges, and an alumna of New Dramatists. She is currently commissioned by Manhattan Theatre Club, Playwrights Horizons, Soho Rep, and Yale Repertory Theatre.

ACKNOWLEDGMENTS

A Devil at Noon premiered at the Humana Festival of New American Plays in February 2011. It was directed by Steve Cosson with the following cast:

Chet Ellis	Joseph Adams
Bob Seward/The Moon Man	Ross Bickell
Lois L	Rebecca Hart
Tom/Don Larkin	Brandon T. Miller
Dennis/Philip Hutchens	David Ross
Colin McAdams/Alien Guy	Matthew Stadelmann

and the following production staff:

Scenic Designer	Brian Sidney Bembridge
Costume Designer	Lorraine Venberg
Lighting Designer	Jeff Nellis
Sound Designer	Matt Hubbs
Properties Designer	Joe Cunningham
Media Designer	Philip Allgeier
Mime Consultant	Emmanuelle Delpech-Ramey
Stage Manager	Stephen Horton
Dramaturg	Janice Paran
Casting	Calleri Casting

Directing Assistant .... Zach Chotzen-Freund
Scenic Design Assistant .... Ryan Wineinger
Assistant Costume Designer .... Lindsay Chamberlin
Assistant Lighting Designer .... Rachel Fae Szymanski
Assistant Sound Designer .... Stowe Nelson
Assistant Dramaturg .... Mik Mroczynski

Development of *A Devil at Noon* was supported by the Eugene O'Neill Theater Center through a residency at the National Playwrights Conference of 2010. Wendy C. Goldberg, Artistic Director; Preston Whiteway, Executive Director.

SETTING
This play takes place in West Berkeley just above San Pablo
and in Sector 8
in a largely accurate 1981.

CHARACTERS
6 actors play the following roles:

CHET ELLIS	56. A writer of Science Fiction.
LOIS L_____	26
COLIN McADAMS	Mid 20s
BOB SEWARD	Late 50s, early 60s
TOM	Man in his 30s/40s, carefully nondescript
DENNIS	Man in his 20s/30s, carefully nondescript
PHILIP HUTCHENS	Executive in his 30s
DON LARKIN	Executive in his 40s
ALIEN GUY	20s. Not an alien, just a guy.
THE MOON MAN	Not the same thing as The Man In The Moon.

ATTENTION!

A design note

so crucial

that it has its own page:

Except where indicated very specifically in the script, in **bold**, all props and set dressings are

imaginary

and are either exactly mimed, or expressively indicated.

(The maneuvering within the imaginary world is supported by sound design.)

The following pieces of furniture are real and are brought onto the set for the scenes indicated and then removed:

Black Metal Folding Chair

Couch

Futon

A FEW ADDITIONAL NOTES

Words in brackets [ ] are thought, but not spoken.

The Moon Man might be wearing a tweed jacket and a sandy moustache.

The two large pieces of actual furniture should be brought on and off by astronauts.

This play draws very heavily upon the life and work of Philip K. Dick.

Rebecca Hart
in *A Devil at Noon*

35th Annual Humana Festival of New American Plays
Actors Theatre of Louisville, 2011
Photo by Alan Simons

A DEVIL AT NOON

ACT I

A coffee maker, and coffee-making set-up, on a little stand.

LOIS *is looking at the percolator as it fills.*

CHET, *nearby on a metal folding chair, is reading **a thick book**.*

LOIS. Is this enough coffee, do you think, for 17 people?

CHET. (*Looking up.*) No.

(*He looks down again.*)

LOIS. But there's more in the carafe.

CHET. (*Shrug of expressive ignorance of the entire situation—coffee-making, carafe volumes, caffeine thirsts.*)

(LOIS *stands there. Looks at **coffee pot**. Stands there. Grinds beans. Hesitates. Swirls **carafe**. Puts it down.*)

LOIS. Yeah, I think this is fine. Besides, some people drink tea.

CHET. (*No response whatsoever.*)

(LOIS *exits.*

Three NINJAS *creep onto stage, quite suddenly leap onto and utterly overpower* CHET, *bind him, throw a black bag over his head and drag him offstage without a peep.*

There is a pause.

They creep back on stage, with extra caution and maneuvering, towards the coffee maker

creeping up behind it…

As they are part of the way there it makes a sound, a percolation sound, they freeze

and stay frozen

for a very

long

time

they start creeping towards it again and then it makes a beep

335

they freeze

it beeps again, again, then a series of rising beeps which sound increasingly frantic

they all look off, to the left

and then they leap upon it

a nod from one to the other, one switches it "off"

the beeps cease

they look left again…for a long moment…

one brings out a black bag, and flings it over the coffee maker

while he is doing this another one of them pulls up his ninja mask to expose his lips, hoists up the carafe, and chugs from it—another reaches out and does likewise—

one hustles the coffee maker off to the right, the other two hustle off the coffee stand.

Only the black folding chair remains on stage.

LIGHT CHANGE.

CHET sits in the black folding chair.)

CHET. I look at a volume of mine in a bookstore sometimes—and I'm not going to deny that I will wander over sometimes, in a bookstore, to sneak a quick peek at my books; first of all I'm always glad they're there, it's always a relief. I think that might make me sound like a humble person and I want to disabuse you of that notion…right away. Because right after that moment of relief, I have a whole series of…requirements that I have to address. It's not enough that they have my books, I always want to see how many of my books they have—it's rare, very rare, that a bookstore will have a complete selection; often, unless it's a specialty bookstore, or a very good bookstore, they will only have a few, and usually of course just the most popular. Then I'm always interested to see how many copies they have of each one. I can take all of this in at a glance. While making like I'm perusing the work of my colleagues. Anyways, when I'm glancing over the titles to my books, even though I'm not making a conscious effort for this to happen, in fact I'd prefer if it didn't, sometimes a character will brush up against me. A character who doesn't feel entirely fulfilled, who doesn't feel entirely expressed—I learned all I need to know about them for the purpose of the novel, the action of the novel, but they don't feel finished and they want to keep going.

I say you're on your own buddy. The cord, is cut. Heartless? Maybe. You're one of my characters I'm your whole life but you've got to be just a part, just the tiniest part, of mine, right? Or I'd spend all my life writing the same book.

But in the beginning—it's a very intimate time, it's a little bit like falling in love, they're a mystery; I really want to know who they are and what the ending of their story is and I think that all of their needs are splendid and I will do anything for them.

So my character—I'm in the middle of this book and my character goes to a Meeting. And then I'm stuck. Just. Stuck. Back at my desk. Brain a complete blank and that does not happen to me. I write quick, I just, I take some time before I start but when I go I go go go go go so it's kind of like, slamming into a brick wall. She's at a Meeting, that's what I know. I'm not aware that she has any kind of major problem with addiction apart from caffeine which she consumes in ludicrous quantities—but she's there. So I'm here.

> (*He is queried.*)

Oh. Well. I myself have taken hallucinogens, ah, you know: in bulk. I currently take stimulants, I drink a fair amount but I suppose in the interest of full disclosure I should admit that I don't myself have a problem. Or, my problem, is not a problem. My problem doesn't prevent me from doing anything I want to do, so how is it a problem? That's how I see it. I could perfect myself, yes I could. I could. But it would take all day, and I've got a vocation to pursue, that's…my feeling about it.

> (*He stands, carefully folds his chair, and takes it off.*
> *LIGHT CHANGE.*
> *As he passes him in the hallway, a young man approaches an older one.*)

COLIN. Excuse me can you tell me where is Sector 8?

BOB SEWARD. Sector 8?

> (*A few beats.*)

Is there a Sector 8?

COLIN. Well I think yes, I think that there might be; at any rate, I'm to report there so. I hope so!

BOB SEWARD. Sector 8… Who *are* you?

COLIN. Oh I'm nobody, I'm new.

BOB SEWARD. Obviously you're new. And you *look* like nobody. But I'll be the final judge of that. What's your name.

COLIN. Colin McAdams.

BOB SEWARD. I've never heard of you.

COLIN. I'm new.

BOB SEWARD. Yes I know that. Who are you reporting to? In Sector 8.

COLIN. Well I'm just, I don't know. I'm to go there and give my name to the receptionist.

BOB SEWARD. Sector 8 has a receptionist.

COLIN. Yes, well I hope so.

BOB SEWARD. Let me try again: who *sent* you to Sector 8.

COLIN. (*Promptly.*) Richard Harrison.

(*A little beat.*)

BOB SEWARD. No.

COLIN. Well...yes.

BOB SEWARD. No.

(*Beat.*)

COLIN. Are you sure?

BOB SEWARD. I'm positive. Let's start from the beginning. You arrived here this morning—after shaving yourself most earnestly. And after attiring yourself. How new are you anyway?

COLIN. (*Promptly.*) First day.

BOB SEWARD. (*Of course.*) Yes. Yes. And so you strode up to the front desk. And you gave them your name—what is it again?

COLIN. Colin McAdams.

BOB SEWARD. And they said yes, Mr. McAdams, who are you here for. And you said—

COLIN. I said I was told to report to Richard Harrison.

BOB SEWARD. And they said.

COLIN. They said oh, good, or something like that.

BOB SEWARD. They did.

(COLIN *fidgets a bit.*)

Richard Harrison.

This very interesting. You may or may not be an interesting person but you have had a very interesting morning.

COLIN. Oh well, thank you?

BOB SEWARD. Probably not. So you went through the office doors.

COLIN. I went through, they buzzed me in, and Mr. Harrison met me

(BOB SEWARD *stops himself from interjecting.*)

and we went back to his office and we had a chat.

BOB SEWARD. Describe Mr. Richard Harrison.

COLIN. Describe him? Well I'm not [so good at describing]

BOB SEWARD. Humor me.

COLIN. Well you know, you know Mr. Harrison?

BOB SEWARD. (*Micropause.*) I do. Yes. Indulge me.

COLIN. Well he's—yea tall maybe, I'd say 5 foot 11 or maybe…6 foot. And gray here, and gray there

  (*Pointing to his temples and the back of his head.*)

and

  (*Running his hand down the air in front of his body.*)

…suit…

BOB SEWARD. A bit of a nose.

COLIN. (*Restrained bit of hesitation.*) A bit of a nose maybe, yes.

BOB SEWARD. Shy of a honker. Eyebrows only a bit out of the ordinary, not extraordinary, but a bit, just a bit of a feature.

  (*Tiny pause.*)

COLIN. Yes.

BOB SEWARD. If he wore thick dark rimmed glasses, if he possessed a dark moustache, he would be in the smallest danger of looking, just a tad, like an anemically realized Groucho Marx Halloween ensemble.

COLIN. *Oh.*

BOB SEWARD. We're talking about the same man.

COLIN. But not in those terms. We're not; *I'm* not—

BOB SEWARD. Of course not. You're his employee; I'm his…colleague. We use different words. But we're talking about the same man.

COLIN. …Yes.

BOB SEWARD. Richard Harrison met you. And you went back to his office. And you had a chat.

COLIN. Yes.

BOB SEWARD. Was it a nice office?

COLIN. Yes.

BOB SEWARD. Describe it to me.

COLIN. A lot of white, I suppose.

BOB SEWARD. White. White—what? Laminate? Marble? Plastic?

  (*Bit of a beat.*)

COLIN. I don't actually, I wasn't paying attention to the office itself you see, first day, I was nervous.

BOB SEWARD. You can't describe it, can you.

COLIN. I'm not a good describer.

BOB SEWARD. You can't remember it can you.

COLIN. I'm not a good, I'm not I have a terrible memory also.

BOB SEWARD. White. A lot of white. And this chat.

COLIN. Yes.

BOB SEWARD. What was it about? Can you remember that? You can't, can you.

COLIN. Well he said—

(*He stops.*)

BOB SEWARD. He said…

COLIN. All kinds of things.

BOB SEWARD. I see.

You're beginning to wonder if this is really any of my business.

COLIN. Well I—

BOB SEWARD. You're wondering just who the hell I am, or think I am.

COLIN. Yes. I am, actually.

BOB SEWARD. Do you know your way out? Do you know your way back?

(*A beat.*)

COLIN. Yes.

BOB SEWARD. Are you sure?

COLIN. (*Looks behind him.*) I could pick it out.

BOB SEWARD. I wouldn't be so sure about that. Listen, I'll do you a favor. I'll escort you back to the front. Send you on your way.

COLIN. Thanks. I think I'll just, make my way to Sector 8, somehow.

BOB SEWARD. (*In earnest.*) I'm quite serious. If you take my advice you'll go: you'll just go.

(COLIN *looks back, stares at him.*)

This job. I know it seems important to you, look at how dressed you are, but it actually, in the grand scheme of things, it means nothing. *Nothing.*

(*A statement:*)

You're not going back.

COLIN. No. Of course not.

BOB SEWARD. Well then: go forward. I'll tell you this, I still don't know if you're someone or not, but you're about to have an experience which is going to be quite something.

COLIN. (*A beat then, terse.*) Thanks.

BOB SEWARD. No. Don't thank me. No.

(COLIN *exits. A moment, then* BOB SEWARD *exits the other way.*
LIGHT CHANGE.
Sound of a prolonged rattling in a lock, a door opening, a screen door closing behind it.)

TOM. Succulents. Hippies, and their succulents. How you growing there, little buddy?

(*He taps at an imaginary plant.*)

Doing okay.

They watering you in a responsible and timely manner?

(*Deciding; decisively.*)

This place is a mess.

DENNIS. (*Taking a better look.*) It's not so bad.

TOM. It's a mess.

DENNIS. I've seen worse.

TOM. Yeah you have, I've been there with you, you've seen places floors all spread over with garbage and fecal matter, flies, and seven-day-old corpses. Regardless, this place is a mess.

DENNIS. It's untidy. But nothing's rotting.

TOM. That's not a standard.

DENNIS. (*Decides to let it go.*) Maybe his wife left him.

TOM. Again?

DENNIS. That was the other one, that one was always leaving him.

TOM. She's probably some kind of creative person as well. What I don't like about a mess—apart from the fact that it's a mess, which is just wrong—is that it is very difficult to tell, from looking at it, is this a mess with or without a system of operating psychology; could you drive a tractor through it and he's never going to notice or is this the kind of thing where you tweak a magazine and his antennae, jump. I mean look at this, look at this sugar bowl, it's like, Nepal, from above, heights, depths, lumps, and that's—

DENNIS. That's coffee.

TOM. That's coffee drips.

DENNIS. Coffee sugar drips.

TOM. What a mess. This sugar bowl is a mess. After I use my sugar bowl in the morning I swirl it.

(*He almost does it with this one, stops himself abruptly.*)

I swirl you know, hard, just for, 'til it's smooth on top, 'til it's perfect anyone in the world could walk into my kitchen and root around in my sugar bowl and then just

(*He does the motion.*)

if they can make it perfect again I'm never going to know it. Damn I wish we had little portable x ray machines, like on *Star Trek*, you know? Point it at this: zooooop. (*Does computer voice:*) "Affirmative." I mean, what.

DENNIS. I don't think he's got anything in the sugar bowl.

TOM. Hippies love to stash things in the sugar bowl.

DENNIS. (*Hasn't heard this one before.*) Do they?

TOM. Joints in the sugar bowl; it's supposed to be a statement about goodness. I think it's a statement about…(*Loses interest in his thought.*) …whatever the fuck. Alright, I'm not going to chance the sugar bowl.

> (*He points a truly imaginary portable x-ray at random locations throughout the room.*)

Zoop, zoop…zoop "Affirmative."

> (*Key in the front door.*
>
> *They freeze, for a second.*)

Fuck.

> (*They tiptoe, super speedily, out the way they came, close the screen door carefully*
>
> *as the door is opening, sound of someone entering, putting packages down momentarily*
>
> *keys dropping onto a table or in a metal dish*
>
> *A light jacket being pulled off, slung somewhere, packages lifted up again*
>
> CHET *enters, carrying groceries, which he puts down on the table, hits an answering machine.*)

ANSWERING MACHINE. (*Curt.*) "This is Chet and Delia."

OLD LADY. "…Hello? Hello? Is this Roland? Roland is this you? That didn't sound like you. (*Pause.*) Well maybe I have the wrong number."

> (CHET *snorts. He pours in beans, twists the top of the coffee grinder, it grinds, empties the contents into the filter section of the coffee maker, fills up the canister with water from the sink, pours it in, hits go, the machine starts percolating;*
>
> *while the coffee is making he unpacks rapidly, a lot of cans—which go into cupboards—*
>
> *a bag of potatoes, which goes into a floor cupboard next to the sink,*
>
> *two six packs of beer which go in the fridge, he pulls one out, takes off the top with an opener, takes a swig, and then puts it back in the fridge; he pulls out a jar of peanut butter which is sort of wedged behind things in the back.*
>
> *a bag of apples which he puts on the counter*
>
> *pulls out a chopping block and a medium-sized knife from the counter near the sink, cuts an apple into wedges.*
>
> *looks around for a bowl, finds a bowl, also grabs a plate, spills the apples from the bag into the bowl, scoots the apple wedges onto a plate*
>
> *leaves the peanut butter jar, the knife, the cutting board on the table*

pulls out a box of dish soap from the bag, puts that under the sink, and debags some boxes of frozen peas which go into the freezer, along with a box of Neapolitan ice cream.

All of these objects, remember, are imaginary.

He crumples up the bags, leaves them on the table

his coffee mug is by the sink, he picks it up, carries it to the machine, pours if it's ready, or waits there, staring at it while it gurgles, until it's done

returns to the table to the sugar, goes back to the sink for a spoon, rummages briefly, finds a spoon, returns,

decides to throw the crumpled up paper bags away now,

sets the mug and spoon on the table

squashes the bags together again, as small as he can get them, and smashes them into the garbage bag, squishing down, returns to the table, and his coffee, looks down at it briefly, remembers about the sugar, dips spoon in several times, sugars the coffee, stirs, places spoon on table, picks up the plate of apple wedges, and is just about to leave the kitchen to go settle down to work when he stops.

He looks around him, as though suddenly the room looked a little strange to him.

He stands there for just a moment or two, head cocked, looking about,

then leaves.

LIGHT CHANGE.

A nondescript man stands in front of the curtain at the back of the stage.)

THE MOON MAN. Moon off.

(*He pulls or, ideally, snaps and causes to be pulled, the curtain.*
There is a **cardboard moon**, *nicely rendered at full and carefully lit, the size of a dodgeball.*
Formally:)

Moon on.

(*He snaps, the curtain closes, he turns to audience.*)

Moon off.

(*He exits.*
LIGHT CHANGE.
CHET, *at a meeting, sitting on a folding chair.*)

CHET. My character, my mysterious little maybe-addict, is named Tracy. Do you like it? As a character name? I think it's a terrible name. I would never name someone Tracy. When I found out that was her name—and this was when I thought she was just a peripheral character that she was this kind of cool friend of a woman who I briefly entertained this idea was the main character—but I found out her name and I was already I was no, no I don't care if she's here on page 12 and then we don't see her again until 73—76 if that, no. I really just don't care for that name. It always strikes me as officious. And, insubstantial. I said let's just see about that name and there was this tremendous resistance. I could not think of another name. Lois. That's no kind of name. Miranda, well that didn't suit her at all. So I just I said well we'll put the name change on hold, for the moment, this is a minor character, this is a minor quandary, let's keep it moving, keep it moving here folks

(*Lost for a moment.*) keep it moving along, nothing to see here.

Anyway, it happens that I discover a few weeks ago that no, Tracy is not a minor character at all, she is a rather major one but by this time it's too late to change the name; I'm in her grip. And this is a woman, if I met her in life, this is not a woman I would immediately want to sleep with, at all. She doesn't have that kind of… sexual charisma, you know, I like a woman with a trim packed ass in blue jeans and long hair with a kind of weight to it and a reefer lilt in her voice, like, mischief but in slo motion that's—or is that too—anyway, that's not Tracy at all. Not at all. I like nice breasts, nice big solid breasts (*He's being interrupted.*) oh I see. I see. Oh all right.

(*He stands, exits, takes his chair in with him.*)

PHILIP HUTCHENS. I thought you should hear this.

Colin, will you—this is Colin McAdams, Colin this is Don Larkin, he's a member of the senior management team for the Capacity project.

COLIN. Hello I'm

(*They shake.*)

pleased to meet you I

DON LARKIN. Welcome to Capacity. Richard says you're highly recommended.

COLIN. Oh well thank you—

DON LARKIN. This is your first day isn't it?

COLIN. Yes. Yes it is. And I'm, I'm this is not how I

PHILIP HUTCHENS. I want you to tell Mr. Larkin what you told me. (*To* DON.) Colin was to report in promptly at 9:30. He arrived at 9:55 and when Stella queried him

COLIN. Yes I'm

PHILIP HUTCHENS. He said that he had been detained, at some length, in the hallway, by

COLIN. I never got his name.

PHILIP HUTCHENS. By an unnamed gentleman who said that he was a colleague of Richard's. He was wearing a bow tie. A blue one. With little, white, anchors.

(*Tiny beat.*)

DON LARKIN. Anchors.

PHILIP HUTCHENS. Older man, in his late 50s early 60s, nicely tailored suit, someone who "looked like someone." When Colin asked him for directions to Sector 8 he expressed incredulity; he said that there was no Sector 8; when Colin said that he was reporting to Richard Harrison he said—

COLIN. He said that I couldn't be.

(*Pause.*)

DON LARKIN. Little white anchors, salt and pepper hair, avuncular, confident. A bit of an air.

COLIN. Yes.

(DON LARKIN *turns aside for a moment. Runs his fingers through his hair. There is a pause.*)

DON LARKIN. (*Turning back towards them.*) Bob Seward. (*To* PHILIP.) Bob Seward.

PHILIP HUTCHENS. He wanted to know about Colin's meeting. With Mr. Harrison.

DON LARKIN. And what did you tell him.

COLIN. I didn't, actually, because that was the point, that was where it all started to seem a little fishy. (*It just comes to him.*) He was sweating a lot, on his forehead. I remember just thinking to myself oh it must be hot in here, and then later on I realized that *I* wasn't hot.

PHILIP HUTCHENS. He told him he should turn around and walk out of the building.

(*A little pause.*)

DON LARKIN. Well.

PHILIP HUTCHENS. Yes.

DON LARKIN. Does Richard know?

PHILIP HUTCHENS. Not yet. I thought it might be better if you—

DON LARKIN. Right.

COLIN. I hope I didn't say anything out of line or inappropriate, he seemed to me, he said he was a colleague of Mr. Harrison's and

DON LARKIN. Bob Seward is a *former* employee.

COLIN. Ah.

DON LARKIN. It's luck for us that you ran into him. It's possible that he's been here for…a time.

(*To* PHILIP HUTCHENS, *conversationally.*)

God, I don't like to think about that.

(*Focusing on* COLIN *directly.*)

Not so fortunate for you. You came in 25 minutes behind and we've kept you here for another...?

PHILIP HUTCHENS. 15

DON LARKIN. So you're 40 behind, already. I don't pretend to understand the mechanics of this but it's my understanding that there are issues of...

PHILIP HUTCHENS. Calibration.

DON LARKIN. Windows of opportunity. We'd better get you in gear or we'll have the Lab on our head. Who's looking after him?

PHILIP HUTCHENS. Marylis—just go down that hall, take the first left, third blue door down on your right. She'll get you started. Listen, why don't I see you there in just a tick.

(COLIN *exits.*)

It's been weeks, since the explosion. Weeks. Has he been here—

(*A gesture all around.*)

for weeks?

DON LARKIN. I don't know. The Lab probably has a theory about that.

PHILIP HUTCHENS. And is this that "strictly localized" effect? I thought "strictly localized" was the Lab. In a pinch, I thought it was Sector 8. Colin didn't run into Bob Seward in Sector 8, he found him in the West hallway down by the H4 staircase.

DON LARKIN. The Lab has a lot of confidence, in their theories. (*Lightly.*) Which is a relief, no?

PHILIP HUTCHENS. I transferred to this division, from Industrial Transmissions, which is going, actually, like gangbusters—but in any case because I thought: ground floor, whole new line of business—do you know what I discovered yesterday, strictly by chance? They're running this entire operation off of a charred notebook. Dr. Tanner's notebook. What's left of it. Sixty-some odd pages of burnt paper.

DON LARKIN. Phil.

(*Beat.*)

It's nothing I'd want to have to think about.

(*There is a little tiny pause.*)

PHILIP HUTCHENS. You're going to tell Richard though.

(*Microbeat.*)

DON LARKIN. Yes.

(*Microbeat.*

Beat.)

It's the funniest thing but you know. When I meet with Richard, these days. I have the hardest time. I have the hardest time remembering. Afterwards. I have the hardest time remembering. Just exactly what we've said.

> (*They look at each other.*
> *They exit in opposite directions.*
> CHET *carefully sets up a **black folding chair**, sits in it.*)

CHET. You know another genre which did not receive respect, back in its initial day? Philosophy. They thought it was stunt thought. Stunt thought.

> (*He stands up, folds the chair up, and carries it off with him.*
> *LIGHT CHANGE.*
> *A man stands in front of the curtain at the back of the stage.*)

THE MOON MAN. Moon off.

> (*He pulls or, ideally, snaps and causes to be pulled, the curtain.*
> *There is **a cardboard moon**, nicely rendered at full and carefully lit, the size of a hula hoop.*
> *Formally:*)

Moon on.

> (*He snaps, the curtain closes, he turns to the audience.*)

Moon off.

> (*He exits.*
> CHET *stands with his **coffee cup** on his front porch.*)

LOIS. Mr. Ellis?

CHET. Oh it's...

LOIS. Lois.

CHET. Lois.

LOIS. Remember? "That's no kind of name."

CHET. ......

LOIS. From the meeting. You were talking about your character, Tracy, and how she came to be named Tracy, and you didn't want to name her Lois because that's no kind of a name. Anyway I'm named Lois. I thought you knew that.

CHET. No. I didn't know that.

LOIS. (*Lying.*) Remember I introduced myself I said "My name's Lois"...

CHET. (*Mostly lying.*) *Oh*, oh. Yes. From the meeting. Hello.

LOIS. Hi, yes.

> (*A bit of a pause.*)

Well I wondered why you weren't coming to the meeting anymore.

CHET. Oh. How did you get hold of my address.

LOIS. It was on that sheet you signed. When you came in.

CHET. Ah. Right. I suppose you're a fan.

LOIS. No, I wouldn't describe myself as a fan.

CHET. Oh. Then…what are you doing here?

LOIS. I became concerned, when you didn't show up at the meeting again.

CHET. Well I didn't see the point of being there.

LOIS. Maybe it was to meet me.

CHET. Oh. Listen. Lois.

LOIS. Yay! You got my name.

CHET. Lois. I very much…I'm married, right, you know that?

LOIS. Where's your wife then?

CHET. She's around. (*Looks around.*) In the city, somewhere; she's definitely in the state.

She likes to think of herself as a free spirit.

LOIS. Does that mean she sleeps with other men?

CHET. Possibly. Possibly. I don't worry about that too much.

LOIS. No?

CHET. No. I figure I'm a very…particular kind of beverage. So if she hath quaffed of me, which she hath, and then stuck around for seconds and for thirds it must be because she has or has acquired a taste for me and if she *has* she's not going to get a taste of that anywhere else.

LOIS. She isn't your first wife.

CHET. No. She is my fourth wife.

LOIS. So you can't be very romantic about the concept of marriage.

CHET. I'm very romantic about it. It's the women I marry. I'm joking.

LOIS. Can I come in?

CHET. No.

LOIS. Not even just for a cup of coffee?

CHET. I'm working right now actually, you've caught me at a very bad time.

LOIS. When's a better one?

CHET. When I'm not working.

LOIS. And that's…

CHET. Hard to determine.

LOIS. Okay. I'll be back then then.

(*She waves, exits.*
CHET *goes back inside.*

LIGHT CHANGE.

TOM *is in* CHET'*s kitchen, rummaging very carefully through a box of cereal.*
DENNIS *enters, leans in the doorway.*)

TOM. How's that study coming.

DENNIS. Slowly. I found his stash of bennies.

TOM. Oh. Where was it?

DENNIS. In a baby food jar, by the computer.

TOM. Keep looking.

DENNIS. Right.

(*Looks longingly over by the coffee maker.*)

I wish we could make coffee, I always forget to bring my own.

TOM. Bring your own you'll leave it somewhere.

DENNIS. Naw, I don't ever forget that.

TOM. I did that once. I brought in a cup of takeout coffee. I wasn't even in a hurry, I did the job, left, middle of the night I wake up I think: did I leave that coffee cup *there?*

I couldn't remember. I'm lying in my bed, middle of the night, I'm thinking no, no, this is paranoia, I took the coffee cup with me, it's crumpled next to the emergency brake. But I can't…I can't remember. I'm sure I took it with me, I know I took it with me, I always take it with me, but where did I throw it away. I'm begging myself: go, back, to sleep. I get up, I get halfway dressed, I go down to the garage, it's not in the car. It's three a.m., I'm in the garage in my apartment building, in my jeans, barefoot, bare-chested, I do the stupidest thing, I get in the car. What are the cops going to do they look over see the guy in the car is bare-chested at three in the morning; they're going to get super agitated and they are going to *find a reason* to pull you over. Right? A patrol car paces me for twelve miles, they are *dying* to pull me over and if it were Oakland they were *going* to pull me over but Berkeley cops, they know that the more bare-chested a guy is at three a.m. the more likely he is to have the penal code memorized and to embroil them in an extensive court battle so they pace me, and I am driving perfectly, impeccably, I'm not an *inch* over the crosswalk, I'm nowhere near the center line, you've never seen such driving they've got nothing, absolutely nothing on me, I'm sweating, I'm dying. Finally they give up. Maybe they get philosophical and decide I've got a reason, theirs not to wonder what or why, maybe they get a call an actual crime. To this day I keep a wrapped Hanes undershirt in my car under the driver's side seat. I'm never going to have to use it because never again will I be that stupid but I always know that it's there, just somehow in case.

DENNIS. Did you ever find the coffee cup?

TOM. Yeah, I found it. I went back. Big old doctor's residence way up on Dana. *Four* a.m. now which I don't like, some people are very early risers, so I do the bedroom first.

DENNIS. Shit.

TOM. Is right. And they're *silent* sleepers: are they out or just laying there awake, scared out of their minds, holding their breath, creepy. I'm in the kitchen, the study, finally it comes to me, it just comes to me, and I march right to the laundry room, this utility laundry room and it's there, right above the machine, on the shelf where they keep the soap. Which is the least horrible place in the entire house I could have left it because if they see it they think the maid left it the maid sees it she thinks they left it—I like to think that I'm thinking even when I'm not thinking. I take it, I get out, I never bring a cup of coffee onto a job again.

> (*Little bit of a beat.*)

DENNIS. You know he's got a really fancy computer.

TOM. Well that's not so surprising, is it.

DENNIS. I guess not. But it's a lot of money, a lot more money than the rest of this place. He's got one of those—what do they call them—one of those wall screens.

TOM. They call them wall screens.

DENNIS. No not where it's mounted on the wall, where the wall itself *is* the screen where it's

TOM. (*Promptly.*) Plaster Plasma.

DENNIS. Yeah that's right, Plaster Plasma. What is that. It's an area got to be five by eight.

TOM. (*Shrugs.*) Twenty thousand.

DENNIS. The screen saver is trippy.

TOM. What it's getting on your nerves?

DENNIS. A little.

TOM. I'll be in there in a bit. The study is going to take both of us.

DENNIS. What if we swapped out for a little while.

TOM. No, nothing doing. I have a Kitchen System I've perfected.

> (DENNIS *watches him for a little bit.*)

DENNIS. What do you think, think he swiped some of those dead sea scrolls from the University?

TOM. (*Shrugs.*) Eh.

DENNIS. (*Staring off into the middle distance.*) Those things are fragile.

> (TOM *ceases.*)

TOM. You think I'm being careless?

DENNIS. (*Startled.*) No. I was just thinking: those things are fragile. I was thinking: they're old.

TOM. (*Resuming.*) A scroll, a coin, a fetish. The Ark of the Covenant. I don't know.

DENNIS. (*Appreciatively.*) That was a good movie.

TOM. That was an idiotic movie.

(*Slight beat.*)

DENNIS. I enjoyed it, actually. Very much.

(*Little pause.*

TOM *continues to work.*)

TOM. I don't mind running an incredibly tight search. Really, it's a pleasure. Give me a haystack, give me a day, I'll find you your needle. (*A beat.*) But tell me I'm looking for a needle. Amateurs. I don't care how much crazy corporate money you've got—

DENNIS. What makes you think they're corporate.

TOM. Please.

(*He nudges his head toward the study.*)

I'll be in there in a bit.

(*DENNIS exits.*

TOM *has finished the cereals and is taking the cookbooks down from the shelf over the stove.*)

DENNIS. (*Offstage.*) Yii!

(*TOM is on high alert.*)

TOM. What's that?

(*Minipause.*)

DENNIS. Nothing. It's nothing.

TOM. What's nothing?

DENNIS. No it's—I thought I saw something. I didn't see anything. It's nothing.

(*A wary beat, and* TOM *resumes examining the cookbooks one by one, brushing through them in a cursory fashion, turning them upside-down and shaking them, running a thin metal implement along the spine; one book he shakes and something falls out from it, he swiftly picks it up from the floor and examines it on both sides before returning it to the book without interest.*

DENNIS, *from off:*)

Hey Tom. Tom.

TOM. Yeah.

DENNIS. Can you give me a hand with this? It's about to topple…

TOM. Right there.

(He carefully returns the book to the shelf. And exits to the study.

LIGHT CHANGE.

CHET's *living room.* CHET *and* LOIS *on a couch with imaginary glasses of scotch.*

Music plays. A very faint bubbling sound is heard.)

CHET. How old are you.

LOIS. 26.

CHET. Isn't that a little young to have an addiction.

(She shrugs.)

Or at any rate, to identify it and overcome it. Hey you're drinking my scotch.

LOIS. You said I could have some. You *gave* it to me.

CHET. But aren't you an alcoholic?

LOIS. *(Shrugs.)* Probably. I mean, what else right? Oh. But that's not why I was at the meeting.

CHET. Oh. So you can drink alcohol.

LOIS. I have that ability. Maybe I shouldn't, but, I'm not a hypocrite.

CHET. Why were you at the meeting then Lois.

LOIS. What's it like to use my name?

CHET. *(Tasting it a bit.)* Lo-is.

LOIS. Does it get a little less improbable each time?

CHET. Lo-is, it does. It slowly, slowly sounds more like the name of a human being, and less like the name of a comic book character.

LOIS. Tell me about it. My whole life.

CHET. Did you answer my question?

LOIS. Which one.

CHET. About why you were at the meeting.

LOIS. Well that's why you should have stuck around for another meeting. I probably would have told my story then.

CHET. Well then let me ask you straight out: are you a junkie.

LOIS. *Oh.* No. Good Lord.

CHET. Good.

LOIS. Why, are you afraid of junkies?

CHET. I loathe them. That's all. The theft, the lassitude. I'm not a big fan of the gauntness.

LOIS. Me neither. The ribs…the ribs.

CHET. I didn't think about it that specifically but yes, the ribs.

LOIS. Can I have some more of your scotch?

CHET. That's sipping scotch.

LOIS. It's delicious.

CHET. You just gulped it.

LOIS. Yeah I wanted to experience it maximally.

CHET. What if I get you some vodka.

LOIS. Vodka's fine.

CHET. It's not cold.

> (*She thinks about it a moment.*)

LOIS. That's fine.

CHET. I can get you an ice cube.

LOIS. That would be great, thanks.

> (*He exits to the kitchen.*
>
> *She calls out:*)

Make it two.

CHET. (*Calling from the kitchen.*) What?

LOIS. Make it two. Ice cubes. (*Micropause.*) Please.

> (*It takes him a little while. He returns.*)

CHET. I gave you three. Guessing, that it's more important to you that the liquid is cold, than that it's a little…watered down.

LOIS. Three ice cubes, great.

> (*She takes it from him.*)

CHET. Cheers. We forgot to cheers, with the scotch.

LOIS. Cheers.

CHET. It's not excellent vodka.

> (*She shrugs.*)

LOIS. (*She's lying, she wasn't.*) I was looking at your book collection, while you were in the other room.

CHET. Oh sure. This is part of it. I should throw half of it away. (*Microbeat.*) See anything you like?

LOIS. You have a lot of books about religion.

CHET. Sure.

LOIS. Are you a religious man?

CHET. That's…a complicated question isn't it.

LOIS. Is it? I feel like that's one of those questions which comes up a lot, is a person religious or not. Most people know either way. You aren't a Buddhist are you? Tell me straight out if you are.

CHET. Why, are you afraid of Buddhists?

LOIS. They are not. My. Favorite.

CHET. And why is that.

LOIS. Mmmmmmm. I feel like that's a Buddhist kind of rejoinder—you aren't answering the question, you're turning my question into another question, technically about me but really actually in fact sort of about you, the person who now mysteriously has the power in the conversation.

CHET. I'm not a Buddhist.

LOIS. Prove it. Kill an ant or something…

> (*She's twisting in her place a bit, looking around.*)

…kill a mosquito.

CHET. (*Amused.*) Happy to do it. Happy to kill— (*He's looking around.*) something, to please a lady…

> (*They're both looking around—maybe the bubbling aquarium sound keys up for a moment.*)

Only not a fish.

LOIS. (*Agreeing.*) Not a fish. There must be ants in your kitchen.

CHET. What makes you think there are ants in my kitchen.

LOIS. Your living room looks like the kind of living room that leads to a kitchen that has ants in it.

CHET. (*Wait: I tidied up.*) What's wrong with my living room?

LOIS. It's not bad at all really, it's just that in my experience your kitchen will have ants in it. Not an infestation. A few. You'll probably find them scouting around the sugar bowl, or by the sink. Go, go look. Find an ant, bring it back to me, kill it, and then I'll know you're All Right.

> (*As he's leaving the room:*)

CHET. I very much doubt it.

LOIS. (*Calling after him.*) What's that?

CHET. (*Calling back.*) I very much doubt I am. All Right.

> (*She makes an exasperated/annoyed face, but doesn't say anything.*
> *A little bit of time…*)

Oh.

LOIS. (*Calls out.*) Find one?

CHET. I found…a few…

LOIS. (*Calling.*) Where are they?

> (*A beat or two.*)

Where'd you find them?

CHET. (*Entering.*) Sugar bowl.

(*He sits down on couch.*)

Okay. Here it is.

(*He twists his hand a bit as it explores around his finger.*)

It's an alive one, as you can see. Just in case you suspected me of bringing in a ringer.

LOIS. A what?

CHET. A previously dead naturally dead ant. Part of my Buddhist cover kit.

LOIS. No, that's a lively one.

CHET. And now

(*He grinds his finger tip against the base of his thumb.*)

it's a dead ant, see?

(*He holds his hand out.*)

All right?

(*She looks at it, looks up at him.*)

LOIS. That was sort of sad, actually. (*Beat.*) Which doesn't make me a Buddhist.

CHET. No. You're a pagan goddess. In the classical sense: passion requires blood.

LOIS. *You* killed it.

CHET. Entirely at your behest.

LOIS. Of course…you could have said no.

CHET. When you asked me? No. I couldn't have. I now anoint you, dear goddess, *propitiate* you, with blood of ant.

(*He smears the dead ant carefully and ritualistically on her cheek, they kiss.*

It's swiftly very ardent.

He takes her into the other room.

LIGHT CHANGE.

THE ALIEN GUY is a man in his 20s wearing an English Beat tee shirt, faded black skinny jeans, dirty checkered Vans. His hair is moussed into a dark springy taffy.

*He's talking on **a phone**. He holds the receiver to his ear, the instrument itself dangles from the fingers of one hand, the cord trails behind him leading to offstage.*)

THE ALIEN GUY. They just, they cannot distinguish between made up and real; they cannot make sense of what is a news broadcast and what is just, you know, programming—and they also can't, they can't distinguish between, historical eras, how we portray historical eras, so they see something on TV about Elizabethan England, or Feudal Japan, or America in the 19th Century…

Yeah they think that it's all going on right now, here, somewhere, they think it's surveillance cameras or something the Sci-Fi stuff has them completely confused I've got HBO—yeah it's good, it's expensive—yeah they do sometimes, it's irritating, but I don't care, I'm not so discriminate, I just like watching movies at home, I don't care so much what it is, that's the terrible truth—yeah my friend has Showtime, it seems like it's okay—I'm just like I'm going to pretend it's six of one and half a dozen of another because I can't decide and I can't afford them both—but anyway guess what just started running: *Alien*. I know, right?—now they're extremely agitated; they very much want to know where it's taking place like the coordinates the space time coordinates I think they want to mount an attack, right, and I just say no, no I can't tell you that, that's state secrets. I have to limit their TV-watching time they can't handle it. I thought the gardening show wouldn't be provocative—my mistake.

No they do because they don't know that I'm not the supreme leader.

No, they haven't worked that out yet.

No at the moment, I'm just going with it.

Yeah at first I thought—yeah—"this is hella gonna blow up in my face" but it was irresistible and then now…it's kind of a burden, man, you have to act a certain way, yeah I thought for sure they'd work it out, instantly, but now I don't know if they're up to the task.

It's not all a gag either I'm trying to be some kind of a cultural ambassador. I tried playing music for them, I'm like: music! This is our music! This is *one* of our kinds of music—I was trying to be responsible: I said "We have *many* kinds"; they weren't into it.

No I think it's like another sound to them. Like traffic, or when the washing machine goes on spin cycle.

No no, they've *got* music I'm sure of it; I feel like Einstein promised us that was a universal constant or something.

They're disappointing, really. I'm talking with Zorkon the Eliminator— (*In response to a query.*) that's what *I* call him. He says "Why do you call me that"; I say "Because that's what you'd call *yourself*, if you had any balls at all, man."

(*He's drifting offstage, growing more indistinct as he does so.*)

Zorkon the Eliminator comes to me with this puzzled expression and I'm: *oh no.* I haven't got any more down time that's like the worst of it it's questions questions questions inane statements and then more questions. So he's all concerned and…

(He exits, trailing phone cord behind.

A ninja bounces onto the stage, low, like a cat, grasps the cord, tugs, and then lunges forward offstage.

CHET *is in the kitchen bending forward and peering at the refrigerator.*

LOIS *appears wearing* CHET's *plaid bathrobe, thick red and black wool with the hem fragmenting off on one side.)*

CHET. You ever have a magnet go stale on you?

LOIS. Go—what?

CHET. Lose its ability, its force, its grip.

I have a whole refrigerator full of magnets they don't do the work any more, they can barely stick to the side let alone support a note or a photograph; you try to use them and they slide right off the thing.

LOIS. That's weird. Maybe they're dirty?

CHET. That shouldn't affect them in the least.

LOIS. Well but if the surface…area…

CHET. I swabbed a few with soapy water it didn't make a difference. Some of them are even dying. Couple weeks ago they started peeling away. Look on the floor. Like leaves at the end of fall.

(She bends down, picks one up, affixes it to the refrigerator, watches it slide down and fall off.

A considering silence.)

LOIS. Maybe the problem isn't with the magnets, maybe the problem is with your refrigerator.

CHET. First of all, that doesn't make sense. Is the refrigerator any less metallic? Second of all, I thought of that already and I left a few stuck to pots, same thing.

LOIS. Bad batch.

CHET. Different brands, different hardware stores, some of these I've had for years and years, house to house, some I bought recently. Few days ago I even got a couple of those daisies they sell by the cash registers. Same thing. They enter the house, strong as the day they were made, a few days inside and they die.

(He picks one up off the floor.)

I've had this magnet since I was…*(Does the mental math.)* 23. That's something, isn't it? I didn't make any special effort to keep it, it just always managed to come along with me. Like a good magnet should I suppose.

(He considers a moment, walks over to some other part of the kitchen, plants the magnet on something—maybe pulls a can out of the cupboard—the magnet sticks for just a moment and then falls.)

Now it's dead.

LOIS. That's weird. That's really weird. That sounds bad, doesn't it?

CHET. Bad. I don't know. It's drastic, I know that much.

LOIS. I mean, is that…healthy?

CHET. I have a theory I'm running around in my head, something I'm formulating but I don't have it, I don't have all of the pieces in place yet.

LOIS. What is it?

CHET. At the moment…it's just a theory.

(*A beat.*)

You sleep okay?

LOIS. You were right there.

CHET. Asleep.

LOIS. Yeah, me too.

CHET. Good.

(*There's a bit of a pause.*)

You want coffee?

LOIS. Uh huh.

(*He goes over and pours it for her.*)

I could smell it, in my dream. This guy I know was (*She yawns.*) trying to tell me something, something really important, and I smelled the coffee and I said, you know, let me get right back to you.

I almost feel guilty about it. Like he's in the other room waiting for me. Mmmh. (?)

CHET. How is it?

LOIS. …charry.

CHET. (*Guiltily.*) I make it strong.

LOIS. Did you reheat it?

CHET. No, it's fresh. There was a little old coffee in the carafe. Do you want

LOIS. Is there cream?

CHET. Half and half. In the fridge.

(*She goes, gets container, opens it eyeballs it shakes it and smells it before deciding to pour it in, replaces container, sips.*)

LOIS. Mmmmm. Much better.

(*She takes another sip.*)

Well.

(*She looks about her.*)

I suppose I should get going.

CHET. Is the coffee that bad?

LOIS. When I finish the coffee.

> (*There's a bit of a pause.*)

Won't your wife get back?

CHET. I doubt it.

LOIS. Mgh.

Do you have—breakfast type things? Cereal?

CHET. I have toast. And butter, and jelly.

LOIS. Or eggs or something?

CHET. Ah, no. I just

LOIS. You don't have an old box of pancake mix somewhere? Doesn't that sound good? Pancakes? With syrup, yum.

CHET. It does, it sounds very good. I don't believe I do.

LOIS. I feel certain, that you do. Everyone has a dusty old box of pancake mix somewhere in the back of their cupboard.

> (*She starts a search.*)

CHET. Won't that make dusty old pancakes?

LOIS. (*A gesture of dismissal.*) It's all about the syrup anyway.

> (*She stops what she's doing; looks over.*)

You have syrup right.

CHET. Ummm.

> (*She marches over to the refrigerator, peers in.*)

LOIS. All right, it's all about the butter and the jam right?

> (*She marches back to the cupboard and resumes her search.*)

CHET. Which is practically toast.

> (*She ignores him.*)

LOIS. And I like to put chocolate chips in. But I can tell already that's not happening today…

you don't have it do you.

CHET. I believe I don't.

LOIS. That's so odd, I could have sworn you did.

CHET. Toast?

LOIS. No. I'm not really hungry. I just like, pancakes I like (*She does a brief mime of the idea of.*) the production. I guess I'll just drink my coffee. And then I guess I'll just go.

If that's okay with you.

CHET. I should probably get back to the work.

LOIS. "the" work

CHET. A book. I'm in the middle of a book.

LOIS. I know but I thought that was kind of great, "the" work, not "my" work "the work" it's like it's…eternal already.

CHET. Oh.

LOIS. "the work"

CHET. I think I meant it as a verb, not a noun.

LOIS. (*Shrugs.*) Nothing wrong with the grandiose.

CHET. Back to the working.

LOIS. Which doesn't involve me.

CHET. Which doesn't involve you.

LOIS. (*Promptly.*) Are you sure?

(*There's a couple of beats.*)

CHET. Why did you come here? Again.

LOIS. Why not, right?

(*A few beats.*)

I wanted to (*Black Urban Patois:*) "get wi'cho," Mr. Ellis.

CHET. And why was that?

LOIS. I found you compelling.

CHET. You haven't read my books.

LOIS. I didn't say that. I said I wasn't a fan.

CHET. Ah.

LOIS. At least, not of the ones I've read.

Hey, this robe is super itchy. I think I'm going to sluice off and then—and you can start working while I'm showering I'm not sentimental about things like that at all.

(*She starts to go.*)

CHET. I don't know your last name. I just now realize.

(*She stops.*)

LOIS. I'd tell you. I'd totally tell you. But it's alliterative.

CHET. Lois…L'amour?

LOIS. No.

CHET. Lois…Langton? Lois Lewis, Lois Lazar, Lee…*not* Lane.

LOIS. *No.* My parents were unkind. But they weren't crazy.

CHET. Why didn't you just change it? Berkeley is full of people with names they weren't born with.

(*Mini beat.*)

LOIS. That's a good question. I'm going to go shower.

> (*She exits.*
>
> *He stands there, for a long time, coffee in hand.*
>
> *There is a small sound.*
>
> *He turns.*
>
> *Bends over, picks up a magnet from the floor near the refrigerator, examines it for a moment, places it on the table, leaves the room.*)

THE MOON MAN. The moon, is dark. Tonight.

> (*The curtain shoots aside: blackness, nothing.*)

The moon!

> (*The curtain closes again.*
>
> COLIN *enters the dark room, slowly. Looking around him.*
>
> *His footsteps echo. There is an underlying stream of continuous and un-uniform white noise.*
>
> *He is wearing a white lab coat, and green tinted goggles, and holding* **a flatscreen computer** *the size of a pad of paper—as though it were a clipboard.*
>
> *He has white booties over his shoes.*
>
> *He is also carrying* **a small slim flashlight-looking device.**
>
> *After a moment he toggles at the flashlight; there is a fragrant response of sound from the clipboard.*
>
> *He taps briefly at the clipboard which responds occasionally with intermittent sounds.*
>
> *He switches at the light, a small focused beam of rose-or jade-colored light comes on.*
>
> *He pulls his goggles down.*
>
> *He runs the beam carefully over the surface; as he does so, a light stream of continuous small faintly discordant music emanates from the clipboard.*
>
> *There is a jarring sound. He stops. He retoggles the flashlightything—as he does so there is an intermittent series of answering chirps from the keyboard which he also taps onto—*
>
> *when he has completed this, he switches on the beam again—it is wider, or narrower, or a different color, or strobe-y—and uses it to finely examine that small area.*
>
> *As he does so a louder, richer series of more musical pulsing noises emanate from the board. Until, with a few meaty clicks, the sound extinguishes.*
>
> *He works away at the clipboard for a minute or so.*
>
> *Then toggles the flashitem back to its original setting [again with answering*

chirps from keyboard] and starts to strobe again.

There is an incredibly loud sound from offstage: it sounds like a key fitting slowly into a lock, and then the lock being pulled back very slowly—but terribly terribly magnified, and underwater as well as with a great deal of adjacent distortion.

He freezes.

A door opens with an incredible slow motion shudder, footsteps just boom, and then an intermittent caterwaul in two tones which we can slowly come to understand is human speech—magnified, underwater, distorted, the values scrambled.

We will only barely make it out, but we hear this:)

DENNIS. My shoe, the side of my shoe…

TOM. That's just

DENNIS. Yeah that's just

TOM. That's just mud.

(*COLIN is frantically toggling at the flashthing and muffling the keyboard chirps by pressing the item against his chest.*

There is an unexpectedly loud "zing!")

Wait what was that?

DENNIS. What was what?

TOM. What was that?

(*As slowly and carefully and rapidly as he can COLIN backs from the room, his footsteps echoing underneath the sound from the next room.*

As he exits the room there is a small "woosh" and our sound returns to normal.

There's still a shifting prickle of sound.)

DENNIS. (*Offstage.*) What?

What?

TOM. (*Low.*) Shut up.

(*TOM enters the room slowly, with DENNIS close behind, guns drawn.*

TOM *puts his finger to his lips. They both look around them.*

TOM *has his head cocked, listening.)*

I heard something. I thought I heard something. I heard something.

DENNIS. I didn't hear anything.

TOM. You were yapping.

DENNIS. "yapping"

TOM. Shhh.

(*A bit of a pause.*)

DENNIS. It's the computer. It's probably the computer.

TOM. Maybe it was a mouse. A real one, I mean.

DENNIS. What? No.

TOM. A mouse, *on* the computer. There's mice here for sure.

DENNIS. (*He doesn't quite like this.*) I didn't see any mice in here.

TOM. They like to hide under papers. Since when do you care about mice?

DENNIS. I don't know they're just, they're there but you don't see them or, I don't know. I've never loved mice.

TOM. How much of our sensory experience is just…hallucination, misfire. You're tired, you think you see a rat it's a bag in the wind, you think you heard someone calling your name you didn't you look at a billboard you think you see one word but actually it's another word. All these instant little freaks of perception. (*He taps his head.*) This is not totally sound. This is not a reliable instrument. But I know I heard something in here.

> (*He is lifting imaginary papers up from the desk with great care and sorting through them.*)

DENNIS. Probably a gadget.

TOM. Right. Well…

> (*He's staring, mesmerized, at the fourth wall.*)

You're right. This screensaver is a problem…

> (*He wrests himself from it.*)

Where's the…

DENNIS. What are you looking for?

TOM. How can the man—with all of these papers— [write/focus] The mouse. I'm looking for the mouse.

DENNIS. (*A little start.*) Oh the computer mouse.

> (TOM *is fingering a pile of papers gingerly.*)

TOM. …I just want to jostle this…

DENNIS. But we're not.

TOM. Yeah I'm not, I'm just eliminating the screensaver.

DENNIS. They were superexplicit about the computer.

TOM. I'm not going to be touching the computer I'm going to be touching the mouse, when I locate it.

DENNIS. But then we're going to see what's on the screen.

TOM. What's going to be on the screen, the desktop.

DENNIS. What if he's left it up, what if he's left a document up.

TOM. We'll avert our eyes.

DENNIS. They were superexplicit.

TOM. I'm a professional. You're a professional. It's my professional opinion that this screensaver is a problem.

(*He's still hunting through the desk.*)

I'm more likely to locate an actual mouse in this mess.

(*A tiny bit of a pause.*)

DENNIS. There's no mouse.

TOM. ?

DENNIS. There's no mouse, there's no keyboard.

TOM. Really?

DENNIS. Uh huh.

TOM. That's crazy. Wait a minute, where's the…where's the, the tower the

DENNIS. It doesn't have one.

TOM. The spot. The consolidated place the I don't know what it's called the home base

DENNIS. The drive. It doesn't have one.

TOM. It doesn't.

DENNIS. Nope.

TOM. Well then how does it *know* anything.

DENNIS. Mist Memory. Aerosolized Information.

TOM. Gaagh, technology.

So it's—

(*He's waving his hands around.*)

—it's here, it's here—

DENNIS. Yeah, it's

TOM. If I'm

(*He's waving his hands through it.*)

what does this do, does it

DENNIS. No it just reforms

TOM. Fine. Okay so there's no power terminal, there's no keyboard, there's no mouse, its brain is fritzing about in the air all around us; how do we *get* at it?

DENNIS. There's a command area, over the desk. It's Air Operated.

(*He steps forward, centers himself, makes a very explicit gesture, the low prickle sound stops.*)

Oh fuck. Oh fuck there's content.

(*He turns around.*)

TOM. That, is wild. Air Operated. That is very very wild.

DENNIS. We're not supposed to be looking at this.

(TOM *makes a very explicit gesture. Nothing happens. He makes another gesture, there is a small "bong.")*

TOM. Woah. What happened. What happened nothing changed.

DENNIS. What are you doing?? They were superexplicit about the computer Superexplicit!

TOM. I'm trying to get the screensaver...

(*He's making a series of random explicit gestures.*)

back up...look, you do it.

DENNIS. I don't know how to do it, I don't know how to operate this thing.

TOM. You operated it.

DENNIS. I saw a demo on the news I saw, that was, that's what I remember I remember

(*He makes the same explicit gesture.*

There's a vibrating thrum.)

Oh no. Oh fuck. Oh no.

TOM. Calm down. Jesus Christ, calm down nothing's happening.

DENNIS. Then what's that sound. What's that sound.

(*The vibrating hum continues a moment longer, then abruptly ceases.*)

TOM. Nothing. Nothing's going on. There's probably something happening on the desktop.

(*He paws downward.*)

The *desktop* is a mess.

I don't think anything looks...there's no way of knowing. But I don't see anything which is obviously...disarranged.

DENNIS. Fuck. Fuck fuck fuck fuck fuck.

(TOM *paws upward. Adjusts position carefully.*)

TOM. Well it's here...I'm just gonna take a look.

DENNIS. At the content? *Ignore* the content.

(*He turns so that he can't see the screen.*)

If you see it, if you happen to see it, that's one thing that's bad enough, if you look at it, that's another thing.

TOM. This is disturbing, frankly. Very disturbing.

DENNIS. Oh fuck.

TOM. (*Making this up.*) "all...work...and...no...play...makes...Jack...a... dull...boy...all...work..."

DENNIS. (*He swivels.*) Are you serious?? No. Fuck.

(*He swivels back again.*)

I don't believe in, I don't believe that if you do one tiny thing if one tiny thing if you do one tiny thing wrong that you just have to that you've blown everything

I believe that life is lived in increments and you have to fight, for the integrity of each increment as it occurs I don't believe that if you are weak if you have a moment of weakness and you give in to it… I don't think you should give up that if you kill one person you're a murderer and you should just decide well, I'm going to kill kill kill because I've blown I've blown everything open I've blown open that…shell…of self-description I don't think we have shells I don't think we're eggs I think we're some layered thing and layers come off and so we work, we fight, to put them back on I believe in moments, frankly, I believe that every moment counts…you're reading the whole thing, aren't you.

(*A bit of a pause.*)

TOM. Uh huh.

(*A beat.*)

Just this page. I'm not…scrolling the document.

(*A bit of time, then he fumbles at the air briefly,*
there are some small noises
he starts tapping at the air
there is a small ratcheting sound.)

DENNIS. (*With dread.*) You're scrolling the document.

TOM. (*Continuing to stare and scroll.*) I know exactly…where…I left…this…puppy.

DENNIS. These people are extremely uptight.

TOM. They can purchase my time…my attention…my considerable expertise…

but they cannot pay me…to ignore…my common…sense.

(*He continues to read.*
DENNIS *suffers in silence.*
Finally:
A literary judgment:)

eh.

(*He looks down at desk. Up again at wall.*)

Plaster plasma. If I had the time I'd write a couple of these. That's good money.

DENNIS. This is a crazy part of town to live in when you've got crazy movie money.

(TOM *shrugs. Looks around.*)

TOM. She says we've got until morning. Go get the cart would you. I'm going to make us some coffee, it's going to be a long night.

(*They leave the room.*

LIGHT CHANGE.

BOB SEWARD *ambles slowly on, looking about him.*

COLIN *enters. He is still wearing the lab coat, and carrying* **the clipboard computer**, *but is minus the goggles, and the flashlight thingie.*

When COLIN *sees* BOB SEWARD *he stops short,* BOB *notices him.*)

BOB SEWARD. Colin. (*Remembering.*) McAdams.

COLIN. …Yes.

(COLIN *is looking around, licking his lips nervously.*)

BOB SEWARD. So this, is Sector 8.

Our meeting piqued my curiosity, and I set out to locate it for myself, this Sector 8. I've been searching for a long time, but actually finding it proved to be surprisingly easy. I was looking in remote areas, regions, [fields of teeth, rivers of blood, that kind of thing] when here it was the whole time. Underfoot. Right under the nose. Document storage areas 9-12 retrofitted and equipped in record time, in a matter of…weeks, am I right?

(*A beat.*

COLIN *clears his throat slightly.*)

COLIN. That's my understanding.

BOB SEWARD. At unimaginable expense. They've given you a coat I see.

COLIN. Yes.

BOB SEWARD. *Richard Harrison,* gave you a coat.

COLIN. Not personally.

BOB SEWARD. Richard Harrison *authorized* a coat for you. Is that right?

(*A little gasping mini beat.*)

COLIN. Yes.

BOB SEWARD. What a nice man. What a nice coat. May I?

(*He gestures for* COLIN's *coat; it takes* COLIN *a moment to understand.*)

COLIN. Oh.

BOB SEWARD. Only for a moment of course. I don't want to keep it.

(*His hand is still held out.* COLIN *struggles out of the coat; passes it over very carefully.*

BOB SEWARD *shrugs it on, it doesn't fit—is short or long, the sleeves are too short—he tidies the collar.*)

My uncle was involved in the War—in World War Two. He was German, a half-uncle actually, and he was involved on the wrong side; I don't know how he weaseled out of it afterwards. When I was six. Or seven. I received a doctor's kit for my birthday—vinyl, you know, with plastic forceps and a plastic syringe and a stethoscope that actually worked, although it was weak in its powers, and a glass bottle of candy pills. He was lying down in the front room preparing to take a nap and I saw him stretched out on the sofa, prone, and I went over to him with the kit and I had the stethoscope on and I said lie very still Uncle, I'm going to operate on you. He swung himself up and he gripped my wrists, very hard and I began to cry and still he gripped my wrists. Children make such a rich complex series of associations in very short bursts, loaded with inaccuracy but potent, and very true. The word lab coat was never mentioned but this is the very first time I have donned…such an attire.

(*He takes it off; holds it up briefly: limp, drained.*)

It's only a bogeyman isn't it. I put it on. I took it off.

(*He hands it over to* COLIN, *who struggles back into it.*)

Look, you're putting it back on.

COLIN. The coat is crucial for spotlessness. I actually have a very well-developed moral sense. If that's what you're trying to imply.

BOB SEWARD. We don't do terrible things because we're immoral, on the contrary. May I see that?

(*He gestures towards the clipboard.*)

COLIN. This? No, of course not.

BOB SEWARD. Oh it's only for a moment. I had a hand in the prototype. Strictly supervisory but I like to think I know my way around a blueprint. Probably vanity.

(*He holds out his hand.*)

COLIN. I'm afraid. No. You're not authorized.

BOB SEWARD. I'm not. Authorized?

COLIN. Well I'm not, I'm not authorized to…

BOB SEWARD. My dear young man. Of course you aren't.

You're going to give it to me anyway.

(COLIN *licks his lips, swallows, looks around him.*)

No, there's no one around. No one, I am afraid.

Look at me. In the eye, that's right. Good.

Here.

(*He reaches out his hand.*)

COLIN. Oh. Fuck. Fuck.

(*He gives it to him.*)

BOB SEWARD. Thank you, Mr. McAdams. Now run.

Like the wind.

(COLIN *stands, gaping at him a moment longer, then as he turns to run,* BLACKOUT.)

End of Act I

ACT II

A low futon bed with sheets, a few candles.

LOIS. What did you write today?

CHET. Are you really interested?

LOIS. I am. I'm curious.

CHET. I thought you weren't a fan.

LOIS. Oh. Of the books. No I'm not. I um, I like stories where people really come into contact with their…peopleness. Not their lack of peopleness.

CHET. Somehow I didn't picture you much of a reader.

LOIS. I'm not a reader. But it's not like I don't read.

CHET. There aren't any books here. Not a single one.

LOIS. I don't keep books, when I read them. I don't want to affirm their "thing"ness.

CHET. Hmmm. The thingness of their peopleness.

So what are these books. That you read. And then discard.

LOIS. I sell them at Moe's.

CHET. That you consign into a purgatory of cigar reek and neglect.

LOIS. Who do you think?

    (Pause.)

CHET. Richard Brautigan.

LOIS. Please.

CHET. "stories where people come into contact with their peopleness" Anne Tyler.

LOIS. Who?

CHET. James Michener.

LOIS. *Oh.* No.

One of them's a Russian. I will tell you that much.

CHET. Dostoevsky.

LOIS. I'm not going to tell you which one.

CHET. Tolstoy.

LOIS. I'm not going to tell you which one.

CHET. Bulgakov.

LOIS. I'm not going to tell you which one.

CHET. Is it one of the ones I've mentioned? Gogol.

LOIS. I'm not going to tell you. I also like nonfiction.

CHET. Uh huh.

LOIS. Sometimes I look at textbooks.

CHET. Textbooks.

LOIS. Used ones, I pick up at the flea market or at garage sales near campus.

CHET. Which ones.

LOIS. Um…not going to say.

CHET. Which fields.

LOIS. Field. I'm only really interested in one field, when it comes to textbooks.

CHET. Does it involve numbers?

LOIS. Not gonna say. Besides, everything involves numbers.

CHET. True enough. True enough. What about you, are you a religious person?

LOIS. Oh my god. No.

CHET. (*Amused.*) That's decisive.

LOIS. See how easy it is to be clear-headed about it?

CHET. Some people would say though, that that essential insight, that everything is numbers, is in itself a spiritual insight with clear religious… implications.

LOIS. Mgn. Not the people I know.

> (*The phone rings.*)

Speaking of which.

> (*She pads off to the other room where we hear her speaking briefly in a low muffled tone.*)
>
> *She returns and stands over the mattress.*)

CHET. One of your admirers?

LOIS. Mh huh. I told him I'd call him back tomorrow.

CHET. Did you tell him that there was a naked man in your bed?

LOIS. He didn't ask.

CHET. If he asked?

LOIS. I would tell him.

> (*Poking him with a pointed toe.*)

Shove over.

> (*He obliges. She doesn't get in.*)

You hungry? Thirsty?

> (*He takes the foot and kisses it.*)

CHET. Uh uh.

LOIS. There's pizza in the fridge.

CHET. No thanks.

LOIS. *I* want me some of that pizza.

> (*She pads off, we hear the refrigerator opening, see a brief glow of light, hear the door closing.*
>
> *She re-emerges with a* **slim, stiff-looking piece of pizza** *and sits cross-legged on the bed next to him chewing while he begins fondling her leg.*)

Mushroom. Mozzarella. Divine. Speaking of religion. Bite?

> (*He opens his mouth, she inserts the tip, he chomps down.*)

This is my communion.

> (*She takes another bite.*)

CHET. (*Through a mouthful.*) This is terrible, where is this from.

LOIS. (*Indignantly.*) It is not. Leaning Tower.

CHET. It's granular.

LOIS. It's two days old.

CHET. Peh.

LOIS. So it's not at its melty tasty peak. (*She chews thoughtfully.*) It's true maybe what I like about it is that it *reminds* me of when it was fresh. But that's good enough for me.

CHET. (*Plato.*) A memory. A shadow experience.

LOIS. That's what religion is a lot of it. Something happened a long time ago, and then it's remembered endlessly. I suppose what I like about my pizza, or what I don't mind about my pizza, is that I'm remembering *my* experience. I called up Leaning Tower, I asked them—or was it Round Table...(*She glazes out for a moment*) shit

> (*She leaps up, back to the kitchen, refrigerator open, glow of light, door closes again, she returns.*)

Leaning Tower. Yes. So *I* called them up, I opened the door to this pizza, I took it in from the cold night, I was so hungry, it was so warm, oh god, it was just perfect. Now, two days later, I eat of it again and I remember, I celebrate that moment again. My moment. That's my religion: my moments. No one else can tell me what they mean. You can't. Ronald can't. A minister can't.

CHET. Ronald's your admirer?

LOIS. Mmph. No. Our President. I call him "Ronald."

CHET. Oh, as a form of protest.

LOIS. Sure, yes. I wouldn't be with someone called Ronald. I mean really? (*She's asking herself this.*) If they were really cool? I just can't imagine it.

CHET. I didn't know you were political.

LOIS. Hmmm, not so much. I just call the man Ronald.

CHET. You're breaking him from within.

LOIS. Yeah I'm the Third Front.

CHET. I thought you weren't political.

LOIS. I just said I'm not political.

CHET. That's a very political term.

LOIS. I've slept with some people who were very political. I osmose. That's how I know, most of what I know. I osmose.

CHET. I think you're the only person in this town who pretends to know less than she does politically.

LOIS. Pretend my ass. You're really going to piss me off. Ask me about any of the current events of the last 26 years of my existence: here's my political history of the part of the 20th century I've been personally involved in: Vietnam: bad. Nixon: tapes, cursing, Watergate: bad. Spiro Agnew—I don't even know who he *is* I just always remember that crazy name. Ford, then Ford is assassinated: Dole. First man on Mars. Gasoline. Hostages. That's it. I mean I'm irritated about… nuclear obliteration, I won't pretend otherwise, but you don't see me out there with signs or buttons or any of that. I have opinions but they aren't informed ones—I sort of think, why bother to spend all that time getting informed when I'm still going to have the same opinion. I bet you're *really* political.

CHET. No I stay out of politics.

LOIS. Hmmm. I bet you *used* to be really political, in the Sixties.

CHET. I was kind of old to be really political in the Sixties.

LOIS. There were a lot of older guys, hanging around. I remember that.

CHET. Sure. It was a seductive time. What the kids were doing, in the sixties, they were homesteading: they determined that society was a wilderness, so that they could carve their own space out of it; they decided that the indigenous people, the adults, were heathens, so they could disregard them and exploit them. These kids had all of this crazy new…mental technology and…and everything was sexy, everything was very very sexy…and I saw fully grown men who just wanted to participate so badly and those kids would play them, they'd give those kids everything for a handful of blue glass beads. So I was very cautious about all of that.

I like young people, girls particularly, but men too, I relate to most anyone better before they really settle into life in a solid fashion—but I never forget that young people are essentially wild animals.

LOIS. Wow. (*Laughing.*) Is that what you think I am? A wild animal?

CHET. A feral beast. No. I don't. But I think you have an…untrammeled set of instincts, and that you have a capacity to vibrate, and a thirst for the wind and an appetite for the earth and the light catches you and clings to you in strange and holy or possibly unholy ways.

(*He is fondling her leg again.*)

LOIS. Huh. Wow. Huh.

You know, the way that I remember it, the blue glass bead trade was pretty brisk on both sides.

Hey, you never answered my question.

CHET. Mgh?

> (*He is nomming her leg now, slowly working his way up.*)

LOIS. About your writing

> (*She moves her leg.*)

About what you wrote today.

CHET. About what I—is this a Requirement?

LOIS. (*Smiling.*) Maybe. Make it with men if you don't want Requirements.

CHET. If they had breasts, if they had silky hair, if they had pussies, *and* no Requirements, I wouldn't care what else was there.

LOIS. "Just push it aside."

CHET. Push it aside, get it involved, I don't care; the only thing I've got against men sexually is that they aren't women.

> (*He's getting a little worked up.*)

LOIS. Hey but you were going to tell me.

CHET. I was?

LOIS. You were.

> (*A slight pause while he reorients.*)

CHET. You don't like my work.

LOIS. I don't like to read it. That doesn't mean I don't want to hear about it. And hey, maybe you'll convert me.

CHET. (*Gathering his thoughts.*) About what I wrote today—I warn you, it wasn't very people-ful.

LOIS. I'll live.

CHET. What I wrote today…(*He squinches his eyes shut.*) I wrote a lot today.

LOIS. A banner day of writing—hurray!

> (*He's not quite paying attention to her.*)

CHET. My main character—

LOIS. Tracy.

CHET. No, Tracy isn't the main character.

LOIS. (*Startled.*) She's not?

CHET. No.

LOIS. I thought she was, I thought she was.

CHET. Tracy is a very important character. And she's my favorite character. And she's my most demanding character, for sure, but she isn't the main one.

LOIS. Well who is then.

CHET. A man named Charles.

LOIS. Charles.

CHET. Charles Klinger.

LOIS. (*Perplexed.*) Wait...who is Charles Klinger?

CHET. He's a civil rights lawyer. A former civil rights lawyer. Lately he's been handling low level lawsuits from well-meaning but ineffective environmental organizations against the refineries at Point Richmond. He's hopelessly handicapped by current environmental regulations as well as a very stiff set of recently passed laws which severely limit the ability of watchdog groups to bring any kind of civil or liability case against corporations with any claim to national security relevance.

LOIS. (*As if trying to make sense of all this.*) Uh huh.

CHET. He cynically accepts fees from these organizations, knowing that his chance of actually winning a lawsuit is pretty much nil; the laws are stacked against them and he knows he doesn't have the zeal for a successful prosecution; equally cynically, the fee he accepts is substantially reduced from his usual one, which is already low; he's descending into a state of financial anorexia.

LOIS. Uh huh. And this is now, right? This is right now.

CHET. It's set in the future, a little more than a year from now; the events take place from February 28 to March 2, 1982.

LOIS. Does that really count as the future?

CHET. It depends on the past.

LOIS. Ah. Uh huh. Uh huh okay. So...

CHET. Charlie's car has broken down. This puts him into a real bind because as I said: he's going to be living out of it in a couple of weeks but if he can't move it he'll be arrested for vagrancy. He can get it fixed, if he spends the money he was saving for his last month's rent and just moves into the car. But that requires a decision, it requires an action whereas he was dimly just waiting for his life to dissolve through inaction.

LOIS. Wait why is he—never mind, go on.

CHET. It's an overcast morning and he thinks if he can just get out from underneath the fog layer he can think more clearly. He's thinking maybe the sun is breaking out, up in the hills. He walks up to Center and Shattuck, puffing, he's out of shape, and he takes the University Shuttle up to Lawrence Hall of Science.

LOIS. I went to the Botanical Gardens once. Someone told me there was a really freaky cactus but if it was there I didn't see it. Sorry, so he goes to Lawrence Hall of Science.

CHET. It's even foggier up there, the whole hillside is shrouded. When the shuttle comes to a stop in the parking lot he almost thinks no, he's not even going to get out, he's going to ride the shuttle back down, but on impulse, as the engine is starting up again, he gets out. It's freezing cold and he's just wearing a sweater. Already he thinks this is a bad idea, it's even more depressing up here, but he goes to the edge of the observation deck, which he can barely see in the mist, and he stands there, shivering at the edge, staring out into the totally nonexistent view when this kid strides out of the mist and stands ten feet away from him, he's in full hippie regalia like you only ever see on Telegraph Ave. anymore: buckskins, tie dyes, hemp cording, bit of old velvet, everything dirty, everything torn, maybe he's 20, his gold hair's in knots, he takes this deep breath and he turns to Charlie with an exhilarated expression and he says "smell that?"

And Charlie basically really wishes he would go away but he takes a breath, and he smells: fog, eucalyptus, scrub.

The guy grins at him and says "Smells…like…planet."

And he turns, and he strides away, back into the mist. Charlie looks after him, then looks out again, into the fog, towards the invisible Bay, and that's when it happens.

>   (*A pause.*)

LOIS. That's when what happens.

CHET. That's what I write tomorrow.

LOIS. What happens tomorrow.

CHET. Don't know yet.

LOIS. What do you mean you don't know.

CHET. I like to leave off at an unknown. It makes it more interesting to go to work in the morning.

LOIS. But—

CHET. Tomorrow wasn't part of the Requirement, only today.

LOIS. Yeah but what—

>   (*He kisses her.*)

CHET. Only today.

LOIS. (*Aggravated.*) Oh…

CHET. Today is today. Tomorrow is tomorrow.

>   (*He kisses her.*)

LOIS. Is it? In your universe?

CHET. No. You're right. It isn't.

>   (*He kisses her, she makes an aggravated protest sound, but kisses him back.*

In the dark:)

THE MOON MAN. The moon!

(As he runs across the stage he pulls the curtain open shouting:)

The moon! The moon! The moon!

*(The **moon** is so vast that much of it is out of frame, we see a bulk of its face, and the curve of the rim, then a bit of the blackness of space beyond. It is very bright.*

CHET and LOIS are sleeping, he rouses, after a bit he sits up on the edge of the bed, nurses his head, the moonlight streams around him, he gets a funny feeling, he turns, he sees the vast vast moon, he gasps or aiies a bit, falls onto the floor, scuttles backwards naked like a crab to get away from it, aiies again, she murmphs, rouses slightly, settles back to sleep.

*He stalls there, for a long time, then creeps slowly over to his **pants**, puts them on, buckling the belt very carefully, can't find his **shirt**, pats all over the bed, very carefully, keeping always an eye on the enormous enormous moon, finally finds it half under LOIS, tries very carefully to extract it, she starts to rouse, he leaves it, scuttles carefully, half naked, from the room.*

Percolator sound

*A match flares, in the light of the **match**, TOM brings a **cigarette** to the flame*

Lights snap abruptly on full, DENNIS stands in the doorway, TOM stands with his back to the audience.)

DENNIS. What are you doing.

(TOM turns around, the cigarette is now imaginary.)

TOM. Smoking.

DENNIS. Are you crazy?

TOM. Keeps me awake.

(DENNIS goes to the back door, opens it, fans air in.)

Shut it.

DENNIS. You're smelling up the place.

TOM. Shut it, it's cold.

DENNIS. This whole place is going to reek are you crazy.

TOM. We've got hours. She said we had all night.

DENNIS. Smoke it outside, for god's sake.

TOM. It's cold. It's freezing cold out there. Shut the goddamn door. You think I don't know what I'm doing?

DENNIS. We're already...

TOM. I know what I'm doing. We've got all night. There are fans in the truck.

>(DENNIS *shuts the door.*
>
>*Several heavy beats.*)

DENNIS. Why not just smoke it outside.

TOM. Because it gives me great pleasure. To smoke it in here. What have you got.

>(DENNIS *holds up a white envelope.*)

DENNIS. I think I've got it.

I think this is it.

>(*He passes it over,* TOM *rifles through it.*)

TOM. Receipts?

Centurion Used Books

Calvary Pharmacy & Medical Supply

Jericho Records

Mediterranean Café

Damascus Road Resurfacing and Driveway Repair

Caesar's Burgers

Caena Wine and Liquors

Jacob's Ladder Hardware

Dead Sea Aquarium Supply

Yeah. That's odd, but.

DENNIS. I think this is it.

TOM. This? No. A bunch of receipts.

DENNIS. Who says we're looking for a thing. For a thing thing thing. Maybe they don't fully know what we're looking for. Maybe that's why they haven't been explicit.

TOM. These are…*receipts.*

Grouped because he found it amusing to group them.

>(*He looks at other side of the envelope, reads from it:*)

"Taxes, '81."

DENNIS. Calvary Pharmacy doesn't exist.

>(*A beat.*)

TOM. In what way.

DENNIS. It just isn't.

TOM. (*Gives him a hard look.*) How so.

DENNIS. My wife works in a title office on San Pablo. I pick her up there all the time. The address is 1672. 1670, to the left, is an apartment complex,

1674, to the right, is a bar, a very old bar, the Hi Life, the kind that little drunk old ladies hang out in all day. (*Irrelevantly.*) Next to that is a dentist.

> (*A beat.*)

TOM. The receipt is wrong. They don't—I don't know how those machines work but the machine prints the receipt and someone, originally, inputs information and whoever it was, got the address wrong, just slipped a digit, so it's on 1679 San Pablo, or on 5674 San Pablo. Or 1684 San Pablo. The possibilities are endless. No one looks closely at these things.

DENNIS. Look it up. Look it up in the phone book.

> (TOM *stomps offstage, emerges with white pages, is leafing to spot, looks, checks for alternate spelling, closes white pages and goes offstage again, emerges with yellow pages, goes to section there scans, scans.*)

I knew about Calvary Pharmacy because of my wife. But when I saw that I got interested. Jacob's Ladder Hardware doesn't exist either. And Dead Sea Aquarium Supply—obviously, I guess.

TOM. But The Med, exists. I eat at Caesar's all the time. And I don't know about Jericho Records but I could swear—yeah, on Dwight, I've never been in there but I've passed by it a million times.

DENNIS. Yeah I've seen it too.

TOM. (*Holding up receipt.*) So then what, is this.

DENNIS. What is it. I think this has got to be it.

> (*A pondering pause.*)

Maybe it's got something to do with the numbers. With the numbers on the receipts. Maybe they add up to something. If they're not all real purchases, if they can't be, because the place itself doesn't exist, then what are the numbers, right? The numbers must mean something.

> (TOM *spreads the receipts out like cards, closes them up, replaces them in the envelope.*)

TOM. (*Quietly.*) It's a conundrum.

Here.

> (*He gives envelope to him.*)

You should take this in. I'll close up.

DENNIS. Shouldn't we keep looking? Maybe there's more of this.

TOM. Maybe, but I think we're done for the night. You take it in, I'll shut this all down and air out the place. Tell them I'll be there in an hour.

DENNIS. Sure? I can help you close up.

TOM. They should have this right away, they're going to want to do analytics, paper analysis, oh I don't even know, but they might as well get started. You take it in, I'll be there when I finish up.

DENNIS. 'Kay. See you in an hour.

> (*He exits. The door closes.*
>
> TOM *goes into the other room and the screensaver sound stops.*
>
> *We hear a thrum, and an intriguing metallic "plip."*
>
> *There's a moment.*
>
> *Then we hear the ratcheting sound of* TOM *scrolling through the document.*
>
> *LIGHT CHANGE.*
>
> THE MOON MAN *stands in front of the back curtain.*
>
> *He stands there for a moment.*
>
> *He parts the curtain very slightly, and peers behind it.*
>
> *Abruptly he shuts it again.*
>
> *He turns to the audience.*
>
> *He walks off.*
>
> *There is a low and problematic growl from a very specific point on the other side of the off-stage.*
>
> *LIGHT CHANGE.*
>
> *The ratcheting sound, as* TOM *scrolls through the document; the ratcheting sound; the ratcheting sound stops.*
>
> TOM *emerges, lights an imaginary cigarette. He remains, smoking, thinking. This takes the length of the cigarette. He ashes on the floor.*
>
> *When he's done he holds the smoldering butt a moment in his fingers, then turns around and stubs it out into something on the table.*
>
> *He returns to the study, emerges in his coat, walks out the front door and closes it.*
>
> *LIGHT CHANGE.*
>
> *Early morning birds.*
>
> *The front door opens.*
>
> CHET *enters, pants as per the night before, entirely unfamiliar shirt—red, satiny, too small, too tight.*
>
> *He stands a moment, in the middle of the room.*
>
> *Then he goes to the percolator, removes the carafe.*
>
> *Stands indecisively in the middle of the room.*

Puts the carafe on the table, moves to the coffee grinder.

Opens a can and shakes beans into it.

Grinds coffee a moment.

Goes to get filter, shakes coffee into filter.

Pauses indecisively by table.

Puts filter into coffee maker.

Gets carafe from table, fills it at sink, at same time takes coffee cup from sink and when carafe is full swirls cup in stream of water, shakes upside-down over sink, places by sink, takes carafe to coffeemaker and pours in, replaces carafe, hits button.

Machine starts to percolate.

He stands near it in a numb tired daze, watching it as the coffee slowly makes itself.

A nostril wrinkles.

He sniffs.

Lifts his upper arm to his nose and sniffs at his shirt.

Replaces his arm, sniffs again.

Looks around briefly, discards sensory impressions.

Relapses into gazing at machine.

Phone rings, three times, the machine picks up.)

MACHINE. (*Curt.*) "This is Chet and Delia."

MARTIN. Chet, this is Martin. I hope you made it safely home this time. Listen, just so you know, the shirt, when you clean it before you return it to me thank you so much it's got to be dry cleaned, it *cannot be washed*, must be dry cleaned, the dry cleaner. Thank you Chet. (*A deep gravelly laugh.*) Do not forget. That is a one hundred and fifty dollar shirt.

(CHET *lets the call just wash over him.*

When the coffee is half-ready he pulls the carafe out

[sound of drops hitting the burner plate and sizzling]

and pours his coffee, replaces the carafe.

He goes to the refrigerator, pours milk in

He goes to the table, goes back to the sink, pulls out a spoon from the dish drainer, returns to the table, fishes in the sugar, draws out a spoonful of sugar with a cigarette butt in it.

He sees the cigarette butt.

He shakes the sugar gently away from it.

He puts down the coffee cup and he lifts the butt away from the spoon.

He puts the spoon down on the table, and lays the butt gently in the palm of his hand.

—all of this, remember, all of it, is imaginary—

And he stands, staring at the cigarette butt in the palm of his hand.

He looks briefly over at the sugar bowl.

He looks back into the palm of his hand.

There's a knock at the back door.

He starts, his hand curls protectively around the cigarette butt.

The knocking again.

He goes off, to let her in.)

LOIS. There you are,

(She enters.)

You weren't there, when I woke up.

So I came to see where you were. You're here.

And you have a new shirt.

(He sort of looks down at it for a moment, as if briefly he sees it for the first time.)

CHET. This is my agent's shirt.

(A pause.)

LOIS. Is it?

CHET. I was driving without mine.

I have a lot of unpaid parking tickets. As it turns out. And I don't carry my checkbook with me. So.

(She decides not to try to process this fully.

Micropause.)

LOIS. Mmmm. I smell coffee.

(Micropause.)

You mind?

(She ferrets out a cup, pours, sips.)

Mmmm. This is good. Not at all charry.

(*Beat.*)

Really fresh.

(*Beat.*)

You been here a while?

CHET. Just got in.

LOIS. Just now?

CHET. Pretty much.

LOIS. Hmm.

(*Sips, looks around, sniffs, sniffs again, stops sniffing.*)

CHET. Something occurred to me. While I was driving home. The second time. From the station house.

LOIS. Hm?

CHET. I didn't write my address down. At the meeting.

LOIS. At the—

CHET. When you came by the first time, you said you'd gotten my address from the sign-in sheet, at the meeting. But of course I didn't write my address down, no one did. Of course they didn't ask for it. It's *anonymous.*

(*A tiny pause. She smiles.*)

LOIS. Yeah. You got me there. I got it out of the phone book.

CHET. I'm not listed.

(*She takes a sip.*)

LOIS. So I skullduggered a bit to get it. No reason to freak out.

CHET. Because I'm compelling.

(*She shrugs.*)

LOIS. Sure. I don't think things through all the time. I'm intuitive.

CHET. Right.

LOIS. Listen, if you don't want me to be here, I can take off. I just woke up, you were gone, I thought: check it out. My mistake. Big day of writing ahead of you, right?

(*She places coffee cup on counter; turns to go.*)

CHET. Were you afraid I'd interrupt someone?

(*She turns back.*)

LOIS. No.

(*A beat.*)

Did you?

CHET. No. But only barely.

(He holds up the cigarette butt.)

I guess I'm wondering who you are.

LOIS. Who am I. Good question.

I am, I think I am, Tracy.

CHET. Tracy.

LOIS. Your character, Tracy, I think that's me. At least, I'm pretty sure that's me.

CHET. Oh.

(A beat.)

Oh.

I don't think so.

LOIS. I actually think so, yes.

(A heavy beat.)

CHET. Listen, maybe you should go. My wife…

LOIS. Is in Sonoma. With a guy named Rick. I wouldn't be concerned, it sounds to me like a strictly temporary entanglement, but she won't be back today, or this week probably.

CHET. I think I should, change this shirt.

(He exits and does so, returning with a red plaid flannel over a white or black tee shirt.)

Did you find what you were looking for?

LOIS. *(Looking around.)* Me?

CHET. All of you.

(A little pause.)

LOIS. Oh—oh all right:

They found a bunch of, receipts, for places that don't exist and they're excited about that.

CHET. Receipts for places that don't exist.

LOIS. A pet store, and a pharmacy on San Pablo and, others, I didn't—you were gone, not that I said that but I called in and that was the point in the conversation when I discovered that—someone—was still here, so I wasn't listening.

CHET. What did they find? Receipts?

LOIS. Like, yes, an envelope of receipts.

(He marches out of the room, briefly, marches back.)

CHET. They took my tax receipts.

LOIS. Woah that was quick.

CHET. For this year.

LOIS. How did you know it was gone?

> (*He blinks at her.*)

How did you know where it wasn't? Do you know where things *are* in that mess?

CHET. I know what I need to know about that mess, yes.

> (*A beat.*)

You're with the IRS.

LOIS. No. No.

CHET. Tax receipts.

LOIS. For places that are imaginary.

CHET. So they think, what, *fraud?* This is patently illegal they broke into my house to...

LOIS. Oh...no.

CHET. Those are all real receipts. For genuine purchases.

LOIS. How can they be? If the stores aren't real.

Not the pet shop. Not the pharmacy. Apparently. I don't remember the others.

CHET. Pet shop? I don't go to pet shops. I don't have receipts for a pet shop. They've doctored this whole thing up, I knew it, this is a governmental con job, a set-up—

LOIS. (*Remembers the precise word.*) Aquarium. Store.

CHET. But that's.

They think that it doesn't exist.

LOIS. Because it isn't there. It isn't in the phone book, there's no business license. They sent a car to the location and it's a typewriter repair shop.

CHET. They're incompetent. That's where—

> (*He waves towards the living room.*)

all of my fish, the tank. Their pellets.

LOIS. Fish tank.

CHET. Yes. The one in the living room.

LOIS. Oh I don't remember.

CHET. We were talking about yes it's huge just the other night, we were talking about the fish.

LOIS. About your fish? No.

CHET. I wasn't going to kill one.

LOIS. I remember that. I thought you were speaking rhetorically. About categories of things you weren't willing to kill. Like pets. Even if they were fish, I thought that seemed reasonable.

CHET. Go, go, it's in there.

LOIS. (*Calls from living room.*) I don't see it, where?

CHET. On the console.

> (*A pause.*)

LOIS. I really don't see it. On the console?

> (*He's already moving offstage.*)

CHET. Yes.

> (*This conversation takes place out of sight, but we hear it.*)

There. Right there.

> (*Beat.*)

LOIS. There's nothing there.

CHET. (*Suddenly hard.*) You're a little bitch.

LOIS. There's nothing—where, where my hand—

> (*He cries out in surprise and fear.*)

nothing.

> (*He re-emerges into the kitchen.*
>
> *He stands there.*
>
> *After a moment, she emerges again, stands just in the doorway.*)

CHET. (*To himself as much as anyone.*) I'm tired. I'm very tired. I've been this tired many times before. Many times before. I've hallucinated, a lot. I've had many hallucinations. Afterwards, it's obvious—oh. *That* was a hallucination. But in the moment, sometimes, rarely, you will be unaware, that a hallucination, is a hallucination. It's rare. But it happens. But, I've had that fish tank for, for over a year.

What else. What was the other…Dead Sea, and what else.

LOIS. (*She struggles to remember.*) A pharmacy. On San Pablo.

CHET. …Calvary.

> (*He goes out the other way, emerges after a moment with a prescription bottle.*)

What about this? Calvary Pharmacy.

> (*A pause.*)

LOIS. No.

> (*He looks at it again, holds it out in her direction.*)

CHET. Really? You can't see this?

LOIS. I'm sorry.

> (*A pause.*)

Do you want me to, I can wave my…hand through this one? Would that help?

CHET. No. No.

> (*He clutches it, protectively.*)

No.

You really can't.

(*She shakes her head.*)

LOIS. Does it look…fuzzy, to you? Or, clear.

CHET. It looks absolutely real. It feels absolutely real.

(*He steps towards her, she steps back from him.*)

LOIS. I'm sorry.

(*He rotates, looking around him.*)

CHET. What else?

(*He shakes the bottle. We hear the sound of pills shaking, somewhat amplified.*)

LOIS. (*Microbeat.*) What? Do that again. What you did.

(*He shakes again.*

An intake of breath:)

I *hear* that.

(*He shakes.*)

I *hear* that.

CHET. You hear it. You *hear* it. What about the

(*Bubbling sound kicks in.*

He's going into the living room, she follows him. We can still hear them.)

the aquarium, the bubbler.

LOIS. I don't. I mean I can hear something, I can't quite tell.

CHET. Let me just, I'm going to pull out the plug.

(*The faint bubbling sound ceases.*)

Now:

(*It starts up again.*)

LOIS. (*A faintly "wigged" sound.*) Ujuh. I *hear* it but I—

Is my hand in it? Right now?

CHET. Yes.

LOIS. Am I moving my hands around in it?

CHET. Now you're to the side, left.

LOIS. Now?

CHET. Yes.

LOIS. And does it, when I, does that change it at all?

CHET. No.

LOIS. Can you see my hands through it?

CHET. No the object is solid. Your hands disappear into it.

LOIS. Pick up a fish. Make it squeak.

CHET. Come.

>   (*They re-emerge into the kitchen.*
>   *He points to the floor near the refrigerator.*)

Do you see that magnet?

>   (*A beat.*)

LOIS. I don't see a magnet there. But I see one

>   (*She points to different area.*)

there.

CHET. You don't see that one, you see that one

>   (*He points to the fridge.*)

there?

LOIS. I see that one.

>   (*He points to a different spot.*)

CHET. There.

LOIS. I see it.

CHET. There.

LOIS. I see that one.

CHET. Here.

LOIS. I don't see that one.

CHET. The daisy? You don't see the daisy?

LOIS. No.

CHET. You don't see any of the daisies. Jacob's Ladder Hardware. A week and a half ago.

>   (*She shakes her head.*)

The sushi?

LOIS. I see the sushi.

CHET. Okay.

>   (*He looks about, on a counter.*)

You see *this* one.

LOIS. No.

>   (*He stops.*)

CHET. You don't see this one? Look carefully. Right

>   (*He picks it up.*)

here.

LOIS. Uh uh.

>   (*Several beats.*)

CHET. This is the one…I've had this one for 30 years.

LOIS. Oh.

CHET. More than 30 years. I don't remember where I got it from. Some store I wandered into. 30 years ago.

Oh fuck. Fuck.

Oh fuck.

I go into Dead Sea Aquarium Supply, oh, every three or four weeks; I pick up pellets or a new filter or an aquatic plant, and I usually get another fish. I don't go in for anything fancy just something pretty, or neat-looking. The guy behind the counter, George Menendez, was in 'Nam. We usually chat about... fish. He describes himself as an... aficionado. That's his standing joke. He's trying to refine my sensibility; long-term he's trying to groom me for salt water; he thinks I've got the head for it. Secretly, I agree.

(*Pause.*)

LOIS. Are there other people there? When you go in?

CHET. Are there other customers? (*He thinks.*) There must be. (*He thinks.*)

I don't know.

I don't have the sense that it's not busy but

I can't quite

I can't

I don't remember.

LOIS. What about the pharmacy? When did you start going there? Was it around when you got the aquarium?

CHET. No (*He's thinking.*) it was earlier. Maybe a year earlier. It's small it's, the prices are pretty good it's convenient. A little dusty...

There's usually an elderly woman, at the counter, she doesn't like to talk much, she has, bifocals, which make her eyes look...enormous. Or there's a kid, early 20s, pimples, no chin, shy, I don't think I've ever heard him speak, I think he's related, I think it's all one family that runs it.

LOIS. Other customers.

CHET. I don't know. I don't think so. I don't know.

(*He's absolutely clutching his skull in his hands, staggering around a bit like a bear.*)

If these places don't, if they don't exist. Then where have I, when I go there, where have I *been?*

(*Pause.*)

LOIS. I suppose they exist...somewhere, right? Just not...here.

(*There's a tiny while, while he clutches his head and fugues briefly. He looks up.*)

CHET. Tell me again. You think that you're—Wait, first of all: are you Lois.

LOIS. No.

No I picked that name, I went to the meeting and you said, and I figured it was an "in," you know?

I think that I'm—yes. Tracy.

CHET. Right. Tracy. Tracy. How could you be Tracy. You're nothing like Tracy. Who doesn't, by the way, actually exist.

LOIS. Yeah, I think you may not actually have a good handle on her. I think you may be projecting or something, a lot of male writers do that with female characters. It's why I do in fact slightly prefer female writers for a certain kind of novel.

(CHET *makes a sound halfway between a "huh" and a "humph."*)

CHET. So tell me. Why you think you're Tracy.

(*There's a pause.*)

LOIS. I'm not me, to begin with. I'm a person, for sure, I mean

(*She indicates herself.*)

Right?

But I don't know who.

A lot of my memories don't make sense.

My mother died. And I can remember—I can remember her dying. I can remember sitting with her, in the hospital, as she was dying—it was three in the morning it was just us two, she (*She starts to well up.*) she did regain consciousness— (*Recovers herself.*) It's a very vivid memory. And afterwards, after she died, I went and I stood by the window, before I called the nurse, and I remember looking out, at the moonlight, on the snow. And a mountain. Lit up by the moon, half cut out from view by a wing of the hospital. But I don't have any memory of—going—to some place where there is a mountain, and snow, to be with my dying mother.

And then I have a memory, just a very ordinary memory, which postdates that one, of talking with my mother on the phone. I remember it because I was trying to bake blondies which was her specialty and I didn't know how to know if they were done or not and she was coaching me I'm crouched down with the phone on the kitchen floor with the oven open and I'm sticking toothpicks into all these different sections of these poor half-baked blondies and she's getting impatient and I remember saying "Mom, Mother... 'We can't all of us be baked goods geniuses,'" something like that. She died when I was 19 and I only moved into that apartment, the one with the stove, in '76 which I know because the super was always coming over, right when I first moved in, to fix the stove, there was some ongoing nonsense with the gas pipes, and he was obsessed with how Ford was going to win the election. When he wasn't criticizing my posters.

And these memories, they're not only contradictory, a lot of them don't function.

I have a great friend, Genna, we've been friends since we were 9, I have a million stories about Genna she is so dear to me, she's nuts, we fight like cats and dogs, she's a total bitch, but we always make up, but I could not, for the life of me, tell you her phone number. If I want to get hold of her, right now, I have no idea how. I saw her a few weeks ago. We were in her kitchen, drinking *White Russians* until four a.m., I can tell you everything about her apartment, that twirky wall-hanging, the rug I helped her pick out at the flea market, what's in her refrigerator, her spice cabinet, which is a disgrace, the kind of soap she uses…but I can't tell you where that apartment *is*. I try to think about it and I just…I just don't *know*.

I don't know where I work. I thought I worked at a law office, on Shattuck, as a secretary, but when I went there to…go to work…some girl was sitting at the front desk. I'm a terrible secretary so I figured I'd just been fired but when I said is Tim there—one of the partners—he came out but he didn't recognize me.

And the memory I have most often is the one which makes the least sense. I'm standing in a corridor, an all-white corridor. I'm standing in front of a door it doesn't have a handle it has, buttons, a, key pad, I'm reaching out to press the buttons, to, I want to go in and I hear a voice behind me and I see a man and it's I don't know who it is but it's someone I know. I've seen his face, over and over and, I have no idea.

And I know you can only think that my brain is ravaged by drugs, or that I'm crazy, and that was what I thought too. I was going to check myself into Herrick and I passed by the meeting. I don't even know why I went in. I thought why doesn't he tell them this about Tracy, why is he only mentioning that. I thought no, this is crazy, but I knew, by the end of that meeting I *knew* I know, things about Tracy, I know I know that she's been having these savage headaches, and fevers.

(*From* CHET: *a sharp intake of breath.*)

I know she grew up in a small town near Shasta. I know that she's been waking herself up, in the middle of the night, muttering things in Koine Greek, I know that her dealer is trying to get her into a new drug, this drug everyone's starting to take it gives you visions and she's reluctant to try it—

CHET. You read my book. While I was asleep.

LOIS. I know things you haven't written down yet, things I'm not sure if you know or not. I get, just, bits: Tracy is seeing a man named Leonard who works for a cultish alternative day school; he's about to tell her he's been deported and is going to have to leave the country—

(CHET *starts.*

She just realizes this:)

Actually, I think it's Leonard who knows Charlie Klinger, is that right? That's how she meets him, later. (*Continuing.*) He hasn't actually been deported, he's actually planning to hole up in Marin at an…(*She's trying to make it out, it's as though she's seeing it fuzzily.*) at an expansion…at a secular consciousness expansion seminary called…Golden…Capacious…?

CHET. Capacity. Golden Capacity.

LOIS. Institute. Golden Capacity Institute.

Golden Capacity.

I know things about you, too. Not so much, probably about as much as you know about me. Tracy. Me. I know about a dream you have. A recurring dream you've had since you were a kid. Where you're standing in a schoolroom, only it's really terribly old fashioned-looking with dark wainscoting and miles of green linoleum, one light bulb and it's night and a huge globe—

(*He puts his hand over her mouth.*

He pulls her to him. He holds her to him. It's not a romantic gesture precisely. He puts his hand on her skull. He might be weeping.)

CHET. Oh Dear Lord. Oh Dear Dear Lord.

(*He has both hands on her skull.*

She takes his hands down and holds them in her own.

They're leaning in towards each other, skull against skull, not kissing, not looking at each other's faces.

After a bit, quietly.)

LOIS. And Chet?

(*A beat.*)

CHET. Yeah?

LOIS. I don't know how it ends, your book. But I think it's important. For me. Tracy. Me.

(*A beat.*)

CHET. Huh.

LOIS. And for you.

CHET. Mmmn.

(*He stands and holds her again. He kisses her, passionately. She kisses him back.*

There is a prickle of sound and a cry of pain from the study.)

They freeze. CHET *slips to a drawer, rummages silently and pulls out a knife [or, it's already on the table, from when he was slicing apples and spreading them with peanut butter]*

After a moment BOB SEWARD *appears in the doorway to the study, he is swaying slightly.*

His clothes, since we last saw him, are very much worse for the wear.)

BOB SEWARD. A moment. Just a moment. Let me just. Let me just.

(*He recovers himself, looks around at the room.*)

This is…pretty bad…You're going to need to get out of here.

CHET. You're going to need to tell me who you are.

(*Beat.*)

BOB SEWARD. I wouldn't know where to begin. Really Mr. Ellis. You should leave. If you could see it, your old familiar home, as I can see it, you wouldn't hesitate, not for a moment.

LOIS. You're the man. I know you. This is the man. In the corridor. In the white corridor. I've seen you over, and over. Do you know me?

(BOB SEWARD *is staring at her, his head cocked, squinting slightly; his face changes, he steps back a pace.*)

BOB SEWARD. Dr. Tanner. That's you, in there.

LOIS. Dr. Tanner?

BOB SEWARD. Or, no. Yes. In part. The explosion must have punched you through. Bits of you. Not all.

LOIS. Bits? Who is Dr. Tanner.

CHET. (*Quietly.*) Another one of my characters.

Dr. Sylvie Tanner heads up Golden Capacity, a secular consciousness expansion seminary in Marin. To all appearances the kind of facility typical of organized fringe thinking in the Bay Area; a delusional self important financially rapacious and entirely sincere mixture of various spiritual practices and modern quasi brain science; half disorganized institute, half mildly dangerous cult.

And, a product of my imagination.

BOB SEWARD. Not quite.

CHET. My current book.

BOB SEWARD. No. This isn't your book, any more. You are no longer its author.

CHET. (*Rousing.*) Like hell.

BOB SEWARD. You don't have an outline, do you—

CHET. No, but I never

BOB SEWARD. You don't know the ending of your book.

CHET. No I like to leave that a surprise.

BOB SEWARD. Yes, I think it will be. An incredible surprise. The next time you sit down to write I believe you will find that Charlie Klinger has borrowed, "borrowed," really, a friend's car and is on 580 heading towards Marin; try to write something else, try—start a sentence on Begonias, or the Russian Revolution, bend down to describe your cat; you will wake with a start to find that pages have gone by and Charlie Klinger has pulled into the gravel parking lot; up ahead, at the end of the white stone path, is the entrance to Golden Capacity.

LOIS. Golden Capacity. That's what's on the other side of the door. The door I'm trying to get into. You're following after me. We're both going in. The demonstration. Right. Yes. The Lab. We're beginning in 20 minutes.

(*She starts forward, stops, her brow crinkles.*)

That's so…strange, I can't.

Dammit, what's the passcode.

Bob would you mind? I'm having a brain glitch.

BOB SEWARD. You want me to open the door.

LOIS. Just punch in your code and we'll get the demonstration started.

BOB SEWARD. The demonstration is over, Dr. Tanner.

LOIS. Bob I don't have time for this.

BOB SEWARD. Where are we.

(*She stops. Registers her surroundings.*)

LOIS. Oh. Oh.

We're not.

BOB SEWARD. No.

LOIS. No. Where are we? We're…right. here. Right.

I'm at the door, my fingers on the keypad, you're behind me in the hallway you've come to attend the demonstration and then I don't…and then I don't…then I don't know what happens next.

BOB SEWARD. There's an explosion. Twenty minutes later. A miscallibration.

LOIS. Fuck.

BOB SEWARD. Dr. Tanner, standing right next to the board, is obliterated. Richard Harrison, the rest of the management team, littered on the floor around me. I assumed that they had died. But then, of course, I also assumed that I had lived.

LOIS. Capacity failed.

(*A beat.*)

BOB SEWARD. No. I'm afraid that Capacity continues. (*To* CHET.) The Capacity project was set up to exploit a temporal sensitivity—a point of opportunity for intradimensional exploration. The explosion in our dimension punched through the weak point in yours.

CHET. The weak point is in my house.

BOB SEWARD. The weak point, initially unbeknownst to Dr. Tanner, is located in your brain. You've been trafficking in unrealities for quite some time Mr. Ellis, and now they are trafficking in you. You can continue to write, if you choose to, I can't stop you, but you'll find that you are now creating a work of nonfiction. Pick up a pen, test the ink flow, just for fun, just a little doodle, just a scribble a little bit of a scrawl and you'll be on the threshold, the sun bright, and crisp, the wind picking up with just a hint of tang from the ocean, the hills rising around yellow and dry, a hawk overhead, oaks.

(*He looks at* LOIS.)

Tracy is already there, staring in front of her, shielding her eyes from the sun reflected off the bright front gate.

LOIS. I've been…whacking at the buzzer. For what seems like forever but I know it's only been minutes. It's so loud, listen—

(*A deep echoing chime.*)

There's an echo, off the canyon. Can you hear voices? I can hear a fountain, bubbling, I think I hear voices, but no one comes.

(*Her face clears, she looks at* CHET.)

Here. You try. Maybe they'll open it up, for you.

CHET. You want me to.

LOIS. Ring the bell. Pass through the gate.

CHET. (*With dread.*) And after that, what. What happens after that.

LOIS. I think that our questions, are answered. I think the things that separate us, become insignificant. I think that we feel whole. (*Not unsardonically.*) At least, that's what the brochure says. I say: why not give it a try.

Come on. Let's go in together.

(*She closes her eyes.*)

Knock on the door. Let's see what happens next.

(CHET *looks at* BOB.)

CHET. What happens next.

BOB SEWARD. Our two dimensions become one. The boundaries of our bodies are broken open. Our souls merge; birds would fall from the sky—if there were still birds, a sky, flight; seas would rage, if there were seas, water, rage. Eternity, Mr. Ellis. Unity. Totality.

(*A beat.*)

CHET. What you're describing, is some people's idea of heaven.

BOB SEWARD. Is it yours?

LOIS. (*Her eyes are closed.*) I can hear voices, definitely. Someone is there, close to the gate.

(*She looks at him.*)

Call out. Maybe they'll hear us. Maybe they'll let us in.

(*He looks at her. Takes her hand.*)

CHET. Do you know who I am?

LOIS. You're Leonard's friend Charlie. It's Charlie, right? Or is it Charles?

CHET. Do you know me?

LOIS. ...Oh.

(*She looks around her.*)

Oh God. Oh God. Oh...Chet.

(*She touches his shoulder, she stops, she pushes him away.*)

Oh. God.

(*Her hands to her face.*)

Oh my God.

(*Looking up, maybe crying.*)

I don't make any sense. I don't make any sense at all.

(*He comes towards her, to hold her, she clutches him, pushes him away, clutches him.*)

CHET. You are the only woman—the only person—who has ever made sense to me. Real sense to me.

(*Her head is on his chest, he's cradling her, she is shaking.*)

You are the realest being I've ever known.

(*He holds her for a long time.*

He reaches behind him, and picks up the knife from the counter.

Still holding her, he stabs her in the chest.

They sink down together.

There is a long Pause.)

BOB SEWARD. (*Quiet.*) You didn't hear that?

It sounds...structural...and (*Holds up a hand.*) I don't like that wind.

(*Another pause. CHET looks up.*)

CHET. Are you an angel?

(*BOB takes a moment to consider this.*)

BOB SEWARD. Only in a very disturbing theology.

If it's a consolation, you have seen into the heart of things. Luckily without understanding them.

(*A beat.*)

CHET. (*He looks down at* LOIS.) I've come close. Haven't I.

BOB SEWARD. I would never say.

(*He disappears into the study, there is a woosh.*

After a moment CHET *stands.*

He looks around for a moment.

Then he walks out.

Sound of the front door slamming.

There is a moment, then a creak, and then the sound of something large beginning to splinter

Structural give and sway; a crash on a distant floor, then another crash, on a closer floor;

The sound of a house, slowly falling in on itself, then the sound of something larger, an office tower, slowly giving way, or an ocean liner, a great structural groan

Then larger possibly cosmic structures twinge and twang

Then the sound of a house slowly luxuriously elaborately collapsing, the sound of debris, and a vast cloud of dust.

At the last of the collapse, LOIS *slowly rises from the imaginary wreckage.*

Bright, eerie light.

And LOIS:

She stretches out her hands. Catches the light.

She sings:)

LOIS. And the light has filled
the room
I know I'm standing
on the moon
Now the light exceeds
the room
And I'm drinking
of the moon
Now I'm the light without

the room
And for a moment
I'm the moon
For just a moment,
I'm the moon…
For this one moment…
I'm the moon.

(*The curtain slowly closes.*)

End of Play

THE END
AN APOCALYPSE ANTHOLOGY
by Dan Dietz, Jennifer Haley, Allison Moore,
A. Rey Pamatmat and Marco Ramirez

Copyright © 2011 by Dan Dietz, Jennifer Haley, Allison Moore, A. Rey Pamatmat and Marco Ramirez. All rights reserved. CAUTION: Professionals and amateurs are hereby warned that *The End* is subject to a royalty. It is fully protected under the copyright laws of the United States of America and of all countries covered by the International Copyright Union (including the Dominion of Canada and the rest of the British Commonwealth), the Berne Convention, the Pan-American Copyright Convention and the Universal Copyright Convention, as well as all countries with which the United States has reciprocal copyright relations. All rights, including professional, amateur stage rights, motion picture, recitation, lecturing, public reading, radio broadcasting, television, video or sound recording, all other forms of mechanical or electronic reproduction, such as CD-ROM, CD-I, information storage and retrieval systems and photocopying, and the rights of translation into foreign languages, are strictly reserved. Particular emphasis is laid upon the matter of readings, permission for which must be secured from the Authors' agents in writing.

Required royalties must be paid every time this play is performed before any audience, whether or not it is presented for profit and whether or not admission is charged.

All inquiries concerning rights, including amateur rights, should be addressed to:

For Dan Dietz's *Promaggedon*: Dramatic Publishing, 311 Washington Street, Woodstock, IL 60098. www.dramaticpublishing.com.

For Dietz's appended material: William Morris Endeavor Entertainment, 1325 Ave. of the Americas, New York, NY 10019, ATTN: Jonathan Lomma.

For Jennifer Haley: William Morris Endeavor Entertainment, 1325 Ave. of the Americas, New York, NY 10019, ATTN: Derek Zasky.

For Allison Moore: Creative Artists Agency, 162 Fifth Avenue, New York, NY 10010, ATTN: Chris Till.

For A. Rey Pamatmat: Abrams Artists Agency, 275 7th Avenue, 26th Floor, New York, NY 10001, ATTN: Polly Hubbard.

For Marco Ramirez: Abrams Artists Agency, 275 7th Avenue, 26th Floor, New York, NY 10001, ATTN: Kate Navin.

ABOUT *THE END*

This article first ran in the January/February 2011 issue of Inside Actors, *before rehearsals for the Humana Festival production began.*

Some say the world will end in fire, some say in ice. Others have their money on a zombie apocalypse.

Since the very beginning, it seems, people have been anticipating the end of all things. The oldest surviving apocalyptic prediction by a human dates all the way back to 2800 B.C. Carved on a clay tablet by a not-very-cheery Assyrian, the ancient message announced the forthcoming disaster in no uncertain terms: "Our earth is degenerate in these latter days. There are signs that the world is speedily coming to an end. Bribery and corruption are common." (One can't help but wonder what that gentleman would have to say about our modern instruments of warfare. Or reality television.)

The prophecies have been flying fast and loose since then. The Book of Revelation foretells the finer points of Armageddon, the Rapture and the subsequent End Times in harrowing, glorious detail. Several Christian sects predicted the apocalypse would coincide with the turn of the first millennium A.D. In the 19th century, a group of American farmers neglected to plant their crops not one, but two years running, assured that the end was near and they would not need the food.

Fascination with the end of the world has not waned in the modern era, as anyone with one eye on the Mayan calendar (or America's carbon output) will tell you. Indeed, apocalyptic mania remains pervasive today, manifesting in popular culture and on the religious landscape in various forms. For some, such thoughts induce panic. For others they are a source of comfort. Others still stand on the sidelines and laugh.

What is it, exactly, about the idea of apocalypse that continues to inspire and terrify? And why, generation after generation, do so many cleave to the conviction that they are living in Earth's final days? We invited playwrights Dan Dietz, Jennifer Haley, Allison Moore, A. Rey Pamatmat and Marco Ramirez to tackle these and other questions. Together with our Apprentice Company of twenty-two young actors, this diverse and energetic group of writers came up with all sorts of answers—and some questions of their own. Their explorations, collected in *The End,* will take you from a zombie-infested Los Angeles, to a basement bunker beneath a John Hughes-style high school, to the very edge of existence, and back again.

It is so nigh.

—Sarah Lunnie

BIOGRAPHIES

Dan Dietz's plays include *tempOdyssey, Americamisfit,* and *The Sandreckoner,* and have been seen in theatres around the country. *tempOdyssey* received a rolling world premiere from the National New Play Network, premiering at Curious Theatre (Denver, CO), Studio Theatre (Washington, D.C.), Phoenix Theatre (Indianapolis, IN) and New Jersey Repertory (Long Branch, NJ). The play was also named a finalist for the 2007 PEN USA Literary Award in Drama. His latest play, *Clementine in the Lower Nine,* received its world premiere at TheatreWorks in October 2011. Dietz has been honored with an NEA/TCG Theatre Residency, a Jerome Fellowship, a James A. Michener Fellowship, a Josephine Bay Paul Fellowship, and the Austin Critics Table Award for Best New Play. He received the Heideman Award from Actors Theatre of Louisville in 2003 for his play *Trash Anthem,* and again in 2010 for his play *Lobster Boy.* Dietz has received commissions from the Guthrie Theater, Actors Theatre of Louisville, and The eXchange. His plays have been developed and presented at the Kennedy Center, the Public Theater, Rattlestick Playwrights Theater, CenterStage, the Lark, PlayPenn, and the Summer Play Festival, among others. Dietz's work has been published by Dramatists Play Service, Heinemann, Playscripts, Samuel French, Smith & Kraus, and Stage & Screen. He is a Core Member of The Playwrights' Center.

Jennifer Haley's current plays include *Neighborhood 3: Requisition of Doom,* which premiered at Actors Theatre of Louisville in the 2008 Humana Festival and continues to see productions around the country; *Breadcrumbs,* which premiered at the 2010 Contemporary American Theatre Festival; *Froggy,* developed at the 2011 Sundance Institute Theatre Lab, The Banff Centre in Canada and American Conservatory Theater; and *The Nether,* developed at the O'Neill National Playwrights Conference and The Lark Play Development Center. Jennifer's work has also been seen at the Summer Play Festival in New York, PlayPenn Playwrights Conference in Philadelphia, Lincoln Center Director's Lab, A.R.T./Moscow Art Theater Institute in Boston, Wellfleet Harbor Actors Theater, Geva Theatre in Rochester, Theatre at Boston Court in Pasadena, Sacred Fools Theater Company in Los Angeles, Brown/Trinity Playwrights Repertory Theatre in Providence, Manbites Dog Theater in Durham, NC and Page 73 Productions Summer Residency at Yale, among other venues. She has been awarded fellowships by the MacDowell Colony and Millay Colony for the Arts, and a 2009 Primus Prize Citation by the American Theatre Critics Association. Her work is published by Samuel French and Playscripts, Inc. She lives in Los Angeles, where she founded a network of dramatic writers called the Playwrights Union and is a member of the 2011-2012 Center Theatre Group's Writers' Workshop. You can find out more about her at jenniferhaley.com.

Allison Moore is a displaced Texan based in Minneapolis. Her play *Slasher* premiered at the 2009 Humana Festival, and has been produced at ten theaters around the country. Other plays include: *My Antonia* (Illusion Theater), *End Times* (Kitchen Dog Theater), *American Klepto* (Illusion Theater), *Hazard County* (2005 Humana Festival and National New Play Network Rolling World Premiere with Kitchen Dog and Actor's Express), *Split* (Guthrie Theater commission), *Urgent Fury* (Cherry Lane Mentor Project), and *Eighteen* (O'Neill Playwrights Conference). Her most recent play, *Collapse*, received a 2011 National New Play Network Rolling World Premiere at Aurora Theater, Curious Theatre and Kitchen Dog, with additional productions in Sacramento, Portland and Cincinnati.

A. Rey Pamatmat recently received the 2011-12 Playwright of New York Fellowship from the Lark Play Development Center. His play *Edith Can Shoot Things and Hit Them* began its rolling world premiere at the 2011 Humana Festival before playing at New Theatre, Actor's Express, Mu Performing Arts, B Street Theatre, and Manbites Dog in the 2011-12 season. His plays have been produced Off-Off Broadway by Second Generation (*Thunder Above, Deeps Below*), the Vortex Theater (*DEVIANT*), HERE (*High/Limbo/High*), and Vampire Cowboys (*Red Rover*). Both *Edith Can Shoot Things and Hit Them* and *Thunder Above, Deeps Below* will be published by Samuel French in 2012. Rey's work has been developed nationwide at The Public, Playwrights Horizons, Ma-Yi, the O'Neill, Victory Gardens, The Magic, Curious Theatre, American Theater Company, Ars Nova, Rattlestick Playwrights Theater, Ensemble Studio Theatre, New Dramatists, and The Lark. He was a recipient of the Princess Grace Fellowship for Playwriting, a New York Foundation for the Arts Playwriting Fellowship, an Ensemble Studio Theatre/Alfred P. Sloan Foundation commission, and is a proud member of the Ma-Yi Writer's Lab. B.F.A.: New York University, M.F.A.: Yale School of Drama.

Marco Ramirez has had plays produced at The Kennedy Center, The Juilliard School, The Black Dahlia, Theatre [502], and Actors Theatre of Louisville's Humana Festival of New American Plays—where he has twice received the Heideman Award for best ten-minute play (*I am not Batman*; *3:59a.m.: a drag race for two actors*). Other honors include a Helen Hayes nomination, the Bryan Award from The Fellowship of Southern Writers, and the Le Comte Du Nouy Prize from Lincoln Center. He's trained at both New York University and The Juilliard School. TV credits include FX's *Sons of Anarchy*.

ACKNOWLEDGMENTS

The End premiered at the Humana Festival of New American Plays in March 2011. It was directed by Amy Attaway and Michael Legg, and co-conceived and developed with Sarah Lunnie, with the following cast:

This is How it Ends by A. Rey Pamatmat
JAKE...Sean Michael Palmer
ANNIE..Emily Kunkel
PESTILENCE ....Daniel Desmarais
DEATH...Victoria Alvarez-Chacon
WAR...Devin Olson
FAMINE..Martina Bonolis

The One About the Asteroid by Marco Ramirez
ENSEMBLE MEMBER ....Peter Vergari
THE BOWLER ....Alex Hernandez

La Reina de los Ángeles by Jennifer Haley
TRENT..Zach Virden
RYAN/BART ....Brandon Peters
LILA..Lizzie Schwarzrock
JILLIAN ....Rebecca Haden
MINDI/JENNA...................................Monica Bergstrand
JAKE...Will Steele
DIRECTOR..Kerri Alexander

The One That Ends Itself by Marco Ramirez
ENSEMBLE MEMBER ....Alex Stage

Apocalypse Apartments by Allison Moore
MICK...Ryan Westwood
ZOE ....Lizzie Schwarzrock
TYLER...Peter Vergari
STACE ....Rebecca Haden
PIPER ....Dinah Berkeley
ERIC ....Zach Virden

La Muerte by Marco Ramirez
SLICK ....Alex Hernandez
MOUSE...Jordan Brodess
LA MUERTE ....Kerri Alexander
MUSICIANS......................................Alex Stage, Ryan Westwood

The One They Call The Bloop by Marco Ramirez
ENSEMBLE MEMBER .... Kerri Alexander

Promageddon by Dan Dietz
GIL..Scott Swayze
THEO ....Jordan Brodess
DOT...Havalah Grace
ALEXIS ....Ellen Haun
KIMMY ....Dinah Berkeley

and the following production staff:

Scenic Designer ....Ryan Wineinger
Costume Designer.. Lindsay Chamberlin
Lighting Designer... Brian J. Lilienthal
Sound Designer .... Matt Callahan
Properties Designer... Alice Baldwin
Wig Designer..Heather Fleming
Stage Manager...Jessica Potter
Fight Director ....Joe Isenberg
Dramaturg ....Sarah Lunnie

Directing Assistants ....Zach Chotzen-Freund, Rachel Paul
Lighting Design Assistant ....Rachel Fae Szymanski
Sound Design Assistant...Dan Cassin
Assistant Dramaturgs................ Mik Mroczynski, Jessica Reese

The End was commissioned and developed by Actors Theatre of Louisville.

Havalah Grace and Ellen Haun
in *The End*

35th Annual Humana Festival of New American Plays
Actors Theatre of Louisville, 2011
Photo by Joe Geinert

THE END

THIS IS HOW IT ENDS
by A. Rey Pamatmat

1.

JAKE *and* ANNIE *sitting on a park bench, sipping Jamba Juices.*

ANNIE. Okay, okay, Jake, here's one. If the world were coming to an end—and I mean everything is ending—every planet (even poor, not-really-a-planet Pluto), every sun, and every galaxy and every everything. Apocalypse. What would you do on the very last day at the end of existence?

JAKE. I don't know. You go first.

ANNIE. I'd call my dad and be at his side. Partly because I feel obligated. But also, he's my dad. I adore my dad.

JAKE. (*Baby talk.*) Awww…Daddy's girl.

ANNIE. Shut up. Your turn.

JAKE. I would find where all the other gays are, and I'd fuck my fucking brains out.

ANNIE. What about your parents and your loved ones—or if you had a boyfriend?

JAKE. I'd call my parents, but they live too far away to get to in a day. And if I had a boyfriend he'd totally be the kind of boyfriend who'd join me at the fucking place to fuck my fucking brains out. Oh, and thanks for reminding me how single I am.

ANNIE. How do you know that there would even be a fucking place?

JAKE. Annie, there's a fucking place now, and it's a Tuesday. Trust me: faced with extinction, gay people are going to have sex. They'll find a place, tell everyone where it is, make flyers that say "Fuck the Apocalypse" or "Armageddon Some Ass," go there, and then fuck and fuck and fuck so they can sync up the final explosions of universe and cocks.

ANNIE. God…why can't straight people be like that?

JAKE. I bet, on the day to end all days, there will be a straight fucking place, too, ke-mo sah-bee. (*Different subject.*) How's Mega Mango?

ANNIE. Eh. How's Peach Perfection?

JAKE. Fairly flawed. Not for me.

ANNIE. Can I make a potentially controversial suggestion, actually?

JAKE. Please do.

ANNIE. I bet I'd like yours, and you'd like mine. We should swap.

JAKE. That is crazy.

ANNIE. I know.

JAKE. That is punk rock.

ANNIE. Right?

(*They switch juices. They sip.*)

JAKE. Mmmmmm…I do like yours.

ANNIE. And I like yours!

JAKE. Wow! It's like you're psychic. Like you have creepy mental powers or something.

ANNIE. I do.

JAKE. You are, hands down, the best roommate I have ever had. I can't believe I found you on Craigslist. The last roommate I found on there was a hoarder. And you know what he hoarded? Condoms. And, yes, you do dare ask, so ask.

ANNIE. Used?

JAKE. Yes.

ANNIE. NO!

JAKE. YES.

ANNIE. SHUT! UP!

JAKE. Everyone on Craigslist is a freak! Honestly, Annie, you're perfect: a girlfriend who's not a fag hag; we have similar dishwashing habits; and this psychic Jamba Juice thing… You're the best.

(ANNIE *is silent.* JAKE *sips his juice and notices that she is uncomfortable.*) What? Annie…are you…?

(ANNIE *turns away and shakes her head.*) I didn't mean to make too big a deal out of it.

(ANNIE *takes a deep breath and then…*)

ANNIE. Jake, you should go. You should… You should find the fucking place.

(ANNIE *turns. Her eyes are glowing with a serene, powerful stare.*)

JAKE. Annie…what—holy shit—what's?

ANNIE. I really think you're the best roommate ever, too. I do. But my name's not really Annie Christmas. I don't even have a name. I'm more like an idea or aspect of Him. My dad.

JAKE. What are you talking about?

ANNIE. I'm saying that you should find the fucking place, Jake. Because I am the Anti-Christ.

JAKE. WHAT?!

ANNIE. Totally. I'm totally the Anti-Christ, and I've got a lot of work to do. This is THE last day, in every world, everywhere. Some will end in fire or in ice or in zombie bloodbaths or nuclear holocausts. One will even end with these random, huge shards of glass falling from outer space.

JAKE. Shards of—huh?

ANNIE. Shards of glass on the world without shrimp. And you know my co-workers?

JAKE. Those four weirdos?

ANNIE. Yeah. They're, like, the Four Horsemen of The Apocalypse.

JAKE. Is this a joke? Because it's fucked up if it

(*Suddenly,* ANNIE *floats above the bench.*)

ANNIE. Not a joke.

JAKE. Whoa…so not a joke.

ANNIE. Go have fun. And don't worry. I know it seems scary, but when it's over everything will be so beautiful.

JAKE. Will I see you again?

ANNIE. We'll all see each other again. We'll be one with the universe, Jake, and no one will ever be alone again. It'll be like the explosion at your orgy, forever. Divine ecstasy outside of space and time. Now: go get yourself some ass.

JAKE. Thanks, Annie.

(JAKE *hugs her feet, still within reach. He runs off. A shaft of light shines down as* ANNIE *ascends heavenward.*)

ANNIE. (*To the audience.*) Ladies and gentleman: this is how it ends.

(*End of scene.*)

2.

A kitchen. DEATH *and* PESTILENCE *sit at a table.* DEATH *is mostly dressed for work in some pretty smart threads.* PESTILENCE *is still in PJs. He's sipping coffee, of which he's already had too much. He's a jittery mess.*

DEATH. Hey, Pestilence. It's okay.

PESTILENCE. Whatever, Death. Like, how is an existential crisis okay? I made AIDS! I totally blew my wad with that one.

(WAR *enters groggily to pour himself a coffee. He just got up and looks it.*)

WAR. Hey, Death. Hey, Pestilence. Good morning.

DEATH. It's barely morning, War.

WAR. Death, please don't be a bitch right now, okay?

(WAR *exits with his coffee, ruffling* PESTILENCE's *hair as he goes.*)

DEATH. He is such a goddamn infant.

PESTILENCE. Can we focus for a minute? I mean, who could have expected that? Percentage-wise, AIDS doesn't kill as many people as the Plague did. Cancer kills more people. That was my MASTERPIECE, you know? And AIDS was, like, a hobby. I was like, I'll just throw this together, it'll be weird, and people will think, "What is that mutate-y sex disease? That is so intensely just BEYOND!" Right? It was just weird.

> (FAMINE *enters. As* PESTILENCE *speaks, she opens the fridge, staring into it.*)

But then people start blaming each other for getting it. They actually stop trying to cure sick people. And now some people even TRY to GET IT. And people TRY to GIVE it to them. On purpose.

DEATH. I know, I know. I'm Death, remember?

> (FAMINE *shuts the fridge and starts going through the cabinets, louder and louder—total passive-aggression.*)

PESTILENCE. I can't top that. It is THE disease. What the fucking hell could I do that would be as motherfucking awesome as AIDS?

> (FAMINE *opens and shuts the same cabinet door again and again.*)

DEATH. Famine, WHAT are you doing?

FAMINE. I am starving.

DEATH. So eat something.

FAMINE. You ate my Kashi. And my soy milk. Or Pestilence did.

PESTILENCE. Fuck you.

DEATH. Lay off him right now. He's going through some shit.

FAMINE. Whatever with his shit. He's always going through some shit. I've been doing the same goddamn thing for millennia, and it works. "No food. You're hungry. You're dead." IT WORKS. Why try to be so creative? I liked when it was just the flu, and it just killed everyone. Can't we just have more flu?

PESTILENCE. Shut up about the flu! The flu was for children.

FAMINE. Well, you're a child.

PESTILENCE. Your mom's a child.

FAMINE. And you told the Anti-Christ that AIDS stuff was intentional. Now you're saying your most brilliant scheme was accidental? Fuck you.

PESTILENCE. What could I do? The A.C. was totally into it.

FAMINE. Wipe the brown off your nose, you shit-eating ass-licker.

DEATH. Famine, lay off.

FAMINE. WHERE'S MY KASHI! I. AM. STARVING!!!!!

> (WAR *stumbles back on with a mug, a used bowl, the Kashi, and soy milk.*)

Keep your hands off my stuff, you slacker pig. You smell like Pestilence's hole after a gangbang.

    (FAMINE *takes the food and exits.*)

WAR. God. Why is everyone so agro today?

DEATH. Shouldn't you be at work already anyway?

WAR. Mental health day. Like, why go in and just check on projects and stuff? Like, my job does itself; I'm so good at it. Start one fight, they keep fighting. I'm, like, not CHALLENGED, and I don't want to just Facebook all day.

DEATH. You two have got to pull your shit together. We are all worldly suffering incarnate. I know how hard it is to look like we're above it, when we're really not above it at all. And of course that is going to wear us all down.

WAR. It doesn't seem to be wearing you down.

DEATH. Believe me, if anything, you—at least—are wearing me down. But look: one day the world will actually end, and the A.C. is counting on us to do it right. I know we can. (*To* WAR.) Even you. (*To* PESTILENCE.) Now, I'm putting on my makeup, and then I'm going to work. You want a ride? You'll feel better, getting stuff accomplished.

PESTILENCE. Yeah. I'll come with you. I'll come in.

WAR. Dude, you won't feel better in your cube. Give it up.

DEATH. WAR. Pick him up, don't keep him down. HE'S IN CRISIS!

    (WAR *lifts up his hands in surrender.*)

What is that?

    (*He keeps his hands up.* DEATH *lifts hers.*)

What is this?

    (*Silence.*)

Pestilence. Five minutes.

    (DEATH *exits.*)

WAR. Just 'cause I'm War I'm supposed to fight back? That shit is for the office. Home is, like, home. Everyone else can fight all they want. I'd rather get stoned and eat Famine's ice cream. Hey—stay home with me, and we'll eat the whole fucking pint for breakfast.

PESTILENCE. What'll the A.C. say if I call in sick again?

WAR. Who gives a shit?

PESTILENCE. She's our boss.

WAR. Yeah, but I was totally blitzed last night—okay, this morning—and kaboom: mondo revelation. The A.C. is the C. with, like, a disguise. Like, Jesus.

PESTILENCE. Stop it.

WAR. For real! We're, like, she's this holy terror, harbinger of the end. But what if… 'cause the Christ was, like, this Messiah from god who saved people. And the Anti-Christ is also from God and saves people. From us. At the end of time, she takes the good people and makes them one with God and OMMM, right? And all the bad people are burnt up in a lake of fire so they cease to be. Which, like, sounds sucky, but really it's the end of suffering. The end of us. At the end, we end.

So I was all BAM! in my head. The Anti-Christ? Totally the Christ. In, like, a wig.

PESTILENCE. You're nuts.

WAR. Believing suffering will end is nuts? Babe, I get how serious this existential crisis stuff is, but it'll end. So fuck it, let it end! Stay home, chill out, and let's eat Famine's ice cream.

PESTILENCE. …Okay.

WAR. Sweetness.

(WAR *makes sure no one's around and then kisses* PESTILENCE.)

PESTILENCE. No. Come on—Stop it!

WAR. But the angst? It's totes adorable. I want to eat you up.

PESTILENCE. We make people suffer. This—YOU do not motivate me to pollute the water supply with Salmonella or engineer creative applications for flesh-eating bacteria. Everyone knows I'm off my game. If they knew about us, that I'm capable of feeling like—

WAR. If you had AIDS, I'd totally want you to give it to me.

PESTILENCE. Holy fuck, I love you.

WAR. Love you, too.

(PESTILENCE *grabs* WAR *and they kiss again.*)

PESTILENCE. Where's that ice cream?

(*A sudden burst of trumpets [seven of them] as a ridiculous light show invades the apartment.* DEATH *and* FAMINE *run on as* ANNIE *flies in.*)

DEATH. Is it time?

(ANNIE *nods, opening her arms to them. End of scene.*)

THE ONE ABOUT THE ASTEROID
by Marco Ramirez

An ENSEMBLE MEMBER. *Direct address. Across the stage, another ensemble member, let's call that one* THE BOWLER, *stares at a bowling pin on the floor forty feet before him/her.*

ENSEMBLE MEMBER. On February 23, 1950,
On the summit of Mount Hamilton,
In the Diablo Mountain Range just east of San Jose,
An astronomer named Carl made the final discovery of his career.

(THE BOWLER *stretches his/her shoulders. Stops.*)

He did not give it a playful nickname, he gave it a serial number.
(29075) 1950 DA.
…
He noted that the asteroid had a mean diameter of 1.3 kilometers,
He noted it was fairly dense and likely composed of nickel-iron,
And he noted that it had the highest known probability,
Of any other asteroid in the known universe,
Of crashing into planet Earth.

(THE BOWLER *hurls a bowling ball across the stage. Misses. The pin stands alone. Vulnerable.*)

Smaller asteroids enter the atmosphere every year.
And some contain as much energy as Little Boy, the atomic bomb dropped on Hiroshima.

(THE BOWLER *hurls another bowling ball across the stage. Maybe he/she gets closer.*)

But once every five hundred thousand years,
An asteroid as big as 1950 DA happens across the Earth's surface.

(THE BOWLER *hurls a bowling ball across the stage. Misses. The pin is helpless.*)

The odds of dying in a plane crash are one in eight million.

(THE BOWLER *hurls another ball across the stage. Misses.*)

The odds of dying by accidental drowning are one in seventy-nine-thousand.

(THE BOWLER *hurls another ball across the stage. Misses.*)

The odds of 1950 DA crashing into the earth?
…
One in three hundred.

(THE BOWLER *hurls a bowling ball across the stage. Misses.* THE BOWLER *hurls another. Misses.* THE BOWLER *winds up to shoot one last shot. Smirks. Black.*)

LA REINA DE LOS ÁNGELES
by Jennifer Haley

Scene One

A high-rise in Los Angeles.

RYAN. What do you mean? This is a great script!

TRENT. There's no genre.

RYAN. The dialogue is gorgeous. The characterizations subtle, moving—

TRENT. It doesn't go anywhere.

RYAN. Maybe it lacks a car chase or two, but emotionally—

TRENT. Emotionally? Emotionally??

RYAN. It's the next step in my career.

TRENT. Ryan, you've made a hit bromance. The next step in your career is leading man, romantic comedy. Then leading man, action adventure. Then leading man, high concept thriller. Then—and only then—can you hang your ass on the line with a script that has nothing going for it but emotion.

RYAN. The main character is looking for something to believe in again.

TRENT. He doesn't do anything.

RYAN. He's fighting a battle for his very soul.

TRENT. Which he loses. He fucking kills himself.

RYAN. It's high tragedy!

TRENT. It's professional suicide! Listen to me, Ryan. I'm your agent. You can't do this. You're not there yet.

(*Pause. RYAN goes to the window. Looks out moodily.*)

RYAN. I was a dramatic actor before I moved to this town.

TRENT. (*Sarcastic.*) You're still a dramatic actor.

RYAN. No. I mean. It meant something.

(TRENT *joins him at the window.*)

TRENT. The original name for this place was *El Pueblo de Nuestra Señora la Reina de los Ángeles.* The Town of Our Lady the Queen of the Angels. The City of Angels. Some people think those angels are here to serve us. Or kill us. But I think we make them. Right here in the studios. We make them for people who pay us. Not to smear ourselves in shit and call it art—but, for two measly hours, to make life look easy and fun. You did that quite well in *Two Bros Go to Mexico.* It's the only reason I'm spending my breath on you right now. I see it here, on the window—my precious breath—and I want you to know it's there because I believe my cut of your next salary will keep me behind this cool pane of glass instead of out there, on the street, having to wrestle another smelly human for a plastic bowl of Frito pie. Now I've got

a stack of scripts from top studios who all want you. If you don't chuck this
low-budget downer and explode with gratitude over your good fortune, I'm
going to sock you in the nuts.

    (*He turns from the window.*)

TRENT. I mean it. Explode.

RYAN. What?

TRENT. Explode with gratitude! Right now!

    (RYAN *stares at him.* TRENT *punches him in the nuts.*)

Now take home these scripts, note how in each one there is a hero who exerts
a force on this world, and an ending that helps us believe our lives are worth
a shit, pick which one you want to star in, and BE HAPPY.

    (RYAN, *doubled over, takes the scripts and exits. In his place,* LILA *appears.*
    She wears sunglasses and a pair of long, white gloves—like costume pieces from
    a 1930s film.)

Do you have an appointment? (*No answer.*) A pretty face alone does not score
you an appointment. (*No answer.*) Look—

    (*She moves toward him. Slowly. Deliberately. A little clumsily. All the while,*
    slowly removing her gloves.)

Do I know you?

    (*She reaches him, puts her hands to his face.*)

Did we sleep together?

    (*She draws his head down to hers. Just as they are about to kiss, her mouth opens*
    really wide, and she bites his face off.)

Scene Two

    JILLIAN *and* MINDI *sit at a metal table. Both suck through thick straws*
    on large lattes in paper cups. Leaning against the table is a baseball bat covered
    in blood.

JILLIAN. I can't think of the end.

MINDI. Do you have to know it now?

JILLIAN. My agent wants it tomorrow. It needs an end.

MINDI. Just make something up.

JILLIAN. You can make something up in the beginning. You can make
something up in the middle. You can't make something up at the end. The
end tells everyone how to think about the whole thing.

MINDI. You've been working on this for two years. Don't you know what
you're trying to say?

JILLIAN. (*A long, mean stare.*) Are you a writer, Mindi?

MINDI. No. I'm a grip.

JILLIAN. Then you just. Don't know. What it's like.

> (JILLIAN *sucks bitchily through her straw. Far opposite them,* TRENT *appears. He wears a pair of sunglasses. He moves toward the two women slowly. So very slowly. Sometimes he stops, off-balance, takes a step back. But always resumes course. The women take no notice.*)

MINDI. Well, what's happening so far?

JILLIAN. (*Sigh.*) As you know, Savannah and Lucas are undercover agents posing as newlyweds on their honeymoon in Pakistan, but their actual mission is to assassinate an arms dealer who's about to sell nuclear warheads to Al Qaeda. Right? So they're wandering around Karachi, holding hands and like, seemingly in love, but they're really tailing this dude who can lead them to Absolem Hamma bin Ali Alladin, the arms dealer, and also—here's the twist—they really are falling in love, but each of them thinks the other one is just playing his or her role, and each of them is like, solitary-hit-man-great-at-killing-people-but-terrible-at-intimacy type, so there are all these awkward, vulnerable moments of confusion—it's really funny. But anyway, they corner this guy in an alley behind a tea shop, and Lucas gets him in an arm lock while Savannah pulls out his fingernails and demands the location of bin Ali Alladin, when a rain of bullets pours down the alley, and they have to use the dude as a sort of bullet umbrella to escape into an underground latrine. Which is where they realize A) they've been set up—there's a mole in the CIA who's compromised their identities because he stands to make a shit-load from the arms deal, and B) they're totally hot for each other. That's the midpoint, because then they start working as a team, chasing down bin Ali Alladin, investigating the CIA, freaking out when it looks like the other one might die, 'cuz it'd be like losing the only person in the world who'll ever love them for who they are. They figure out this deal with the CIA goes all the way to the Vice President and that one of the warheads is going to be launched at us the moment Al Qaeda gets ahold of it, and these shady government figures want it that way because they own all the weapons companies. So, I mean, there are these car chases and stuff, but basically Savannah and Lucas deactivate the warhead, expose the Vice President, and pretty much SAVE THE ENTIRE WORLD.

MINDI. So.

JILLIAN. So what?

MINDI. So that's the end right?

JILLIAN. No, Mindi. This is a romantic comedy. The end is when we find out what happens to the couple.

MINDI. Don't they get together?

JILLIAN. That's what I can't decide.

MINDI. Why wouldn't they get together?

> (*A longer, meaner stare.* TRENT *is very close to the table.*)

JILLIAN. Because, Mindi. That is so. Fucking. Cliché.

> (JILLIAN *launches herself from the chair, grabs the bat, and swings it at* TRENT's *head, which sort of explodes as his body whips around and falls onto the ground.* JILLIAN, *howling, beats him viciously with the bat. She flings the bat away, breathing heavily.*)

MINDI. (*Gently.*) I think you should let them end up together.

JILLIAN. Yeah?

MINDI. Life is already rough. I don't think you need to go against how everyone wants it to end.

JILLIAN. You are so right. Thank you.

> (*She sobs.* MINDI *stands, hugs her, exits.* JILLIAN *pulls herself together. She reaches for her coffee. She can't move her foot because* TRENT's *hand is on it. Uh oh.*)

Scene Three

> JAKE, *weeping, comes crawling across the stage toward* RYAN. JILLIAN, *wearing sunglasses, lies lifeless in the path of* JAKE's *crawl.*

RYAN. Stop right there.

JAKE. Please.

RYAN. I said, right there.

JAKE. You know me. It's Jake.

RYAN. I don't know anybody anymore.

JAKE. Please, Ryan. We made a bromance together.

RYAN. The grounds are mined. If you keep moving forward, you'll set one off.

> (JAKE *freezes.*)

JAKE. Let me talk to Michael. He'll let me in.

RYAN. Michael's decided the house is full.

JAKE. He was our director! He can't separate the bros!

RYAN. You should have gotten here sooner.

JAKE. The 405 is a nightmare! I crawled here on surface streets—

RYAN. I'm sorry.

> (*Pause.*)

JAKE. Aw fuck! You're not still holding that against me, are you man?

(RYAN *is silent.*)

Ryan! Buddy! My manager thought it would be a good publicity stunt! You know, make it seem like we hated each other so that when we got back together again, it would be a big deal! It was funny man—that's how we got to know each other—telling bad jokes! I thought you'd get it!

(RYAN *remains silent, hard.* JAKE *notices* JILLIAN.)

Wow. She's hot.

RYAN. Yeah, she's hot.

JAKE. Too bad she's dead.

RYAN. Yeah.

JAKE. Even dead, she's really hot.

RYAN. Super hot.

JAKE. Almost as hot as that chick we both—remember? Out there, on location in Mexico? We were so—innocent—so caught up in the process. That's the stuff that mattered. Not the stupid shit that went on afterwards. Listen, man, I know this because I saw her. The Queen of the Angels. She was floating above the 405, between the city and the valley. She had long, black hair covering her face. But I could hear her speaking. She said: Now is the time to choose between my children! My light angels! My dark angels! Once you could take a lifetime to choose, but the earth has no more lifetimes! So choose now! Light or dark! She shimmered there in the dark sunlight, her hair pouring into the shadows growing over the canyon. And I cried, man. I cried right there in the dirt. For all the stupid things I've said and done. I prayed to see the light. And here I am. And I want you to know—I've never had so much fun doing a movie with someone. I mean, none of my other movies came close to that budget… I never got to blow shit up like that before. But it wasn't about blowing shit up. It was about blowing shit up with you.

(RYAN *is visibly torn.*)

RYAN. It's not me, man. It's Michael. He's still pissed about what you said in *Variety.*

(JILLIAN *suddenly grabs* JAKE's *foot. He shrieks.*)

JAKE. RYAN!!!! PLEASE!!!!!

(JAKE *continues to scream and call* RYAN's *name as* JILLIAN *hauls herself up his body.* RYAN *watches in horror.*)

Scene Four

Some street. We'll say La Brea and Fairfax. MINDI stands in the middle, still. Her long hair falls over her face. From offstage we hear:

RYAN. Lost! Everything lost! Everything gone! Even my dreams!

(He wanders on, wailing. He clutches his headshot.)

Nothing to hope for! Nothing to live for! Lost!

(He spies MINDI.)

There you are! My queen! Queen of the angels of death! Take me under your leathery wings! Extinguish my desire to be. I don't deserve it anymore! I made a bromance! I slept with starlets! I stood and watched while my friend was eaten alive! Who would have thought playing Hamlet at Sherman High School would lead to such…confusion?

(He throws himself at her legs. MINDI's head rises. She wears a pair of sunglasses. RYAN looks up at her. He shudders when he sees the glasses.)

Oh! You are terrifying! But I am not afraid! Please take away this loathsome thing I call myself!

MINDI. *(Hissing.)* Go. Away.

RYAN. What?

MINDI. Go. Away!

RYAN. But. My Queen…

MINDI. I don't know what you're talking about. *(Pulling down her glasses for a moment.)* I'm in camouflage. Sorry to douse your Oscar-winning performance. Now piss off. You're attracting attention.

(Sure enough. Some slow-ass ZOMBIES have wandered on and seem vaguely interested in them.)

RYAN. But.

MINDI. I said go.

(RYAN looks around. Starts to wander off.)

RYAN. Lost! Everything lost!

MINDI. Oh for Christ sake.

RYAN. Everything gone! Even my dreams!

(MINDI storms over to him.)

MINDI. Are you just giving up?

RYAN. I'm so tired!

MINDI. Tired of what?

RYAN. Tired of the struggle!

MINDI. How old are you?

RYAN. (*Sniffles.*) Twenty-four.

> (MINDI *slaps him forehand. Then backhand. She rips up his headshot.*)

MINDI. Welcome to reality! Life is a struggle. And you're the hero. We want to see you do something. Now put these on…

> (*She holds out a pair of sunglasses.* RYAN *eyes them.* ONE OF THE ZOMBIES *is getting close.* RYAN *finally swipes the sunglasses, puts them on, turns to the approaching* ZOMBIE—*which happens to be* JAKE. JAKE *sniffs him over.* RYAN *trembles, but keeps still.* JAKE *wanders off.*)

RYAN. Wow. What's your name?

MINDI. Mindi.

RYAN. Mindi, I think you just gave me a reason to live.

> (*The mood is suddenly romantic. Cue music. They lean in for a kiss.*)

DIRECTOR. (*From off.*) Annnnnd CUT!

> (ZOMBIE CHARACTERS *come back on, casual, chatting, removing their sunglasses.* DIRECTOR *enters.*)

That's a wrap for today. Extras, we'll see you at 4:30 tomorrow morning for the great zombie steamroll scene. And I hope you two have been gearing up to get naked!

> (*She makes a lascivious gesture at* RYAN. *Everyone exits. The stage is dark except for a spot on* MINDI *and* RYAN, *whose real names are* JENNA *and* BART.)

JENNA. Wanna ciggy?

BART. I'm trying to quit.

JENNA. (*Mock sigh, tries again.*) Wanna ciggy?

BART. Okay, just one.

> (*They light up.*)

(*Very bitter.*) God knows I need it. This film is such a pile of crap. It's gonna bomb so hard. Besides, no one likes movies about the biz. My agent insisted I take it. There's nothing else out there right now. What with, you know—

BART & JENNA. the economy—

JENNA. —totes—

BART. Now I'll wish again I could hack into IMDB and take another piece of shit off the list of what I've done in the past ten years…

JENNA. The problem with this flick is it has no genre.

BART. What do you mean?

JENNA. Genre meets its own expectations. We can believe, for a couple hours, that we have control over time. And we know how things will end.

BART. Huh. All I know is it fucking burns my ass.

JENNA. Exactly. We don't know how things will end. We just know they will. I mean, they've found plastic at the cellular level in deepwater marine organisms.

BART. So?

JENNA. That means in another forty years... (*She makes a slitting gesture at her throat.*)

BART. Are you trying to cheer me up here?!

JENNA. Bart, we're in the midst of a global apocalypse. Do you have to make it a personal one?

(*He stares at her.*)

Take a load off! We're in a movie about zombies! It's funny!

BART. Funny...

JENNA. Why strut and fret our last hour on the stage. Why not laugh?

BART. Huh... Why not laugh?

(*They laugh. And laugh and laugh and laugh.*)

THE ONE THAT ENDS ITSELF
by Marco Ramirez

Another ENSEMBLE MEMBER *onstage. Direct address. Dead serious.*

ENSEMBLE MEMBER. The first case happened one morning in the winter of 1902,
When the residents of Cape Cod woke to find 98 fully grown pilot whales dead on their coastline.

…

At a town hall meeting that evening, a biologist from the University of Massachusetts attributed the "mass stranding" to rough seas,
The Canadians,
And the whales' own navigational error.
He reminded those in attendance that pilot whales beached themselves year-round,
And that even though the death toll—for that morning—
Was three times the amount of pilot whales beached in Massachusetts that calendar year,

…

There was no cause for concern.
> (*Illuminate* TEN ENSEMBLE MEMBERS, *who stare—listening—waiting.*)

The second case happened at approximately 10:30 p.m.,
Just 35 miles south of Little Rock, Arkansas,
On a very recent New Year's Eve,
When more than 3,000 red-winged blackbirds dropped out of the sky.
The national government attributed the event to unusual migration patterns,
The state blamed firework smog,
And the city council—at the mayor's insistence—remained completely silent.

…

> (*One* ENSEMBLE MEMBER *opens his/her hands and releases a wind-up toy. It waddles or rolls its way across the stage.*)

The third and final case—
The one that went ignored by most media outlets,
But which attracted investigative teams from The Center for Disease Control,
The United Nations,
And The Vatican—

> (*Another* ENSEMBLE MEMBER *opens his/her hands and releases a wind-up toy.*)

Happened in a small river basin in Mozambique,
Where a tiny,

Unicellular organism dubbed RS13 started dying in quantities so large that sixty tons of it were said to have accumulated—clogging several river channels near Lago Corzao.

…

> (*The remaining* ENSEMBLE MEMBERS *pull out their toys and begin to wind them up.*)

The cells and the river were analyzed,
But the results surprised even the most open-minded members of the scientific community.

…

Because no one could trace the mass death to pollutants or even changes in climate.

> (*The* ENSEMBLE MEMBERS *release a flurry of wind-up toys on the floor before them. The* NARRATOR *speaks above the buzzing sound of toys on the floor.*)

Because—
In fact—
The poisonous substance responsible for killing RS13,
Was being produced by RS13 itself.

…

> (*Perfectly timed—the wind-up toys start falling limp. First one, then the rest.*)

As if even this,
A single-cell life form,

> (*He/she looks at the wind-up carcasses on the floor.*)

Had the instinct to know when its time on Earth
Was over.

> (*Black.*)

APOCALYPSE APARTMENTS
by Allison Moore

One.

Apartment 1A. MICK, TYLER *and* ZOE.

MICK. Imagine it.

TYLER. I don't want to imagine it.

ZOE. (*To* TYLER.) Come on, Tyler.

MICK. Patti Smith, Robert Mapplethorpe and Sam fucking Shepard, having a threesome. It happened. You know it happened.

TYLER. (*To* ZOE.) See?

ZOE. Who's Robert Mapplethorpe?

MICK. You don't know who Robert Mapplethorpe is?

TYLER. Don't encourage him.

ZOE. I'm asking a question. I'm interested, okay? I mean, I was listening to Patti Smith's "Gloria" when the first wave started.

MICK. Which is so fucking rad.

TYLER. Because it's important for the apocalypse to have a good soundtrack.

MICK. Okay, Robert Mapplethorpe was a photographer, a very famous photographer—

ZOE. Like, what are his famous pictures?

MICK. The lilies? The giant lilies?

(TYLER *gets up, checks the towels shoved in the windows and doors.*)

Or the cover of *Horses*, right? The photo on the cover, Patti Smith, with the jacket and the tie and she's looking right in the camera with a face that's like—

ZOE. Okay, I mean, it's on my iPod, but I never really looked at the cover—

MICK. All right, he was a photographer. And he and Patti Smith were best friends, they lived together—he was mostly gay, but sometimes, you know? And then Patti and Sam Shepard had some kinda crazy intense thing going at the same time. So it's like three geniuses, all together one night at the Chelsea Hotel, stoned out of their minds, radiating their genius-ness all over each other…? You cannot tell me that they didn't have a threesome.

ZOE. Maybe.

MICK. Not maybe.

TYLER. (*To* ZOE.) I can't believe you.

ZOE. What?

MICK. And you can bet that Sam Shepard fucked the shit out of Robert Mapplethorpe—

ZOE. (*To* TYLER, *annoyed.*) What?

(MICK *is oblivious to the fight.*)

MICK. And then Patti strapped on her dildo and fucked 'em both. Oh my God she was hot. She was like a man she was so hot, you know what I mean?

ZOE. Totally.

MICK. That aggressive, that unapologetic. She was a force. I mean, have you ever seen her perform?

ZOE. No.

TYLER. Neither have you.

(MICK *shoots* TYLER *a stare.*)

MICK. I'm talking about footage, from back in the day?

ZOE. I've never seen it.

MICK. It's unbelievable. There's this clip I found online: she's on stage, with her hand down her pants, finger fucking herself, while she's singing. It's amazing. Sends chills down my spine just thinking about it. It's like: Fuck yeah! Choke on that, Jack Johnson. Justin Bieber. Or fucking Fergie, shaking her ass for the camera. Let me tell you something, Patti Smith was not putting on a show. She wasn't trying to sell anything, she wasn't trying to get on fucking "Entertainment Tonight," or—she didn't care! She didn't care that she was on stage, with all these people watching, she didn't care what anybody might think—I mean like that fucking matters anyway, but we all walk around most of the time acting like it does matter. We're so fucking scared all the time, but she just—she just felt like it. And so she did it. I mean think about that for a minute.

(ZOE *does.*)

ZOE. Yeah.

MICK. It's powerful, right?

ZOE. Yeah.

TYLER. (*To* ZOE.) Are you, like, into him now? Is that what's going on?

MICK. What?

ZOE. I'm having a conversation—

MICK. What's your problem, man?

TYLER. You mean aside from the fact that you and my girlfriend are talking about threesomes between DEAD PEOPLE?

ZOE. Right, instead of re-sealing the windows, or checking to see how much of our water supply has evaporated from the bathtub for the fifth time today—

TYLER. At least I'm doing something instead of listening to this shit! How can you listen to him going on and on about these people like—

MICK. Whoa, buddy—

TYLER. (*To* MICK.) You weren't there! Okay? You. Weren't. There. So get over it.

MICK. What, so I can't talk about it? I can't be inspired?

TYLER. You weren't even alive! You never saw Patti Smith or the Ramones—

ZOE. Tyler—

MICK. I didn't see Jesus, I can't be inspired by him?

TYLER. (*Overlapping.*) Whoever, you never saw any of them except on YOUTUBE! You weren't there at CBGB's to see them launch the Punk revolution and then go fuck each other! So stop talking about it! Both of you! Half the people we know are dead, or incinerated, or—I don't know if my mom, or my brothers are alive, if Seattle even exists anymore, maybe the entire Pacific Northwest has just, disappeared. I don't even know how long it is until the next wave because nobody has a fucking watch anymore!

ZOE. It's okay—

(ZOE *moves to touch* TYLER, *he shakes her off.*)

TYLER. It's not okay! None of it is okay! The world is ending and Patti Fucking Smith isn't going to save you!

(*A moment.* MICK *is bummed.* ZOE *slides her hand down her pants.*)

What are you doing?

ZOE. I feel like it.

TYLER. Stop it.

ZOE. I am unapologetic.

TYLER. I said stop—

ZOE. I am a force.

MICK. Yeah. Fuck yeah.

(MICK *slides his hand down his pants. There is nothing sexual between* MICK *and* ZOE.)

ZOE. I am a force.

(TYLER *grabs his jacket and leaves. Immediate shift to—*)

Two.

Apartment 2C. STACE *and* PIPER. STACE *wears rubber gloves, and holds a large frying pan that she was either scrubbing or preparing to use as a weapon, it's not clear which. As* PIPER *speaks, she peels the kerchief from her face, shakes it out, takes off her backpack, sunglasses, etc., makes herself at home, oblivious to the mess she's making. She has a Starbucks cup she sips from occasionally.*

PIPER. It's crazy, what's happening. You have no idea.

(ERIC *enters from the back of the apartment with a knapsack, stops cold when he sees* PIPER.)

ERIC. Oh shit.

[handwritten: 2 dif views of leaving gsp]

STACE. I think I have some idea.

PIPER. I mean, have you been out there? It's like some parts of town have been totally obliterated, and then other parts: it's like nothing's happened. It's like Whittier? Gone. Kenwood? Perfect. I mean perfect—well, except for the ash, you know, that's pretty much everywhere, and the occasional piece of tentacle. But as I was walking through it all, I kept thinking: where's the justice? I mean, seriously. Why did the poor neighborhood get obliterated? Why couldn't the rich people get it for once? Although, you have to give it to those Kenwood moms, they had the Starbucks up and running like a well-oiled machine.

[handwritten: mystery]

(Beat. She notices STACE glaring.)

[handwritten: coffee workers]

Sorry I didn't bring you anything.

STACE. (Of ERIC's knapsack.)What is that?

PIPER. Full-fat latte, they were out of skim—

STACE. What's in there?

ERIC. I'm trying to do what you want, Stacc.

(Microbeat.)

STACE. What?!

PIPER. Oh my God, he told you.

[handwritten: Stages of grief]

STACE. What I want?

PIPER. Please tell me you did not tell her.

STACE. You're so fucking stupid sometimes.

PIPER. I'm her sister! Why would you tell her we slept together?!

STACE. He's my husband! Why would you sleep with him?!

(Beat.)

PIPER. Want the rest of my latte?

(STACE snatches the cup from PIPER.)

(Disappointed.) Oh.

(STACE freezes PIPER with a death stare. STACE takes a long slurping drink.)

Okay, in my defense—

STACE. Shut up.

(PIPER does. STACE does not look at ERIC through this next section.)

I am furious with you. I want to be clear about that. It's not that I don't expect this kind of shit from you. I mean, I didn't expect this particular shit, I had hoped that you would refrain from spewing your own special brand of chaos all over my marriage? But it's not entirely out of character.

> *incest?*

(PIPER *has to agree.*)

And I am really, really angry.

(STACE *starts to crack.*)

But for Eric to do this to me?

ERIC. Stace, what do you want me to say?

STACE. With you, of all people! I just…

PIPER. Oh sweetie.

(PIPER *and* STACE *hug it out.*)

I told him not to tell you, never to tell you.

> *Amen*

STACE. Yeah, well, we all know he's not the ~~brightest~~ bulb on the tree.

ERIC. Excuse me?

STACE. I used to like that about him, that he was kind of simple and uncomplicated? I mean, I'm complicated enough. My family is complicated enough.

> *sso was light hearted but later its sad*

PIPER. Well, yeah.

ERIC. I'm sorry, I am so sorry—

STACE. He probably didn't even realize that half of the thrill for you—three quarters, even—was just knowing you were fucking your sister's husband.

ERIC. Okay, why am I the bad guy? Why are you still talking to her?

PIPER. Because I didn't tell her.

ERIC. I thought the world was ending!

> *irony*

PIPER. It's still ending, asshole.

ERIC. But I thought it was ending, like, immediately! Like we were gonna be vaporized in a split second. I didn't want to die with this thing on my conscience.

STACE. No, you wanted me to die pissed off.

> *but you would anyway*

ERIC. No!

PIPER. So fucking selfish.

STACE. Right?

ERIC. No!

STACE. I mean right?

> *how can you forgive cheating*

ERIC. I told you ~~like that~~ because I love you! And when the world is ending, you're supposed to, like, FORGIVE EACH OTHER! You're supposed to be, BIGGER than all the petty bullshit we walk around with every day, you know? And I know I

> *it isn't petty*

screwed up, and things haven't always been easy, and we have BOTH done things, and said things that we shouldn't have. But no matter what happened before, or whatever is coming next, I love you. (*Heartbreakingly genuine.*) I love you, Stace.

(*Beat.*)

> *still not justified*

STACE. Why couldn't you have said that?

ERIC. What?

STACE. Why couldn't you have said exactly what you just said and left out the part about how you let my sister fuck you? Huh? Did it ever occur to you that maybe, just maybe, I didn't need all the details? *DAMN!!*

(*Beat.*)

ERIC. Okay that probably would have been better.

PIPER. So fucking stupid.

ERIC. I am not stupid!

PIPER to ERIC & STACE to PIPER. Shut up.

(ERIC *pulls on his jacket, gets his knapsack.*)

STACE. What are you doing?

ERIC. What does it look like I'm doing.

STACE. What are you—you're leaving? *good*

ERIC. That's obviously what you want. I mean / you can't even look at me—

STACE. You keep talking about what I want, like it's really important to you but if you were thinking / about what I wanted—

ERIC. What am I supposed to think? You spend the last six hours either holed up in the bathroom, screaming and sobbing, or, or AGGRESSIVELY CLEANING—

STACE. Excuse me for not living up to your apocalyptic forgiveness fantasy! Clearly, I'm the bitch in this situation for actually being hurt!

ERIC. She didn't even apologize! I've done nothing but grovel and beg but she's here two minutes—

STACE. I didn't marry my sister, I married you!

I should kick you out into—whatever is left out there, so that you know what it feels like to have your heart crushed by the person you trusted most in the world.

ERIC. You don't have to.

(ERIC *walks out the door.*)

STACE. Oh god.

(*Immediate shift to—*)

Three.

Hallway. ERIC *and* TYLER. *They both wear jackets, stand near the front door of the building.* ERIC'*s bandana is around his neck, ready to go over his face. A moment.*

ERIC. You been out there? I mean, since…?

    (TYLER *shakes his head.*)

Me either. You going?

TYLER. In a minute.

ERIC. Yeah. Me too.

    (*Beat. They look through the little window in the door.*)

Ash almost looks like snow, huh? All drifted against the buildings?

TYLER. Toxic snow.

ERIC. Bet there's a kid with a sled out in the park.

    (*A beat.*)

I hope there's a kid with a sled.

TYLER. I wasn't sure anybody else was still in the building. I heard someone on the stairs, but—

ERIC. My sister-in-law.

TYLER. Mm.

ERIC. You're in…?

TYLER. 1A.

ERIC. We're 2C.

    (*They nod, as people do at such moments.*)

I think we may be the last ones. Kristin and Blake, up in 4B, went to her parents' house, and the older guy—

TYLER. 1B?

ERIC. Someone came and got him this morning.

TYLER. I think it was his daughter?

ERIC. I guess. The guys across the hall from us are actually on vacation. In Hawaii. How's that for good timing?

    (*They share a brief smile.*)

TYLER. Yeah. (*Reconsiders.*) I mean, maybe.

    (*They both think about Hawaii, and its unknown fate.*)

ERIC. Where you going?

TYLER. Um. I don't know. I just, wanted to get out. You know? But. Maybe I'll stay.

ERIC. Yeah. Me too.

    (*They look out the little window in the door.*)

LA MUERTE
by Marco Ramirez

CHARACTERS

SLICK, our protagonist. A protector.

MOUSE, his meek brother. "Little Man."

LA MUERTE. Fucking terrifying. More of a suggestion of a nightmare than an outright picture of one.

POSSIBLE INSTRUMENTS

ELECTRIC GUITARS, BASS GUITARS.
DISTORTION PEDALS, AMPS WITHIN REACH.
A DRUM SET.
PERCUSSION.
Or maybe just—
A CHORUS OF HUMS.

> *Feet stomping.*
> *Finger snaps.*
> *BREATH.*
> *BOOM.*
> *BOOM.*
> *BOOM-CHIK-CHAKA-BOOM.*
> *A quick fuzz of feedback.*
> *Breathing.*
> *Running.*
> *A pinspot on* MOUSE—*counting, in the present.*

MOUSE. Sixty-one,

Sixty-two,

> (*A pin spot on* SLICK—*dirty, sweat on his brow, something heavy in his hands.*)

Sixty-two,

Sixty-three,

SLICK. We started running,

> (SLICK *speaks directly to the audience.*)

MOUSE. Sixty-three,

Sixty-four,—

SLICK. —Started running like a week ago,

Me and Little Man.

MOUSE. Sixty-five,—

SLICK. —And he ain't exactly right in the head,

Never has been,—

MOUSE. —Come on,—

SLICK. —But these dreams,

The ones that started burning late at night,—

      (*BREATH.*)

—Burning through him?—

      (*BREATH.*)

—They were something else.

…

And our whole life has been me takin' care of him,

My whole life I've been shakin' off street-rats and punchin' in teeth for his sake.

      (MOUSE *abruptly looks up.*)

But last week something changed.

MOUSE. Move.

SLICK. Last week something changed 'cause he said—

MOUSE. —We should go—

SLICK. —And I was like "Since when do you tell me to go?" but he said—

MOUSE. —WE SHOULD GO,

RIGHT—

NOW—

SLICK. —And as we did, the building collapsed.

      (*BREATH.*)

As we made our way outta the city,

These streets we call home,

As we moved between the crowds of crying screaming trembling people he said—

MOUSE. —This way,

This way,

This way,—

SLICK. —And as he said—

MOUSE. —Don't drink that,—

SLICK. —The milk turned to acid.—

MOUSE. —Get under this,—

SLICK. —The rain turned to poison.—

MOUSE. —Don't stand there,—

SLICK. —The shards of glass fell and sliced old ladies straight down the middle,

Clean.

MOUSE. …Don't stand there.

SLICK. And my whole life—you see—has been me takin' care of him,—

MOUSE. —Run—

SLICK.—Only reason this little fool is alive is 'cause he's the closest thing in this shithole city I got to family—

MOUSE. —Now—

SLICK.—But when he said—

MOUSE. —Pick up that crowbar,

Now,

And run,—

SLICK.—We started running.

      (Music. Mysterious. Echoes.)

MOUSE. Sixty-five,

Sixty-six,

SLICK. We're stutter-stepping our way downstairs,

Down these tunnels,

Deep under the city 'cause he said so.

Crowbar in hand,

Heavy as shit,

But he said—

MOUSE. —We gotta carry that—

SLICK. —Over and over—

MOUSE. —We gotta carry that—

SLICK. —And the lower we go, the less we hear the screams,

Cars crashing,

Men sobbing.

The lower we go, the safer we are.

      (Quiet. Then a WEIRD WHISPER.*)*

WHISPERS. La,

SLICK. And in the middle of the night,

In the tunnels under tunnels,

He can feel what's going on,

WHISPERS. La,

SLICK. Ear to the ground,

Connected to some other-universe shit,

To the stories people forgot,

WHISPERS. La la,

SLICK. In the tunnels under tunnels,

Little Man looks up,

Skin burning,

And he gives it a name.

>(MOUSE *looks at* SLICK, *doesn't move his lips.*)

WHISPERS. La Muerte.

>(*A beat. This terrifies* SLICK.)

SLICK. With a voice that wasn't his, he says—

WHISPERS. —La Muerte—

SLICK. —Has a cape like Darth Vader.

She eats neon light so she could fly,

>(*BREATH.*)

Hands like leather,

Eyes so—

WHISPERS. —Black—

SLICK. —Even in the—

WHISPERS. —Dark —

SLICK. —You could tell she's lookin' at you.

>(*BREATH. BREATH.*)

She lives in junkyard refrigerators,

In the trunks of squad cars,

And if you pick up a payphone in the middle of the night you could hear her breathing.

>(*An* EERIE NOISE *slowly builds.*)

The people in this city, they were surprised.

>(*It builds.*)

When the milk turned to acid,

Rain to poison,

Glass sliced old ladies down the middle,—

MOUSE. —Don't stand there,—

SLICK. —He says the people in this city,

It's been so long,—

MOUSE. —They don't remember monsters.

  (*Quiet.*)

SLICK. And he says all of this in his sleep.

  (*Quiet.*)

When it's quiet.

…

When I start to think maybe none of this is happening,

…

When I start to think maybe he dragged me down here two city-lengths carrying a heavy-ass crowbar for nothing,

…

When I start to wonder what I'm even doin',

'Cause Little Man?

He ain't exactly right in the head.

  (*Suddenly, another weird* WHISPER.)

WHISPERS. La.

SLICK. He ain't exactly—

WHISPERS. —La. La.

  (*A rumble.*)

SLICK. Something rumbles so bad it hurts my cavities,

WHISPERS. La, La, La, La, La,

SLICK. An underground wind that comes without sound and without warning.

  (*SOUND.*)

And then I see her.

  (*RUMBLE. WIND.*)

Creeping forward,

Eyes so black even in the dark you could tell she's lookin' at you.

WHISPERS. —La Muerte.

  (*Something terrifying. An indication of* LA MUERTE. SLICK *tries to wake his brother.*)

SLICK. Little Man.

Little Man get up.

It's my turn.

Get up,

Move,

Move,

Little man I SAID MOVE.

> (*RUMBLE. THUNDER.*)

And I'm not leaving without him.

I'm not going nowhere and I'm not dying and I'm not leaving without him,

> (*LA MUERTE appears. She's terrifying.*)

My whole life has been me takin' care of him,

Shakin' off street-rats and punchin' in teeth so—get up!

Little Man are you—

> (*Suddenly* LA MUERTE *has* SLICK *by the throat. Maybe it's as simple as a person in silhouette across the stage with an outstretched arm. Sound builds.*)

She's got me by the throat—

> (LA MUERTE *squeezes.*)

—Hands like leather and my feet ain't even touching the floor,—

> (*The sound of wind.*)

—HER GRIP GETS TIGHT AROUND MY NECK AND I COULD FEEL MY PULSE ABOUT TO JUMP THROUGH MY SKIN AND LA MUERTE'S BLACK EYES ARE LOOKIN AT ME WITH ALL THE HATE THE DEVIL HAS FOR THE WORLD

BUT I AM NOT GONNA DIE—

> (*—SLASH—*)

—'CAUSE I REMEMBER MONSTERS—

> (*—SLASH—*)

—'CAUSE I WAS THERE WHEN THE BUILDING FELL AND THE MILK TURNED TO POISON,—

> (*—SLASH—SHE SQUEEZES HARDER.*)

—I MADE IT OUT AND I'M GONNA KEEP MAKING IT OUT UNTIL I'M GODDAMN READY!—

> (*—SLASH, LOUD EVERYTHING—*)

—I AM NOT GONNA DIE!—

> (*—SLASH!!!!—*)

—AND I SEE A RIP THROUGH THE TOP OF ITS HEAD—

> (*—SLASH—*)

—AND NEON LIGHT IS COMING OUT THROUGH THIS GASH ON ITS FACE AND IT LETS OUT A SCREAM LIKE—

> (*—A SCREAM—*)

—Like motherfuckin'—

> (*—A SCREEEEEEEEEEEAM!!!!!—*)

—And it's gone.

> (*Quiet.*)

WHISPERS. La, La,

> (*Quiet.*)

SLICK. And there's Little Man.

> (*Lights up on* MOUSE.)

Crowbar in hand.

> (MOUSE *drops the crowbar.*)

Standing tall in a neon blood puddle.

> (MOUSE *takes a breath.*)

MOUSE. …We gotta carry that.

> (SLICK *takes a breath. Stares at his brother—who stands taller than before. Some kind of hero. A breath.*)

SLICK. And our whole life,

Our whole everything has been me takin' care of him.

MOUSE. Sixty-six.

Sixty-seven.

SLICK. Shakin' off street-rats and punchin' in teeth for his sake.

MOUSE. Sixty-seven.

Sixty-eight.

SLICK. But last week something changed.

MOUSE. Keep moving.

…

Come on.

> (MOUSE *looks* SLICK *in the eyes—earnest.*)

We've gotta keep going.

> (A beat. SLICK looks at his brother—and makes a promise.)

SLICK. And we do.

> (*Black. End of play.*)

THE ONE THEY CALL THE BLOOP
by Marco Ramirez

One ENSEMBLE MEMBER *onstage. Direct address. Dead serious.*

ENSEMBLE MEMBER. They called it The Bloop,
The people who recorded it,
Researchers who spent countless hours monitoring the travel patterns of seaweed and algae,
People with a sense of humor.
…
It was traced to somewhere in the Pacific Ocean,
Off the southernmost tip of South America.
…
An underwater sound, classified as ultra-low frequency, its exact location kept strictly confidential by seven different national guards.
…
The Oceanic Association did not believe its origin was mechanical—completely ruling out submarines, oil drills, and undetonated World War explosives.
But neither did they believe it was geological—not a volcano, a tectonic shift, or any kind of earthquake.
…
According to audio engineers, the acoustic profile of The Bloop is biological—but not like any living creature they can identify.
…
> (*The* ENSEMBLE MEMBER *holds out a small roll of paper.*)

A waveform profile: a physical way of mapping out the magnitude of sound.
…
This is a nine-year old screaming.
> (*The* ENSEMBLE MEMBER *rolls the paper out. It's three feet in length. Drops it.*)

This is a blue whale.
The largest animal ever known to have existed.
> (*The* ENSEMBLE MEMBER *rolls out a twenty-foot length of paper. Drops it.*)

And this is what they recorded,
Out there,
Alive,
Somewhere in the Pacific Ocean.
> (*Ten rolls of paper fall from ceiling. They bounce on the floor and keep rolling. Four hundred feet.*)

"The Bloop."
> (*Black.*)

PROMAGEDDON
by Dan Dietz

A storage room in a public school basement. ALEXIS, 18, and DOT, 17, are in formal gowns. ALEXIS wears hers well, DOT significantly less so. THEO and GIL, both 18, are in tuxedos. GIL stands in front of the door, guarding it. THEO strums an acoustic guitar and sings a sad folk tune.

THEO. WENT TO THE DANCE ALONE
TOOK A CHANCE, I SHOULD HAVE STAYED HOME
NOW I'M TRAPPED IN RIVERSTONE
MMMMM-HMMMMM

(He finishes with a flourish.)

ALEXIS. That's it? The entire song?

THEO. Song*let.* They're called "songlets." I'm pushing the envelope of brevity.

ALEXIS. Yeah? Well, try pushing something useful—like him. *(Trying to shove GIL aside.)* Move it, meat bag.

GIL. I told you: nobody's going anywhere till I say it's safe.

ALEXIS. You may be the star quarterback up there on the field, Gil, but down here you're not the boss of anything except industrial-sized rolls of toilet paper, anti-bacterial soap, and…the janitor's half-used can of chewing tobacco EW!

GIL. You're a cheerleader, Alexis. You're supposed to cheer me *on,* not like, *off.*

ALEXIS. If you're so cheer-worthy, how come you showed up tonight with your little sister on your arm? Oh wait, that's right: I dumped you for Zander Perkins.

GIL. She couldn't get a date. It's called a favor.

ALEXIS. It's called you got arrested last week for streaking around the neighborhood butt naked yelling, "Look at me! I'm a freak!" so now me and everybody else at this school want nothing more to do with you.

GIL. You can't crush my spirit. I'm a natural born leader. And I'm gonna lead us out of this.

THEO. I seriously doubt the playbook for the Riverstone Civets has in any way prepared you for what's on the other side of that door.

GIL. Shut that mopey little face of yours, dude, or so help me I will find the nearest water source and swirly you into oblivion.

ALEXIS. Yeah, Theo. We don't know what's out there. It could all be fine. Like a false alarm or something.

THEO. Did you not hear the wailing screams half an hour ago? Feel the earth-shattering thuds? Enjoy the delicious buzz of a mild to moderate concussion as the floor slammed up to meet your face?

ALEXIS. Okay, I know you like to think of yourself as some musical poet…

THEO. Folk rock singer-songwriter.

ALEXIS. …but I'd appreciate a little less hyperbole and a little more "keeping your panties dry."

THEO. (*Singing with a snarl.*)
SHE TOLD ME TO KEEP MY PANTIES DRY
THINKS SHE'S THE QUEEN BITCH OF RIVERSTONE HIGH

GIL. Enough, you two! We're a team, and we're gonna start acting like one. Now can I get a "Go Civets"?

ALEXIS. Oh, I'll give you a "Go Civets."

DOT. Please.

ALEXIS. In fact, if you don't step two feet to the left and get out of my way…

DOT. Everybody please.

ALEXIS. …I'm gonna take my hotly manicured tensies here and claw the words "Go Civets" right into your—

DOT. COULD EVERYBODY PLEASE SHUT UP? (*They stare at her.*) We all could have died. We all could have died and we all still could die and we ought to have respect enough for the sledgehammer of that fact to be quiet for five fucking minutes. I mean Christ: THERE WAS A NUCLEAR WAR ON OUR PROM NIGHT.

　　　　(*Beat.*)

GIL. So what does that mean for like, tux rental?

　　　　(ALEXIS *pulls out her cell phone and starts texting.*)

ALEXIS. "Status update: Trapped in basement storage room with ex-BF, emo freak, and a prom dress that appears to have eaten 1990s Janeane Garofalo. Please advise."

DOT. Do you really think anyone's gonna get that?

ALEXIS. Send. (*She stares down at her phone.*) Come on… Come on…

　　　　(*Nothing.* ALEXIS *hurls her phone to the floor. Silence.*)

THEO. God. Nuclear war? It's so… (*With disdain.*) retro.

ALEXIS. I know, right? That's our parents' apocalypse. Can't we have anything of our own?

DOT. Okay. I'm not sure the reality is sinking in with you guys. So I'm gonna try one more time: Up above us, everyone that used to be alive is either dead or dying. The heat from the blast has turned many people into a fine atomic mist and given many more people burns from which they cannot possibly survive. Buildings are now rubble. Water is now steam. The sky is in perpetual twilight. Civilization has ended.

(*Pause.*)

ALEXIS. Or…Up above us, people are dancing. Music is thumping. Booze and pot and other amazing things are secretly trickling into the bodies of all our classmates like answered prayers. Zander is looking for me. Squeezing his tightly-muscled frame through a crush of velvet and sequins and ill-advised hair. The world is turning. All is rad. And any minute, they're going to announce the King and Queen. I have to go. I have to go!

(ALEXIS *wrestles with* GIL.)

DOT. Alexis. We all heard the sirens. We all got the texts. We all saw Mr. Havister stop the band, get up on stage, and make the announcement. And then we all did exactly what he told us not to do: run. There's nothing up there now.

(ALEXIS *stops wrestling and gives a howl of frustration.*)

ALEXIS. I was supposed to be Queen! Fucking China!

THEO. Well, more accurately, Iran. Then Israel. Then Pakistan. Then India. Then China.

ALEXIS. Then Us. Then fucking Us. (*Pause.*) I'm a cheerleader. I have a 4.0. I have a new boyfriend so hot his tweets burn my retinas. This can't be how it all ends for me. If I'd have known I was going to spend my last days on earth stuck in a storage room with three of the biggest freaks ever to roam the Riverstone halls, I'd have taken Kimmy Whitman's hand when she jumped off that bridge last year and gone with her, all the way down.

THEO. Wow. Where do I begin? First, if you think being a cheerleader with a hot boyfriend is a guarantee against a bleak and meaningless future, check out our parents' Facebook profiles. Second, you only have a 4.0 because pathetic geeks are willing to let you cheat off them in exchange for a couple of lousy sexts. And third, shallow, self-obsessed people like you are the reason Kimmy Whitman jumped in the first place.

(*Quiet.*)

DOT. That was the worst day ever. Well, besides…

THEO. Yeah. It really was.

DOT. And that YouTube video? Of the guy finding her?

ALEXIS. He throws up like forever. It was disgusting.

THEO. Not the point, Alexis.

DOT. Seaweed and algae and stuff dripping off of her. Her skin was the color of the moon. And the weirdest expression on her face. Like the tiniest smile. Like she knew something we all didn't.

THEO. Are we ever gonna see the moon again?

GIL. Yes. I'm gonna make sure of that.

ALEXIS. Well I know I'm relieved.

THEO. The point, Alexis, is that none of us would have chosen this as our way to go out. But none of us knew this was going to happen.

GIL. Well... Maybe one of us did.

DOT. Gil. Don't.

GIL. Are you gonna tell them, Dot, or am I?

THEO. Tell us what?

DOT. Nothing.

GIL. Nothing? We're on our way here in the stretch Hummer Mom and Dad rented for us when suddenly Lil Sis here says, "Do you hear something?" And I say, like what, and she says like a bell, like multiple bells being rung or struck or something.

DOT. A) It was one bell three times, and B) shut up.

GIL. And then she jolts up straight, raises her palms to the heavens and recites this, this...I don't know what. "Prepare for the End of All Things"... "Fire Shall Rain Down from the Heavens"..."The Breath of the Beast Shall Linger 999 Days"...stuff like that. On and on. Her voice was like Metallica. Limo driver pretty much shit his uniform.

(*They all stare at her. Pause.*)

DOT. You're all making me feel very uncomfortable.

THEO. How long has this been going on? These, I'm assuming, visions?

DOT. Since...I don't know...

GIL. Puberty. Basically since puberty.

DOT. Goddammit, Gil!

ALEXIS. You've been having visions of the apocalypse for like five years and didn't tell anybody? This isn't your period, Dot. When it starts happening you can't just shut up, go buy a stack of maxis and get back to photoshopping yourself making out with Zac Efron. (*Beat.*) Like some people might have done at that age.

THEO. What about you, Gil? Why didn't you speak up?

GIL. She begged me not to say anything.

DOT. Yeah, thanks for keeping your promise.

GIL. Um, Nuclear War? Your social status is no longer my top priority. My top priority is leading us all to safety. First things first: documenting our party of survivors. (GIL *pulls out his camera and photos himself.*) There. Now you, Sis.

DOT. Me what, traitor?

GIL. I'm keeping a record of how we look now. That way if there are drastic changes in our appearance—you know like from radiation, poison…

THEO. …starvation, death by giant mutant rat…

GIL. …we can detect the problem early and maybe do something about it.

DOT. I hate to admit it, but that's actually pretty smart.

GIL. Say cheese. (*He snaps a photo.*) You. Emo.

THEO. Theo.

GIL. Whatever. Smile for posterity.

> (THEO *gives him a gesture that is anything but a smile.*)

Good enough. You're up, Alexis.

ALEXIS. Absolutely not.

GIL. You're still doing this? It's the end of the freaking world!

DOT. Doing what?

GIL. Little Miss Prom Queen here won't let anyone take her picture but her.

THEO. Last guy who tried got an iPad in the face.

ALEXIS. Unlike you losers, I know how to keep myself from being tagged in incriminating photos.

GIL. I'm taking this whether you like it or not. One…

ALEXIS. Get away from me.

GIL. Two…

ALEXIS. Leave me alone!

DOT. Look, Zander's tightly-muscled frame!

ALEXIS. Where?!

GIL. Three! (*He snaps a photo.*) See? That wasn't so hard, was…

> (GIL *stares at the picture on the screen.*)

DOT. Gil? What is it?

GIL. I don't know. Some kind of distortion. Like a weird circle of light around her head.

> (THEO *pulls out his phone and takes a picture.*)

ALEXIS. That's right! Everybody gather round! Get your picture of the freak!

THEO. Mine has it too.

DOT. Let me see. Is that…? A halo! Alexis, does this happen in all your pictures?

ALEXIS. Ever since puberty. My mom destroyed all her photos of me from like age thirteen on because in every single one of them I look like some kind of Madonna.

GIL. Gross!

THEO. She means a figure from a religious painting, dumbass.

GIL. Oh.

DOT. Hang on. Alexis has a halo that only shows up in photographs. I have visions of the apocalypse. Does anybody else have something weird about them? Maybe something that started right around puberty? Gil? Have you been hiding something from me?

GIL. No.

DOT. You're lying. Look at your face. He's lying.

THEO. What is it?

ALEXIS. Yeah, mister shutterbug, what is it? A beam of heavenly light coming out of your butt?

DOT. A chorus of angel voices coming out of your mouth?

THEO. A sentient third nipple that speaks in tongues coming out of your chest?

> (*They all stare at* THEO.)

I have no idea where that came from.

GIL. Fine. You really want to know? It's…this!

> (GIL *tears off his shirt, revealing an otherworldly tattoo on his back. It's a map of the school, with a large "X" indicating the storage room. Above the map are big letters that read, "LEAD THEM HERE."*)

ALEXIS. What is that?

GIL. You see it too? Nobody else ever has before.

THEO. That "X" marks the room we're in right now.

DOT. How long have you had this?

GIL. It appeared on my thirteenth birthday. It must only be visible to people like us.

DOT. No wonder you refused to take your shirt off around me!

THEO. You asked him to take his shirt off around you?

ALEXIS. Incest much?

DOT. No, I…shut up!

> (DOT *retreats to a corner.*)

ALEXIS. So when Mr. Havister said the bombs were on their way and you turned and charged down the stairwell into the basement…you were following your mystical back map?

THEO. I only followed him because I had this strange sense that I needed to.

ALEXIS. Me too!

GIL. Now do you see why I'm the leader? I've been preparing for this my whole life. That's why I streaked across the neighborhood that night. The pressure…all these years…it was just too much. I wanted someone, anyone, to see what I've been carrying around.

(DOT *is crying in a corner.* GIL *goes over to her.*)

GIL. Dot? What's the matter?

DOT. For years I've felt like a freak because of these stupid visions. And now I find out that at any moment my popular, football hero brother could have reached out and made me feel less alone. Why didn't you tell me?

GIL. I don't know, Sis. I think something in me knew you'd see the map, when no one else could. And then it would be real. If I didn't show it to you, I could pretend I was normal. Just another run-of-the-mill really really really really really talented athlete.

ALEXIS. Wait a minute. Theo. You can see the map?

THEO. Yeah, so?

ALEXIS. So that means you're like us.

(*They all turn to him. Beat.*)

THEO. I'm nothing like you people, okay?

DOT. Come on, Theo. We've all had to cough up our darkest secrets here. Why hide yours?

THEO. Because it's none of your business.

GIL. Theo, if we're gonna function as a team of survivors—

THEO. Who says we're survivors?

ALEXIS. And who says we're a team? I'm not *with* you guys, okay? Just because I'm suffering through the apocalypse doesn't mean I'm *desperate*.

THEO. Me neither. Let's just wait in our separate corners for the roaches to evolve hyper-intelligence and plot our demise.

ALEXIS. Yeah. And if any of you losers even think about infiltrating the cool corner over here—

DOT. NO! Nobody gets to be cool anymore! (DOT *grabs* THEO*'s guitar and swings it at them. They scatter.*) For as far back as I can remember, I've been the awkward one. The friendless, fashionless, socially disastrous one. And now, here we are at the End of the World, and you, and you, and even you Gil, are all still acting like you're better than me or anyone else. Miss Hotter Than Thou. Mister Master of Detachment. Big Man on Irradiated Campus. Well no more! You hear me? NOBODY GETS TO BE COOL!

(DOT *raises the guitar up and starts to bring it crashing down.*)

THEO. WAIT! Please, Dot. I'll tell you. Or actually, I'll have to show you.

(*Slowly,* DOT *lowers the guitar.* THEO *gently takes it from her.*)

There's a reason I only perform songlets. Ever since I was about thirteen, if I sing for more than thirty seconds…something takes over. It's not me. It's kind of horrifying actually. You sure you want to see this?

> (*Everyone nods.*)

Okay. Brace yourselves.

> (THEO *takes a deep breath. Then he sings a morose urban folk song.*)

I SEE YOU ON THE BALCONY
CIGARETTE AND COLD BLACK COFFEE
MY LATTE'S SPIKED WITH BITTER IRONY
MMMMM-HMMMMM

FRIENDING YOU WAS WRONG FROM THE START
YOUR SKINNY JEANS ARE BLUE AND SO IS MY HEART

> (*Suddenly,* THEO *begins to convulse. Some supernatural force is taking over his body. He shakes, he trembles, he moans. Then all at once, his hips lock into a swagger, he lays down a sassy rockabilly guitar riff, and he starts singing. It's a big, bold 1950s rock'n'roll song—think Elvis/Buddy Holly/Jerry Lee Lewis.* THEO *explodes around the room, grinning and hopping and bopping it up.*)

ONE HAS THE VISIONS
ONE HAS THE LIGHT
ONE HAS THE MAP
SO BABY IT'S ALL RIGHT

GO ON NOW
REPOPULATE THE EARTH
YOU SURVIVED ARMAGEDDON
SO GO ON AND REPOPULATE THE EARTH

YOU FOUR HAVE BEEN CHOSEN
BY THE HEAVENS ABOVE
SO JUST WAIT FOR THE MESSENGER
OF LOVE LOVE LOVE

AND THEN GO
REPOPULATE THE EARTH
WHEN THE MESSENGER COMES
IT'S TIME TO REPOPULATE THE EARTH

POP-A-POP! REPOPULATE IT!
POP-A-POP! DON'T HESITATE IT!
POP-A-POP! REPOPULATE THE EARTH!

> (THEO *collapses in a heap. Long dumbstruck pause.* THEO *slowly regains consciousness. He looks around.*)

What happened? What did I say?

GIL. Um…Basically, you told us all to bang each other until we've made enough babies to kickstart humanity.

THEO. Fuck.

GIL. Exactly. Apparently a messenger is supposed to come give us the all clear. Then we can go and, you know…

ALEXIS. No. No way.

GIL. Come on, Alexis. You can't say no to the halo. You're like, the holy mother of humanity now.

DOT. I'm with Alexis. That's insane. I mean, the four of us? I'm in AP Calculus right now, and even I am daunted by the mathematics of what you're suggesting.

GIL. But this is our destiny. Look, it's simple. Dot and Theo, Alexis and me. Theo, back me up here, bro.

THEO. Forget it.

GIL. It's not like it can be me and Dot.

THEO. I don't know what I said, but there's no way I'm supposed to do that.

GIL. Look, my sister has a beautiful heart…

DOT. Oh for God's sake.

GIL. …and if you think I'm gonna let some goth-folk goober like you stomp all over it…

DOT. Gil, you're not helping!

GIL. Say it! Say you'll have apocalypse babies with my sister!

THEO. No!

GIL. Why not?

THEO. You know, I was thinking to myself, there's only one way today could get any worse…

GIL. Because you don't like my sister?

THEO. Because I don't like anyone's sister!

   (DOT's *and* ALEXIS' *eyebrows shoot up. They get it. Pause.*)

GIL. I still don't—

ALEXIS & DOT. HE'S GAY!

THEO. The end of THE world and the end of MY world on the very same day, how convenient.

GIL. Then…this isn't gonna work. We can't, I mean (*Indicating* DOT.) *we can't,* I mean (*Indicating* ALEXIS.) *we* could—

ALEXIS. Forget it. I'd rather hook up with Zander's melted corpse.

GIL. But, the song said—

DOT. It's over, Gil. Let it go.

GIL. So that's it? We give up? When the aliens invaded Earth in *Independence Day*, did Will Smith give up? When the asteroid invaded space in *Armageddon,*

did Bruce Willis give up? And when Ben Affleck invaded *Armageddon*, did the
movie give up?

DOT. Gil…

GIL. DID THE MOVIE GIVE UP? We're better than this, people! You
know, I've learned a few things about civets in my four years playing football
for Riverstone High. Number One: they're named for the foul-smelling
secretion that comes from a gland near their genitals. And Number Two: they
never give up. We survive, when others perish. We carry on, when others fail.
Now hear me, Universe! I know you've given us each a holy token to carry
around, marking us as chosen. But we need one more signal from you—just
one—to let us know we're on the right path. As the Leader of the Final Four,
I'm asking you, please: GIVE US A SIGN!

>   (*Big, earthshaking rumble. Plaster falls from the ceiling. The door busts off its
>   hinges. Beyond, a hall filled with smoke and mist. Slowly, a figure emerges from
>   the haze. A seventeen-year-old girl. Dorky glasses, dumpy clothes. Her skin is
>   dead white, and there's seaweed dripping off of her, yet her lips betray a tiny,
>   Buddha-like smile. It's* KIMMY WHITMAN.)

ALEXIS. Oh my God…

DOT. Kimmy? Kimmy Whitman?

THEO. But you're dead. We all saw it.

>   (KIMMY *enters the room, staring at each of them with profound grace. When
>   she speaks, her voice echoes with otherworldly power.*)

KIMMY. Once, I was Kimmy Whitman. Now I am The Messenger.

GIL. Dudes, I fucking told you!

ALEXIS, DOT & THEO. SHUT UP, GIL!

KIMMY. I have been sent to draw you four out into the new dawn.

THEO. By who? Who sent you?

>   (KIMMY *offers a small, enigmatic smile.*)

KIMMY. There are things you cannot now know. Not while you occupy these
human shells.

ALEXIS. Some of us happen to like our shells.

DOT. Alexis!

KIMMY. Alexis. You will find it difficult to maintain your beauty where you
are about to go. Be strong, and allow your true radiance to unfold.

>   (ALEXIS *is speechless at this.*)

Dot. You will now learn what I did. That being an outcast has given you
profound strength. Very soon, your smile and your guidance will by sought
by all.

>   (DOT *is blown away.*)

Theo. You have chosen isolation for so many of your brief years. In this new world, you will no longer have to use music to keep others away. You will no longer be alone.

(THEO *is calmed.*)

Gil. You bravely led, when no one else would stand tall. So…good job.

(GIL *is confused, but okay with it.*)

Now. Follow me. The time has come to begin your great work.

ALEXIS. Hold up. I'm not signing on to be a baby generator in some nuked-out hellscape.

DOT. Yeah. If we're really supposed to repopulate the Earth, we should be able to do it on our own terms, not like…I mean…I MEAN, I COULDN'T GET A DATE FOR MY JUNIOR PROM, NOW I CAN'T GET A DATE FOR THE POST-APOCALYPSE?

KIMMY. Allow me to alleviate your concerns. There are others just like you, waiting in different high school basements, all over town. Those who were once freaks are now the chosen ones. And I, the biggest loser of all, shall lead you on your way. Even here, in this very basement, there is another. The one known as Zander is alive.

ALEXIS. YES!!!

THEO. But what good does all that do me? What if none of those other survivors is like me?

KIMMY. I just told you. The one known as Zander is alive.

ALEXIS. But, Zander doesn't like boys.

(KIMMY *offers her enigmatic smile.*)

KIMMY. Come. The end is over. The beginning begins.

(*With* KIMMY *in the lead, everyone heads out into the mist of a new dawn. End of play.*)

THIS IS HOW IT ENDS
by A. Rey Pamatmat

3.

PESTILENCE, FAMINE, *and* WAR *at the edge of existence.*

PESTILENCE. The diseased have succumbed.

FAMINE. The hungry have starved.

WAR. The militant have totally waxed each other. Like, wipe-out.

FAMINE. So…what do we do now?

(Silence.)

Seriously. At the edge of existence, they got their dubious salvation from us: they died. No more disease for the dead. Or anger. Or hunger. Even for zombies. Even for brains.

And suddenly I don't have time to do anything, and I can't think of anything I want to do.

Am I really THAT girl? The minute those creatures knew it was over, they ran around to confess one last truth, fight one last fight, try everything they never tried without hesitation or regret. All I did was work: suck power from their muscles, suck stability from their bones. All I did was suck. It's like I'm already non-existent. I don't even want something. I want to want something. I'm starving.

(FAMINE is breaking down. WAR enfolds her in a comforting embrace. She clings to him for a moment and then notices PESTILENCE looking at them, longingly. She pushes WAR away.)

Ugh, you smell like homeless, you hippie bong-sucker. Go fuck your boyfriend, before the whiny man-baby pisses himself.

PESTILENCE. Boyfriend? Huh! What do you…pffft. I mean? Pfft. I don't…you're CRAZY.

FAMINE. Oh, please. Stealing glances, sneaking into each other's rooms, fucking on the floor so the bed won't creak? It's pathetic. Cowards.

WAR. Yo—living and working together eternally is a totally sensitive situation.

FAMINE. Who cares? Just do it. Leave me here fucked in the head and go bumfuck each other into oblivion. I'm alone. I'm fine being alone. GO.

(A beat.)

PESTILENCE. How did you know?

FAMINE. Webcam. You gave half of Central America dysentery and then called in one of your five billion sick days, leaving me to starve them of nutrients by myself. So I Skyped you to give you a piece of my mind, and the webcam flips on to pony boy drilling you like Halliburton in Afghanistan.

WAR. (*Laughing.*) No shit!

FAMINE. So I sat back and enjoyed the show.

PESTILENCE. How. Dare. You.

FAMINE. You give babies cerebral palsy! He makes orphans out of them! We are so beyond good and evil. And, you know what? I did it again. And again. And again.

PESTILENCE. I CANNOT BELIEVE YOU. Yeah, well…I ATE YOUR ICE CREAM. SO FUCK YOU.

FAMINE. YOU WHAT?!

(*FAMINE grabs PESTILENCE but stops herself.*)

Oh, who gives a shit? We don't have time. YOU don't have time. Fuck. Him. Go. Do it.

WAR. I don't think leaving you is a great idea. Not now.

FAMINE. You won't, orphan-maker. I'm going to watch.

(*FAMINE takes a granola bar out of her pocket, sits cross-legged on the floor, and starts to unwrap it.*)

PESTILENCE. You can't watch! We'll go somewhere else.

FAMINE. There isn't a lot of somewhere else left to go to. You want to be with him? This is your last chance. And I… I would really like to blink out of existence experiencing love, even if it's not my own. All I've seen for eternity is their need. Their desire left unfulfilled. I would really like… I would appreciate it if I could…

I would really like to see love.

Please.

(*PESTILENCE gawks at her, stunned, until WAR places a hand on his cheek. PESTILENCE swats his hand away.*)

PESTILENCE. I'm not going to do this, she—

WAR. P, it's the end of the world.

So the A.C. was all, "Get cracking!" But, like I said, job does itself. So I was like, am I gonna spend the end pretending to work? So, like, NUH-UH. So I…wrote you a sonnet.

PESTILENCE. Wrote…? For me?

WAR. It's called, "Lovesick."

(*Reciting.*) I'm ill at ease. My head, my chest, my heart,
All flutter when your body presses mine.
With flush of fever, shakes, and chills it starts,
A sickness savaging both frame and mind.
Uneasy now, my body you defile,
Each once strong limb by your infection wracked.

Your touch bacterial, your viral smile,
By beauty beyond fatal I'm attacked.
Then, foul disease a strange surprise unveils,
By giving strength to me as I succumb.
Immunity surrenders and health fails,
To leave me strong in love and yet undone.
The pow'r of illness felled oh greatest War,
So he'll be Pestilence's ever more.

(*Speaking.*) Love you, babe.

(PESTILENCE *pulls* WAR *in for a kiss. It's beautiful.* FAMINE *cries, quietly.*)

PESTILENCE. I remember that first time I saw you wading in blood, covered in entrails, smiling that goofy grin at me. (*To* FAMINE.) You're right: AIDS doesn't matter. Neither does cancer or the flu. This matters.

(WAR *and* PESTILENCE *begin to make love as* FAMINE *watches, crying and nibbling on her granola bar.*)

FAMINE. Thank you.

(*End of scene.*)

4.

DEATH *appears, as does* JAKE, *who is half-dressed.*

DEATH. It's time, Jake.

JAKE. Annie said you'd come. She said it wouldn't hurt.

DEATH. It won't. But everyone else left is either the holiest saint or the vilest sinner. Why are you here at the universe's end?

JAKE. I did what I told Annie I would. I told my parents and friends I loved them, some friends came over, and we all fucked our brains out. Then the universe started ripping apart, and everyone panicked.

So I was like, "Hey, relax. Annie is, like, the best roommate ever. And this one time I was a total dick to her, because she'd used up all my cayenne pepper. But she took it in stride and totally ran to the store for me in the middle of the night. Annie's the coolest, and she says we're going to become one and be totally at peace, and I believe her."

DEATH. And that's all it took.

JAKE. No. But we started talking about how we loved our roommates, friends, and family. About how happy we were to be with people now, and not running scared like everyone else.

We talked and cried and made love like I have never made love before. So many people becoming one. Afraid, ecstatic, and alive… Together.

What'd you do?

(DEATH *stares blankly, and then…*)

DEATH. What did…? Oh. I've been cleaning up the messes my comrades have left behind.

JAKE. No, I mean, it's THE last day. Did you do something for yourself before time ran out? I guess, I mean: how are you? This is, like, the Apocalypse.

DEATH. Oh, well, I… I'm…fine.

JAKE. You sure?

DEATH. It's just…people fear me, even though I've spent my whole existence helping them on their way. I'm not used to being asked after.

JAKE. But now you're on your way, so someone should help you out, too, even if it's just me. Right?

DEATH. Right. And I'm…fine. I'm not like the others. I've seen so many suffer; I'm just glad I never had to. I'm happy now, at last, to rest.

JAKE. Awesome.

(DEATH *grins for the first and last time in all eternity.*)

DEATH. You are a saint, Jake. An everyday saint, but still: a saint.

(*A beat.*)

JAKE. You sure it won't hurt?

DEATH. For people who fear too much, death hurts. For people who love too much, death hurts, too. But for those few who know they're no different on this side than on the other—that they're the same as a parking meter and the infinite cosmos—for them I'm nothing more than a friend who helps them out of their clothes.

(DEATH *holds out her hand.* JAKE *takes it. She helps him "out of his clothes." JAKE stands naked before her [metaphorically, please]. ANNIE appears with two Jamba Juices. She holds one out to* JAKE.)

JAKE. O-M-G… Hi, Annie! All done?

ANNIE. Almost, Jakey. But before it's all over, I have a present for you. I saved a DVD for us to watch in the last few hours of eternity.

JAKE. Let me guess: *Nowhere*, the third movie in Gregg Araki's…

BOTH. Teen Apocalypse Trilogy!!!

JAKE. Best. Roommate. Ever. And from Craigslist! What the hell? Anything's possible.

(JAKE *and* ANNIE *link arms and exit.*)

DEATH. (*To the audience.*) No more prom night messiahs. Or re-awakened gods. Or apartment revelations before THE Revelation. Now I bring everyone to paradise, close my eyes, and sleep. This is how it ends.

End of Play

APPENDIX:
Additional Material

The following short plays, scenes and monologues were written during the course of the workshop process, but did not appear in the Humana Festival production.

4B
by Marco Ramirez

CHARACTERS

MIKEY, 20s-40s. The fuck-up brother.
PETE, 20s-40s. The other one.

> *A rooftop. A big city. A shabby four- or five-story apartment building. MIKEY leans on the ledge, drinking his second beer. He stares out. Wind. Eerie quiet. Shouldn't there be sirens? Shouldn't there be something? A metal door swings open. PETE enters. Smart haircut. Smarter watch. Both men stare at each other. Recognition. Tension. MIKEY half-smiles. This is the last thing either of them expected.*

PETE. Should one of us go?

MIKEY. You mean should I go.

PETE. That's not what I mean,

> *(That's exactly what he means.)*

MIKEY. We got like ten minutes, I can't exactly take the train back,

PETE. Right,

MIKEY. And I ain't gonna waste it on some street corner or in some fuckin' bodega.

PETE. I get you, I just—

MIKEY. …

PETE. …I'll go.

MIKEY. C'mon Pete,—

> *(PETE looks at MIKEY. MIKEY looks right back. PETE doesn't make the decision to stay—but doesn't really go either. Quiet. MIKEY grabs another beer. He quickly pops it open up against the ledge—ritual. He passes it to PETE, who catches it without blinking.)*

You should see what they did to the place.

PETE. What place?

MIKEY. 4B.

PETE. You broke in?

MIKEY. There wasn't no one inside,

What was I supposed to do.

PETE. Not break in?

MIKEY. Wish I hadn't.

…

Ma's sewing machine's gone,

There's new hardwood,

Porcelain tub,

Blotchy art shit hanging on the walls,

The stuff hoytytoyty assholes call painting,

They got a fuckin',

> (*With disgust.*)

Espresso machine.

> (PETE *smiles politely. He has one, too.*)

Good beer in the fridge, though.

PETE. Yeah.

> (*A beat. They drink.*)

MIKEY. Shouldn't you be with Maggie or somethin'?

PETE. …

MIKEY. Day like today,

Fuckin' end-of-the-world-grief everyone's been going through,

Shouldn't you be with your wife?

PETE. …

> (PETE *stares off.* MIKEY *gets it.*)

MIKEY. Alone or with somebody else?

PETE. Alone, I think.

She just—

She didn't even pack a bag.

> (MIKEY *stares off with him, sympathetic.*)

MIKEY. …

PETE. …

MIKEY. They let us go,

I didn't break out,

In case that's what you're thinkin'—

PETE. —I'm not,—

MIKEY. —Just opened the front doors.

…

Didn't make an announcement or anything,

Just unlocked the cage and took off, went home,

No more wasted seconds on the scum o' the earth.

…

Some o' the guys,

They've been dreamin' about gettin' out since the goddamn seventies,

You think we'd've rushed outta there,

But it was nothin' like that—

…

It was slow.

…

Like a funeral.

…

Lettin' us out with twelve hours left,

Talk about a *Twilight Zone* ending, right?

> (PETE *cracks half a smile.*)

PETE. I think I'm gonna go,—

MIKEY. —Too good to blow the last—what—eight minutes on the scum o' the earth?

Even if he's your brother?

PETE. I'm not "too good."

MIKEY. (*Toast to the sky.*) I'll drink to that,—

PETE. —I just don't want this.

…

I'm sorry I bothered you.

It's unfortunate we chose the same place to spend this,

It's strange that we both ended up here,—

MIKEY. —How's it fuckin' strange?—

PETE. —Mike,—

MIKEY. —I lost a fingernail reaching into that gutter,

Looking for a baseball mitt you hid there 'cause Phil Pickens used to beat your ass,—

PETE. (*Grow up.*) —Really?—

MIKEY. —There are pieces of us in this building,—

PETE. —You know what I mean,—

MIKEY. —"Unfortunate?"—

PETE. —I don't wanna have this—

MIKEY. —In eight years you come visit me once,—

PETE. —I came, didn't I?—

MIKEY. —To bring the old man by,

To stand in the back like you were just his driver,—

PETE. (*Checking his watch.*) —Seven minutes,—

MIKEY. (*Upset.*) —You got somewhere else to go, Pete?

You fuckin' go!

You go,

You spend this.

I won't keep you.

(PETE *doesn't move. A beat.*)

PETE. (*Only half-sincere.*) It was good seeing you.

MIKEY. …

PETE. I'm sorry you got in trouble,

I'm sorry you got caught,

I'm sorry I didn't visit.

I'm sorry if it caused you any pain.

I'm sorry if that makes me an asshole,

…

I hope you have a great rest of the world.

(PETE *moves to leave.*)

MIKEY. Guys were cheering,—

PETE. —I'm walking,—

MIKEY. —For the first day or two,

When the news hit?

Like good-riddance-fuck-the-world-anyway kinda cheering,

Like maybe-now-everyone'll-know-what-it's-like-to-be-trapped-in-a-box cheering,

But the cheering got louder,

Then it just became screaming,

Then it just became sobbing,—

PETE. (*Checks that watch.*) —Six minutes,—

MIKEY. —Nonstop, two weeks,—

PETE. —Can we not do this,—

MIKEY. —When their bodies ran outta tears they kept crying,

Eyes swollen,

Infected-looking,

And I told myself it was catching,

I told myself it was some kinda sickness and if I caught it I'd be fucked,

So I fought it,

(And jail sucks, Pete.

Like a lot.

Like even more than you think it sucks?

It sucks.)

But I fought it,

I told myself it just wasn't possible,

The world wouldn't let me die without seeing home again,

…4B.

PETE. …

MIKEY. I made this bet,

Out loud,

I said "Universe, you can kill yourself,

You can implode and explode and hang yourself by the goddamn throat,

But you gotta let me go home."

…

And then it happened,

PETE. What.

MIKEY. They just opened the front doors.

Let us go.

…

'Cause of me.

…

If I'd stayed I might've saved everything,

If I'd stayed in that cell and given in, I might've saved us all.

But on the one day when the whole world's makin' the same wish,

The Universe chose to listen to one asshole,

And here I am.

…

And here you are.

…

And it ain't strange.

…

…

It ain't unfortunate.

> (*A beat.* PETE *makes the decision. Leans against the rooftop. Maybe he sits. Next to his brother. Where he belongs. A beat.* PETE *checks watch.*)

PETE. We got four minutes left.

MIKEY. We got one beer left.

> (*A breath. They stare at the beer.*)

PETE. Maybe if we don't drink it, it won't happen.

> (MIKEY *smiles, hopeful.*)

MIKEY. Yeah.

…

…

Maybe.

> (*They look up at the sky. They wait. Together. And black. End of play.*)

RAPTURE

by Jennifer Haley

BELLE's small children are gathered before her. She is taking great pains to remain calm.

BELLE. You know where Mama keeps the cereal? Where Mama keeps the Cheerios? In the big cupboard? Yes? Well, there's lots of cereal there for you. There are fifty boxes of Cheerios. I know—wow—but you shouldn't eat them all at once. Mama put them all there so they will last you a long time, right? Grace, you make sure they don't eat them all at once. And the milk. You know how we drink cold milk from the refrigerator? Well you can do that for about a week, and then you can't do that anymore. There are two gallons in the refrigerator, which should last you a week. Unless the refrigerator stops working. Do you know what will happen if it stops? All the food will be warm. And the milk will be warm. Which means what? You can't drink it. Grace, make sure they don't drink warm milk. And make sure you don't drink it after a week. Okay? After a week, you can use the powdered milk. Do you remember when we used that before? Remember when your daddy was here, and lost his job, and we pretended we were camping? And we had that milk that tasted a little funny? But you got used to it, didn't you? Well now you'll be making it yourselves. Which will be fun, right? There are five boxes of powdered milk in the cupboard with the cereal. You add three tablespoons to a cup of water, and you have milk. It's very easy to understand. There are instructions with pictures on the back of the powdered milk box. I've left the measuring spoons and cup out by the sink. Grace, you may have to make it, but I know you can do it, okay? It's very easy to understand.

(BELLE *turns her head to a sound outside. Her panic rises. She tries to keep it down.*)

I want you to stay inside the house, okay? We put all those boards over the windows so nothing can get in, but it's not going to mean anything if you go out. This is where you will be safe. For a long time, Mama hopes. Long enough for the first wave to blow over. You can't trust anyone during this time. They may come to the door seeming all nice, but you must tell them quite forcefully that you have guns and you will use them. That's why we loaded all of Daddy's guns and put them around the house. That's why we made those holes in the boards. Right? Grace, we went over how to load all the guns, and where the extra ammunition is, so you're in charge of that. You show the boys. If the house is surrounded, you take the living room. It will be harder for anyone to get in the back with Bucky out there in the yard. You must leave him out there to guard you for as long as possible. Don't let him in. You can't play with Bucky like you used to. He's a guard dog now, not a friend. There is one bag of food for him under the sink, and that must last as long as possible. Grace, only feed him one quarter cup a day. People are already afraid of Bucky, and they will be more afraid when he's hungry. And listen to me—if someone shoots him—I'm praying to our Good Lord that won't happen, but if it does—if someone shoots him, and you can get to his body, you should bring him inside and cook him. You've seen how Mama does the chickens and squirrels? With the big knife? You take off the skin and carve the muscle, and you can put him in a soup or in the oven. Be very careful with the oven. And if it stops working, just eat him quickly that day. Eat all of him. You will need your strength to last. Mama knows you're strong—each of you. But you will need a special kind of strength to get through the first wave. After that, things may settle down. There may be some decent people out there, even if they're atheists. They may be ignorant and misguided, but they can still do kind things. And Mama has great faith that kind people will come along and take care of you. Just don't believe it if they tell you there's no God. There is a God—it's very simple—it's easy to understand.

(*Again, she turns her head toward a sound. Again she controls her panic. She turns back.*)

Where am I going? Mama's going... Mama's going to Heaven. Mama's going to be taken to Heaven by our Lord. She may disappear before your eyes. She doesn't want to leave you. She wishes you could come with her. She wants that so badly. She wants that so badly. Why can't you go? Because... Because you are not old enough to know what it means to accept Jesus Christ as your Savior. I asked Father Bill about it. I told him you've all been baptized, you all believe in God. But he says you have to be at least nine years old before you can make a choice using your free will. So all of the children...all of the children must stay here. And...it's not easy to understand. I don't understand why God must separate us. Maybe if he separated us for just a little while, but...this is Eternity. I want to lie to you and tell you I will see you again. But if God can't give me that hope to me, I can't give it to you. And it's not easy... (*She tries to control her emotion.*) ...it's not easy to understand. I don't understand His plan. But I have to believe in it. We all have to believe in it. Because the plan is greater than we are. Greater than we can even imagine. There is so much...splendor that we cannot even imagine. And if we must say goodbye to achieve that splendor, then we must be brave and say goodbye. Remember I love you. Remember God loves you. Even your lost souls are precious to Him. I believe that. I don't understand...but I believe. You believe that, too? Promise me you'll keep believing all of this means something, even though it's not easy. Promise me.

(*Another sound—louder than the rest. She puts her hands together.*)

Oh God! Promise me!

WE ALL KNEW IT WAS COMING
by Allison Moore

Either mid- or post-apocalypse, depending on how you date such an event. ALEX *is alone. Maybe he has one other change of clothes, maybe just the clothes on his back.*

ALEX. We all knew it was coming. But the best minds, the smartest people on the planet were on the job. They were gonna fix it, that's what they kept saying. They were gonna literally save the world.

In other places the crazy cults appeared, especially after the first intercept failed. I saw it on the news, the mass suicides, looting, riots. But somehow, we avoided most of that. I mean, it turns out Garrison Keillor was right. Minnesotans don't really go in for that sorta thing.

In our neighborhood, it was really quiet. Northeast is an old Polish neighborhood, very working class. Small houses with long, narrow lots. Most people didn't have fences, so you could see your neighbors in their yards. And as it got closer, we all drifted outside to watch.

(OTHERS *begin to appear in the dim spotlights of memory, scattered around the theater. Some in family groups, some singly. They all watch the same sky. Maybe the faint drone of Brian Williams.*)

Left CNN and Brian Williams talking to empty living rooms and stood in our yards in the moonlight. Mark and Amy and Zander. Keith the bachelor gardener two houses down, Maxeline Jellybean, and Hyde who used to go barreling down the sidewalk on his Big Wheel.

And I'm holding my son in my arms. He keeps putting his hands on my face, pressing his little palms against my cheeks as we look at the sky. And when the meteor appears, streaking toward its target it is so…silent. There are no cars, no sounds of traffic. Just the hum of the power lines and our collective breathing, each in our own patch of grass as we watch this slow motion collision happening millions of miles away. And when it strikes the moon, I feel it, in my veins, my organs, all the water in me being pulled with it, the way my son pulls on my arm, until his hand slips, and the invisible line snaps, and the moon disappears from sight, released from orbit, careening off into the ever-expanding universe.

(*Lights out on all but* ALEX. *He is once again alone.*)

And we are left standing in our yards in the dark.

RADIANT DINAH
by Marco Ramirez

DINAH *is exhausted, but her spirit's not yet crushed. Direct address.*

DINAH. I'm holed up at a Starbucks on Amarillo and Third.

And not even a real Starbucks,

At one of those shitty half-service counters attached to an office building.

…

I'm living off of Bran Muffins, Apple Fritters and Asiago Bagels.

Blueberry Scones, Banana Loaf, and Iced Lemon Pound Cake.

I'm allergic to pumpkin but I tried the Pumpkin Bread too, because I got so fucking bored.

I threw up.

That was yesterday.

…

I'm a temp at a graphic design firm where everyone is pretentious and they talk about

Vassar

And

NYU

And

It's occurred to me that I've wished (more than once) that they all die horrible deaths.

…

So it felt weird when it happened.

…

I was trying to find the toner in the supply room and I heard it—

An ear-piercing scream the likes of which you'd normally welcome on any other office day,

Like SHIT, something's happening,

(Something other than clocking in and clocking out and getting stared at by Jeff in I.T.)

But when I looked out—

Katie's face was on the floor,

Fred was leaning headfirst (but without a head) onto one of those inspirational posters that says "Joy is—"

Kunal had peed himself,

Gay Matt was calling his mother,

And that fat Dominican security guard was sitting in a corner, holding in his own intestines.

…

I saw a black tentacle feel its way down the hallway and crush the water cooler,
And my first thought (weird?)
But my first thought wasn't "Why's there a black tentacle in the hallway?"
It was "Sweet, I don't have to refill the water cooler."

…

There were five or six tentacles altogether,
Some bigger than others,
All terrifying,
And I somehow made my way outta the office,
In and out,
Just a temp.

…

…

It's been three days.
The power hasn't gone out,
And I'm at Starbucks,
And I can't figure out how to turn off the Norah Jones.

…

Once in a while I hear a scream.
Once in a while I look out and see another tentacle taking out a grown man,
A child,
Squeezing them until their insides come out through their throats.

…

…

I've been doing a lot of thinking,
Which you don't do much of—as a temp—
About how maybe, in another dimension,
I'm one of those women who married young and maybe has a baby,
None of this ten-years-outta-college shit,
I was one of those gorgeous pregnant 20-somethings and people called me radiant.
I have a son or a daughter and his name is something literary like Anton and he's one of those quiet babies,
The kinds mothers talk about later when they look lovingly at their grown-up-

baby and say "He never gave me any trouble."
>   (*She gets emotional.*)
Maybe it's all the Norah Jones?

...

I passed by that goddamn poster thirty times a day and never read it.
I clocked in and clocked out and couldn't wait to leave,
But today—
The day I needed it,
Half of it was covered with Fred's brain particles,
"Joy is—"

...

"Joy is—"

...

...

What does it say, Fred.
>   (*Black.*)

"OT"
by Dan Dietz

Part One

The entire company of actors stands onstage, each holding a single object. Maybe it's an object from the play itself. Maybe it's an object from their own lives. Either way, it is clearly precious to them. One of the objects is a bottle of champagne. These lines can be divided up any way you like.

in the end, it really was a good idea
such a good idea
each person
this was back when the apocalypse was, like, nigh
each and every person
we're talking on the planet here
every single person
chooses a single object
to carry with them into the new world
this is besides food and clothes and stuff
one thing
obviously it can't be too big
the operative word here is "carry"
so not too big or heavy or awkward
or fragile
and nothing living
so like, rare and beautiful houseplants: no
but a packet of their rare and beautiful seeds: yes
your beloved pet goldfish: no
the little castle at the bottom of its little glass bowl: yes
champagne: no
a cork from a bottle of champagne

> (*An actor tries—and fails—to pop the cork from a bottle of champagne.*)

you get the picture
it started small
this idea
a few people talked about it online with each other
and then in like no time flat
it became a worldwide movement
the One Thing movement
everyone was doing it
everyone agreed it was such a good idea

such a good idea
we all posted pictures of our One Things online
and we all felt kind of like one planet for once
instead of the fractured, buzzing mess we actually were
One World, One Thing
that's what we named it
and yes eventually judgment started to set in
and yes we looked at each other's postings and
"liked"
and
"disliked"
them
and ranked them according to visual
slash
emotional
slash
ironic appeal
because the thing about the apocalypse is
it always takes longer to arrive than you think
and if you leave enough people in a room
in a world
long enough
they're gonna make a beauty pageant out of something
but still
it was One World
for once
for *once*
so when the disaster came
when the oceans rose and drowned our cities
when the asteroid came and shattered half the planet
when the aliens
the missiles
the supervirus
came
we all took our One Things
into our shelters
onto our rafts
within our sterilized government bubbles
and we rode it out
and those of us who died
their bodies were burned
buried

slipped into the sea
and their One Things were left behind with them
it seemed only right
we all agreed
it was the right thing to do
it was amazing
there was like an unconscious, worldwide agreement on this
people just knew
if you died
your One Thing
died with you
even if it was useful
even if the new world might need it
we all understood the fragility of worlds
the empty promises they made
so if you shuffled off your coil
the new world would just have to do without
your One Thing
and if you were trekking along
in the post-melted-icecap-asteroid-shattered-nuclear-wasted-alien-raped-virus
        ravaged landscape
and you found what was obviously someone's One Thing
obvious because everyone agreed to write the letters "OT" onto their One
        Thing
there was a handy list of what this looked like in multiple languages
if you found one
everyone unconsciously agreed
you passed it by
it became a shrine to that soul
that person who like you
like me
Was Here
and it was kind of beautiful
this landscape of occasional mundane objects
photographs
a jar full of marbles
(*Struggling to pop champagne bottle.*) a cork from a bottle of champagne
popping up in the middle of nowhere
with the letters "OT" written on them
fountain pens
a single lace doily clinging delicately to a charred tree
(*Struggling harder.*) a CORK from a BOTTLE of chamPAGNE

you'd see all these things and more
as people resettled
rebuilt
re-knit themselves into new societies
and told stories of how
long ago
everything in the whole wide world
went—

> *(The cork POPS out of the bottle and an explosion of light and/ or music and/ or movement erupts around the stage. It feels like the biggest party in the world has just started, and we have a front row seat.)*

Part Two

> *The actors return to their places onstage, objects in hand.*

it's a funny thing
to find yourself at The End
lingering
wondering:
is this the part where we restart the party
or the part where we drift out the door
into the sheets
saving cleanup till morning
till dawn

> *(One by one, the actors set their objects down on the floor.)*

i like to think that
even if we fail
to rebuild
to go on
and the last one of us
finally falls
and the End of the World truly does
you know
exactly that
these things will remain
i like to think that another race
a group of aliens from a far off galaxy
a future life-form evolving its way up from the post-apocalyptic muck
something in no way resembling the hairless apes who got to run things for
    a while

might arrive on the surface of the planet
and look around
and see them
all the One Things
scattered before them
like a map of longing and desire
and experience a moment of absolute

(*Overlapping whispers, ricocheting around the room.*) wonder/confusion/terror/joy
   love/annoyance/amusement/disgust/rage/affection/despair/hope
before moving on

   (*One by one, the actors start to leave the stage.*)

i like to think these things
that what we do
what we say
what we struggle
and clutch at
and smile
and sing at
will be like that
a slowly fading
but never disappearing
echo

   (*The sound of a champagne cork popping out of a bottle. It echoes…lingers…*)

instead of
an instant
unforgiving
blackout
blackout
blackout
blackout
blackout
blackout
blackout
good night

   (*The final actor leaves the stage. Is there a blackout? Or are we left looking down at the landscape of objects left behind, like the remains of the biggest party of your life, where everyone was dancing, singing, loving, having fun, and never noticing how very late it's getting…*)